The
FINGER LAKES
Book

A Complete Guide

The Columbia *tours Seneca Lake from Watkins Glen.*

THE
FINGER LAKES
BOOK
A Complete Guide

Katharine Delavan Dyson

Berkshire House Publishers
Lee, Massachusetts

On the Cover and Frontispiece
Front Cover: *Waterfalls are a highlight of the Finger Lakes experience.* Photo © Peter Finger.
Frontispiece: *The* Columbia *tours Seneca Lake from Watkins Glen.* Photo © Peter Finger.

The Finger Lakes Book: A Complete Guide
Copyright © 2001 by Berkshire House Publishers
Cover and interior photographs © 2001 by credited sources

Library of Congress Cataloging-in-Publication Data

Dyson, Katharine D.

The Finger Lakes book: a complete guide / Katharine Delavan Dyson.
      p.   cm — (Great destinations series, ISSN 1056-7968)
Includes bibliographical references and indexes.
ISBN 1-58157-018-X
  1. Finger Lakes Region (N.Y.)—Guidebooks. I. Title. II. Series.
F127.F4 D95 2001
917.47'80444—dc21   00-049415

ISBN 1-58157-018-X
ISSN 1056-7968 (series)

Editor: Sarah Novak. Managing Editor: Philip Rich. Text design and typography: Dianne Pinkowitz. Cover design and typography: Jane McWhorter. Maps: Ron Toelke.

Berkshire House books are available at substantial discounts for bulk purchases by corporations and other organizations for promotions and premiums. Special personalized editions can also be produced in large quantities. For more information, contact:

Berkshire House Publishers
480 Pleasant St., Suite 5; Lee, Massachusetts 01238
800-321-8526
Website: www.berkshirehouse.com
E-mail: info@berkshirehouse.com

Manufactured in the United States of America

First printing 2001
10 9 8 7 6 5 4 3 2 1

No complimentary meals or lodgings were accepted by the author and reviewers in gathering information for this work.

Berkshire House Publishers'
Great Destinations™ travel guidebook series

Recommended by NATIONAL GEOGRAPHIC TRAVELER and TRAVEL &
LEISURE magazines.

Smart, literate, well-reported, and incredibly comprehensive.
— MID-ATLANTIC COUNTRY

. . . a crisp and critical approach, for travelers who want to live like locals.
— USA TODAY

Great Destinations™ guidebooks are known for their comprehensive, critical
coverage of regions of extraordinary cultural interest and natural beauty. The
authors in this series are professional travel writers who have lived for many
years in the regions they describe. Each title in this series is continuously
updated with each printing, in order to insure accurate and timely information. All of the books contain over 100 photographs and maps.

**Neither the publisher, the authors, the reviewers, nor other contributors
accept complimentary lodgings, meals, or any other consideration (such as
advertising) while gathering information for any book in this series.**

Current titles available:
The Adirondack Book
The Berkshire Book
The Charleston, Savannah & Coastal Islands Book
The Chesapeake Bay Book
The Coast of Maine Book
The Finger Lakes Book
The Hamptons Book
The Monterey Bay, Big Sur & Gold Coast Wine Country Book
The Nantucket Book
The Newport & Narragansett Bay Book
The Napa & Sonoma Book
The Santa Fe & Taos Book
The Sarasota, Sanibel Island & Naples Book
The Texas Hill Country Book
Wineries of the Eastern States

If you are traveling to, moving to, residing in, or just interested in any (or all!)
of these enchanting regions, a **Great Destinations**™ guidebook is a superior
companion. Honest and painstakingly critical, full of information only a local
can provide, **Great Destinations**™ guidebooks give you all the practical
knowledge you need to enjoy the best of each region. Why not own them all?

*To the memory of my father, William H. Delavan,
who grew up in Seneca Falls and moved to Skaneateles
where he raised his family. I remember our walks in the fall along
leaf-strewn paths; sled rides down our back yard to the lake;
and sailing, swimming, and burying him up to his neck in piles
of sand on our little beach. His love and great enthusiasm for the
Finger Lakes area live on to brighten my world.*

Contents

CHAPTER ONE
Imprint of the Spirit
HISTORY
1

CHAPTER TWO
Highways, Byways, and Waterways
TRANSPORTATION
10

CHAPTER THREE
Picture Perfect
SKANEATELES, OWASCO, AND OTISCO LAKES
21

CHAPTER FOUR
Vineyards, Colleges, & Museums
CAYUGA LAKE
62

CHAPTER FIVE
Deep Water and Gorges
SENECA LAKE
115

CHAPTER SIX
Split Personality
KEUKA LAKE
152

CHAPTER SEVEN
Western Frontier
CANANDAIGUA LAKE
Canadice, Conesus, Hemlock, and Honeoye Lakes
183

CHAPTER EIGHT
Gold Medal Grapes
WINERIES
219

CHAPTER NINE
Host Cities
SYRACUSE, CORTLAND, ELMIRA, CORNING, AND ROCHESTER
237

CHAPTER TEN
Finger Lakes Facts and Figures
INFORMATION
262

Acknowledgments

In the process of researching and writing this book, I continually met people who went out of their way to help me.

First I must thank my publisher, Jean Rousseau, for believing this project would work and for giving me the time and resources to do it properly. I also want to thank Sarah Novak and Philip Rich at Berkshire House who were indispensable in providing thoughtful input, patience, kindness, and support throughout the many months it took to write the book.

As I explored the Finger Lakes from lake to lake, town to town, filling up my car with brochures, flyers, menus, and other materials, there were many who took the time to meet and speak with me. Lynn "Spike" Herzig, president of the Finger Lakes Association, was most helpful in giving me an overview of the region. Gene Pierce of Glenora Wine Cellars explained what was happening in the wine industry; Jim Bramble of the Ithaca/Tompkins County Convention and Visitors Bureau helped me discover the nooks and crannies of Ithaca; Laurie Nichiporuk of the Finger Lakes Association was always available with enthusiastic help and ready answers; and Barbara Adams opened doors along the Seneca Wine Trail.

I am grateful to Carol Kammen, Historian and Senior Lecturer, Department of History, Cornell University, for giving me input and resources to complete the history segments. I also must thank Idelle Dillon, executive director of the Yates County Genealogical and Historical Society, for providing a wealth of historical information on Yates County and Valerie Knoblauch, director of the Ontario County Tourism Board, who gave me an insider's tour of her region as well as valuable insights into the history and happenings in the area.

I appreciate the help I received from many others, including Eva Mae Musgrave, owner of The Edge of Thyme and secretary of the Finger Lakes B&B Association, who told me about some special places in and around Ithaca; Pauline Weaver, Weaver-View Farms, Penn Yan, who gave me new insight into the Amish/Mennonite people in the region; and Peter Jemison, director of Ganondagan State Historic Site, Victor, who helped me better understand the history, contributions, and place of the native American people in the Finger Lakes.

Also thanks to Carol Eaton of the Syracuse Chamber of Commerce who opened my eyes to the many interesting things in Syracuse, Pat White of the Steuben County Conference and Visitors Bureau who showed me around the Corning area, Meg Vanek of Cayuga County Tourism, and Jim Dempsey of the Cortland County Visitors Bureau. Another big thank goes to Diane Wenz, a Geneva native and friend, who gave up many hours to show me her "home town."

Well deserving of accolades are Sarah Novak, my editor, who was indispensable in pulling it all together, and Ellen Delaney, who spent hours fact-checking the hundreds of phone numbers and other details. Lezli White of the Corning Museum of Glass deserves the credit for coming up with "Host Cities" to replace the former chapter title "Gateway Cities."

As I drew on the local knowledge and expertise of family and relatives, a hearty thank you goes to Nelson "Pete" and Edith Delavan for their help on Seneca Falls; to Byron and Caroline Delavan for sharing their thoughts on Canandaigua; to my brother Bill Delavan and his wife, Terry, for insider's information on Syracuse; and to my sister, Holly, who spent some exhausting hours driving with me and writing down special things as we went along.

The hospitality and "camping rights" bestowed on me by my son, Christopher, and his wife Cathy Pinckney in Skaneateles made my job so much easier. Their cheery and sunny home was always a welcome haven after many long days on the road.

Above all, I want to extend my heartfelt thanks to my husband, John, who encouraged me, month after month, to do what I had to do to get the job done and patiently endured many evenings of late dinners and general chaos and piles-of-paper overload. I could never have completed this project without his support.

Introduction

As you drive through the rolling hills and valleys of the Finger Lakes, a region of tidy villages like Skaneateles where summer brings Friday night band concerts, as you stop to sip a glass of Riesling from one of the eighty vineyards that blanket the hills or to take a dip in the crystalline waters of any of the eleven lakes, you are mindful that this region is one of the most beautiful on earth. Horses graze in meadows, corn and wheat fields pattern the landscape, and, in many places, it's open sky country with miles of vistas in every direction. Gorges, waterfalls, and slim fingers of blue water highlight the landscape.

Summer brings fleets of sailboats tacking from shore to shore; endless fields of tasseled corn, alfalfa, and wheat; flashes of goldenrod, china blue chicory, purple horse mint, and buttercups lining the roads, turning dusty as warm weather wanes. High school and college football games kick off the orange-red glow of fall which quickly turns brisk as grapes and apples are harvested and dry bundles of corn stand like sentries in the countryside against deep lapis skies. Winter ushers in drifts of snow and ice-covered trees. Skiers take to the slopes; skaters clear the snow off lakes and ponds and glide onto the ice. Spring blossoms with sweet-scented blue, pink, and white lilacs, tulips, daffodils, and clouds of forsythia; hundreds of waterfalls burst over outcroppings of rock plunging to icy pools below, taking your breath away.

Then there are things man has created: picture-postcard villages with wide front lawns, white clapboard houses with front porches furnished with wicker furniture and windowboxes brimming over with petunias, ivy, and geraniums; renowned colleges and universities; mansions like Rose Hill in Geneva and Sonnenberg in Canandaigua; the amazing Corning Glass Center; Watkins Glen International Racing Circuit; and a handful of old-fashioned ice-cream parlors, wooden-floored hardware stores, and outdoor movie theaters stubbornly hanging in there from the 50s.

One of the most exciting cities in the region, Ithaca, has a revitalized downtown area including a pedestrian street lined with trendy cafes, boutiques, art galleries, and gift shops. Cornell University and Ithaca College play a strong role in creating a vibrant atmosphere of continual growth and cultural opportunities.

Other colleges and universities in the Finger Lakes — Wells College, Hobart and William Smith Colleges, and Keuka College — also contribute greatly to their communities.

Many of the original settlers in the region were farmers, and today there still exists a strong farm population. As you drive along country roads, you'll see billboards advertising farm machinery, tractors and combines parked in fields near barns that easily dwarf nearby dwellings, huge blue Harvestore silos, and a patchwork of plowed fields that create a crazy-quilt pattern defined by tightly woven stands of trees.

Signs along the road warn of cows or tractors crossing and advertise home-produced products: stacked rows of split firewood, fruits and vegetables, cut flowers, and piles of corn. Always corn.

At the end of the day as the sun melts into the horizon, you are sure to see black and white Holsteins crowding the gates, their udders heavy with milk, as they wait for the farmers to take them into the barn and relieve them of their bounty.

The legacy of the past is evident in Moravia, where much eighteenth-century architecture has been preserved. Auburn is a repository of American history and historic homes. If native American history is your passion, there is Ganondagan State Historic Site in Victor, a seventeenth-century native American settlement, and Sainte Marie among the Iroquois, a living history museum in Liverpool.

Many of the pleasant little towns like Homer, Avon, and Dresden are nice places to live, but don't necessarily attract passing travelers, nor do they count on transient tourists for their livelihood. Anchored by farm lands on either end of the main route that runs through them, these little towns might have a shop or two worth browsing, a barn of antiques piled helter-skelter, or perhaps a place to eat or a nice B&B. Some shops may even post their hours as "open by chance or appointment."

For some, this lack of commercial hype is enough of a reason to come — the promise of a few days escape from the corporate treadmill. In the Finger Lakes the pace is kinder.

This does not mean there isn't plenty to see and do. There are vineyards to visit, cruises to take, historical sites and attractions such as the Erie Canal Museum and the Women's Rights Park to explore. There are great restaurants, festivals and fairs, beautiful villages and cities, and places to stay ranging from wonderful B&Bs to large hotels and boutique spa resorts. And always, people that smile and greet you warmly even if you are just stopping for a look.

G rowing up in Skaneateles and living in this village for more than half my life, I can trace family roots back six generations. My father was born in Seneca Falls and relatives live throughout the region from Rochester to Syracuse. As a travel writer, I am fortunate to be able to visit places all around the world, from Africa to China to Brazil to Europe. Perhaps because of these experiences, I have been left with a deep appreciation for the Finger Lakes, a part of our world that combines some of the best characteristics of those places I have enjoyed the most.

Whether traveling through southwestern Ireland with its wide open fields, the Lake District in England, the lochs of Scotland, or the vineyards banked along the Rhine in Germany, I am continually reminded that back home, there too is a place where the hills soothe, lakes dazzle, and the people are warm and comfortable with themselves and where they live. It's a good feeling to know in our own country there is such a place as the Finger Lakes.

Katharine Dyson
Ridgefield, Connecticut

THE WAY THIS BOOK WORKS

This book covers the region of the Finger Lakes around or within easy driving distance of the eleven lakes, an area that falls roughly inside the perimeter of a rough circle drawn along the New York Thruway (Rte. 90), Rte. 81, Rte. 17, and Rte. 390 and stretching from Syracuse to Rochester and south to Ithaca. It encompasses eleven lakes (plus a few smaller lakes) in an area of about ninety miles by sixty miles.

A general history of the region opens the book, followed by an overview of the best routes into the area, by land, air, and water. The lake areas are described in five chapters: Skaneateles, Otisco, and Owasco; Cayuga; Seneca; Keuka; and Canandaigua, Honeoye, Hemlock, Canadice, and Conesus. Within each of these chapters, you will find information about everything from history to lodging, restaurants, recreation, shopping, and cultural attractions. A separate chapter highlights a selection of the area's wineries and vineyards. Features of major cities — Syracuse, Rochester, Corning, Elmira, and Cortland — are described in the *Host Cities* chapter. Ithaca, also an important city, is described in the Cayuga Lake chapter. The final chapter, *Information*, gives Finger Lakes facts and figures.

In the Index you will find lodging and dining facilities organized by lake area and listed according to price and type. Every effort has been made to place towns and villages in the chapter that covers the lake (or lakes) nearest to the place. Still, there are coin tosses on some places that straddle the area almost dead center between two lakes. In this case, the index can be your best friend.

Although all information was as accurate as possible as of publication date, we suggest you call ahead before visiting; circumstances could have changed in the meantime. Please note that many places are open only during the warmer months, usually from mid-April through mid-October.

PRICES

Since the Finger Lakes region is most active with visitors during the warm weather months, you can expect prices to be higher at that time, especially for lodging. In addition to higher prices during the popular months, you may also find that some places require a two- or three-night minimum. Cabin or house rentals may require one week's minimum. Off-season is a different story.

A general price range is given instead of exact prices, which often change. Lodging prices are per room, double occupancy, and may or may not include breakfast or other meals. Restaurant prices indicate the cost of a meal for one person including an appetizer or salad, main course, and dessert. Bar beverages are extra.

Lodging price codes:
$: Up to $75 per couple
$$: $76–$150 per couple
$$$: $151–$250 per couple
$$$$: More than $250

Dining price codes:
$: Up to $10
$$: $11–$25
$$$: $26–$40
$$$$: More than $40
Prices are estimated per person for appetizer and dinner entrée without tax, tip, or alcoholic beverages.

We welcome your comments on the content of the book and any personal experiences you care to share. A major effort was made to include all key historic sites and attractions as well as a wide variety of lodgings, restaurants, retail establishments, and other places of interest. The purpose of this book was not to include every store, every bed-and-breakfast, every restaurant, and so forth, but to give you a guide to the places you should know about along with first-person descriptions and enough information to help you make educated choices. However, if places have been left out that should be considered for the next edition, we would be happy to hear about them.

The
FINGER LAKES
Book

A Complete Guide

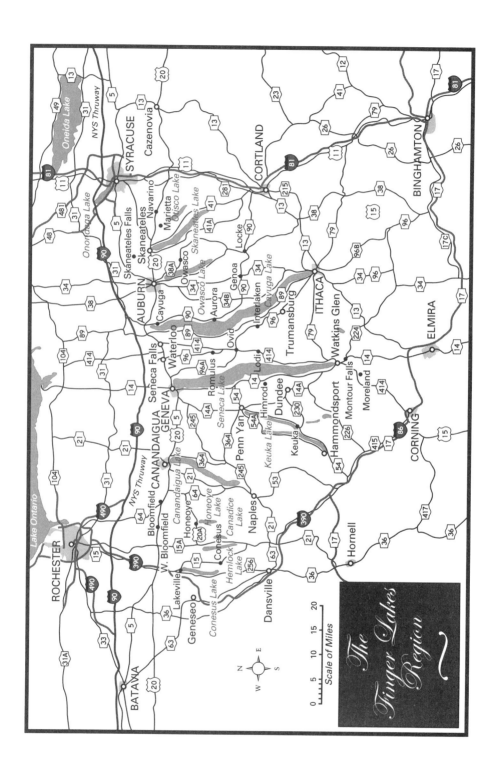

The Finger Lakes Region

Scale of Miles
0 5 10 15 20

CHAPTER ONE
Imprint of the Spirit
HISTORY

Sailing on Skaneateles Lake.

According to legend, when the Great Spirit laid his hands on this land to bless it, the imprints left by his fingers filled with water to form lakes. Hence the "Finger Lakes." You can believe this or the geologists' explanation: more than 550 million years ago, during the Pleistocene Ice Age, glaciers crept through the area from north to south, carving deep slices in the land. The ice pushed the land and rocks southward. Gradually the ice melted and the glaciers withdrew, leaving shale-bedded valleys of water so deep in some places that their bottoms are below sea level.

As the glaciers receded, the pile-up of rocks in lakes like Skaneateles and Cayuga created a fiord-like terrain with steep sides and deep waters. Spectacular waterfalls such as the 215-foot-high Taughannock Falls off the southwestern shores of Cayuga Lake and the deep gorges of Watkins Glen at the southern end of Seneca Lake also developed as the glaciers retreated.

The glacial landscaping — the lakes, the moraines (the debris field left by the glaciers), and the small "kettle lakes" (bowl-like depressions) — created a uniquely stunning landscape and fertile agricultural lands.

The clarity of the water of the Finger Lakes has gained a worldwide reputation. So clean is the water in Skaneateles Lake, some homes and camps along the shores still draw drinking water directly from the lake. Keuka Lake is also known for its exceptionally pure water.

Peter Finger

Fishing in the crystal-clear waters of the Finger Lakes.

FIRST THERE WERE THE NATIVE AMERICANS

One summer day when I was twelve years old, I dove off our dock into Skaneateles Lake. That day, the water was calm, and I could see right to the bottom. Swimming out a ways, I looked down. There, half-buried in the sand and shale, I saw a few pieces of pottery. Having learned about the Onondagas who had lived on these shores, I let my imagination free-fall: had I discovered a piece of history?

Later, in a canoe, I tried to find that spot again. I never did. Still I remember that day and the excitement of my discovery.

Even a brief run through the area will leave no doubt as to the Finger Lakes' native American heritage. The names of lakes and many villages, streets, restaurants, inns, and even today's families are derived from tribal language: Taughannock, Ithaca, Montezuma, Genesee, Cayuga . . . the list goes on.

Before the American Revolution in 1775, 20,000 members of the Haudenosaunee (six nations of the Iroquois Confederacy) lived in communities throughout the Finger Lakes region. In the east, there were the Mohawks, the warriors and keepers of the eastern door of the Long House; the Onondagas were the fire keepers and the story-belt "secretaries" of the tribes. The Senecas, hunters and keepers of the western door, and the largest of the nations, were the most fiercely protective of their territory. There were also the Oneida and Cayuga, the farmers, and later the Tuscarora.

Before the first white settlers found their way along the trails and passageways created by the native Americans, life in the Finger Lakes was remarkably

---

Mary Jemison

Katharine Delavan Dyson

When Mary Jemison's family was attacked by a Shawnee war party, everyone was killed except two brothers who escaped and went south and Mary, who was just eleven years old. Mary was captured and later adopted as a Seneca sister and as such was treated as one of their own. Living with them until she was an adult, she married a Delaware chieftain and lived with him and his people in Pennsylvania near Gettysburg. She apparently loved him a great deal and they had a son known as Buffalo Tom. In 1758, after her husband was killed when he was hunting, she walked 300 miles with two of her Seneca brothers back up north to the area now known as Letchworth Park, where she rejoined her adoptive family. Eventually she married an older man, a Seneca named Hiakatoo, who was known to be a fierce but wise warrior. Together they had many children. In her later days, Mary had only good things to say about him.

Her final home was along the Genesee River, which runs through Letchworth Park in the western part of New York State. A statue in the park of Mary Jemison pays tribute to this remarkable woman. One of Mary's several times great-grandsons is Peter Jemison, director of the Ganondagan Historic Site in Victor.

Peter Jemison, director of the Ganondagan Historic Site, Victor, is in full dress for the annual native American festival.

democratic. The native Americans' "Great Law" gave their people free speech, religious liberty, and the right to bear arms to protect the security of each person. The women were influential and their war chiefs were subordinate to the highly respected elected civil chiefs such as Joseph Brant, a Mohawk, and Cornplanter, a Seneca.

In 1794, the Pickering Treaty, an agreement between the United States and the Haudenosaunee (Iroquois Confederacy), marked the beginning of the native Americans' retreat from their lands. The treaty confirmed the Phelps and Gorham Purchase of 2,600,000 acres east of Genesee for $5000 plus an annuity of $500 forever. It was very important to the Haudenosaunee because it established their sovereignty as independent nations; from that point on, they would be considered independent from the United States.

At the Wood Memorial Library in Seneca Falls is a piece of faded old parchment. It's the native Americans' copy of the original Pickering Treaty, signed by Red Jacket, Little Beard, and Cornplanter. In Canaan a boulder on the courthouse grounds marks the place where the signing took place.

These were turbulent times. Whites against the natives; natives against whites. Families on both sides — including women and children — were killed or taken prisoner. Some, like Mary Jemison, were assimilated into the tribal community.

During the Revolutionary War, General George Washington, believing that the native Americans were siding with the British, ordered generals Clinton and Sullivan to wipe out Indian activity in the region around Seneca and Cayuga Lakes. In carrying out their assignment, more than 5,000 men with 4,000 horses torched villages and corn fields, cut down trees, and exiled the people. Not a single Indian settlement or field of corn was spared. Their wave of destruction broke the backbone of the Iroquois community.

A plaque on the west side of Cayuga Lake near Burroughs Point reads, "Site of an Indian Village destroyed during the Sullivan campaign 1779." Arrowheads and bits of pottery still occasionally turn up in the fields and around the lake shores and are now prized by collectors.

SETTLERS MOVE IN

In the late 1700s, people like Job Smith and John Cuddeback drifted into the area, settled down, and became the first settlers in communities such as Seneca Falls and Skaneateles. Most of these early settlers were farmers who found the soil fertile and well-drained. They cleared the forests and plowed the land for wheat, corn, and other crops as well as dairy operations.

Dwellings then were simple structures built around a central fireplace, perhaps with a beehive oven in the back. Sleeping quarters might be up in a loft. There were usually no carpets, no pumps in the wells, and no stoves. Cooking was done in the fireplace using wood for fuel; pine knots were burned for light instead of candles.

In 1781, the main transportation routes were along trails created by the native Americans. After the Revolutionary War, growth was spurred when the United States government granted lands here to officers and soldiers who had fought for independence.

For a while, especially after the opening of the Erie Canal which allowed goods to travel easily from the region to New York City's markets, farmers thrived. Businesses developed along the waterways: mills, retail establishments, banking institutions. The most imposing buildings of the period were the grist and saw mills along rivers and outlets such as on Keuka Lake at Penn Yan.

Most people moved their families into the region during the winter months when the rough roads were frozen hard and smoothed by snow making it easier going for wagons carrying household goods. With the construction of the Seneca Turnpike in 1803, from Utica to Canandaigua, traffic increased and stagecoaches rumbled across the miles on regular routes. A bridge built across the northern end of Cayuga Lake soon became one of the wonders of the state. It meant that travelers on the Great Western Turnpike no longer had to go the long way around the Montezuma Swamp, cutting the east-west travel time considerably. At either end of the bridge, taverns and general stores blossomed, creating a mini-boom-town. Today, the bridge is gone, and that area known as Bridgeport is barely on the map, consisting mainly of a firehouse, old cemetery, and a park.

Following the Great Depression of 1929, many farms were abandoned. Some areas, such as the land southwest of Skaneateles Lake, were purchased in the 1930s and replanted by the Civilian Conservation Corps. Today these state forests are used for hiking, biking, and other recreational purposes and are also preserved as open land for wildlife, trees, and unusual plant species.

Many villages were scarred by major fires, especially in the early 1900s when most buildings were constructed of wood and firefighting equipment and transportation of water were primitive. Seneca Falls, Skaneateles, and Geneva all fell prey to destructive fires. New buildings were built of brick and constructed with firewalls. These are evident particularly in the business block along Genesee Street in Skaneateles.

THE ERIE CANAL

One of the most important manmade features of the region was the Erie Canal, at first derided as a major folly. Stretching from Albany to Buffalo, "The Big Ditch," as it was not so affectionately called, took an army of laborers eight years of blasting rock, digging earth, felling trees, and building locks to complete. The first ceremonial shovel of dirt was dug in Syracuse near the spot where the Erie Canal Museum now stands.

When the canal opened in 1825, sending a rush of water flowing from Lake Erie and the Hudson River, cannons spaced five miles apart along the 363-mile canal heralded this grand event.

What's in a Name?

Many places in the Finger Lakes have undergone several name changes, for sometimes obvious reasons. For example, Phelps was once Vienna, Hemlock was Slab City, Perry was Shacksburg and Ninevah, Honeoye was Pitt's Flats, Vincent was Muttonville, and Bristol Springs was first called Cold Springs. Geneva was once Kanadesaga which translated as "dog town," and Naples was first called Watkinstown.

It was a brilliant idea sparked by a man from his jail cell who dreamed of a waterway that would link Lake Erie to the Hudson River. As the story goes, Jesse Hawley, once a man of substance in the freight forwarding business, found himself languishing in the Canandaigua jail after his failed attempts to transport grain from farms in the area to the mills in Seneca Falls and finally to New York City. It was too expensive and too treacherous. After his operations collapsed and he found himself behind bars, he used his down time to devise a better way to move his products: a manmade waterway. He made sketches and wrote several articles detailing how it could be done. Eventually these materials landed in the hands of New York City mayor De Witt Clinton.

Clinton became obsessed with the idea and, in 1817, ground was broken for the new canal. Lacking proper engineering talent, the project became a huge on-the-job-training exercise. Special challenges included the construction of locks, development of waterproof cement, the need to blast through rock, construction of aquaducts across the Genesee River in downtown Rochester and the valley in Pittsford, and solving the problem of keeping the water from drying up in areas prone to drought (feeders were built from lakes and streams).

As one obstacle after another was overcome, American workers developed expertise in engineering. The need for professional schools was met when the Rensselaer Polytechnic Institute in Troy, the Civil Engineering Department of Union College, and the Rochester Institute of Technology were founded.

When the canal was completed, goods could be moved from Buffalo to New York City in just ten days instead of six weeks; a ton of freight cost $10 instead of $100. Products moving easily from west to eastern markets meant that immigrants came to the area and business thrived.

In 1835, the canal was widened and deepened and locks doubled to handle the gridlock from the increasing traffic. Continual improvements over the next few years included rerouting a portion of the canal to incorporate existing rivers and lakes. A "spur" was built, the Cayuga-Seneca Canal, which connected the two lakes. In 1918, the Erie Canal became the Barge Canal.

The canal brought new prosperity to the state and especially to the villages along the waterways, including Syracuse, Port Byron, and Seneca Falls. Seven years after it opened, the canal was the main method of travel from east to west. Travelers could go from Buffalo to Albany, then connect with the Post Road and continue to New York.

Peter Finger

The Women's Rights National Historical Park celebrates the work of area women in championing women's issues.

Portions of the canal are open today and it is an important recreational waterway.

WOMEN'S RIGHTS

Women's rights appeared on the nation's agenda at a convention held in 1848 at the Wesleyan Chapel in Seneca Falls. Led by a determined Elizabeth Cady Stanton and Lucretia Mott, the Declaration of Sentiments and Resolutions was read to 300 people, including forty men. One hundred people signed the Declaration. The women dealt with issues such as temperance, abolition, suffrage, and dress reform.

Amelia Jenks Bloomer, who appeared in the village in her bloomers, raised many eyebrows, but she persisted in setting a fashion trend of sorts. A small bronze marker on a building on Fall Street, Seneca Falls, marks the location where it all started.

Seventy-five years later, in 1923, when the town celebrated the anniversary of the first Women's Rights Convention, my Aunt Lee (Elizabeth) Delavan was one of seven young girls that took part in an outdoor pageant.

Peter Finger

More than 250 Amish and Mennonite families live in the Finger Lakes.

MENNONITES AND AMISH

The central Finger Lakes region is home to more than 250 Amish and Mennonite families, who originally came from Pennsylvania. Here around Seneca and Cayuga lakes, they continue to practice their strong religious beliefs. Their black, horse-drawn buggies occasionally seen on the roads are a reminder that there are still those who have no electricity, phones, or television, by choice. Such things, along with cars, planes, and trains, are seen as threats to breaking up the family unit, corrupting the values they hold dear.

This does not mean they do not live well. On the contrary, because of their hard work, close-knit families, and sense of community, the Amish and Mennonites most often flourish. They own their own land, are very self-sufficient, take great joy in their children, and make strong contributions to their communities.

Most earn their living through farming and building; some have shops, work in restaurants, and make and sell quilts and other craft items. Most work very hard, live simply, educate their children in one-room schoolhouses until they reach their late teens, and bring up their boys and girls to have a strong work ethic.

FAMOUS FINGER LAKES RESIDENTS

This region has had its share of important and wealthy personalities. Francis Bellamy, who wrote the "Pledge of Allegiance," lived in Mt. Morris; Clara Barton established the first American chapter of the Red Cross in Dansville; Ezra Cornell founded the college of the same name in Ithaca. Residents of Auburn include Harriet Tubman, abolitionist; Theodore Willard Case, founder of Twentieth Century Fox; and William H. Seward, governor of New York and the man responsible for the purchase of Alaska. Mark Twain lived in Elmira, and Amelia Bloomer of bloomer fame was born in Homer.

Katharine Delavan Dyson

The agricultural traditions of the Finger Lakes continue to shape the land; barns and silos dot the countryside.

CHAPTER TWO
Highways, Byways, and Waterways
TRANSPORTATION

Katharine Delavan Dyson

Boats tie up at the canal dock in Seneca Falls. Canal boats are available for weekly charters.

With the Finger Lakes region just a one-day drive (about 300 miles) from about fifty percent of the United States population, many visitors arrive by car. Some come by rail via Amtrak which links the region with major areas throughout North America. The route across New York State roughly follows the east-west route of the New York Thruway from Albany to Buffalo. Finger Lakes area stations are in Syracuse and Rochester.

Major airports in Syracuse, Rochester, Elmira/Corning, and Binghamton make the region accessible to the rest of the world.

The Greyhound/Trailways bus system offers point-to-point service throughout all the major cities (800-231-2222).

Approximate distance to the center of the Finger Lakes Region:

From Albany: 214 miles
Buffalo: 138 miles
New York City: 295 miles
Rochester: 55 miles
Washington DC: 337 miles

Approximate miles between key cities:

Corning—Albany: 206
Corning—Boston: 373
Corning—New York City: 267
Corning—Rochester: 103
Corning—Syracuse: 99

Rochester—Albany: 232
Rochester—Buffalo: 78
Rochester—New York City: 360
Rochester—Philadelphia: 351
Rochester—Syracuse: 91

Syracuse—Albany: 136
Syracuse—Boston: 299
Syracuse—Buffalo: 147
Syracuse—Corning: 90
Syracuse—New York City: 253
Syracuse—Philadelphia: 255
Syracuse—Toronto: 248
Syracuse—Washington DC: 350

Penn Yan—Buffalo: 100
Penn Yan—New York: 250
Penn Yan—Philadelphia: 250
Penn Yan —Syracuse: 75
Penn Yan—Toronto: 150

BY CAR

Many roads today follow old native American trails and go along waterways. For example, Rte. 5, which runs east-west through the region and becomes Rte. 5&20 much of the way, was once a native American footpath only about eighteen inches wide. The route was indicated by hatchet marks on trees. The Great Central Trail led to the longhouse on the shores of Onondaga Lake. A cavalcade of colonial settlers, French priests, traders, explorers, adventurers, and pioneers widened the trail as their wagons rumbled along the road.

East-West Routes

Major east-west routes include scenic Rte. 17, the New York Thruway (I-90), and Rte. 20 and 5&20. From New York City, it's about a four or five hour drive to the easternmost part of the Finger Lakes following these routes.

Rte. 17: From Jamestown to Orange County just north of New York City, this divided highway offers rest areas and picnic areas along the way. Although the road seems to be continually under repair at some point, for the most part the surface is good and the scenery along the rivers and through the

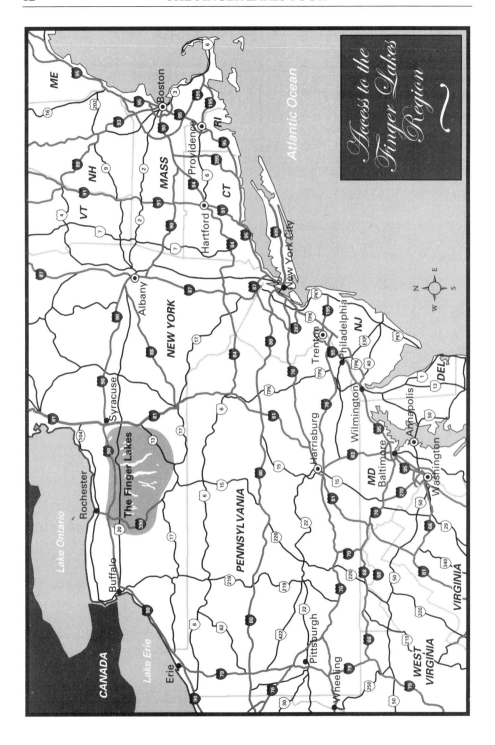

Access to the Finger Lakes Region

Catskills and southern tier of the state to Erie, Pennsylvania, makes it well worth going this way unless you are into high-speed driving. Gas stations and other services are well marked on the route.

The New York Thruway (Interstate 90): Runs along the top third of the state from Albany to Buffalo and south to Erie. It's rather boring, but efficient with speed limits up to 65mph in places. Service areas are at regular intervals about every fifteen to twenty miles. This is a toll road.

Rte. 20: The old route used extensively before the Thruway was built links Albany to Buffalo. It runs right through the center of many of the Finger Lake's most beautiful towns. If you have the time — village speed limits and stop lights will slow your pace — but want to capture the flavor of the region, I recommend you take the time to go this route. Major towns along Rte. 20 include Skaneateles, Auburn, Seneca Falls, Waterloo, Geneva, and Canandaigua. Feeders into the lake roads run off the route.

North-South Routes

Major north-south routes are I-81 bordering the eastern lakes region and Rte. 390 going from Rte. 17 to Rochester.

I-81: Running along the easternmost border of the region, this divided highway has fair to good roads and well-marked exits. There are two lanes each way along most of route. Some services on the road.

Rte. 15: Runs from Washington DC through central Pennsylvania, Harrisburg, and through the heart of Amish country to Corning.

I-390: Skirts the western part of the region from Rte. 17 to Rochester.

BY WATER

Erie Canal

Running east-west from Albany to Buffalo, the New York State canal system contains 524 miles of canal and waterways connecting Albany, Utica, Syracuse, Rochester, and Buffalo. Systems include the Erie Canal, the Champlain and Oswego systems, and the Cayuga-Seneca Canal built in 1821 to connect the two lakes.

The canal, which is usually navigable April through November, has sixty locks making it possible for canal boats and pleasure craft to go across the state by water. Boat launches are located at points along the way. For more information, contact the NYS Canal System: 518-471-5011; www.canals.state.ny.us.

Pleasure boats go through the lock at Waterloo as they cruise the Erie Canal.

Peter Finger

Boating

In line with the Federal Boating Act, every boat using auxiliary power must be registered and numbered. Licenses are issued for a three-year period.

Those bringing in boats from other states do not need to get a license for ninety days providing these boats are numbered according to federal law. If you don't have a proper registration, you need to get one. Contact the Dept. of Motor Vehicles, Div. of Motor Vehicle Regulation, Empire State Plaza, Albany NY 12228. A free pocket guide and map brochure on the Canal and Lakes System is available by calling 800-KIT-4-FUN.

Speed Limit: 5 mph within 100 feet of shore, except on Canandaigua and Keuka lakes where the limit is extended to 200 feet from shore.

ARRIVING AT HOST CITIES

CORNING

By Air

Elmira/Corning Regional Airport (607-739-5621; Exit 51 on Rte. 17, Corning NY 14830) Scheduled air services with USAirways and Northwest Airlines. Corning is also about equal distance from the Syracuse and Rochester airports.

Chartering a Canal Boat

Erie Canal Cruise Lines: Half-week and full-week charters on the Erie Canal are available from $1,500. Up to six adults are included in the fare along with linens, fuel, housewares, lock fees, itinerary, and applicable tax. The forty-foot custom-built canal cruiser features two private suites with a vanity, toilet, and access to the shower, a dinette that converts to a full-size berth, and a fully equipped galley. The boat is air-conditioned and there is a television/vcr and cd/casette player. Social and lounging areas are located aft and on the top deck. The interior of the boat has a knotty-pine homey feeling with curtains on the windows.

You can begin your trip in Seneca Falls on the Cayuga-Seneca Canal where you will experience the double lock, lifting you fifty feet in back-to-back lock chambers. You'll join the Erie Canal just beyond the Montezuma National Wildlife Refuge. A 200-mile bike and hiking path traces the original Erie Canal towpath. You can also start in Fairport, southeast of Rochester and cruise west toward Pittsford and Lockport. 800-962-1771.

Mid-Lakes Navigation Company: Two- and three-night canal cruises with accommodations at ports along the way. For example, the forty-passenger *Emita II*, which sails from Buffalo to Syracuse and Albany, has a bar, library, open front deck, and upper deck.

For those who prefer to captain their own boat, Mid-Lakes charters Lockmaster Canalboats ranging from thirty-three feet to forty-four feet long and ten feet wide with a top speed of about six mph. The boats are fairly simple to operate and navigate the locks in about twenty minutes. The boats come with fully equipped galleys, VHF radio, ice cooler, gas range, refrigerator, binoculars, linens, cleaning supplies, and two bicycles. Some have two cabins. Weekly charters costs from $1700 to $2300. Starting at Cold Springs harbor near Syracuse, you can choose to cruise three different canals. One of the most popular is the Cayuga-Seneca Canal; tie up in Seneca Falls for the night. 800-545-4318.

By Train

Corning is about equal distance from the Rochester and Syracuse Amtrak stations. The distance is approximately seventy-six miles in either direction.

Rental Cars

Avis, Hertz, and National car rentals are available at the airport.

ELMIRA

By Air

Elmira/Corning Regional Airport (607-739-5621; Exit 51 on Rte. 17, Corning NY 14830) Scheduled air services with USAirways and Northwest Airlines. Elmira is also about equal distance from the Syracuse and Rochester airports.

The Corning Museum of Glass bus shuttles customers back and forth from Corning's Market Street.

Peter Finger

By Train

Elmira is about equal distance from the Rochester and Syracuse Amtrak stations. The distance is approximately seventy-six miles in either direction.

Rental Cars

Avis, Hertz, and National car rentals are available at the airport.

ITHACA

By Air

Tompkins County Airport (607-257-0456; www.tompkins-co.org/airport or www.co.tompkins.ny.us/airport/airport.hmtl; 72 Brown Rd., Ithaca NY 14850) The airport is served by USAirways with jet service to Pittsburgh and forty-five other daily flights to Philadelphia, New York City, and Boston. The airport has a café, conference room, computer/fax/modem jacks, and a limousine shuttle.

By Train

Ithaca is about forty-seven miles from the Syracuse Amtrak station.

Rental Cars

Avis and Hertz rental cars are at the airport terminal.

ROCHESTER

By Air

Greater Rochester International Airport (716-464-6000; www.rocairport.com; 1200 Brooks Ave., Rochester NY 14624)) On the south side of Rochester fifteen minutes from downtown, the airport has one main terminal with two concourses. More than 220 flights a day fly to twenty-two cities nationwide. On-site services include shuttles to the hotels, car rentals, taxi and bus service, sheltered parking garage, business center, meeting rooms, restaurants, and gift shops.

Rochester Shuttle Express (888-663-3770, 716-663-3760) Round-the-clock, door-to-door service between your home and the Greater Rochester International Airport. The shuttle also offers mini-tours of Rochester, and trips to Niagara Falls, Buffalo, and Toronto.

By Train

Amtrak Station (800-USA-RAIL, 800-872-7245; www.amtrak.com; 320 Central Ave., Rochester NY 14605) Services: Ticket sales, Quik-Trak Ticketing Machines, checked baggage. The trip to New York City takes about six and a half hours; the run from Rochester to Syracuse is one hour, sixteen minutes.

By Bus

The Regional Transit Service (RTS) (716-288-1700, 888-288-3777; 187 Midtown Plaza) A quick, convenient way to get around. NY State Trailways and Greyhound bus terminals here.

By Car

A color-coded sign system aids drivers in navigating downtown Rochester. Convention Center (red); Eastman Theatre (blue); Shopping (orange); Strong Museum (brown); War Memorial (green). Auto rentals — Alamo, Americar, Avis, Budget, Enterprise, Hertz, National, and Thrifty — at the Greater Rochester International Airport and other outlets.

By Taxi

Taxis can be found at the airport, bus station, train terminal, hotels, and on call.

SYRACUSE

By Air

Syracuse Hancock International Airport (315-454-4330; Rte. 81, Exit 27, Syracuse) More than 270 passenger flights arrive and depart daily from the airport which is serviced by six major airlines and three commuter lines.

By Train

William F. Walsh Regional Transportation Center (General information: 315-

478-1936; 131 P&C Pkwy., Syracuse NY 13208) Services include ticket sales, checked baggage. **Amtrak** (800-USA-RAIL; 800-872-7245; www.amtrak.com) provides rail passenger transportation for an East Syracuse terminal with eight daily departures. The trip to New York City takes about five and a quarter hours.

Ontrack (315-424-1212) Originally started to get Syracuse University students around, its services have been expanded to include an extensive network of routes through historic areas, fall foliage tours, even cowboy holdups and a Santa's train.

By Bus

Greyhound/Trailways: 800-231-2222

Centro Bus/Central New York Transportation Authority (315-442-3333) provides public transportation in the city and to the suburbs. Onondaga Coach, Greyhound, Syracuse & Oswego, and Trailways also have inter-city passenger service.

By Taxi

Taxis can be found at the airport, bus station, train terminal, hotels, and on call.

By Water

The Port of Oswego on the southeast shore of Lake Ontario is thirty-four miles northwest of Syracuse. The New York State canal system encompasses 524 miles and runs east-west across the state linking the Niagara River with the Hudson River. The Onondaga Lake Barge Canal Terminal is just north of Syracuse.

By Car

Alamo, Americar, Avis, Budget, Enterprise, Hertz, National, and Thrifty auto rentals are available at Hancock International Airport and other outlets.

SCENIC ROUTES

The entire Finger Lakes region is laced with roads and highways providing some of the most scenic views in the country. Here are some suggestions.

Keuka Lake

Shoreline Route: Rte. 54A, which runs 22.6 miles from Penn Yan to Hammondsport along the westernmost shore, clings closely to the shoreline, winding and twisting around coves and rock outcroppings. For this reason, it is considered one of the most scenic drives in the world. Several restaurants are along the route with open decks close to the water.

Middle Road Overlook: Middle Rd., along with Rtes. 74/76, runs through the hillside vineyards, revealing stunning views of the lake. I suggest you do a loop, going one way on Rte. 54A and returning on Rte. 76, Middle Rd. and 74. Going south from the northern end, Rte. 54A splits at Branchport. Go right on Italy Road then left on 74/76. Follow the signs to Dr. Frank's Vinifera Wine Cellars, Heron Hill Winery, and Bully Hill, which will jog you over to Middle Rd. and south to Hammondsport. Then return along 54A where you will get so close to moored boats you can read their names.

East Bluff Drive and Skyline Drive: These roads run between the Y branches of Keuka Lake. At the crook of the Y, there are some spectacular views of the lake in all directions.

New York to Finger Lakes Rte. 17: This has been designated as one of the most scenic highways in the country. The highway winds through the Catskills and along many gushing, rugged streams.

Canandaigua Lake

Lake Loop: Starting from Rtes. 5&20 in Canandaigua, take Rte. 364 south. After about 13 miles, go straight on West Ave., then take a quick short left onto Coward Cross Rd., then a quick right at the stop sign on Rte. 245 south into Naples. At the end of Rte. 245, take a right onto Rte. 21 and go north and take it back into Canandaigua. Stop in Naples to visit the Arbor Hill Grapery and Widmer's Wine Cellars.

Cayuga Lake

Lake Loop: Take Rte. 90S off Rte. 20, drive down the eastern shore of Cayuga Lake, stop at Aurora for a bite to eat or shopping, continue on to Ithaca at the southern end of the lake then return along the western shore past Taughannock Falls to reconnect with Rte. 20. This loop around the lake can take a couple of hours of a whole day if you stop for lunch and check out the vineyards and attractions along the way.

New Scenic Byway: The portion of Rte. 90 that runs from Montezuma to Homer has been officially designated a scenic byway. This is the first segment of a proposed scenic route that will circle Cayuga Lake.

Conesus Lake

Lake Loop: From Lakeville, go west on Rte. 20A then left onto Rte. 256 (W. Lake Rd.) Follow this to south end of the lake then turn left onto Slyker Hill Rd. and left again onto East Lake Rd. Go north back to Lakeville. Round-trip is about 19 miles.

Skaneateles Lake

Lake Loop: From Rt 20 in the village, take Rte. 41A south along West Lake Rd. You'll pass Mandana and New Hope on your way to the south end of the lake. At New Hope watch for Glen Haven Rd. and turn left. Turn right at the T-junction and continue on Glen Haven Rd. Turn left at the stop sign, Rte. 41A and go north along the east side of the lake back to the village. You'll enjoy many lake views and pass several farms. Fun stops along the way include New Hope Mill in New Hope and the old Glen Haven Hotel (watch for sign). Round trip is about 40 miles.

CHAPTER THREE
Picture Perfect

SKANEATELES, OWASCO, AND OTISCO LAKES

Gazebos, water, and boats are familiar features of the Finger Lakes; Clift Park in Skaneateles offers all three.

Close to Syracuse, and the most eastern of the Finger Lakes, Skaneateles, Otisco, and Owasco are all quite different in style and spirit.

SKANEATELES LAKE AND SKANEATELES

At sixteen miles long and just one to two miles wide, Skaneateles Lake lives up to the meaning of its name, "long lake." Tucked in and around the lake are the small villages of Skaneateles at the north end, Mandana and New Hope on the west side, Glen Haven at the south end, and Spafford and Borodino on the east side. Because of its depth, up to 350 feet, the color of the water can change dramatically from deep cobalt to brilliant turquoise. Set against this stunning backdrop, the white sails of boats gliding noiselessly through the water are a magnificent sight.

At its northern end of the lake, Skaneateles reigns as the prima donna of Finger Lakes villages. Time and wise local policies have dealt kindly with it over the years. This pampered and prosperous picture-perfect place — about 2,800 in the village, 4,800 in the town — attracts doctors, contractors, academics, manufacturers, lawyers, sales representatives, and other affluent types who vie for choice and pricey homes that fan out around the northern tip of the lake, up the hills behind Genesee Street and along the shoreline.

The streets of Skaneateles are lined with Victorian houses.

Katharine Delavan Dyson

The village sidewalks pass by white Victorian and colonial houses; some with cupolas, others with wide porches furnished with wicker rockers. All are impeccably maintained, many are of historic interest. (It is interesting to note that early records indicate the first houses in town were painted red.)

A few years ago, Skaneateles hit the national news for its stress-free environment program. Those parked along Genesee Street had no reason to panic if their meter time had run out: the meter police would drop in an extra coin for them so they would have more time to shop, eat, and linger.

Throughout the year is an ongoing array of hometown fun. Every Friday evening in the summer in Clift Park, a community band plays from the round gazebo, entertaining villagers with rousing Sousa marches, show tunes, and other upbeat music. Sunday afternoons in July and August there are polo matches in a field off West Lake Road; the last weekend in July is the Antique and Classic Boat Show, and every weekend in August, the Skaneateles Musical Festival showcases music under the stars.

At Thanksgiving there is the Turkey Trot, a fun run for charity; at Christmastime Dickens characters stroll the sidewalks greeting shoppers who come to browse and buy from the many boutiques, galleries, and gift stores. Memorial and Labor Day weekends roll out old-fashioned parades, parties, games, rides, and fireworks.

Manufacturing companies just north of the village in Skaneateles Falls are Welch Allyn, Inc., a highly respected medical instrument and fiber optics company, Scapa Filtration Inc., and Habermaass, a wooden toy company founded by Marshal Larrabee in 1936 as Skaneateles Handicrafters and known for its high quality hardwood pull trains, blocks, and toys. When Larrabee sold the company to the German-based company in 1980, the product name was changed to T.C. Timber.

The village has three lakeside parks: Clift Park, Thayer Park, and Shotwell Park, as well as Austin Park on the north end of town with tennis courts and ball fields. The Allyn Arena is used for ice skating in the winter and special events in the warmer months. A small ski area is just outside town; Syracuse is eighteen miles northeast.

Skaneateles is the place to shop. Genesee Street, with its brick sidewalks, brick buildings, and period lighting, is lined with interesting boutiques, craft shops, galleries, and cafés. The village welcomes hundreds of tourists each year who come mainly in the warmer months to browse and buy.

SKANEATELES: GROWTH AND DEVELOPMENT

In 1791, Skaneateles contained forty-one military lots given to Revolutionary War soldiers, surveyors, and early settlers as compensation.

The land the village now occupies was originally lot #36 purchased by Jedediah Sanger, who constructed a log dam in 1797 in the center of town where the outlet from the lake flows under a bridge and the main street. The increased water flow created power to operate a grist and saw mill. Most recently the mill has contained a restaurant and pub. (As of this writing, it was closed.)

In 1794, John Thompson settled on military lot #18 and that same year Abraham A. Cuddeback took the forty-three-day wagon journey from Orange County, New York, to Skaneateles, bringing his wife, eight children, three yoke of oxen, a horse, and twelve cows. He built a log cabin on a heavily wooded piece of land on the west side of the lake and more families followed.

An ideal location to attract settlers, Skaneateles was at the junction of two major routes, Rte. 20, the Cherry Valley Turnpike, and the Great Genesee Road, which followed the old trail of native Americans from Utica and Canandaigua (later the 1800 Seneca Turnpike improved the same road).

This land held much promise. The outlet to the lake provided water power for mills and other industries; the soil was fertile for crops such as corn, beans, and wheat; and the lake not only supplied settlers with water, but the scenery also soothed the soul. Gradually the town grew; tanneries, bark mills, distilleries, cigar making, blacksmiths, and other businesses opened up, some clustered around Mottville, just north of the village center. Farms specialized in crops like tobacco for cigars, cabbages for sauerkraut, and teasels.

Skaneateles's first store was opened in 1803 by Winston Day and by 1830 there were seven stores, a Masonic Hall, three hotels, two sleigh and carriage factories, five flour mills, six saw mills, two iron foundries, and one brass foundry.

There was also the Sherwood Inn. Dominating the lakefront on the west end of the village, the sprawling blue inn started life as Isaac Sherwood's Tavern in

> ### Teasels
>
> For more than a hundred years virtually all teasels cultivated in American came from the Skaneateles area and nearby Marcellus. Teasels look like thistles, but the stiff natural awns (hooks) on the burr head grow down, making it an excellent "tool" to raise the nap of woolen cloth. Some teasel barns have been converted into private residences. One is on East Street; another on a side road off Academy Street.

1806, welcoming travelers arriving by stagecoach. Over the years the hotel expanded and changed names several times, from Sherwood's Tavern, to Lamb's Inn, Houndayaga House, Packwood's National Hotel, Packwood House, Kan-Ya-To-Inn ("beautiful view"), and back to the Sherwood Inn, thanks to Chester (Chet) Coates, one of the previous owners, who lived in a wing on the second floor with his wife and daughters. Today the Sherwood Inn is owned by William Eberhardt.

A man of large proportions and vision, Sherwood also owned the Old Mail Line stage coach company which carried mail between Utica and Canandaigua. More than fifteen stages stopped daily at the Sherwood on their route.

Carriage and boat building were very important to the village's early economic growth. Carriage builders included Seth and James Hall, John Packwood, and former blacksmith John Legg. Boat companies founded here included the Bowdish Boat Company, the Edson Boat Company, and George Barnes' Skaneateles Boat and Canoe Company where the first Lightening Class sailboat was built. The Lightening in those days was a seventeen-foot double-planked centerboard-style wood boat. A lighter version in fiberglass is today a popular recreational craft on the lake.

In the late 1800s, Syracuse, seventeen miles to the northeast, started tapping into the lake for its drinking water. The water in the outlet slowed down, waterwheels turned more sluggishly, and industry was curtailed. Although Skaneateles Lake is known for its purity, a critical period for the village occurred in the 1920s when Syracuse's withdrawal of water brought the lake level to a dangerously low point, upsetting the sewage system. A typhoid epidemic broke out when the water became contaminated and village leader Charles Major, Sr., had to pipe water into the community.

THE COMING OF THE RAILROAD AND STEAMBOATS

In 1840, a railroad with horse-drawn cars shuttled passengers back and forth between the village and Skaneateles Junction five miles north of town, where they could connect to the Syracuse-Auburn Railroad. The Skaneateles Railroad, a steam line, was launched in 1865, replacing the equine version. The line was so short that when some became concerned about snow and rain, one man replied, "Hell, build a roof over it."

Around 1900, the Auburn and Syracuse Electric Trolley began, shuttling people between cities. Both the train and later the trolley tied into the lake steamboats. The first steamboat, the eighty-foot *Independent,* began carrying passengers up and down the lake in 1831, and was later joined by the forty-foot *Highland Chief,* the *Homer,* the *Ben H. Porter,* the 180-foot *Glen Haven, Ossahinta,* and *City of Syracuse-on-the-Lake,* which carried passengers to the south end of the lake to Glen Haven, where there was a spa-style resort and a small village with a hotel, restaurant, and a couple of stores. The hotel is gone, but there is still a small community and a lakeside restaurant.

The large steamboats ceased to exist in 1917, but smaller boats took up the slack for important services such as mail delivery to the lake-bound cottages. Mailboxes were placed on the end of docks, and the boat would cruise alongside and deposit the mail all around the lake. Sometimes passengers packed lunches and went along for the ride. Today this practice continues on the U.S. Mailboat Cruise operated by Mid-Lakes Navigation Company.

Among the early boat operators were Mr. A.J. Hoffman who ran the *Florence,* and the Stinsons who ran the Stinson Boat Line from 1938 until 1968 when the boat *Pat II* was sold to Peter Wiles of Mid-Lakes. Today the *Judge Ben Wiles,* a handsome double-deck diesel craft resembling the old steamboats, offers dining and sightseeing cruises on Skaneateles Lake. Over the past thirty years, Mid-Lakes has branched out from Skaneateles with a lake and canal boat operation throughout the Finger Lakes.

FAMOUS VISITORS AND RESIDENTS

Famous visitors to Skaneateles have included General de Lafayette, statesman and orator Daniel Webster in 1825, and General Jonathan Wainwright, who was feted in his wife's hometown in one of the grandest parades the town has ever seen, when he returned from a World War II concentration camp. Most recently, the former President and Hillary Clinton vacationed here at a private home on East Lake Road.

Skaneateles was the home of a lot of Roosevelts. Nicholas Roosevelt lived in town from 1831 to 1854. His relative, Samuel Montgomery Roosevelt, and later his son, Henry Latrobe Roosevelt, spent summers in an imposing pillared Greek Revival mansion called Roosevelt Hall. Famous guests included Theodore as well as Franklin and Eleanor Roosevelt. The Roosevelts would

---

Big Doings in Skaneateles

"We haven't had this much excitement since Banjo Greenfield's son, Dozer, towed his double wide through town and they had to raise the street lights." (Matt Major referring to the impending arrival of President Bill and Hillary Clinton who came to vacation on the lake in 1999.)

often bring showgirls to the property to perform on a grassy flat stage near the shore: friends and guests enjoyed the entertainment from seats set on the tiered hillside facing the lake.

William H. Delavan, who purchased the home in 1942, renovated the mansion and restored a large conservatory-style greenhouse filled with tropical trees and flowers. After Delavan sold the estate in 1959, the new owner divided the land into a few building lots. Today the greenhouse is gone and the property, originally covering twenty acres, contains a handful of luxury homes. The last private owner, Dennis Owen, deeded the mansion to the Catholic Diocese and it is now occupied by the Christian Brothers.

GONE WITH THE WIND

O ver the years a number of sports activities have risen and fallen in popularity. Once hot, now gone, are horse racing, ice boating, rollerskating, and Microd racing. Microds were an interesting phenomena. From 1954–1965, young boys, with help from their dads and the Robinson family who built the first prototype in their barn, constructed miniature automobiles made of plywood and powered by lawn mower engines. All summer long, weekly races were held on the track where the Allyn Arena now stands. Each car was sponsored by a member of the business community. If you think Little League baseball gets competitive, you should have seen this crowd: the sidelines were jammed with people cheering on their favorite cars as they raced around the track.

When the Lyric Circus came to town in 1952 and erected its huge blue tent on a site just east of the village, professional actors, actresses, and musicians from New York would perform in a summer series of musicals on a round stage surrounded by tiers of seats. Residents got involved in many aspects including marketing, financing, and ushering. In the late 50s, attendance declined. The final blow came from a hurricane which took the tent down; by 1960, the theater shut down.

OWASCO LAKE AND AUBURN

T he largest populated area in this three-lakes region, the city of Auburn, is two and a half miles north of Owasco Lake. In native American, Owasco means "the crossing." Those passing through town along Route 20 do not get so much as a peek at the twelve-mile-long deep blue lake. Reward yourself with some magnificent views of the water by taking a detour via Lake Avenue to Emerson Park.

Owasco Lake is surrounded by rolling farm lands, lakeside homes, and camps. At the southern end is Moravia, a small village of nineteenth-century homes and long-time residents. One of its biggest assets, Fillmore Glen State Park, is blessed with nature trails, picnic areas, deep gorges, and waterfalls. Moravia is the birthplace of our thirteenth president, Millard Fillmore, and childhood home of John D. Rockefeller. A blue historical marker notes the place where Rockefeller's house once stood.

Auburn has exceptional art and historical museums as well as more than 200 homes and buildings of architectural interest. Established in 1793, Auburn was once a busy, growing city. In the early 1900s, small manufacturing companies made their headquarters here producing products such as shoes, rope, and farm machinery. In the last fifty years, most of these companies have moved out, leaving behind a slower-paced, perhaps less affluent town, but still one with a great deal of charm offering a pleasant, affordable style of living, a fine lake, and a handful of lovely parks.

Tree-shaded neighborhoods of substantial turn-of-the-century houses with wide front porches leading to sidewalks recall the days when Auburn was on the move. In particular the South Street area, a National Register Historic District, is home to several important buildings including the Seward House, former residence of William H. Seward, governor of New York, Lincoln's secretary of state, and the man responsible for purchasing Alaska for $2 an acre (they called it "Seward's Folly"). Harriet Tubman's modest dwelling and the home she built for her mother is farther down the street on the edge of town. Tubman, a Maryland slave, escaped to the north where she became a leader in the Underground Railroad movement, hiding runaway slaves until they could find freedom in Canada.

On summer evenings concerts take place in Hoopes Park with its pretty pond and spouting fountain. In Emerson Park the Merry-Go-Round Playhouse stages professional musical productions in a building which formerly housed a fabulous carousel which my children loved to ride on — it had a real brass ring and splendid wood horses. The carousel seemingly disappeared overnight when it was sold and quietly moved out-of-state. An amusement park and games arcade, once a source of family fun in the park, is also gone but the large pavilion — once the scene of many a big band cotillion — still exists and is often rented out for weddings and other large parties and events.

Auburn's shopping activity has largely moved from Genesee Street to the Finger Lakes Mall outside the village center, and indeed a bypass road encourages that movement. Insurance companies, banks, real estate offices, and other businesses have taken the spaces once occupied by retail stores. The whole area is neat and businesslike, but still some retail establishments in the old center

---

Auburn Prison

Looming in a corner of the city, the gray walls of the Auburn Correctional Facility, a maximum security prison, continue to draw curious onlookers. Site of the first electric chair (now a museum piece) and the place Chester Gillette of *An American Tragedy* was put to death, the prison is an important part of Auburn's history and still in operation.

such as Nolan's Shoe Store and the Liberty Store continue to hang in there. A few newer stores, such as Ardvarks and Zippers, and restaurants like Parker's, a new bistro-style restaurant, and the eclectic Kangaroo Court bar and restaurant continue to attract loyal patrons to the once thriving "downtown."

Peter Finger

Otisco Lake is one of the smallest — and quietest — of the Finger Lakes.

OTISCO LAKE

The easternmost lake, Otisco, is small, quiet. The largest village, Amber, on the east side, has only a few stores and homes. At the northern end, water spills over a dam into a river. Just six miles long, Otisco is surrounded by wooded hills; a pretty place for a drive or a picnic. Better yet, if you have a canoe in tow, it's a perfect lake for paddling. Other than a couple of snack stands, Footprints restaurant on the water, and marinas, there isn't a whole lot more going on here.

LODGING

Although the Sherwood Inn, the Lady of the Lake, and Hobbit Hollow have views of Skaneateles Lake, there are no places to stay directly on the water. Lodging choices range from country inns and a smart new resort-spa to bed & breakfasts and 50s-style motels; a few chain hotels are in Auburn.

Syracuse, about a half hour drive from Skaneateles and Auburn, has a wider choice of accommodations (see Chapter Nine, *Host Cities*, for more information about Syracuse lodgings).

LODGING RATES

$: Up to $75 per couple

$$: $76–$150 per couple

$$$: $151–$250 per couple

$$$$: More than $250

Skaneateles

INNS AND HOTELS

THE BIRD'S NEST MOTEL
315-685-5641
Rte. 20, 1601 E. Genesee St.,
  Skaneateles NY 13152
Innkeepers: Patricia and
  Eugene Creech
Rooms: 30 rooms, suites,
  apartments
Open: Year-round
Price: $–$$
Credit cards: Most major

On the edge of Skaneateles, this is your basic motel with seventeen rooms, ten junior suites, and three efficiency apartments, all on ground level. Cool off in the outdoor pool tucked between Rte. 20 and the parking area: not scenic but useful.

MIRBEAU INN AND SPA
315-685-5006,
  877-MIRBEAU;
  fax 315-685-5150
www.mirbeau.com
851 W. Genesee St.,
  Skaneateles NY 13152
Innkeeper: Toby Franklin
Rooms: 34 rooms, cottages,
  suites
Open: Year-round
Price: $$$$
Credit cards: Most major

Tucked into a hillside on the edge of Skaneateles, the new resort Mirbeau is targeting affluent travelers with a full-service spa with ten treatment rooms and a choice of a wide variety of therapies. An elegant resting area is modeled after a Roman bath with soft lighting, columns, lovely wall frescoes, soft comfortable chaises, and radiant-heated floors. European in feeling, Mirbeau has deep ochre stuccoed walls with blue trim and shutters, high-pitched tile-like roofs, arched windows, and massive 300-year-old timbers which have been designed into the buildings.

Rooms face inward around a pond reminiscent of Monet's water garden at Giverney. There is an arched bridge, water iris, and many other flowers and shrubs. Arched iron trellises with climbing roses and wisteria create a romantic entry to many of the cottages. A grove of tall trees, wildflowers, and a few benches beckon to those who want some quiet time; a meditation trail and tea house are to come. A personal valet escorts you to your room and helps you with whatever you might need including golf tee times or dinner reservations.

Peter Finger

The Mirbeau Inn and Spa in Skaneateles, the region's newest luxury hotel and spa.

Guest rooms are spacious and superbly appointed. Fabrics were designed in France; linens, including Frette, come from Italy, and duvets are filled with Canadian down. Armoires with fine inlays, period pieces, antiques, and fireplaces add to the ambiance. Many rooms have beamed ceilings and are painted in deep red or gold. Each room has a fireplace and a patio or balcony with wrought iron table and chairs. Baths come with deep French-soaking tubs on feet, large showers, and double vanities. The sound system is Bose with a cd player. Some of the public rooms are faux-painted by hand in deep ochre; one has a ceiling border of grape vines. The dining room features "Mirbeau Estate Cuisine" — see the *Restaurant* section below for more information.

SHERWOOD INN
315-685-3405,
  800-3-SHERWOOD;
  fax 315-685-8983
www.thesherwoodinn.com
26 W. Genesee St./Rte. 20,
  Skaneateles NY 13152
Innkeeper: William
  Eberhardt
Rooms: 20
Open: Year-round
Price: $$–$$$
Serving: Continental B, L, D
Credit cards: Most major

Located on the southern end of the lake just across from a waterside park, this historic inn — built in 1807 and once a stagecoach stop — is a rambling blue three-story building right in the center of town and shops. It has wide porches and a pub-like bar. The rooms and suites are all different; some overlook the lake, others the back yard and parking lot (the views may not be the greatest but the rooms are very quiet). Decor is eclectic colonial with a bit of early American and Victorian thrown in. Avoid the room over the tavern unless you're into late night music. As the floors creak, the third floor rooms tend to be more serene. For sheer style,

The Sherwood Inn, Skaneateles, which dates back to 1806, was once a stop on the stagecoach route.

Katharine Delavan Dyson

my favorite is Room 21, a lakeside suite with a fireplace and wet bar. The 1807 suite has four bedrooms, two baths, living room, dining room, and kitchen: perfect for families or groups who want to share space and costs. Recent renovations have been completed in the public areas. Eat in the dining room or tavern.

BED & BREAKFASTS

ARBOR HOUSE INN B&B
315-685-8966, 888-234-4558
www.arborhouseinn.com
41 Fennell St., Skaneateles
NY 13152
Innkeeper: Renee Valentine
Rooms: 5 with private baths
Open: Year-round
Price: $–$$
Credit cards: Most major

This mid-nineteenth-century brick Federal-style house was recently converted to an inn with great style. Although it's across from a supermarket, it hardly matters. It's just a five minute walk to the lake and the center of town; a quiet back yard has gardens and a barn (formerly filled with teasels). Four rooms and one two-room suite come with private baths, four with jacuzzi tubs, two with gas fireplaces; all are air-conditioned and beautifully furnished with a combination of antiques and reproductions as well as Oriental rugs. Breakfast is served on the sun porch and there's a wet bar in the kitchen. Non-smoking.

THE GRAY HOUSE
315-685-0131
47 Jordan St., Skaneateles
NY 13152
Innkeepers: Val and Bob
Gray
Rooms: 3 with private baths
Open: Year-round
Price: $–$$
Credit cards: Most major

Just one block from Genesee St., the main shopping area, and the lake, this beautifully decorated Victorian home has two large living rooms, air conditioning, two porches, and gardens. There is one suite with a queen-size bed and a day bed that converts into two twins. A full breakfast is served. Seasonal suites and short-term rentals are also available.

Peter Finger

Hobbit Hollow Farm Bed & Breakfast overlooks Skaneateles Lake.

**HOBBIT HOLLOW FARM
BED & BREAKFAST**
315-685-2791;
  fax 315-685-3426
www.hobbithollow.com
3061 W. Lake Rd.,
  Skaneateles NY 13152
Innkeeper: Richard Fynn
Rooms: 5 with private baths
Open: Year-round
Price: $$–$$$$
Credit cards: Most major

Set high on 320 hillside acres overlooking the lake just five minutes from the village center, this beautifully furnished 100-year-old colonial house has all the amenities of a lovely private home — which it once was. Rooms overlook horses grazing in white-fenced fields, vineyards, and the lake. Each room has a private bath, floors are beautifully polished, and the appointments are elegant — gilt mirrors, Oriental carpets, white-painted deep moldings, hand-painted wall murals, and matelasse and Frette linens. The Master Suite faces the lake and horse stables and contains a four-poster king-size bed, fireplace, two-person whirlpool, and a private veranda furnished with wicker chairs and tables. Chanticleer is decorated in French country and is spacious and sunny. It has a queen-size pencil four-poster bed and European soaking tub. This room also overlooks the lake and fields. A full breakfast is served in the elegant yellow dining room.

LADY OF THE LAKE
315-685-7997,
  888-685-7997
2 W. Lake Rd., Skaneateles
  NY 13152

An ideal location on the corner of Genesee Street and West Lake Road within a block of the lake, park, and shopping area, this nineteenth-century Victorian house features details like a front

*The Lady of the Lake, a B&B
in the center of Skaneateles.*

Katharine Delavan Dyson

Innkeeper: Sandra
   Rademacher
Rooms: 3 with private baths
Open: Year-round
Price: $$
Credit cards: Most major

porch, stained glass windows, gracious wide stair-case, and lovely parlor and dining room. Guest rooms are each different and furnished with a collection of period furniture and antiques. The Stella, the largest room, has a white iron king-size bed set into an alcove where you get a peek at the lake. Full breakfasts are served.

Owasco Lake and Auburn

HOLIDAY INN
315-253-4531;
   fax 315-252-5843
www.holiday-inn.com/
   auburnny
75 North St. (corner Rte. 34,
   Rte. 20, & Rte. 5), Auburn
   NY 13021
Manager: Linda Knight
Rooms: 166
Open: Year-round
Price: $$
Credit cards: Most major

Centrally located in the business part of town, this is a popular choice with those on the road. Don't expect many surprises in decor; the inn is typically Holiday Inn. Still the newly renovated rooms are comfortable and some come with jacuzzis and some overlook the courtyard. There is a very nice indoor pool and courtyard; for an area that can get some rather cold weather, that's a big plus. Some locals have been known to check in with their kids for the weekend for some relaxation and swimming. There is also a fitness center, business center, restaurant, game room, and lounge. Ripples restaurant serves breakfast, lunch, and dinner. Scores Lounge offers entertainment on weekends. A convention center and meeting rooms accommodate up to 700 people.

**MICROTEL INN AND
   SUITES**
315-253-5000, 888-771-7171

This new hotel is in the center of town on Rtes. 5 and 20, making it a good base for those on business. The hotel features suites with separate living

Peter Finger

Springside Inn, Auburn, offers food and lodging.

12 Seminary Ave., Auburn
    NY 13021
Manager: Michael Lucas
Rooms: 79
Open: Year-round
Price: $–$$
Credit cards: Most major

SPRINGSIDE INN
315-252-7247;
    fax 315-252-8096
www.springsideinn.com
6141 W. Lake Rd., Rte. 38,
    Auburn NY 13021
Innkeepers: Sean and Beth
    Lattimore
Rooms: 8
Open: Year-round
Price: $–$$
Credit cards: Most major

rooms and kitchenettes equipped with microwave ovens and refrigerators. Furnishings are modern and efficient. Amenities include dataports, voice-mail, television, guest lounge, and fitness center. A complimentary breakfast is included in the rate, Monday through Friday.

With new owners, the jury is still out on this four-story mid-1800s frame inn built first as a boarding school and in subsequent years used as private residence, summer resort, and, finally, year-round hotel. It is believed that runaway slaves were once hidden in the house and in the thickets behind. Over the years, Springside has had its ups and downs. Now it is undergoing renovations and an infusion of enthusiasm from owners, Sean and Beth Lattimore. The rooms are pleasant, and deco-rated with period pieces and quilts. But the beds (which to be fair may already have been replaced since I checked them out) need a bit of Goldilocks scrutiny: some are too soft, some too hard. Room #6 has one that is just right and lake views as well. Springside is better known as a place to eat and for group functions.

RESTAURANTS

Otisco Lake offers only a handful of seasonal restaurants and snack bars. Auburn on Owasco Lake and Skaneateles are quite a different story. Places to eat range from the pricey and elegant Mirbeau and Rosalie's in Skaneateles, to more casual restaurants like the Blue Water Grill on Skaneateles Lake, Doug's Fish Fry just a block away, and the family-owned and run Mandana Inn, famous for its scrod, further down the lake. In Auburn, there are a number of excellent steak houses, Italian-style cafés, and long-established restaurants including Balloons, Riordan's, and Lasces.

Anyone who has passed through Skaneateles, if only for a brief period, usually remembers Krebs. On Genesee Street in a modest two-story clapboard house with a large front porch, this restaurant has been famous for more than 100 years for its bounteous family-style meals ever since it was founded by Cora and Fred Krebs in 1899.

Prices are estimated per person for appetizer and dinner entrée without tax, tip, or alcoholic beverages.

$: Up to $10 $$$: $26–$40
$$: $11–$25 $$$$: More than $40

Skaneateles Lake and Skaneateles

BLUE WATER GRILL
315-685-6600
11 W. Genesee St.,
  Skaneateles NY 13152
Open: Daily 11:30–10
  depending on season
Price: $–$$
Serving: L, D
Cuisine: Bistro American
Credit cards: Most major

One of the hot spots in town, Blue Water Grill is the place locals head when they don't want to cook. The sandwiches are huge: I always share with whoever is game to do it. In the warm weather, ask to sit on the deck. It's right on the outlet to the lake so you get a good water view; you can practically pull up in your boat and tie up just below the deck. The menu is loaded with good things like grilled chicken pesto wrap, turkey wrap — lots of wraps — hamburgers, ravioli, fajitas, BBQ chicken, steak sandwiches, and nachos. Vegetarians will find plenty of tempting items. I especially like the pizza topped with fresh basil, tomatoes, and mozzarella. The grill features a good selection of beer and wines along with shooters from the freezer. Sauza Commemoritivo Tequila? Now there's a challenge.

DOUG'S FISH FRY
315-685-3288
8 Jordan St., Skaneateles NY
  13152

They line up around the corner in the summertime for what some consider the best fried fish and chips outside of England. It all started in 1982 when Doug Clark opened up on a side street in a

Open: 11am–10pm in season;
 closes earlier off-season
Price: $–$$
Serving: L, D
Cuisine: Fish, chicken,
 seafood
Credit cards: No

small place with just two booths and a narrow counter with a couple of stools. The original place is still the heart of the operation but now you can take your meal to an adjacent antique brick building where there are tables and chairs; in the summer there is a roped-off picnic area in the parking lot where you can eat and mingle with locals and tourists alike. I always look forward to the fish sandwich ($4.09 or $6.25 with fries and slaw). There is also Doug's dippin' chicken dinner at $6.25, shrimp, scallops, lobster, clams, and sometimes frog legs. Also good is the homemade chowder, onion rings, franks, draft beer, and ice cream. It's my mother's favorite place.

**THE INN BETWEEN
 RESTAURANT**
315-672-3166
2290 W. Genesee Turnpike,
 Rte. 5, Camillus NY 13031
Open: Tues.–Sat. from 5,
 Sun. from 2, closed Mon.
Price: $$–$$$
Serving: D
Cuisine: Continental
Credit cards: Most major

Knotty-pine walls with an eclectic mix of furnishings and pastel-colored wall coverings and fabrics set the moods in this cheery restaurant housed in a well-maintained colonial house with three fireplaces. Meals are artfully presented and feature items such as baby rack of lamb, fresh seafood, and veal dishes.

**JOHNNY ANGEL'S
 HEAVENLY
 HAMBURGERS**
315-685-0100
22 Jordan St., Skaneateles
 NY 13152
Open: Daily 7am–8pm,
 Fri.–Sat. until 10
Price: $
Serving: B, L, D
Credit cards: MC, Visa,
 AmEx

It's the place to be for breakfast eggs, bacon, and New Hope Mills pancakes. Lunch and dinner feature half-pound burgers, homemade soups, fish, chicken, hot sandwiches, battered fries, Texas chili, pies, ice cream, beer, and wine. Order and pick up your food from the counter and take it to one of the long tables with red and white checkered tablecloths. Some families make breakfast here a Sunday morning habit. Adjacent to the main room is a new bar and dining area with smaller tables.

KABUKI
315-685-7234
12 Genesee St., Skaneateles
 NY 13152
Open: Daily 11:30–10
Price: $–$$
Serving: L, D
Cuisine: Japanese
Credit cards: Most major

For all those people who crave Japanese good, at last the Finger Lakes has a winner. One of the newest restaurants in town, Kabuki brings sushi and other Japanese specialties to Skaneateles. The design of this small restaurant is refreshingly clean, modern, oriental in flavor but not overdone, with yellow walls, a red ceiling, and soft green setting the tone. Sushi such as the California rolls and Hamachi (yellow tail) is fresh and tasty — you may decide to make a meal out of it. There are many other choices, including the Kabuki roll, which is filled with spicy shrimp and scallions; chicken sate made with marinated chicken, which you dip into a spicy peanut sauce; and the miso marinated sea bass, one of the restaurants most popular dishes. There is a full-service bar and takeout is available.

THE KREBS
315-685-5714, 315-685-7001
53 W. Genesee St.,
　Skaneateles NY 13152
Open: Open daily early
　May–late Oct.; D from 6,
　cocktails from 4, Sun.
　brunch 10:30–2; Sun.
　dinner from 4; Sun.
　cocktails from 12
Price: $$$–$$$$
Serving: Hearty American
　cuisine and lots of it
Credit cards: Most major

Arguably the most famous restaurant in the Finger Lakes, Krebs has been long known for its eat-all-you-want multi-course prix-fixe dinners. In the foyer, letters and signatures of several important people have been collected and framed, including notes from Franklin Roosevelt, who sat in one of the wicker rockers on the porch, and Charles Lindbergh and George Bernard Shaw, guests at the restaurant. Seven-course dinners are served on linen-covered tables in the rooms on the first floor.

Two rooms upstairs, furnished with Victorian settees and chairs, are used for pre-dinner cocktails. Another room contains a bar and dining room for casual dining with a pub menu. Outside, white wrought iron chairs and tables surrounded by lawns and gardens provide yet another place to sip a drink.

I was pleasantly surprised that even after all these years, most items are still very good, and homemade, such as the sticky rolls, soups, and pastries. With most courses, you have two or more choices including items like shrimp cocktail, soup (the tomato soup was excellent with huge chunks of fresh tomato), and the lobster newburg, which was loaded with lobster. The main course is served family-style, a parade of dishes filled with fried chicken, roast beef with horseradish sauce, mashed potatoes, yams, and other comfort foods; seconds are available, though with several courses already behind you, I can't believe anyone would ask for more.

Wines range from several less expensive wines such as a $13.95 white Niagara table wine from Wagner Vineyards and a $14.95 Sauvignon Blanc, Casa Lapostolle (Chile) to a $56.95 Moet & Chandon White Star champagne. Reservations are desirable.

MANDANA INN
315-685-7798; 315-685-6490
1937 W. Lake Rd., Rte. 41A,
　Mandana (on west side of
　Skaneateles Lake)
　Skaneateles NY 13152
Open: Apr. 1–Dec. 31, Mon.,
　Weds.–Sat. 5–10, Sun.
　3–8:30, closed Tues.;

A casual long-established family-owned and operated restaurant on the west side of the lake. I grew up with a strong dislike of fish until I was talked into eating the scrod here: Mandana Inn is famous for this dish prepared with a broiled crumb topping. I've been hooked on fish ever since. The homey interior, which has changed little over the past thirty years, is furnished with pine

winter open Weds.–Sat.
5–10, Sun. 3–8:30, closed
Mon. & Tues.
Price: $$
Serving: D
Cuisine: Fish, seafood,
    steak, Black Angus beef
Credit cards: Most major

tables and chairs and contains two dining rooms
and the Cherry Pub.

MARIETTA HOUSE
315-636-8299
Rte. 174S, Marietta NY 13110
Open: Apr.–Jan. 1 Fri. & Sat.
    from 5pm
Price: $$
Serving: D
Cuisine: American
Credit cards: Most major

Just north of Otisco Lake, one of the best features of this large restaurant is the beautiful brick patio and gazebo set in gardens: a perfect setting for a wedding or special occasion. The facility can accommodate up to 250 guests. The dining room and pub are open for dinner on weekends; it's open year-round for weddings and functions.

**MILLARD'S AT THE
    SUMMIT**
315-673-2254
Rte. 41, Borodino (9 miles
    south of Skaneateles on
    east side of lake)
Open: Weds.–Thurs. 5–9, Fri.
    and Sat. 5–10, Sun. 12–8
Price: $–$$
Serving: D
Specialities: Cajun dishes,
    seafood
Credit cards: Most major

Get here in time to watch the sun set over the lake. The inn sits on a hill with a splendid view of the lake stretching out beyond. Once a farm, inn, and private home, Millard's has been a restaurant for several years. It serves good, not fancy, food such as roast beef, garlic mashed potatoes, and mixed vegetables. (At the time of publication, Millard's was up for sale, although still operating.)

MIRBEAU
877-MIRBEAU,
    315-685-5006;
    fax 315-685-5150
www.mirbeau.com
851 W. Genesee St.,
    Skaneateles NY 13152
Open: Daily
Price: $$$–$$$$
Serving: B, L, D
Cuisine: Mirbeau estate
Credit cards: Most major

Chef Edward J. Moro comes from Hotel Hersey and is already chalking up an impressive track record here. Those who have eaten at Mirbeau feel the cuisine is worth the price tag: a three-course dinner is $39; a five-course meal is $59. Choices include butter-roasted Maine lobster tail with melted leeks and carrot ginger sauce, Fallow Hollow Farm venison with apple conserve, rosemary fingerling potato and sour cherry sauce, and wild berry soufflé. Lunch and breakfast choices are equally tempting. My recommendation: pick a nice evening, reserve a table on the terrace, and enjoy a splendid dinner. Perhaps a warm potato and goat cheese terrine with baby arugula, champagne vinegar, and olive oil, followed by Chesapeake Bay softshell crab with spicy corn, red pepper, and fennel coulis, then charred beef tenderloin with foraged mushrooms and truffle mashed potatoes, or perhaps Scottish salmon with crispy rosti potato cake and littleneck clam chowder climaxed by a wild berry soufflé.

ROSALIE'S CUCINA
315-685-2200
841 W. Genesee St.,
  Skaneateles NY 13152
Open: Daily Mon.–Thurs. &
  Sun. 5–9, Fri. & Sat. 5–10
Price: $$$
Serving: D
Cuisine: Italian
Credit cards: Most major

Relatively new in town, this adobe taverna-style restaurant was built by Philip Romano in memory of his sister, Rosalie. The menu begins, "We are very proud of our chefs, wait staff, bartenders, and all of our crew for keeping Rosalie's legacy alive and her cucina filled with great food, friendly service, and, most important, happy guests." This restaurant lives up to its promise. Although one person commented, "The best place to eat when someone else is buying," the higher than average prices for the area don't seem to faze the continual stream of people who come here to eat. The Italian cuisine is excellent and plentiful. It's upper crust Italian (which seems a tad out-of-place in such a traditional central New York village), but who's to care. Rosalie's is wildly popular among those looking for a special meal, including rich pasta dishes, good breads, succulent meats, and pizza from a wood-fired oven. Among the pasta specialities are farfalle con pollo (bowties, chicken, pancetta, asiago cream, red onions, and peas) and risotto con funghi (arborio rice, with portabella and shiitaki mushrooms, parsley, and reggiano). For your main course you might order arrosto con porc (slow roasted pork, oregano, garlic, and cannellini beans) or aragosta alla Rosalie (grilled lobster tails, orzo, spinach, and artichokes). An extensive wine list ranges from a $19 White Zinfandel to a $120 bottle of Cuvée Dom Perignon. Reservations are taken for parties of six or more.

SHERWOOD INN
315-685-3405,
  800-3-SHERWOOD;
  fax 315-685-8983
26 W. Genesee St./Rte. 20,
  Skaneateles NY 13152
Open: Year-round
Price: $–$$ tavern, $$–$$$
  dining room
Serving: B, L, D
Cuisine: American
Credit cards: Most major

The Sherwood has three places you can eat: the main dining room, the lakeside terrace, and the tavern. The ambiance is traditional in the dining room; the tavern is more casual and resembles an English pub with a long bar, a few booths, and tables. Menu items in the dining room include classics such as herb crust rack of lamb, horseradish crusted filet mignon, and grilled salmon with pommery mustard sauce. Tavern fare is more basic: grilled chicken sandwich, veggie burger, portabella burger, caesar salad, tavern burgers, and a variety of finger foods such as potato skins and fried calamari. Often on weekends, there is live music in the tavern.

CASUAL FOOD

Blue Water Chill (at the Blue Water Grill, 315-685-6600; 11 W. Genesee St., Skaneateles NY 13152) Ice cream; open daily.

Grammie's Breakfast Tea or Victorian Tea (315-636-8111, 607-749-6434; 1126 Woodworth Rd. off Rte. 41, Skaneateles NY 13152) It's a bit down East Lake

Road out of Skaneateles and you have to watch for the sign on the right side of the highway, but it's worth the trip. Typically, breakfast tea includes tea or gourmet coffee, crêpes, scones, breads, fresh fruit condiments, lemon curd, jams, and Arbor Hill Claret Wine Sauce at $9.75 per person. Grammie's Victorian tea treats you to coffee or tea, scones, lemon curd, fruit, cucumber sandwiches, feta cheese spread, and dessert. Open Tues.–Sat. 9–4. Call ahead for reservations.

Patisserie (315-685-2433; 4 Hannum St., Skaneateles NY 13152) There are just a few tables on a patio in this delightfully small bakery shop tucked into a corner behind the Sherwood Inn. Freshly made breads, cakes, pies, and pastries along with coffees and teas.

Skaneateles Bakery (315-685-3538; 19 Jordan St., Skaneateles NY 13152) Homemade bakery products and good coffee bring locals in for breakfast and light lunches. Specialities are doughnuts, sandwiches, soups, and rolls. Not much in the way of ambiance unless you like to watch the people walk by outside the large front windows. Doughnuts, especially the ones they call "headlights" with white frosting, are yummy and death on diets. Cookies, cakes, and other bakery products, too. A village institution. Open Mon.–Sat. 6am–5:30pm.

Skan-Ellus Drive-In (315-685-8280; 1659 E. Genesee St., junction Rtes. 175&20, Skaneateles NY 13152) A snack bar with indoor seating area offering ice cream, deli sandwiches, burgers, hot dogs, and fries. It's been around for more than thirty years and it's still going strong. Open daily 10–9, later in summer.

Valentine's (315-685-8804; 18 West Genesee St., Skaneateles NY 13152) When I just have to have pizza, I come here. They also have calzones, sub sandwiches, wraps and salads along with beer. And they deliver.

Owasco Lake and Auburn

RESTAURANTS

AUBURN FAMILY RESTAURANT
315-253-2274
161 Genesee St., Auburn NY 13021
Open: Mon. & Tues. 6am–3pm, Weds.–Thurs. 6am–9pm, Fri.–Sat. 24 hours, Sun. to 6pm
Price: $–$$
Serving: B, L, D
Cuisine: American
Credit cards: Most major

The name says it all. This is a casual, friendly place where kids are welcome. Decor is basic restaurant; nothing fancy — just good value for money.

BALLOONS
315-252-9761
65 Washington St., Auburn
  NY 13021
Open: Tues., Weds. &
  Thurs. 5–9:30pm, Fri. &
  Sat. 5–10pm, Sun. 5–9pm
Price: $–$$
Serving: D
Cuisine: Hearty American;
  steaks
Credit cards: Most major

This small steak house, which lies in the shadow of the Auburn prison, is still delivering good food at reasonable prices. Many of the waiters have been here long enough to seem immortal. Specialities include prime rib, steaks of all kinds, and salads. It's small, intimate. Bring your appetite.

CRISTY'S LAKE HOUSE
315-497-1602
Rte. 38 Cascade on Owasco,
  Moravia NY 13118
Open: Year-round
Price: $–$$
Serving: L, D
Cuisine: American, seafood
Credit cards: Most major

It's a casual, fun place to come. Pull up by boat or come by car. Eat overlooking the lake on the open deck or inside. Great hamburgers, sandwiches, chicken, and salads.

CURLEY'S RESTAURANT
315-252-5224, 315-252-5277
96 State St., Auburn NY
  13021
Open: Mon.–Sat. 11–2,
  Mon.–Thurs. 5–9, Fri. &
  Sat. 5–10; tavern menu in
  bar all day
Price: $$–$$$
Serving: L, D
Cuisine: Italian, pub fare,
  steaks, seafood
Credit cards: Most major

A long-time winner among locals, Curley's has been serving food and drink to patrons since 1934. Weekends there is often some entertainment. Ask to sit on the outdoor deck in the summertime.

**SWABY'S KANGAROO
  COURT**
315-258-9693
6 South St., Auburn NY
  13021
Open: Mon.–Sat. 3pm–2am,
  Sun. 4pm–2am
Price: $
Serving: D
Cuisine: Pub, sandwiches
Credit cards: Most major

It looks like it's been here since the late 1800s. The decor is eclectically odd and includes artwork, gilt chairs, a ship's figurehead, wooden arms, fans, globes, model dinosaurs, an old electric chair, and barber chairs along the bar. There are lots of interesting antiques and memorabilia . . . a real trip. Great beer and pub food completes the picture.

LASCES
315-253-4885
252-258 Rte. 5, Grant Ave.,
  Auburn NY 13021

Enjoy huge portions: if you don't go home with leftovers, you'll be disappointed. Specialities include deep fried scallops, shrimp scampi,

Open: Tues.–Thurs. 5–9, Fri.
&Sat. 5–10, Sun. 4–9
Price: $$–$$$
Serving: D
Cuisine: Italian
Credit cards: Most major

Gramp's eggplant parmigiana, and chicken piccata. For an appetizer, try the antipasto Nicholas or deep-fried mushrooms. Entrées come with salads, vegetable, and potato, rice, or pasta. A good deal.

PARKER'S GRILL AND TAP HOUSE
315-252-6884
129 Genesee St., Auburn NY
13021
Open: Daily 11–midnight
Price: $
Serving: L, D
Cuisine: Bistro-style
Credit cards: Most major

One of the few restaurants on Genesee Street in the heart of the business district, Parker's is the newest kid on the block and packed at lunch time. In addition to a long bar there are high-top tables, booths, Tiffany-style lamps, lots of wood trim, and regular tables. Although I found the service a bit on the casual side, the servers were friendly and food was good pub style: finger foods, hamburgers, Philly steak sandwiches, pita pockets, soups, and twenty beers on tap.

THE PIONEER RESTAURANT
315-252-9721
RD4, E. Genesee St., Auburn
NY 13021
Open: Tues.–Sat., Sun. 12–8
Price: $–$$
Serving: D, Sun. L
Credit cards: Most major

A long-time favorite of locals — I had to include it for old time's sake.You can't eat here and not try its crispy-fried foods. Popular with families and very homey — they sell a lot of turkey dinners. The decor has not changed much in fifty years and the outside looks like it could use a facelift. Seniors love it. If you're not into grease, this may not be your place.

RIORDAN'S
315-252-7175
10 E. Genesee St., Auburn
NY 13021
Open: Daily 5–10; closed Sun.
Price: $$
Serving: D
Cuisine: American
Credit cards: Most major

Another Auburn institution, this is owned by the same people who have created the Blue Water Grill in Skaneateles. A bistro-style restaurant, it caters to those who like fine dining with items such as steak au poivre, Mediterranean pasta, St. Louis-style ribs and BBQ pork. There is both a dining room and a more casual pub.

SPRINGSIDE INN
315-252-7247;
fax 315-252-8096
www.springsideinn.com
6141 W. Lake Rd., Rte. 38,
Auburn NY 13021
Open: Apr.–Dec. Tues.–
Thurs. 5–9, Fri. & Sat.
5–10, Sun. 10:30–7;
Jan.–Mar. call for hours.
Price: $$–$$$

An institution in Auburn, this red-painted inn with its rambling porches and awnings offers several dining choices. You can dine in the cozy pub room or in the cathedral-ceilinged dining room decorated with turn-of-the-century lamps and English carpets where the menu features traditional hearty items such as roast beef, baked Virginia ham, baked chicken, lobster newburg, duck flambé, and popovers. Salads use local produce in

Serving: D, Sun. brunch
Cuisine: Classic American
Credit cards: Most major

season and the inn prepares its own salad dressing. There are a variety of rooms available to accommodate intimate dinners as well as large functions.

CASUAL FOOD

Green Shutters Drive-In (Corner Owasco Rd. & Rte. 437 across from Emerson Park, Auburn NY 13021) Remember the car hops? Or movies that feature car hops? This is the place where it has been happening all these years. At the time I stopped by, new owners were still trying to get their act together. They were serving, barely, but still weren't sure of their hours. They promise the same great onion rings and burgers as well as car service the place is known for.

Hunter's Dinerant (315-255-2282; 18 E. Genesee St., Auburn NY 13021) One of the last of its kind, Hunter's has been serving customers all hours of the day and night for more than fifty years. Try the homemade pies and puddings as well as the meatloaf, mashed potatoes, and other comfort foods. Open 24/7.

Reese's (Rtes. 5&20, west of Auburn) A candy-colored dairy bar and miniature golf links with picnic tables. Ice cream, hamburgers, and other snack foods.

Wegman's (315-255-2231; 40-60 Genesee St., Auburn NY 13021) A cappuccino and latte bar is in this full service grocery store. Buy a dessert, bagel, or sub, and head to the seating area. Open 24/7.

Otisco Lake

Lake Drive-Inn (315-636-8557; corner Otisco Valley Rd. and Otisco Rd., Otisco Valley) A snack stand with picnic tables and small indoor area offering ice cream, hot dogs, hamburgers, fries, pizza, and other quick food. Open in summers Weds.–Thurs. 12–9, Fri. & Sat. 12–10, Sun. 12–8.

Chief Logan

Where Auburn now stands was once a native American village, the home of Logan (Tah-gah-jute). A sachem of the Shamokins and Cayuga tribes, Logan was known as a peaceful and wise man. Because of his great oratorical skills and good sense, he often represented the Six Nations at powwows with whites. This all changed when his entire family was brutally slaughtered by a renegade band of settlers. In retribution, he lashed out taking the lives of some white families; although it is said he did not allow his people to apply torture to the victims, at that time a common practice among his people. Logan is buried in Fort Hill Cemetery in Auburn. His grave is marked by a limestone obelisk.

CULTURE

Skaneateles Lake and Skaneateles

John D. Barrow Art Gallery (315-685-5135; 49 E. Genesee St., in the village
library, Skaneateles NY 13152) The life work of one of the area's most pro-
lific nineteenth-century poets and painters. Numerous oil portraits and early
scenes around the area. This exhibit should be of interest to anyone who
likes local history. Open July and Aug. Mon.–Sat. 12–4; Jan.–Mar. Sat. 2–4.
(Or ask the librarian and you might get a peek.)

The Creamery and Skaneateles Historical Society (315-685-1360; 28 Hannum
St., Skaneateles NY 13152) Once the place farmers came to sell their milk,
cream, butter, and other dairy products to the public, this 100-year-old building now houses the local historical society as well as hundreds of artifacts, a
research and archives department, gift shop, and meeting room. Open summers Thurs.–Sat. 1–4; the rest of the year open Fri. 1–4 or by appointment.

Owasco Lake and Auburn

MUSEUMS, EXHIBITS, AND HISTORIC SITES

Peter Finger

The Cayuga Museum, Auburn, is in the former Willard Case home, circa 1840.

Cayuga Museum and the Case Research Laboratory (315-253-8051; fax 315-253-9829; cayuganet.org/cayugamuseum; 203 Genesee St., Auburn NY 13021) Permanent and changing exhibits about life in Cayuga country are attractively displayed in the Willard Case mansion (circa 1840). Case, an important creator of his time, perfected the tube that made sound movies possible. In fact, the first commercially successful system of sound film was invented in the Case Research Lab in 1923. See Tiffany windows, paintings, Victorian-era furnishings, and a 1928 Movietone news film along with other memorabilia. It's a great place to learn about native American art.

Cayuga-Owasco Lakes Historical Society Museum (315-497-3906; 14 W. Cayuga St., Moravia NY 13118) The "History House" is a treasure trove of more than 500 items focusing on local history and genealogy. Most of the pieces on display have been donated by area citizens. Call for hours.

Fort Hill Cemetery (315-253-8132; 19 Fort St., Auburn NY 13021) Several important Auburn people are buried in this cemetery which around 1100 was used as a fortress by the Iroquois and Cayuga tribes. The remains of the last fortifications are still evident and a monument to Chief Logan, one of the great native American leaders, is in the cemetery. Other prominent leaders buried here include William H. Seward, whose grave is on a slight hill near the Wadsworth and Aikin family monuments, and Harriet Tubman. To find her grave, from the Fort Hill entrance, keep right along the lower border of the cemetery and look on your left when you round a bend. Her stone is under a tall pine, flanked by two small shrubs.

The Harriet Tubman Home, Auburn, pays tribute to the brave woman who brought many slaves from the south to freedom in the north.

Peter Finger

Harriet Tubman Home (315-252-2081; hthome@localnet.com; Harriettubman home@aol.com; www.nyhistory.com/harriettubman; Rte. 34, Auburn NY 13021) This is the museum and home of Harriet Tubman, a heroic woman and former slave from Maryland often called "the female Moses" and the "Joan of

Arc" of her race. She made nineteen dangerous trips south to rescue more than 300 slaves. During the Civil War, she became a Union spy, scout, and nurse, bringing 700 of her people from plantations to join the Union army. The house she built for her mother and small hospital is open and contains Tubman's sewing machine, her coal stove, a number of pieces of furniture, linens, and other memorabilia. A modest museum is also on the property. Although her private home is also here, it is not yet open to the public. Every year more than 2,000 people from the A.M.E. Zion Church Connection (African Methodist and Episcopal) make an annual pilgrimage to the site over Memorial Day weekend. Open Feb. 1–Oct. 31 Tues.–Fri. 10–4, Sat. 10–3; Nov.–Jan. by appointment. Admission $3 adults, $1 children under 16, $2 seniors.

Peter Finger

Schweinfurth Memorial Art Center, Auburn, features several annual exhibits as well as permanent collections.

Schweinfurth Memorial Art Center (315-255-1553; fax 315-255-0871; smac@relex .com; www.cayuganet.org/smac; 205 Genesee St., Auburn NY 13021) An extensive museum displaying all periods and kinds of art. There are six major shows a year including the annual "Quilts=Art=Quilts," "Made in New York," "Both Ends of the Rainbow" (children's and seniors' artwork), and other fine arts exhibitions, revolving exhibits, and crafts shows. The museum has an excellent gift shop with several one-of-a-kind items on sale and offers a number of classes, lectures, and trips. The facility is state-of-the-art, and a great asset to the city. Open Tues.–Sat. 10–5, Sun. 1–5.

Seward House (315-252-1283; www.sewardhouse.org; 33 South St., Auburn NY 13021) Griffins flank the entrance of this museum and imposing early nineteen-century home of William H. Seward, New York governor, U.S. senator, and secretary of state for presidents Lincoln and Johnson. Seward was instrumental in the purchase of Alaska and one of the founders of the Republican party. The museum contains period and Civil War pieces and there is a lovely garden and gazebo. Guided tours are given Feb.–Dec. Open July 1–Oct. 14 Tues.–Sat. 10–4, Sun. 1–4; off-season Tues.–Sat. 1–4; closed Mon. and all Jan. Admission $3.25.

Ward W. O'Hara Agricultural Museum (315-253-5611; Cayuganet.org/agmuseum; Emerson Park and Rte. 38A, Auburn NY 13021) This is much more than a museum of important farm implements and tools circa 1800–1930. There is a blacksmith shop, general store, woodwork shop, and cooperage, 1900 country kitchen and veterinarian's office. Special events include a draft horse show, antique tractor rodeo, miniature horse and pony show, and dairy and old ways days. Children will enjoy the "Try & Touch" exhibits. Open June, Sat. and Sun. 11–4, July–Aug. daily.

Willard Memorial Chapel (315-252-0339; 17 Nelson St., Auburn NY 13021) This is the only complete and unaltered Tiffany chapel in the country. It is constructed of gray limestone and red sandstone in the Romanesque Revival style of architecture; the Tiffany interior contains a nine-paneled rose window depicting religious symbols and figures, a three-paneled stained glass window, fourteen opalescent nave windows, nine leaded glass chandeliers, a memorial mosaic bronze and gilt tablet, mosaic floors, a jeweled pulpit,

---

Photo Ops

Skaneateles Lake: One of the best views of the deep blue lake is from a spot about 2.8 miles north of Scott on Route 41.

Carpenter's Falls: To find the 100-foot falls near New Hope, go 11 miles south on the west side of Skaneateles Lake to Apple Tree Road and cross over the falls at the east-west escarpment.

New Hope Mills: Hardly a blink in the road along the west side of Rte. 41A — watch for a small sign, New Hope Mills, just past Mandana going south. The old mill wheel still turns, although for a while, at least, we're told the grinding of grains has been curtailed. The shop, housed in a weathered barn, is filled with flour products, organic grains, spices, honey, and other locally produced items.

Otisco Lake: Taking East Lake Road from Skaneateles, take a left on Eibert Road two miles from Rte. 41. As you round a corner and pass a 10 mph sign, you'll get an expansive view of the lake ahead.

and gold stenciled furniture and ceiling. It's simply dazzling. The Tiffany Summer Concert Series takes place in the chapel every Wednesday at noon July and August. Open Tues.–Fri. 10–4 or by appointment; closed holidays. Admission $2.

THEATER

Auburn Players Community Theater (315-258-8275; Empire State College–State University of New York, 197 Franklin St., Auburn NY 13021) Drawing from local talent, this group offers four productions a year.

Finger Lakes Drive-In (315-252-3969; Clark St./Rte. 20&5, Auburn NY 13021) One of the few remaining outdoor movie theaters left in the region. Open seasonally.

Merry-Go-Round Playhouse (315-255-1785, 800-457-8897, off-season 315-255-1305; Rte. 38A, PO Box 506, Emerson Park, Auburn NY 13021) Four Broadway musicals come to the Finger Lakes each summer. Productions such as

Peter Finger

Broadway comes to Auburn at the Merry-Go-Round Playhouse in Emerson Park.

42nd Street and *Annie Get Your Gun* are held in the former carousel pavilion in Emerson Park. Ticket prices are $19 to $26.

RECREATION

Skaneateles Lake and Skaneateles

BIKING

Skaneateles Lake Loop: Starting from the village, go south on West Lake Road, then continue on Rte. 41A to Glen Haven Road. Return to the village by cycling north on Rte. 41. Key stops along the way include New Hope Mills (just south of Mandana on Rte. 41A), Glen Haven at the end of the lake, and Borodino on Rte. 41. 40 miles.

BOATING

A member of the Skaneateles Sailing Club gets ready for evening races on Skaneateles Lake.

Katharine Delavan Dyson

Skaneateles Sailing Club (315-685-7541; 2745 E. Lake Rd., Skaneateles) On the east side of the lake in a protected cove, this club holds informal races weekly and other sail events. There is a membership fee and fee for boat storage or mooring. Members can use the clubhouse and dock facilities. The club was founded by long-time expert sailors Janet and Richard Besse.

CRUISES:

Mid-Lakes Navigation Company (315-685-8500, 800-545-4318; www.mid lakesnav.com; 11 Jordan St., PO Box 61, Skaneateles NY 13152) Mid-Lakes

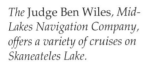
The Judge Ben Wiles, *Mid-Lakes Navigation Company, offers a variety of cruises on Skaneateles Lake.*

Katharine Delavan Dyson

offers a variety of cruises on Skaneateles and on New York State's canal system. Two boats, the two-decker *Judge Ben Wiles* and the *Barbara S. Wiles,* a smaller classic wooden craft, feature two-hour lunch and three-hour dinner cruises, 50-minute sightseeing excursions, wine-tasting cruises, a three-hour Sunday brunch lake outing, a 32-mile, three and a half hour U.S. Mail Cruise delivering mail to camps around the lake, and special group cruises. The dinner cruise gives you a choice of four entrées and a glass of champagne. Mid-Lakes also offers cruises departing Syracuse, Albany, and Buffalo on the Erie Canal. Two- and three-day cruises are priced from $299 including meals and accommodations. For those who want to go it alone, there are canal boats for charter.

MARINAS AND LAUNCHES:

Skaneateles Marina (315-685-5095; fax 315-685-1738; 1938 W. Lake Rd., Mandana) Full service marina, services, ship store, gas, pontoon boat rental.

Sailboat Shop (315-685-7558; 1322 E. Genesee St., Skaneateles NY 13152) Sailboat and canoe rentals and sales.

Town of Skaneateles Boat Launch (315-685-3473, Rte. 41A, Mandana)

GOLF

Most golf courses in the region are open from about April 1 through November 1.

The Midlakes Club (315-673-4916; Bockes Rd., Skaneateles NY 13152) 18-hole public course overlooking the lake.

Foxfire at Village Green (315-638-2930; One Village Blvd., Baldwinsville) Near Syracuse, the well-manicured par 72 championship Foxfire wanders through a community of homes and condos. Elevated tees, narrow fairways, water, and bunkers make it a challenge. Golf, cart, and lunch is priced from $29. There is a driving range on the property.

The Links at Sunset Ridge (315-673-2255; Rte. 175, Marcellus NY 13108) This young course is fairly flat with high roughs designed to resemble a links layout. Jeff Clark, head professional, points out that the tees are gender-neutral: where you tee off from depends on your handicap — i.e., if your handicap is less than 12, you tee off from the orange or black tees; 12 to 25 you drive from the green tees; and more than 25 from the gold tees. Water comes into play on four holes and the course is well bunkered. Greens fees are $19; $26 with cart on weekdays; on weekends $22, $32 with cart.

Radisson Greens Golf Club (315-638-0092; 8055 Potter Rd., Baldwinsville NY 13027) A Robert Trent Jones course that's high on quality, low in greens fees (less than $45 with cart). Tough par 5s and great greens and fairways. A good bet for better players.

West Hill Golf Course (315-672-8677; 2500 W. Genesee Tpk., Camillus NY 13219) One of the best par 3 courses in the state. A virtual arboretum, there are an enormous variety of trees planted along the fairways. The front nine is much easier and less dramatic than the back nine which has a lake bringing water into play on several holes. Greens fees are $13; a half cart is $7. If you're going to play more than three rounds, buy the $25 yearly membership fee. Greens fees drop to $9 per round for members.

HIKING

Baltimore Woods (315-673-1350; From Skaneateles center, take Rte. 20 east, left on Rte. 175, Lee Mulroy Rd. Take another left on Bishop Hill Rd. to the upper parking area and pavilion.) Several loop trails from .25 to .7 miles are laced through this 170-acre area owned by Save the Country, Inc., and operated by Centers for Nature Education. Moderately difficult trails go up and down hills, across brooks, across flood plains, through woods and fields. The Violet trail contains a .3-mile maze containing labeled plantings of wildflowers and plants.

Bear Swamp State Forest (607-753-3095 ext. 217; to find the long loop, going south on Rte. 41, turn left on Iowa Rd. after Reynolds Rd. and take the first left on Bear Swamp Rd. to the parking area on the right. To find the short loop, going south on Rte. 41A, after Reynolds Rd., turn left on the next unmarked dirt road and look for a D.E.C. sign on the right side of Rte. 41A; park where you see the trailhead near a wooden kiosk.) Off the southeast end of Skaneateles Lake, this 3,316-acre state forest is home to thirteen miles of well-marked trails. Take the rather difficult 3.4 mile loop or the longer, also difficult 7.8 mile loop. Both go through forests of pine and spruce, over streams and bridges, and up and downhill, some steep.

Cayuga County Erie Canal Trail (315-253-5611; starts just east of Port Byron off Rte. 31 at Randolph J. Schassel Village Park) You can take a 9.3 mile walk (one way) along the former towpath and abandoned canal bed or tie into another 14.8 miles through Erie Canal Park in Camillus for a twenty-mile walk. The walking, although rough in places, is pretty level and easy except for a few rough places but will take you a good part of a day to do it. One of the highlights is Lock 52 west of Port Byron. This trail is available to hikers, bikers, and horseback riders.

Charlie Major Nature Trail (315-685-3473; from center of village (Rte. 20) go north on Jordan St., then left onto Fennell Rd. Look for a parking area and "Nature Trail" sign just after Old Seneca Turnpike.) A prominent Skaneateles leader from the 1950s through the 1990s and a great advocate of hiking, Charlie Major came up with the idea for this 1.6 mile easy trail which follows an abandoned rail line. Part way down, look for the falls on your right and take the path that goes across some large foundation stones to the falls. There you'll find a perfect place to stop and have a picnic right over the water as it spills over the rocks.

OTHER ATTRACTIONS

Allyn Arena (315-685-7757; 1 E. Austin St., Skaneateles NY 13152) The ice rink is open from late September to early April.

Carpenter's Brook Fish Hatchery (315-689-9367; Rte. 321, Elbridge NY 13060) See the hatchery where thousands of brown, rainbow, and brook trout eggs are hatched and the small fish are put into ponds to grow. Picnic tables, workshops (by reservation), and fishing programs (for senior citizens and special needs groups).

Polo Matches (Off W. Lake Rd., turn right on Andrews Rd., Skaneateles NY 13152) Polo held Sundays at 3pm July and August. Small parking fee.

Skiing: Greek Peak (800-955-2754); **Skaneateles Family Ski Hill** (315-636-8486) open to winter ski members; **Song Mountain Ski Center** (315-696-5711).

Owasco Lake and Auburn

BIKING

Owasco Lake Loop: A 32-mile loop around the lake starting at Emerson Park, going south on Rte. 38 along the west side of the lake, to Moravia and Fillmore Glen and returning north on Rte. 38A. Key stops include Moravia and Fillmore Glen. Bring your suits for a swim in Emerson Park at the end of your trip.

Polo games are held off West Lake Road, Skaneateles, in July and August.

Peter Finger

BOATING

Lake Country Outdoors (315-497-3006; Moravia NY 13118) Full services and launching facilities.

Trade-A-Yacht Marina (315-258-9096; 147 Pulsifer Dr., Auburn NY 13021) Sales and service.

GOLF

Arnold Palmer Golf (315-253-8072; Gates Rd. off Rte. 5, Auburn NY 13021) Bring the family. Driving range, mini-golf, batting cages, game room, and snack bar.

Dutch Hollow Country Club (315-784-5052, Benson Rd., Auburn NY 13021) When you play Dutch Hollow Country Club, a ten-minute drive from town, remember your retriever: there's water water everywhere. Dutch Hollow Brook comes into play on eight holes and the fourteenth, par 3, can beat you up if you miss the 130-yard drive and land in the gully that lies between the tee and the green. Be prepared for lots of ups and downs; it's hilly. Several clinics are offered each year.

Fillmore Golf Course (315-497-3145; Tollgate Hill Rd., Locke NY 13092) This is a pretty basic public course with the advantage of its location in Fillmore Glen. The 18-hole course is open seasonally. There are riding carts, pro shop, and snack bar. Greens fee are about $11.

Highland Park Country Club (315-253-3381, Franklin St., Auburn NY 13021) Popular with locals, this semi-private, well-maintained course has its share of quirky holes and lovely views of the countryside. It is considered one of the better courses in the area.

Sailing is a popular sport on Owasco Lake, Auburn.

Peter Finger

Indian Head (Rte. 5 and 20, Auburn) A public 18-hole course. Rather flat and not too exciting, but good place for beginners.

HIKING

Auburn-Fleming Trail (315-253-5611; from Rtes. 5&20 in Auburn, go south on Columbus St. and park on Dunning Ave. just after Clymer St.) This straight two-mile dirt and stone trail up and back is an easy walk along an old tree-lined railroad bed just west of the northern end of Owasco Lake.

Fillmore Glen State Park (315-497-0130; Just off Rte. 38 south of Moravia. Use the back parking lot.) Near the south end of Owasco Lake, there are three 1.8 mile (one way) moderately difficult dirt trails in this 938-acre magnificent gorge and valley. The trails start in the valley and rise 349 feet to a dam. The North and South Rim trails follow the rims of the gorge; the Gorge trail goes along Dry Creek (which is actually not dry at all). At the turning point of the trails, there is a two-level dam. The lower pool of water is great for swimming. Check out the Cowsheds, a cavern carved out of rock by the tumbling waterfall. The scenery — deep-cut gorges, forests, streams, ponds, and great boulders and rock formations — is wonderful.

PARKS, NATURE PRESERVES, AND CAMPING

Casey Park (315-253-4247; N. Division St., Auburn NY 13021) A multi-purpose sports and recreation facility with tennis courts, Olympic swimming pool, and bicycle and walking trails. Picnic areas, playgrounds, horseshoe pits, and bocce courts.

Emerson Park (315-2553-5611; Rte. 38A, Auburn NY 13021) A large, sprawling grassy park on the shores of Owasco Lake. Swimming, beaches, boat launches, picnic facilities, playgrounds, bathhouse, restored pavilion. Also on grounds is the Cayuga County Agricultural Museum.

Fillmore Glen State Park (315-497-0130; Rte. 38A, Moravia NY 13118) A lovely deep limestone and shale glen comprising 857 acres with many waterfalls, nature trails, sixty campsites, three cabins, picnic pavilions, ball fields, and swimming pool. The original factory where the first cast iron plow was invented by Jethro Wood is still standing near the falls.

Peter Finger

Montezuma National Wildlife Refuge harbors many species of birds.

Montezuma National Wildlife Refuge (Rtes. 5 and 20; west of Auburn) A rich ecological environment and haven for birds and other wildlife. Trails, roads, observation tower, and visitor center make this exceptional resource easily accessible.

OTHER ATTRACTIONS

Balloon Rides (315-252-9474; Sunset Adventures, Box 6863, Beech Tree Rd., Auburn NY 13021) Drift in a colorful balloon over the Finger Lakes. Balloons depart at sunrise or about one and a half hours before sunset. Price: $135 per person for a one-hour flight and champagne.

Cayuga County Fairgrounds (315-834-6606; www.dirtmotorsports.com; 1 Speedway Dr./Rte. 31, Weedsport NY 13166) A variety of events are staged here throughout the year such as fairs, dirt track motor races, demolition derbies, monster truck competitions, agricultural exhibits, horse shows, concerts, and arts and crafts. It is the home of Dirt Motorsports Hall of Fame and the Classic Car Museum containing vintage racing vehicles and memorabilia (315-834-6667).

Falcon Park (315-255-2489; 130 N. Division St., Auburn) See super baseball and enjoy a hot dog in a 2,044-seat baseball stadium where the Auburn Doubledays, a Class A farm team for the Houston Astros (in the NY–Penn League) play June–Sept. The team is named after Abner Doubleday, baseball's legendary founder, who grew up in Auburn.

Otisco Lake

Otisco Lake Marina (315-636-8807; Otisco Valley Rd., Marietta NY 13110) Boat sales, service, rentals, and storage.

SHOPPING

The shopping mecca of the area is Skaneateles, no doubt about it. The attractive brick sidewalks and period lighting that line Genesee Street, the main street, is lined with upscale gift shops, art galleries, boutiques, antique shops, and cafés that invite you to stop and linger. When you need a break, you need only stroll down to either end of the stores for a lake break on a wooden bench by the water.

There are a few shops worth visiting on the western end of the area, up Jordan Street and around the corner past the Sherwood Inn where there is a marvelous clothing store and bakery tucked into quarters in a big old house.

Except for the Finger Lakes Mall and a few bright lights in the former retail district such as Aardvarks & Zippers and Swaby's Kangaroo Court, Auburn doesn't offer much in the way of a major shopping experience.

Skaneateles and Skaneateles Lake

ANTIQUES

Antique Shoppe (315-685-2779, 18 W. Genesee St. across from the gazebo, Skaneateles NY 13152) This is a multi-dealer shop selling china and glass, books, paintings, jewelry, folk art, and collectibles. The shop also offers appraisals and takes consignments. Open 11–5; Sun. 12–5.

Skaneateles Antique Center (315-685-0752; 12 E. Genesee St., Skaneateles NY

13152) You can spend hours browsing through the antiques and collectibles of more than thirty dealers located on two floors. Find furniture, pottery, books, jewelry, linens, lighting, primitives, militaria, coins, decorative arts and crafts, accessories and other things. Open Mon.–Sat. 10–5:30; Sun. 12–5.

White & White (315-685-7733, 18 E. Genesee St., Skaneateles NY 13152) Stephen and Beverly White continually look for unique antiques, both furniture pieces and collectibles. Most are high-end items. Open Mon.–Sat. 10–5.

ART AND BOOKS

Gallery Luna (315-685-0430; 7 Jordan St., Skaneateles NY 13152) Focusing on contemporary work and custom frames, here you can find prints and original art and craft work.

McCarthy's Finger Lakes Photography and Gallery (315-685-9099; 9 Jordan St., Skaneateles NY 13152) A fine selection of regional books, posters, notes, prints, and gifts by noted photographer John McCarthy.

CHILDREN'S AND TOYS

The Bookie (315-685-3322; 24 E. Genesee St., Skaneateles NY 13152) The name is a bit deceiving (the store used to sell mostly books); now it sells some books, but mainly offers toys, including the T.C. Timber line and arts and crafts materials.

Habermaas Corp. T.C. Timber (315-685-6660, 4407 Jordan Rd., Skaneateles NY 13152) Formerly Skaneateles Handicrafters, this company has inherited a strong tradition of wooden trains and toys. These hardwood tracks, trains, and other butter-smooth wood toys are about the best you'll find anywhere in the world. T.C. Timber is available in good quality toy stores but here on Saturdays from 10am–1pm, you can load up on engines, train cars, and other toys, some items at factory prices.

The Kinder Garden (315-685-2721; 3 E. Genesee St., Skaneateles NY 13152) Lovely children's clothes and toys, including frames, stuffed animals, kiddie banks, pictures, and games.

CLOTHING

Complements (315-685-3272; 32 W. Genesee St., Skaneateles NY 13152) Trendy women's clothes, shoes, and accessories.

CRAFTS

The Cat's Whiskers (315-636-8284; 1477 Willowdale Rd., Skaneateles NY 13152) This shop specializes in arts, crafts, quilts, folk art, and prints. Open Tues., Thurs. Sat. 11–5.

Elegant Needles (315-685-9276; 5 Jordan St., Skaneateles NY 13152) Everything for those who want to knit, crochet, needlepoint, etc. Fine yarns by Rowan, Classic Elite, Dale of Norway, and Renaissance. Handknit Norwegian sweaters.

FOOD

Burdick Sugarbush (315-685-5501; Hencoop Rd., off Rte. 41A, Skaneateles NY 13152) See maple syrup being tapped from the trees; farm animals.

Essentially Bread (315-689-1200; 245B E. Main St., Elbridge NY 13060) This is the place to come for pastries and artisan breads made from scratch. Varieties include sourdough, semolina, raisin walnut, peasant, mozzarella and dill, bacon and cheddar, ciabatta, and potato and onion.

Farmer's Market (Allyn Arena, Skaneateles NY 13152) A variety of farmers and bakers bring their wares to this open market. Right of the back of their trucks you can buy vegetables, fruit, flowers, herbs, cheese, and breads. Held each Thurs. during the summer months, 3:30–6:30.

Goat Hill Farm (315-655-3014; goathill@dreamscape.com; 2915 Gulf Rd., a right off Rte. 20 east of Skaneateles just past Pompey Center, Manlius) More than 150 goats are milked twice a day on this fifty-seven-acre goat farm owned by Steven and Jennie Mueller. Products for sale include goat cheese. Open noon–7.

New Hope Mills on the west side of Skaneateles Lake sells a variety of flours and organic grains.

Finger Lakes Association

New Hope Mills (315-497-0783; RD#2, off Glen Haven Rd., north of Mandana just off 41A) A small country mill store and museum specializing in stone-ground grain products, unbleached and enriched products such as bulgar, baking supplies, fruits and nuts, honey, potato flour, and pancake mixes. No fancy packaging, but you can't beat the prices: one pound of buttermilk pancake mix is $1.50; five pounds $2.60; two pounds of oat bran is $1.50; five pounds of buckwheat $3. Open Apr.–Dec. Mon.–Fri. 9–4, Sat. 9–3; Jan.–Mar. Mon.–Fri. 9–4, Sat. 9–noon.

Rhubarb (315-685-5803; 59 E. Genesee St., Skaneateles NY 13152) In a former book shop, here is a treasure trove for those who love to cook. It contains all kinds of kitchen gadgets, cookbooks, gourmet foods, cutlery, aprons, espresso makers, cookware, and salsas.

Tierra Farm Café-Bakery (315-496-2602; 6407 Glen Haven Rd., New Hope NY 13118) Find organic vegetables, café, and bakery on a working farm. The farm features specialty pizzas, ice cream, and vegetarian entrées.

Vermont Green Mountain Specialty Company (315-685-1500; 50 E. Genesee St., Skaneateles NY 13152) I dare you to come in here and leave empty handed. There are just too many good things all around: handmade chocolates, gourmet coffees and foods, pastries; old fashioned lollipops, cookies, cakes, gift baskets, and novelties. Open Mon., Weds., Sat. 6:30–7; Tues. 6:30–5, Thurs. & Fri. 6:30–9 in summer; Sun. 12–6.

GIFTS

Aristocats and Dogs (315-685-4849; 62 E. Genesee St., Skaneateles NY 13152) One of the stars in the shop are the one or two kittens up for adoption through the SPCA. All the merchandise is cat- or dog-oriented. There are collars, ceramics, toy animals, even a life preserver for a dog.

Chestnut Cottage (315-685-8082; 75 E. Genesee St., Skaneateles NY 13152) The store, which rambles through rooms that were once a private home, contains a wealth of Christmas ornaments and wreaths. There are also many red, white, and blue Americana-style items.

1st National Gifts (315-685-5454; 2 E. Genesee St., Skaneateles NY 13152) It's housed in the lofty former bank building, hence the name. Lots of souvenir and local items set up in gift stations.

Gallop On Saddlery (315-685-5232; 38 E. Genesee St., Skaneateles NY 13152) Filled with equestrian items: clothes, stuffed and toy horses, saddles, gifts, t-shirts, and more.

The Hitching Post Gift Shoppe (315-685-7304; 2 W. Genesee St., Skaneateles NY 13152) Since 1957, this corner gift shop has been doing a brisk tourist trade. It's the place to go for cards, pewter, early-American items, candles, brassware, and souvenirs.

Imagine (315-685-6263; 8 E. Genesee St., Skaneateles NY 13152) The merchan-

*Chestnut Cottage,
Skaneateles, is a gift shop in
a former home.*

Peter Finger

dise lives up to its name. Find dazzling handblown glass, pewterware, silver
jewelry, puzzles, oil lamps, prints, charms, and other interesting things.

Pomodoro (315-685-8658; 877-POMODORO; 61 E. Genesee St., Skaneateles NY
13152) As you enter, you'll see a sign that says, "Your husband called; said
to buy anything you want." This should not be a problem if you like primitive art, candles, ornaments, candies, cards, and other unique gifts. There are
also several brand-name collectibles such as Mary Engelbreit, Land and
Wise, and Portmeirion.

Thinking of You (315-685-3023; 3 W. Genesee St., Skaneateles NY 13152) Just
the wonderful scents of candles, soaps, and spices entice. Personalized gift
items include baskets filled with goodies such as fruit, condiments, chocolates, cheese, and other hard-to-resist things.

The White Sleigh Christmas Shoppe (315-685-8414; 1 W. Genesee St.,
Skaneateles NY 13152) Everything here is for Christmas: Dickens's Village,
Byers' Carolers, Old World santas, trees full of ornaments and candles.

Owasco Lake and Auburn

FOOD

Grisamore Farms (315-497-1347; Goose St. off Rte. 90 between Locke and Genoa south of Moravia) This is a large complex with fields, greenhouses, farm store, and Christmas shop. Pick your own strawberries, blueberries, raspberries, apples, cherries, vegetables, and pumpkins, and cut your own Christmas trees. In the fall there are hayrides, a halloween maze, and a working cider press. Open May.–Oct. Mon.–Fri. 8–7, Sat. 8–5, Sun. 10–5; Nov. & Dec. Mon.–Sat. 9–5, Sun. 10–5.

GIFTS

Aardvarks and Zippers (315-252-6613; 83 Genesee St., Auburn NY 13021) Since this new store opened, Auburn residents don't have to drive to Skaneateles for that special gift. Owner Susan Marteney has assembled an imaginative collection of painted furniture, local craft items, glass, quilts, new and "previously enjoyed" jewelry that is smashing, candles, bottles, vases, one-of-a-kind goblets, flowerpots, home accessories, cards, soaps, boxes, frames, historic postcards, even buckwheat pillows.

MALLS

Finger Lakes Mall (315-255-1188; Rte. 5 & Rte. 20) More than fifty speciality stores, restaurants, and department stores.

For More Information

Cayuga County Office of Tourism: 315-255-1658, 800-499-9615; cctourism@cayuga net.org; www.cayuganet.org/tourism; 131 Genesee St., Auburn NY 13021

City of Auburn Historic Sites Commission: 315-258-9820, 877-343-0002; Memorial City Hall, 24 South St., Auburn NY 13021

Skaneateles Area Chamber of Commerce: 315-685-0552; Skaneateles-chamber @worldnet.att.net, www.Skaneateles.com; PO Box 199, Skaneateles NY 13152

CHAPTER FOUR
Vineyards, Colleges, & Museums
CAYUGA LAKE

The Ithaca Gorge, a natural wonder created by glaciers moving through the region.

Anchored on the southern end by Ithaca, home of Cornell University and Ithaca College, and at the north by Seneca Falls, birthplace of the women's rights movement, Cayuga Lake is the longest of the Finger Lakes (forty miles) and the second deepest (435 feet). It is also the lake closest to sea level, with an elevation of 384 feet.

To get an overview of this beautiful body of water, you can drive around it or even bike the distance. As you go south along the western side of the lake, the road comes very close to the water at places like Burroughs Points and Aurora. On your trip around the lake, you'll pass many permanent homes and a large number of summer camps and houses. You'll also drive through smaller villages like Union Springs, Cayuga, and Ludlowville on the east side, and Trumansburg, Interlaken, Sheldrake, and Canoga on the west side. The Wells College town of Aurora is on the mid-eastern shore. Groton is east of the southern end of the lake.

Many of the lake's hills are embossed with vineyards marching down to the water's edge. Dramatic waterfalls spill over rugged cliffs and down into deep pools, and rivers gush through gorges carved by ancient glaciers. Hikers, bikers, and all those who appreciate nature can enjoy these spectacular natural assets in the parks that lie around the lake, particularly near the southern end.

Cayuga means "boat landing" in native American, which is still most appropriate judging by the number of cabin cruisers on the lake. Because of the lake's access to the New York State canal system via the Cayuga-Seneca Canal, Cayuga harbors many boats, large and small, since the possibilities for long-distance cruising are endless.

ITHACA

Ithaca, one of New York State's most energized cities, is bustling with activity from the colleges as well as tourism. Yet its neighborhoods provide a low-key small-town ambiance for its close to 30,000 residents, a number that swells by almost 25,000 when Cornell University and Ithaca College are in session.

Cornell and Ithaca are, in fact, Tompkins County's largest private employer: Cornell has a work force of 8,600; Ithaca 1,300. Cornell, with its prestigious Ivy League reputation, is an educational leader, particularly in the fields of veterinary medicine, hotel management, biotechnology and agriculture, and life sciences. Ithaca, the largest private residential college in the state, is known for its strong programs in music, communications, and health science.

Much of the commercial action takes place in the center of the city known as the Commons, a pedestrian-only shopping and recreational area with a mix of boutiques, speciality shops, art studios, restaurants, bars, cafés, and offices. It's a very upbeat, hip area worth exploring.

The city also has a thriving arts community, with several theaters, galleries, and museums. In Ithaca, something seems to be going on every night — a play, concert, poetry reading, or opening of a new art exhibit. Much of the action takes place in and around the colleges. A new program is designed to develop Ithaca's downtown as a center for the arts. In this direction, the outdoor sculpture exhibition "Art in the Heart of the City" has been installed on the Commons and Cayuga Street. Renovations are also ongoing in Ithaca's historical scene. For example, the restoration of the old State Theater is just one of the projects on the drawing board.

For outdoor enthusiasts, there are three major state parks with 150 waterfalls all within a ten-mile radius of town. There are also plenty of biking and hiking trails and great lake fishing.

The Tompkins County Airport, which is served by USAirways, is just about ten minutes from Ithaca's city center.

ITHACA'S BEGINNINGS AND GROWTH

The first residents of the area that is now the city of Ithaca were the Cayuga native Americans. They farmed the fertile lands around the southern end of the lakes which lay between the swampy flats and the steep hills. In 1779, when General Sullivan swept through on his mission to destroy the native American villages, the men were impressed by the vast cornfields and orchards. When military land tracts were awarded in the late 1700s, offered by New York State to soldiers who had served in the Revolutionary War, some of these men, including Jacob Yaple, Isaac Dumond, and Peter Hinepaw, returned to build their log cabins on lot 94, on the beautiful lands they had seen ten years before.

Land was cleared, grist mills built on Cascadilla Creek, and, by 1800, the area was soon buzzing with activity. Some referred to it as "Sin City." At this time, Simeon DeWitt, the state surveyor general, acquired much of the land. In addition to dividing the land into lots and putting them up for sale at most reasonable prices, DeWitt drew up a plan for the town and in 1804 named it "Ithaca" because of its location within the town of Ulysses. (The ancient Greek hero hailed from the island of Ithaca.)

By 1810, the population was up to 250 and there were thirty-eight houses, a post office, hotel, schoolhouse, stores, and a library as well as a doctor, lawyer, and miller. The First Bank of Newburgh opened up in a frame building in 1815, now on East Court Street.

When in 1817 it became the seat of a new county, Tompkins, the freewheeling town sobered up and knuckled down to serious business. After all, as a county leader, it had a new image to establish and uphold.

In the subsequent years, many factors contributed to Ithaca's growth. The steamboat *The Enterprise* was launched on the lake in 1821, and the boats that followed like *Telemachus* and *DeWitt* along with the daily service provided by the stage coach system, helped Ithaca develop a strong commercial base. By 1830 the population had swelled to 3,592. The railroads arrived in 1842, further enhancing the transportation of goods and passengers in and out of the region. The electric street railway system was established in 1884 eventually linking the hills and the flats.

EDUCATION

The community emphasis on education was launched in 1823, when the Academy opened its doors. Then, in 1865, Ezra Cornell, who had made a fortune in the telegraph industry, donated a public library to the county and, with help from the Morrill Land Grant, he went on to establish Cornell University in 1868 on farmlands on East Hill.

In 1892, when local violin teacher William Grant Egbert rented four rooms and arranged to teach eight students, another important educational institution was created, the Ithaca Conservatory of Music. Gradually it expanded its curriculum and was chartered as a private college in 1931. It changed its name to Ithaca College and moved in 1960 to its present site on South Hill.

Other schools in Ithaca include the Tompkins Cortland Community College, which started in Groton and moved to Dryden in 1974, and a branch of the Florida Lakes School of Massage which came to town in 1994.

RENEWAL AND PRESERVATION

The 50s and 60s saw out-of-town shopping malls draw people out of the city center, and the business district deteriorated. But by the 60s a massive urban renewal program brought new life into the inner city. To make room for the new buildings, entire city blocks were cleared. Unfortunately in the process of a most ambitious program, several buildings of historic interest were razed including the Old City Hall, circa 1843. The resulting uproar from historic preservationists put the brakes on further destruction of noteworthy structures and spurred the formation of the Historic Ithaca organization.

In 1974, Ithaca Commons was created, a pedestrian zone of shops, offices, restaurants, and other commercial businesses. Older structures were rehabilitated including the Clinton House, Clinton Hall, and the DeWitt Mall, as well as neighborhood houses. Joseph Ciaschi deserves credit for purchasing, saving, and renovating the Clinton Block and Clinton House in 1985.

Peter Finger

The Ithaca Commons is a thriving pedestrian shopping and cultural center in the heart of the city.

SENECA FALLS

Seneca Falls — which actually is closer to Cayuga Lake than to Seneca Lake — has played a surprisingly strong role in a number of developments. Home of the first pump, the first fire engine, and site of the first women's rights conventions, this quiet modest-sized village has seen periods of rapid growth and periods of decline.

Today Seneca Falls appears to be on the upturn. The revitalization of the Cayuga-Seneca Canal area which runs behind the main business district, the opening of a new museum, the Seneca Museum of Waterways and Industry, and the other historical sites and parks in town make this a place worth visiting.

Major local industries today with roots in the past are the Seneca Knitting Mills and Goulds Pumps.

NATIVES, SETTLERS, AND ENTREPRENEURS

In the center of the hunting grounds of the once powerful Haudenosaunee (six nations of the Iroquois Confederacy), Seneca Falls was the first town to be settled in the wilderness between Utica and Buffalo. Then it was called "Sha-se-onse," meaning swift waters. And indeed, it was the rapids running in the Seneca River that created the waterpower for the mills and other businesses shaping the growth and character of Seneca Falls.

The first "official" white settler, Job Smith, came to the area in 1787. He was a man of questionable character and there were suspicions among some that he was fleeing from justice. He existed by trading with the native Americans, assisting travelers over the falls, and eating wild game, river salmon, and corn. Later Smith would move to Waterloo and marry a Miss Gorham.

The downtown area of Seneca Falls has many historic buildings.

Peter Finger

When Sullivan swept through the region on his mission to destroy the native American villages, with his army was Lawrence Van Cleef. When he first saw the lake, the story goes, he was so taken by its beauty that he planted his poplar staff in the ground, vowing to return. When he came back ten years later in 1789, the staff had grown into a tree. Van Cleef, who came from Albany, settled with his family near that tree which stood for more than 100 years. When it came down in a storm, a piece of it was preserved. That piece of wood can now be seen in the Seneca Falls Historical Museum.

For a while, Van Cleef and Smith partnered in a business to transport goods and boats around the falls. Then Van Cleef began to make boats and became well known for his skill at piloting craft over the rapids. He was generous, well liked, and one of the early entrepreneurs. He kept the first tavern in his log home and built the first frame building for his family. The Parkus family from Connecticut moved into Van Cleef's log cabin.

Others followed. Records show that several lots were sold as early as 1796 and it is believed that the first saw mill was built about 1794. Seneca Falls was growing up. A log school house was built in 1801 with Alexander Wilson as the first teacher. Dr. Long, the first village physician, settled here in 1793 and the First Presbyterian Church was organized in 1807. In 1814 G.V. Sackett, Seneca Falls' first attorney, opened his law office, completing the village's professional roster of "doctor, lawyer, merchant, chief."

Colonel Mynderse constructed a house, established a store, and built the Upper Red Mills in 1795 and in 1807 the Red Mills on the lower rapids. The company was known as the Bayard Company. By 1825 the Bayard land also contained a few small farms, a cooper shop, blacksmith shop, and a community of about 300 people.

By 1818 locks allowed boats to avoid the rapids; ten years later the Cayuga-Seneca Canal was tied into the Erie Canal, opening vast transportation possibilities for goods and produce originating in Seneca Falls.

As people came and stayed, businesses began to develop, mostly along the river where there was water power. But it is because of the attitude of the Bayard Company that Seneca Falls did not develop more mills and businesses more rapidly at this time. The company controlled the water power in Seneca Falls and, fearing competition, refused to sell any portion of the land. Thus rival villages along the river developed and Seneca Falls with its wonderful natural assets was left to flounder. It was only in 1825, when the company fell on hard times, that it was forced to divide its property and sell its holdings.

During his time with the Bayard Company, Col. Mynderse had amassed great wealth thanks to his network of business connections, and was a man of great influence in Seneca Falls. In 1832 he donated land to build the Seneca Falls Academy, and died in 1836, leaving his family a large fortune.

Early businesses included paper mills, a cotton factory, knitting mills, a clock factory, stone flouring mills, a harness shop, hotels, carriage makers, lumber mills, and leather, tool, and woolen mills, including the successful Seneca

Knitting Mills. One of the most important operations came to Seneca Falls in 1839: manufacturing pumps. In 1855, Mr. Birdsall Holly received a patent for his rotary pump and engine which would gain a worldwide reputation for its use in building steam fire engines.

WOMEN'S RIGHTS

In April 23, 1831, Seneca Falls was incorporated as a village. Twenty years later, the village was gaining a reputation in the state and beyond for dealing with social and religious reform issues including abolition of slavery, temperance, and women's rights. One of the earliest gatherings for women's rights in the United States was a convention in 1848 at the Wesleyan Chapel in Seneca Falls, organized by Elizabeth Cady Stanton and Lucretia Mott. The Declaration of Sentiments and Resolutions, based on the Declaration of Independence, was read to the assembly. The declaration asserted that women and men should be treated equally, and that women should have the right to vote. The site of the convention and Elizabeth Cady Stanton's Greek Revival home are now part of the Women's Rights National Historical Park.

A photo of Stanton, her daughter, and granddaughter is part of the archives of the Seneca Falls Historical Society. Even as a grandmother, Stanton, with her white finger curls, shawl, and full face, still has the look of one fiercely independent and committed.

FIRE AND GROWTH

A devastating fire took place in the summer of 1890, a cruel irony as it occurred in the town that had given the world its first fire engine. Starting in the center of the business area, the flames fanned out, ultimately destroying sixty-seven stores, residences, and offices, leaving half of Main Street in ashes.

The Cayuga-Seneca Canal runs along the rear of the business district buildings in Seneca Falls.

Katharine Delavan Dyson

The buildings were rebuilt and Seneca Falls continued to grow. In 1860 the population was reported to be 4,000.

During the early twentieth century, travel on the lake was by steamboat. Vessels such as the *Kate D. Morgan*, the *T.D. Wilcox*, and the grand *Frontenac* plied the waters between Ithaca and Cayuga. On July 26, 1907, encountering stormy weather, the *Frontenac* caught fire. The captain steered the ship towards shore, running it aground about three fourths of a mile north of Levanna. Panic set in and eight people drowned. The charred remains of the ship still show just above the water, a grim reminder of the tragedy.

In 1915, the old Cayuga-Seneca Canal was widened, the smaller locks replaced with two larger locks, and the area known as "The Flats" flooded, becoming Van Cleef Lake, to be used as a reservoir for the locks. In the process, more than 115 industrial buildings and sixty homes ceased to exist. It is appropriate that the lake was named after Van Cleef; it was on The Flats where he built his first dwelling.

AURORA

Founded on the site of the Cayuga village "Deawendote," which means "village of constant dawn," Aurora is on the eastern shores of the lake. Many of the buildings in this delightful college town, along with Wells College, are listed in the National Register of Historic Places.

Apparently some very special visitors find Aurora highly desirable. About mid-October, the skies above Cayuga Lake shimmer with the arrival of more than 500,000 wild geese heading south from Canada for the winter. Some 80,000 birds make the shores around Aurora their winter headquarters.

In addition to the pottery, furniture, and glass studios of McKenzie Child just north of the village center, there is Aurora Place, a complex of shops in the center of town housed in vintage buildings. The Aurora Inn is also an important Aurora institution.

INTERLAKEN

Its former names, McCall's Tavern, Farmer Village, and Farmer, tell the tale of its origins, a simple community with a strong farming population. Incorporated in 1904 as Interlaken, the village has grown along both sides of Rte. 96 on the western side of the lake north of Trumansburg. The Hinman Memorial Library, Interlaken Historical Society, the Farmer's Museum, and many family-owned businesses line Main Street.

It would be a perfect movie set for a typical down-home village; here they roll out American Legion breakfasts, parades, Old Home Day, an antique car show, and a flurry of flea markets.

TRUMANSBURG

About ten miles north of Ithaca, on the west side of Cayuga Lake, the pleasant village of Trumansburg was founded in 1792 by Abner Truman and now has a population of about 1,600 people. It is adjacent to the spectacular Taughannock Falls State Park. The village is home to a number of historic houses and buildings as well as several unique shops such as Black Sheep Designs, The Blue Heron Gallery, and T-Burg Toys. The Trumansburg Conservatory of Fine Arts provides educational opportunities for all ages and the annual Trumansburg Fair held in August is a week-long festival featuring a demolition derby, stock car football, horse pulls, colt stake and harness racing, draft horse show, a fireman's parade, and fireworks.

LODGING

Most of Cayuga Lake's places to stay are in Ithaca at the southern tip, Seneca Falls on the northern end, and Aurora on the eastern shore. Small inns and B&Bs are scattered in or near the vineyards which ring the lake and there are several 50s- and 60s-style motels along Routes 5 and 20. The largest hotels include the Holiday Inn Executive Tower in Ithaca, the Statler Hotel right on Ithaca's Cornell campus, and the new Courtyard Marriott. Major historic inns include the Aurora Inn and Taughannock Farms Inn. For fun there is the Station Restaurant Sleeping Cars with accommodations in old railroad cars in downtown Ithaca.

LODGING RATES

$: Up to $75 per couple
$$: $76–$150 per couple

$$$: $151–$250 per couple
$$$$: More than $250

Ithaca Area

HOTELS AND RESORTS

**BEST WESTERN
   UNIVERSITY INN**
607-272-6100
E. Hill Plaza, Ithaca NY
   14850
Manager: Terry Terry
Rooms: 101
Open: Year-round
Price: $$$
Credit cards: Most major

Next to Cornell University, the hotel is just fifteen minutes from the Tompkins County Airport. Rooms are all on one level and are newly redecorated in pleasing beige and mauve colors. Rooms come equipped with refrigerators, televisions with video players and HBO service, coffee makers, and irons/ironing boards. Some rooms have cathedral ceilings. Executive rooms offer microwaves, data ports, and gas fireplaces. There is an outdoor pool and an exercise room with 24-hour availability. Rates include continental breakfast and shuttle service to everywhere in Ithaca. This is a convenient, comfortable place but there is nothing remarkable about the grounds or setting.

COURTYARD BY MARRIOTT
800-228-9290
29 Thornwood Dr., Ithaca NY 14850
Rooms: 106
Open: Year-round
Price: $$–$$$
Credit cards: Most major

This new property (due to open by publication date) is in the Cornell Business I Technology Park. It is designed to bring business travelers state-of-the-art amenities such as dual-line speaker phones with dataport and voicemail. The rooms are air-conditioned and come with climate control, coffee maker, hair dryer, and iron/ironing board. There is an indoor pool, whirlpool and exercise facility along with a guest laundry, business services, restaurant, and conference room.

EMBASSY INN
607-272-3721, 607-272-3722
1083 Dryden Rd./Rte. 366, Ithaca NY 14850
Manager: Nick Patel
Rooms: 25
Open: Year-round
Price: $–$$
Credit cards: Most major

Conveniently near the airport, downtown Ithaca, and the colleges, this is a straightforward motel with one-and two-story buildings. It is a bit off the street, so is quiet with a lawn in front. All the rooms have been recently redecorated from carpets and wallpaper to bathrooms. Rooms are air-conditioned and come with cable television, posturepedic beds, and courtesy coffee. Some rooms have two double beds, other have a queen bed, and a few have kitchenettes and a sitting area.

HOLIDAY INN-EXECUTIVE TOWER
607-272-1000, 800-HOLIDAY; fax 607-277-1275
222 S. Cayuga St., Ithaca NY 14850
Manager: Joseph Kelly
Rooms: 181
Open: Year-round
Price: $$–$$$$
Credit cards: Most major

Location, location, location. This full-service hotel is right in the heart of Ithaca, one block from the Commons and within sight of East Hill and the Cornell University campus. The rooms are continually being redecorated and the current themes are French and cherry. The hotels has a restaurant, lounge, indoor pool, and fitness center. Rooms are equipped with irons/ironing board, coffee makers, hair dryers, air-conditioning, and in-room movies. Cornell University, Ithaca College, and airport shuttles are complimentary.

LA TOURELLE COUNTRY INN
607-273-2734; fax 607-273-4821
www.latourelleinn.com

This is not your typical hotel. Set on seventy acres with hiking trails, two tennis courts, and patio, La Tourelle looks and feels decidedly European. Each set of rooms has its own character. Queen-bed

1150 Danby Rd., Ithaca NY
  14850
Innkeeper: Leslie Leonard
Rooms: 35
Open: Year-round
Price: $$–$$$
Credit cards: Most major

rooms have Mexican wood furniture and dark green carpet; king rooms are larger with light Haitian wood furniture and peach carpets. Some rooms have two king beds, others two queen beds. Honeymooners might ask for the special accommodations which come with round beds, mirrored ceilings, disco balls, and jacuzzis. The large room with a four-poster king bed, a woodburning fireplace, and a small balcony is also popular with romantics. The rooms that overlook the valley have the nicest views; the others face the front yard. Rooms come with refrigerators, televisions/vcrs, movies, phone, air-conditioning, and free morning coffee. The John Thomas Steak House is next door and the inn is three miles from the center of town.

THE STATLER HOTEL
607-257-2500, 800-541-2501;
  fax 607-257-6432
www.hotelschool.cornell.e
  du/statler/
11 East Ave., Cornell
  University, Ithaca NY
  14850
Managing director: James
  Hisle
Rooms: 150
Open: Year-round; closed
  major holidays (follows
  Cornell schedule)
Price: $$$–$$$$
Credit cards: Most major

If you can't get spit and polish service here, you probably can't get it anywhere: the Statler is the teaching hotel of Cornell University's School of Hotel Administration. On the Cornell campus, this multi-story hotel has a very business-like ambiance with marble floors, dark woods, and solid-color decor. The rooms are modern and have large picture windows with views of the campus and countryside. The Statler offers kitchenette suites, business desk with phone and dedicated data line, cable television, and in-room coffee makers. Guests have access to the Cornell University athletic facilities including the Olympic pool. Banfi's restaurant serves breakfast, lunch, and dinner as well as Sunday brunch. The Regent Lounge has a full service bar and serves casual food.

BED & BREAKFASTS

**ANGEL ARMS B&B
  WELLNESS RETREAT**
607-838-0497
www.lightlink.com/angel
481 LaFayette Rd., Groton
  NY 13073
Innkeeper: Suzanne E.
  Camin
Rooms: 5, some with
  shared baths
Open: Year-round
Price: $–$$
Credit cards: Most major

On six acres in a newly renovated barn with soaring cathedral ceilings and rustic exposed beams, those who are spiritually minded will find this place a true haven. Specializing in spiritual retreats and classes for individuals and small groups, Angel Arms is ideally situated amidst gardens, fields, and trees. There are wildflowers and herb gardens, and paths through groves of greens and shrubbery. Suzanne's gardens continue to develop. Her newest one, she says, came to her in a dream: a spiral garden leading to a healing and mediation garden. There are also Feng Shui gardens including a lovers' garden and a lovers' walk. Among the spiritual and body sessions are cranio-sacral therapy, ear candling, herbal body wraps, bodytalk, psychic readings, pleiadian light work, reiki, shamanic healing, and ayurvedio cleansing. Rooms are furnished with queen, double, or twin beds, quilts, and some have fireplaces and jacuzzis — everything is new but the antiques. The Rose Room is very feminine in its appointments; others are more straightforward. A marvelously complete breakfast is served enhanced by fresh edible herbs and flowers. Warm fruit compote, apple crisp, pears amandine, egg dishes, lots of homemade muffins, juices, and hot oat cereals are examples of what is offered. Tea and coffee are available all day and there are always cookies, muffins, or other goodies to nibble on. If you want to get married here, Suzanne is a licensed minister and can officiate at the ceremony as well as arrange the details for tying the knot in her gardens. Alternative lifestyles are welcome.

BUTTERMILK FALLS B&B
607-272-6767;
  fax 607-273-3947
110 E. Buttermilk Rd.,
  Ithaca NY 14850
Innkeeper: Margie Rumsey
Rooms: 5 with private
  baths
Price: $$–$$$$
Open: Year-round
Credit cards: Cash, check,
  or money orders

This classic white brick 1820s house is just two miles from the heart of Ithaca, on two acres of landscaping with huge trees and gardens. Set near the entrance to Buttermilk Falls State Park, it's an ideal base for exploring the trails and gorges of the park. The house, which has belonged to six generations of the Rumsey family, is furnished with family heirloom antiques and accessories along with sixteen Windsor chairs and a large pine table which look antique but were actually made by Margie Rumsey's son. Rooms are furnished with queen, king, or twin beds and handmade quilts; one king room has a jacuzzi, woodburning fireplace, and nice sitting area. Upstairs there is wall-to-wall carpeting while downstairs the floors are covered by lovely Persian rugs. All rooms are air-conditioned. Breakfast is served on the screened porch, in the dining room, or even at the picnic table under the large tree in the back yard. The full breakfast includes hot entrées, lots of fruit, and warm muffins and pastries. In the summer you can swim at the foot of the falls and hike and bike; in the winter you can go cross-country skiing. The Rumsey family has a fine collection of antique games including Uncle Wiggley, checkers, chess boards, and others. Margie says she will make every effort to accommodate special requests such as early morning breakfasts for those who have to leave for the airport early. When she's asked if she takes children, Margie says quietly that though she is finished raising her own children, if the parents agree to watch their youngsters carefully to make sure they do not abuse the precious things that are in the house, then they are welcome. Smokers and pets, however, are not.

**THE CODDINGTON
  GUEST HOUSE**
607-275-0021
thecoddington@aol
130 Coddington Rd., Ithaca
  NY 14850
Innkeeper: Denice
  Karamardian DeSouza
Rooms: 3 suites with
  private baths
Open: Year-round
Price: $$ (weekly, monthly
  rentals available)
Credit cards: Most major

This new guest house in the style of a turn-of-the-century Italian villa is on the border of the Ithaca College campus on South Hill, five minutes from Cornell University, and next door to Angelini Centini's Restaurant. All guest rooms have a superb lake views and two of the accommodations have a private entrance. All rooms give you plenty of privacy, as each accommodation is in a separate wing. The upstairs suite is a three-room family suite with large bedroom, full kitchen, living room, veranda and bath. There are three living rooms for everyone to use including one for reading, meetings, and live music (with a piano), one for media (television, cd player, movies) and one exercise/tv room. The exercise/sitting room doubles as an optional second bedroom to one of the suites for large parties. There are also porches and verandas for enjoying the view. A generous continental breakfast is served in the dining room and there is an extra kitchen downstairs and refrigerators in all rooms. Tour packages and learning workshops are available. Children are warmly welcomed.

THE EDGE OF THYME
607-659-5155, 800-722-7365;
  fax 607-659-5155
www.edgeofthyme.com
6 Main St., Candor NY
  13743
Innkeepers: Prof. Frank and
  Eva Mae Musgrave
Rooms: 5 with both private
  and shared baths
Open: Year-round
Price: $$
Credit cards: Most major

Although the house was built in 1860, when John Rockefeller's executive secretary came to town in 1908, Rockefeller's architect transformed the building into a Georgian-style home. Accommodations include a suite with a queen-size bed and a separate sitting room with a pull-out single bed, two large rooms with private baths, and two rooms that share a bath. The house is decorated with tapestries, quilts, period wallpapers, Oriental rugs, and lots of antiques and family heirlooms. Over the years, when various family members have asked Eva Mae if she would like a particular antique, she says, "I have never said no." Her favorite pieces include a rosewood side table with carved lion's feet now in the dining room, a number of lovely paintings, and the original slaw-making machine invented by her great great grandfather which now sits in the library. There are also marble fireplaces, a parlor, an enclosed porch and outside porch, gazebo, and pergola. One of its most charming aspects is the enclosed porch with leaded windows. When they need scraping and repainting, Eva Mae insists on doing the painting herself: "I won't let painters go near them." Apparently the panes alone cost $250 to replace. In a quiet rural village on an acre of landscaped grounds, this B&B lives up to its name: the Musgraves have an herb garden which provides extra flavor for the gourmet breakfasts which might include coddled eggs, baked apples, and apple blueberry tarte. And you can expect great food. Eva Mae loves to cook and is the author of *Tastes at the Edge of Thyme* cookbook. The inn welcomes well-behaved children, but no smokers please. Eva also serves high teas with three-days' notice.

THE ELMSHADE GUEST HOUSE
607-273-1707
402 S. Albany St., Ithaca NY 14850
Innkeeper: Lillie Teeter
Rooms: 8, some with shared baths, plus an efficiency apartment
Open: Year-round
Price: $–$$
Credit cards: Most major

This cozy in-town guest house has been welcoming visitors since 1930. If you don't have a car, this would be a good choice. It is right on the Ithaca Transit bus line and just two miles from Cornell University and Ithaca College. Three of the rooms have private baths, the rest are shared. This is a comfortable, clean place to stay offering a good value. One room has twin beds, four have doubles, and the rest are queens; mattresses are good. Furnishings include quilts, chenille spreads or comforters, lots of pillows, and fairly simple furniture: very few antiques are used. Rooms are air-conditioned and are equipped with cable television. A hearty continental breakfast is served, often on the first or second floor porches in warmer weather, in the dining room in the winter. There is a guest kitchenette with microwave, refrigerator, cupboard, and small counter and cupboard. Coffee, a large assortment of teas and snacks, milk, and orange juice are offered. A large hallway is set up with sofa and chairs for guests' use. Off-street parking is available and Elmshade is three blocks from Ithaca Commons. Children are welcome, but no pets please.

THE FEDERAL HOUSE B&B
607-533-7362, 800-533-7362
www.federalhouse.com
innkeeper@clarityconnect.com
175 Ludlowville Rd., Lansing NY 14882 (6 miles north of Ithaca)
Innkeeper: Diane Carroll
Rooms: 4 with private baths
Open: Year-round
Price: $–$$$
Credit cards: Most major

One of the more romantic B&Bs in the area, this 1815 inn is steps away from Salmon Creek and Falls. Constructed by Abijah Miller, it was here that William Seward, secretary of state under President Abraham Lincoln, courted his wife, Frances Miller, niece of Squire Miller. Rooms are exquisitely furnished with antiques and artwork and the house features original wood and a hand-carved fireplace. The Lincoln Suite has a queen canopy bed, gas fireplace, and private staircase.The two-room William Seward Suite has a queen bed, fireplace, sitting room with tv/vcr and a view of the garden and falls. All rooms are air-conditioned. You can relax on one of the porches or steal some privacy in the gazebo or gardens. A full breakfast is served and there are bikes available for guests' use.

HANSHAW HOUSE B&B
607-257-1437, 800-257-1437
www.hanshawhouse.com
15 Sapsucker Woods Rd.,
   Ithaca NY 14850
Innkeeper: Helen Scoones
Rooms: 4 with private
   baths
Open: Year-round
Price: $$–$$$
Credit cards: Most major

This rambling 1830s two-story restored farmhouse is set amidst exuberant perennial and herb gardens and lawns with views of a pond. There are flowers and birds everywhere. Air-conditioned rooms are light and airy, and furnished with English country antiques, fine bed linens, goosedown comforters, and artwork. Bedrooms are decorated with beautiful wallpaper and chintz in colors that are light and fresh and some rooms have white walls. Two of the rooms have sitting areas. Full hearty breakfasts are served; each morning's offering is different and depends on the season. Menu examples include French toast with caramel sauce and walnuts, scones, baked eggs, potato cakes, melon soup, biscuits with dill, and tomato tart with fresh basil. Iced lemon tea and biscotti, hot mulled cider, chocolate brownies, and cookies are served in the afternoon: your hosts make sure you are well taken care of. The yard and gardens invite you to relax in a hammock, one of the chairs, or gliders. There is a sitting room and television room (the only room with teddy bears who are lined up on a bench). The dining room, although traditionally furnished, has delightful whimsical touches including painted furniture pieces and McKenzie Child glassware, dishes, and vases. Hanshaw House is within walking distance of Cornell's Laboratory of Ornithology.

**HOUND AND HARE
   B&B**
607-257-2821, 800-652-2821
www.houndandhare.com
1031 Hanshaw Rd., Ithaca
   NY 14850
Innkeeper: Zetta Sprole
Rooms: 5 with private
   baths
Open: Year-round
Price: $–$$
Credit cards: Most major

Built by Samuel Boothroyd on military tract property deeded by General George Washington in 1793, this white brick colonial is steeped in history and tradition. Victorian antiques, laces, and family heirlooms are found throughout the house along with Queen Anne wing-backed chairs, fresh flowers, and glittering chandeliers and gold-gilt mirrors. Some rooms have brass beds and all have down comforters, eyelet sheets, down pillows, and are air-conditioned. The bridal suite has a jacuzzi. The guest living room has a fireplace where you can enjoy a spot of tea or you can retreat and catch up on your reading in the library. The grounds are beautifully landscaped and contain herb gardens, rose beds, and an old-fashioned lily pond and fountain. It's a good place to come home to at the end of a day of sightseeing or other activities. In the morning you can look forward to bounteous breakfasts served by candlelight in the formal dining room.

LOG COUNTRY INN B&B

607-589-4771, 800-274-4771
wanda@logtv.com
www.logtv.com/inn
PO Box 581, Ithaca NY 14851
Innkeepers: Wanda and Slawomir Grunberg
Rooms: 5 with private baths
Open: Year-round
Price: $–$$$
Credit cards: Most major

It may be a log house, but the amenities are far from basic. Rustic in looks with soaring cathedral ceilings, massive log walls and fireplaces, yet containing every modern amenity, this house is set at the edge of a 7,000 acre forest. It should appeal to those with a love of the outdoors. A full European-style breakfast may include blintzes or Russian pancakes and a good selection of home-baked breads, pastries, and jams. Enjoy features like a sauna, fireplaces, jacuzzi, and afternoon tea. Hiking and cross-country trails are easily accessed and there is a vegetable garden and orchard.

RITA'S 1843 COUNTRY B&B

607-257-2499, 800-231-6674
http://wordpro.com/ritas/, ritasb&b@lightlink.com
1620 Hanshaw Rd., Ithaca 14850
Innkeepers: Bob and Rita Boothroyd
Rooms: 3 with private baths
Open: Year-round
Price: $–$$
Credit cards: Most major

A 1843 Greek Revival country home on twenty-eight acres close to downtown Ithaca, this is a charming old house with a picket fence and pine and aged chestnut floors. It sits amidst cedar trees, pastures, and meadowlands on a hill above Ithaca. There are two large living rooms, a den, dining room, breakfast solarium, and three bedrooms, a bit on the cozy side, but well appointed. Enjoy super breakfasts with homemade cinnamon rolls and pastries and while you're eating you may see people horseback riding from Rita's barn to nearby meadowlands for some exercise. Take time to wander through the herb and flower gardens and perhaps explore nearby Sapsucker Woods.

ROSE INN

607-533-7905;
fax 607-533-7908
roseinn@clarityconnect.com or info@roseinn.com
www.roseinn.com
813 Auburn Rd./Rte. 34, Ithaca NY 14851
Innkeepers: Sherry and Charles Rosemann
Rooms: 21
Open: Year-round
Price: $$–$$$
Credit cards: Most major

This stately Victorian B&B country inn sits on twenty acres amidst gardens and lawns. Rooms are in the main house and in a nearby carriage house. Built in the 1840s, the house is designed around a stunning circular Honduras mahogany staircase which took two years to build by a master craftsman. It extends from the main hall up through two stories to a cupola. There is a piano in the parlor, hand-carved oak doors, parquet floors, high ceilings, and marble fireplaces. Brandy, the inn's dog, is often on hand to give you a friendly greeting. Each room is different, most lavishly decorated. Some rooms feature four-poster beds covered with silky down duvets and one suite has a jacuzzi tub, mirrored armoires, and French doors which open onto a private patio furnished with white wrought iron furniture. No. 11, the Bridal Suite, has a king-size bed,

Peter Finger

The Rose Inn and Carriage House, Ithaca, is set on twenty acres of gardens and lawns.

down duvet, fireplace, and arched windows overlooking the garden. The library is well-stocked (noted was a sizable collection of Dickens) and there are several board games. Outside is a wood swing for two; nearby a profusely blooming mandevilla climbs a trellis. Amenities include an honor bar, air-conditioning, and televisions in some rooms. Weddings are often held in the formal gardens under a flower bedecked arbor. The restaurant serves breakfast, and dinner Tues.–Sun.; see the entry in the Restaurants section below for more information.

SCANDIA HOUSE
607-898-3799
holson1@twcny.rr.com
137 E. Cortland St., Groton
  NY 13073
Innkeeper: Helen Olson
Rooms: 2 with shared baths
Open: Apr.–Nov.
Price: $
Credit cards: Most major

This pleasant Queen Anne Victorian is in the village of Groton across from the library and two doors down from the Groton Hotel Restaurant. It features a wrap-around porch as well as an upstairs porch, and the interior has much of the original oak in the dining room, sitting room, entrance foyer and stairway, a virtual flow of golden wood. The house is eclectically furnished with a collection acquired by the family through the years. One bedroom has a queen bed; another a twin. There are televisions in the upstairs and downstairs sitting rooms, a piano, and an organ.

Breakfast is served in the dining room when guests prefer it, early or late. In keeping with her Finnish heritage, Helen serves preserves from Finland such as cloudberry, as well as cheeses, eggs with dill, croissants, muffins, and fruits. Guests usually eat in the dining room, but in nice weather, can take coffee out to the porch. It's a pretty house that has not been overly decorated or had its integrity destroyed by over-ambitious modernization. It's simple, nice, laid-back. With only two rooms, this B&B is desirable for a small family as they can have entire use of the second floor.

THE STATION RESTAURANT AND SLEEPING CARS
607-272-2609
www.ithacastation.com
806 W. Buffalo St. at Taughannock Blvd., Ithaca NY 14850
Innkeepers: Terry and Barbara Ciaschi
Rooms: 3 private sleeper cars
Open: Year-round
Price: $$
Credit cards: Most major

Imagine your own private sleeping car: it's on track, but doesn't go anywhere. Converted to guest suites in 1998 and designed by architect Claudia Brenner and V. Romanoff and Associates, real honest-to-goodness vintage sleeping cars are decorated in period decor and much of the original cabinetry and interior woodwork is intact. One suite has balloon shades on all the windows and each car has a private entrance and full bath, phone, cable television, fireplace, air-conditioning, and coffee maker. A continental breakfast is included in the rates. Just outside the cars, the hands on the tall fifty-year-old Seth Thomas clock are wound every eight days. The cars are next to the restaurant in the former Lehigh Valley Railroad Station. The former waiting room is the main dining room where you will find chandeliers from the Ithaca Hotel. The benches are from the original waiting room, the tile floor is original, and the rest rooms retain the old marble partitions and hardware. The accommodations could be considered basic, but fun.

VERALMA, THE 1850 HOUSE
607-275-9519
211 Hudson St., Ithaca NY 14850
Innkeeper: Beverly Beer
Rooms: 3 with private baths
Open: Year-round
Price: $$
Credit cards: Most major

This elegant 1850s Italianate estate, which once belonged to a mayor of Ithaca, features twelve-foot ceilings and a striking three-story walnut staircase leading to a cupola. It's an unusual house because it's virtually the same as when it was built in 1850. Rooms are air-conditioned and have either queen beds or twins and are furnished with family antiques and period accessories, some from the owners' great great grandparents. There is a guest parlor with a marble fireplace, phone and television, formal dining room, a large front porch, and lovely one-acre grounds. There is also a pool and carriage house. A full breakfast is served and features such items as pecan waffles with maple syrup and speciality omelets. This is a light, bright house conveniently near the Commons and colleges. The Veralma does not accept smoking, pets, or children under twelve.

**THE WILLIAM HENRY
  MILLER INN**
607-256-4553, 877-256-4553;
  fax 607-256-0092
www.millerinn.com
303 N. Aurora St., Ithaca
  NY 14850
Innkeepers: Ken and
  Lynnette Scofield
Rooms: 9 with private
  baths
Open: Year-round
Price: $$–$$$
Credit cards: Most major

Built as a private home in 1880 by William Henry Miller, Cornell's first student of architecture, the house is richly detailed with stained glass windows, American chestnut woodwork, fireplaces, and a spacious parlor, dining room, and music room. The house has a wonderful pointed corner tower and Tudor details. Located in a pleasant residential area just off the Ithaca Commons, guests can walk to shops, theaters, and restaurants. Rooms are beautifully furnished with antiques and period reproductions. For example, Dane's Room, large and sunlit, has a king bed; the Library has a corner fireplace, bookshelves, sitting area, and queen bed. The Turret, a third-floor room, has a cozy reading alcove and a queen bed; the Retreat has lots of windows and a nice seating area; the Carriage House has two rooms, one with a jacuzzi, and is ideal for honeymooners or for families traveling together since it is quiet and secluded. All rooms have hair dryer, air-conditioning, telephones, cable television. A full candlelight breakfast is served in the dining room or in the adjoining parlor. It might be baked pear with cream and sun-dried cherries or a three-cheese casserole. You can also have a continental breakfast in your room. Early risers can enjoy a fresh cup of coffee and a read of the *New York Times*. In the afternoon tea is served in the parlor; evening dessert is also offered. Children over twelve welcome; pets and smoking are not.

Seneca Falls Area

GUION HOUSE B&B
315-568-8129, 800-631-8919
www.flare.net/guionhouse
32 Cayuga St., Seneca Falls
  NY 13148
Innkeepers: Sherry Laney
  and Rodger Burnisky
Rooms: 6, 4 with private
  baths
Open: Year-round
Price: $–$$
Credit cards: Most major

This three-story Second Empire home is in the Seneca Falls Historic District, a lovely residential area just a block from the town's main shopping area. Outside the house boasts a mansard roof and a huge front porch detailed with elaborate arches; inside it's furnished with a mix of antiques, period reproductions, chandeliers, converted gas lighting fixtures, and family collectibles, all beneath twelve-foot ceilings. A massive mahogany and black walnut staircase leads to the second floor. The first and second-floor bedrooms have their original plaster rosettes in ceilings. The third-floor bedrooms have slanted ceilings and a charm all their own. All the guest rooms are air-conditioned. A full breakfast is served by candlelight in the dining room and includes hot entrées and several kinds of fruit plus muffins or sweet rolls and cookies to go — Sherry is an admitted "cookie monster." A favorite pastime of

Guion's guests is sitting on the front porch in the bottom rockers (bigger than normal wooden rocking chairs), putting feet up on the railing, sipping a glass of wine, and watching the world go by. This house could be called elegant without pretension.

HUBBELL HOUSE
315-568-9690
http://members.aol.com/
  hubbellhse/index.html
42 Cayuga St., Seneca Falls
  NY 13148
Innkeepers: Karl and
  Joanne Elliott
Rooms: 4, 2 private, 2
  shared baths
Open: Year-round
Price: $$
Credit cards: Checks or
  cash only

This Gothic-style cottage, built in 1855, is on Van Cleef Lake in the historic district of town. Filled with authentic Victorian furniture and memorabilia, including electrified gas lights, it invites the visitor to step back in time without sacrificing modern comforts like air-conditioning and showers. Close to museums, the canal, and shops, the house sits on a hillside so the main rooms are on a middle level along with a lovely wrap-around porch. The common rooms include a large double parlor, library, and dining room. The largest room, the Laura Hoskins Hubbell Room, overlooks the lake and dock. It has a large ornate brass California king-size bed, private bath, Eastlake marbletop dresser, and commode. The smaller Lottie Pollard Room, featuring five beautifully arched windows in a bay, is full of Jenny Lind furniture and accessories such as a Victorian tea set. This room shares a bath. A full breakfast is served in the dining room by candlelight. Items served include fresh fruit, homemade breads or muffins, and hot entrées such as croissant à la orange, Victorian baked toast with light caramel topping and fresh berries, and stuffed French toast. There is a dock, paddle boat, and canoe.

**VANCLEEF
  HOMESTEAD B&B**
315-568-2275, 800-323-8668
www.flare.net/vancleef
86 Cayuga St., Seneca Falls
  NY 13148
Innkeepers: Joice and
  David Fredenburgh
Rooms: 3 with private
  baths
Open: Year-round
Price: $–$$
Credit cards: Most major

This two-story clapboard 1825 Federal-style home was built by the first permanent settler of Seneca Falls, Lawrence Van Cleef. Later the house became the residence of Wilhemus Mynderse, one of the village's most influential citizens of his time. In 1837, the house was transferred to Frederick Swaby, another of the village's original industrialists, whose family then occupied the house for over 100 years. It opened as a B&B in 1996. White with black shutters, it is close to the center of town. Rooms are attractively furnished with antiques and period reproductions. The living room has oversized chairs and a sofa surrounding the fireplace as well as a piano. It is decorated in upbeat blues and whites. The dining room features colorful floral wallpaper and a fireplace. On the first floor, the light, airy Van Cleef Room features a queen bed in a room with a working fireplace and bath. The Mynderse Room on the second floor has a wonderful king bed, and private bath; the corner Swaby Suite has a queen bed with an adjoining sitting room which has a double bed. The private bath for this room is across the hall. Down comforters cover the beds in the winter. A full hearty breakfast includes a variety of cereals, juices, coffees, and teas as well as fresh fruit, home-baked breads or coffeecake and a daily special main course, perhaps "from scratch" blueberry buttermilk pancakes, stuffed French toast, waffles with real maple syrup, sausage strata, quiche, and made-to-order omelets, all served with bacon or sausage. There is an in-ground swimming pool and rooms are air-conditioned. No smokers, please.

Other Area Lodging

THE ARCHWAY B&B
607-387-6175, 800-387-6175
www.fingerlakes.net/arch
   way
7020 Searsburg Rd.,
   Trumansburg NY 14886
Innkeepers: Meredith
   Pollard and Joe Prevost
Rooms: 3, 1 with private
   bath
Open: Year-round
Price: $–$$
Credit cards: Most major

Ever sink your nose into freshly laundered linens just unpinned from the clothes line? Well, those clean, air-fresh sheets are alive and well at the Archway: Meredith Pollard line-dries her bedding whenever possible, a special treat her guests appreciate. The Pollards' gracious 1861 Greek Revival is a very pretty home with a curved staircase, white fences, arbor, and gardens. Guests have the run of the downstairs including a television room, formal living room, and dining room. Guest rooms come with double, queen, king, or twin beds and the house is furnished with antiques and period fabrics as well as work by local artists — for example, the two-foot hand-painted wooden rooster. A full "light gourmet" breakfast is served with the emphasis on the healthy side, such as French toast, strata, and oat bran banana pancake. This is not an eggs and bacon kind of place. Breakfast is served in the sunroom overlooking the Trumansburg golf course, but many guests like to gather at the counter in the kitchen by the fireplace while Meredith and Joe cook the food. If you want to play golf, you get a free cart with greens fees. The house is on the edge of the village and is a perfect place to start the Cayuga Wine Trail. Children are welcome but no pets.

**AURORA INN AND
   RESTAURANT**
315-364-8888
Main St., Rte. 90, Aurora
   NY 13026
Rooms: 14, including 5
   suites
Open: Year-round
Price: $–$$
Credit cards: Most major

Right on the lake, the Aurora Inn, owned by Wells College, has been the place of choice for overnight visitors to the area for many years. Opened in 1833, over the years it has gone through many expansions and renovations. At one time it even served as a residence hall for Wells College. The most recent work was completed in 1992. Bedrooms are pleasant and large but a tad on the dark side. They have private bathrooms, cable television, and telephone, and some have water views. The Times Café serves lunch and dinner; Henry's, the tavern, is a good place for a drink or a light meal. There are plans for a new dock. (Editor's note: As of the publication date, the inn was closing and expected to reopen in the spring of 2001 under new management.)

FOXGLOVE B&B
607-844-9602,
  888-436-8608
www. odyssey.net/
  subscribers/foxglove
28 Main St., Freeville NY
  13068
Innkeeper: Suzanne
  Hoback
Rooms: 5, 3 with private
  baths, 2 shared; separate
  suite
Open: Year-round
Price: $–$$
Credit cards: Most major

This pretty Victorian place (circa 1900) with high roof peaks, large porch, and a bay window is surrounded by gardens, lawns, and nature trails leading past berry bushes to Fall Creek. Here, 100 years ago, the steamboat *Clinton* would carry passengers to the Old Mill and back for 5 cents. Located in the Greater Ithaca area, Foxglove is on the historic site of Riverside Park, a popular resort in the 1890s, where freethinkers and adventurers came to escape the city's summer heat. Today it is a special place for artists, actors, writers, musicians, photographers, poets, and nature lovers. Performances are often staged in the gardens. At the back of the property a seven-circuit labyrinth, forty-five feet in diameter, with gravel paths and more than 600 herb and flower plants, is a good place to meditate, picnic, or just enjoy. The house is furnished with a mix of old and new; rooms are clean and airy, and more on the modern than Victorian side (that is, without the usual doodads). The Tiger Lily Room accommodates one to four with television and private bath with jacuzzi tub. The Rose Room has a queen-size bed, television, and private bath. The Forget-Me-Not Room has a double bed and shared bath, while the Sunflower Room has a queen-size bed and shared bath. The Dogwood Suite, in a separate building next door, features a king-size bed, folding futon couch, kitchen, bath with shower and tub, living room with television/vcr, a screened porch, and private entrance. The guest rooms are air-conditioned. The library invites guests to play chess, read, or sit by the woodstove. A refrigerator with complimentary beverages is provided and there is an eight-person jacuzzi on the outside back deck. Choose what you want for breakfast the night before.

GOTHIC EVES B&B
607-387-6033, 800-387-7712
www.gothiceves.com
112 E. Main St., Trumans-
  burg NY 14886-0095
Innkeepers: Rose Hilbert
  and Roman Pausch
Rooms: 5
Open: Year-round
Price: $–$$
Credit cards: Visa, MC

This pretty 1855 Gothic Revival home is in the historic area of Trumansburg within walking distance of shops and restaurants. Although elegant and furnished with antiques, Gothic Eves is one of the few B&Bs that welcomes children of all ages. Some rooms connect so children can be in the adjacent room; in the yard are swings, picnic tables, and flower and herb gardens. Just behind the house is an elementary school with a large castle playground. In fact, there are young children in the owner's family, so the place can get a bit lively at times. The house is decorated with period fabrics and is air-conditioned. Fresh flowers are everywhere in the summer months; dried flowers and gourds from the garden are used to brighten up the house in the colder months. The rooms are quite large and five have en suite baths; the other bath is private but just out in the hall. The king rooms have an iron bed and a cherry sleigh bed, the double room has a brass bed, and the queen rooms feature a four-poster and sleigh bed. A generous breakfast is served with interesting variations on old standbys — for example, a version of eggs benedict includes lots of fresh vegetables, and most entrées are garnished with fresh edible flowers from the garden or fruit.

LAKE COUNTRY ESTATES
607-869-5182
www.lakecountryestates.
   com
Timber Lake Terrace, off
   Rte. 89, Ovid NY 14521
Innkeepers: Eva and
   Charlie Bennett
Rooms: 4 townhouses and
   small apartment
Open: Year-round
Price: $$–$$$
Credit cards: Most major

Rent a room, apartment, or townhouse in a private community of attractive brick townhouses along a 800-foot private beach. One, two, and three-bedroom units come with modern and pleasant fully equipped kitchens. Suites include bedroom, private bath, common living room, dining room, and balcony. The three-bedroom townhouse has a living room with fireplace, television, dining room, kitchen, powder room, and balcony overlooking the lake. The townhouses are on ten and a half acres of lawns, woods, and nature trails. There is a dock, a barbecue, and tables for picnicking. There are also plenty of lawn tables and chairs beneath the towering oak and maple trees.

ROGUE'S HARBOR B&B
607-533-3535
www.roguesharbor.com
2079 E. Shore Dr., Corner
   Rtes. 34&34B, Lansing
   NY 14882
Innkeeper: Eileen Stout
Rooms: 6, 4 with private
   baths
Open: Year-round
Price: $$
Credit cards: Most major

Although these rooms are in an old inn over the Rogue's Harbor restaurant, a recent insulation program has successfully locked out any noise you might anticipate from the dining crowd downstairs. Rooms are large, all decorated with antiques such a Victorian marble-topped dresser and sleigh bed. Robes are provided for the two rooms that share a bath; other rooms have private baths. Room #5 is one of larger room with a king-size wrought-iron bed and a lovely Maxfield Parrish print on the wall. It has a day bed for an additional guest. Grounds are not extensive, but the B&B is just a mile from Cayuga Lake and close to vineyards and many antique shops. A phone and fax as well as a guest refrigerator are in the common area.

SILVER STRAND AT SHELDRAKE
800-283-LAKE

This restored lakefront Victorian, built in the mid-nineteenth century, has a lovely old porch, five very attractively furnished bedrooms, and a

www.silverstrand.net
7398 Wyers Point Rd., Ovid
    NY 14521
Innkeeper: Maura
    Stamberger
Rooms: 5 with private
    baths; 3 bedroom/2 bath
    guest house
Open: Year-round
Price: $$–$$$
Credit cards: Visa, MC

guest cottage. Each room is quite different but all have private baths, air-conditioning, and private balconies; some have fireplaces. Room #1 has a very bright feeling with French doors that open onto a private balcony overlooking the lake and furnished with cushioned wicker porch furniture. Room #2 has a private "turret" style balcony affording views of over twenty miles of open water. It has a dramatic period queen bed, Casablanca fan, writing desk, comfortable reading chair, and a double jacuzzi. Room #3 is decorated in a Caribbean theme in cool blues and whites and comes with a six-foot double jacuzzi open to the room and a gas fireplace. The private circular balcony has two cushioned chaise lounges. Room #4 has a private balcony, queen canopy bed, Casablanca fan, comfortable reading chair, and a walnut bureau with marble top. (This is the only room without a bathtub and views of the water are from the porch.) Room #6 is open and airy with windows facing three directions. The room features a cherry sleigh bed, Casablanca fan, two comfortable reading chairs, and cushioned seating on a private sun deck. The three-bedroom, two-bath guest house has use of a 150-foot beach with dock, deck, rowboat, and two-person kayak, and has a four-person hot tub, pool table, satellite television/vcr, stereo, dishwasher, microwave, washer and dryer and two decks with gas and charcoal grills. Boats and bicycles are generally available for guest use.

TAUGHANNOCK
FARMS INN
607-387-7711, 888-387-7711
www.T-Farms.com
2030 Gorge Rd., Rte. 89 at
    Taughannock Falls State
    Park, Trumansburg NY
    14886
Innkeepers: Susan and Tom
    Sheridan
Rooms: 13; 5 rooms, 3 guest
    houses
Open: Closed Jan. 2–Apr. 1
Price: $$–$$$
Credit cards: Most major

This lovely Victorian country inn, with its porches, cupola, and high-pitched roof, is tucked into a hillside next to Taughannock Falls State Park. Many of the original furnishings brought here in 1873 by the wealthy owner, John Jones, are still in the house. Some pieces came from Philadelphia, others from England and Italy. During the 1930s, Jones deeded most of the sprawling 600-acre estate to New York State for the creation of Taughannock Falls State Park. In 1945, the mansion was sold and became an inn. Of the thirteen guest accommodations, all rooms are air-conditioned and five are decorated with Victorian antiques. There are also three guest houses for families and small groups. Some rooms have phones and televisions; some do not. The dining room has exceptional lake views through its long bank of windows.

WESTWIND B&B
607-387-3377;
  fax 607-387-5655
www.fingerlakes.net/west
  wind
1662 Taughannock Blvd.,
  Rte. 89, 1/2 mile south of
  Taughannock State Park,
  Trumansburg NY 14886
Innkeeper: Sharon R. Scott
Rooms: 4 with shared baths
Open: Year-round
Price: $$
Credit cards: Visa, MC

A 1870 Victorian farmhouse with lovely porches in a setting of meadows, woods, and ponds, Westwind sits on a hillside above the lake. Rooms share baths with either a clawfoot tub or whirlpool bath and shower. Twin, double, queen, and king-size beds are available. Full breakfasts are served.

RESTAURANTS

Most college towns offer a wide variety of places to eat, from casual bars to more formal restaurants. Ithaca is no exception and, for its size, has a large number of restaurants in the downtown area as well as closer to the campuses themselves. Outdoor dining has blossomed during the past few years in patio courtyards, along the streets, and in Ithaca's pedestrian market area, the Commons. Seneca Falls has a few places including the historic Pumphouse, and Aurora has a handful of restaurants including the lakeside Aurora Inn.

Prices are estimated per person for appetizer and dinner entrée without tax, tip, or alcoholic beverages.

$: Up to $10
$$: $11–$25

$$$: $26–$40
$$$$: More than $40

Ithaca Area

**ANGELINA CENTINI'S
  ITALIAN
  RESTAURANT**
607-273-0802
124 Coddington Rd., Ithaca
  NY 14850
Open: Tues.–Sun.
Price: $–$$
Serving: Tues.–Fri. L,
  Tues.–Sun. D
Cuisine: Italian
Credit cards: Most major

If you eat outdoors in the Grape Arbor Garden, in warm weather, of course, you will get a nice view of Cayuga Lake. Inside it is fine dining with linen table cloths and candles. Help yourself to the antipasto and salad makings from the gondola serving bar. Almost everything is made in-house, including sauces, pasta, sausage, meatballs and desserts. It is for this reason that Angelina Centini is popular among locals. Some evenings there is entertainment such as an accordion player.

**GIOVANNI'S OSTERIA
PAESANA**
607-273-2818
126 N. Aurora St., Ithaca
NY 14850
Open: Daily 5–10, Sun. 5–8;
Sat. and Sun. brunch
12–4
Price: $$
Serving: D, brunch
Cuisine: Northern Italian
Credit cards: Most major

"My alter ego is a rooster," says chef/owner Giovanni Freesia. "I used to raise a lot of dust, just like a rooster." So it is that you'll see a lot of roosters in this great Italian restaurant — on the window, on the walls, on shelves. Giovanni, who was born on a farm in Italy and worked as a chef on several Italian Line cruise ships, opened his restaurant in 1993. Brick walls, lots of plants, butcher-block tables, and candles ("To keep you warm," he says) set the mood for casual dining. All the food is cooked to order. Ravioli, meat, sauces, goat cheese, sage pesto, and everything else is prepared fresh. Dishes include unusual fare such as wild boar, rabbit, venison, pasta, and a huge variety of seafood. Much of the pastas and all the sauces are made in-house; organic pastas are specially ordered from New York. "We make all own desserts such as chestnut sauces, tiramisu, cherries Barolo; and also make our own ice cream, semi-freddo," says Giovanni. One month's flavor was figs soaked in marsala wine; another chestnut ice cream. When you make a reservation here, your table is waiting on your arrival and then you are invited to linger as long as you wish over your food. Some like to stretch the dining experience up to two hours, explains Giovanni. Only Italian wines are served, although Giovanni says some of his customers told him he was breaking down when he added American Italian wines to the list. "We don't serve French wines but we do have a chardonnay from an Italian company," he explains. Several wines by the glass are available, including Amarone. Giovanni says that when his lease is up in 2003, he plans to move the whole operation under a tent. "All cooking can be done on a charcoal grill," he notes. Reservations are requested.

ITHACA YACHT CLUB
607-272-9171
Rte. 89, Ithaca NY 14850
Open: May 1–Aug. 31
Tues.–Sun., Sept.–Oct.
Thurs.–Sun.
Price: $$
Serving: D, Sun. brunch
Cuisine: American
Credit cards: Most major

This club, which is open to the public for dinner, is on the lake. There are picnic areas, swimming facilities, and boat piers.

JOE'S RESTAURANT
607-273-2693
602 W. Buffalo St., Ithaca
NY 14850
Open: Mon.–Thurs.
11:30–10pm, Fri. & Sat.
11:30–11, Sun. 2–10

One of the hot spots in town, this casual family-style restaurant has been serving reasonably priced Italian food since 1932. Everything is fresh and prepared on site. Joe's offers chicken, seafood, veal, pastas, steak, casseroles, and Joe's Black Angus top sirloin. Eggplant parmigiana, manicotti,

Price: $–$$
Serving: L, D
Cuisine: Italian
Credit cards: Most major

red and white clam sauce, Italian grilled shrimp, chicken marsala, and three cheese spinach and artichoke crostini are just a sample of the items offered. Except for a roasted vegetable quesadilla and coconut shrimp that somehow snuck into the extensive menu, Joe's is totally Italian. And if you don't like what you see on the menu, you can customize your meal. There are two dining rooms; the one in the back is a bit more formal with candles. Joe's doesn't take reservations but you can call after 3:30pm and get on the priority waiting.

JOHN THOMAS STEAK HOUSE
607-273-3464
1152 Danby Rd., Ithaca NY 14850
Open: Daily, Sun.–Thurs. 5:30–10, Sat. & Fri. 5:30–11
Price: $$–$$$
Serving: D
Cuisine: Steak house
Credit cards: Most major

This 150-year-old farmhouse, set in meadows and gardens, has five dining rooms — two have fireplaces, one is an enclosed porch with many windows and wonderful views of the gardens, and the upstairs lounge and pub-like room is a favorite among repeat guests. It has lots of beams, a bar, and a fireplace that is kept burning during the colder winter months. In the summer, you can eat outside on the deck. One thing that sets this restaurant apart from other steak houses is Mike Kelly, owner and long-time restaurateur. Not only does he age all the prime beef himself, he also cuts it. Great lobster, chicken dishes served with French-style sauces, salmon, and vegetarian dishes are also offered. Priced at the high end of the Ithaca food chain, this is the place to bring your best clients when you're on an expense account or a place to come for that special occasion. Besides super beef and seafood, the restaurant also dispenses premium cigars, an excellent selection of wines, single malt scotch, and fine bourbons.

JUST A TASTE WINE AND TAPAS BAR
607-277-9463
116 N. Aurora St., Ithaca NY 14850
Open: Mon.–Fri. 11:30–3:30, 5:30–10:30; Sat. & Sun. 11–3, 5:30–11
Price: $–$$
Serving: L, D
Cuisine: Spanish American
Credit cards: Most major

If you like to order something for yourself and taste a bit of everyone else's meal at your table, you are in luck at this place — that's the whole idea. Tapas are a Spanish tradition of tasting and sharing a variety of appetizer-size dishes. Just a Taste's menu is so long, you probably should have it faxed to you and check it out before you arrive. You can get unusual items like garlic and sherry braised baby octopus with marinara sauce and fried angel hair, or quail stuffed with black beans, garlic sausage, and rice with citrus aïoli and chard, or something simpler like eggplant tomato soup with mint. In the Old Port Harbor.

MADELINE'S RESTAURANT AND BAR

607-277-2253
215 the Commons, corner
of N. Aurora & E. State
St., Ithaca NY 14850
Open: Daily for dinner
5–10, Fri. & Sat. 5–11; bar
open until 12 Mon.–
Thurs., until 1 Fri. & Sat.
Price: $$–$$$
Serving: D
Cuisine: Asian fusion
Credit cards: Most major

This upbeat, stylish bistro is decorated with bold artwork. The menu features many Asian-style dishes. For example, you can nibble on fresh chilled Asian soybeans (edemame) in the pod — try them, they're really good — or start with poke, fresh seafood served sashimi-style and seasoned with seaweed, chilies, and onions. Entrées might be wasabi herb encrusted salmon filet with mango salsa served with Asian black beans and sesame oil seasoned bean sprouts, or perhaps seared marinated sushi-grade tuna over green tea rice. You can eat inside or outdoors. Be sure to save room for one of their great desserts.

MAXIE'S SUPPER CLUB AND OYSTER BAR

607-272-4136
www.maxies.com
635 W. State St., Ithaca NY
14850
Open: Sun.–Thurs. 4–1am,
food served Sun.–Thurs.
5–midnight, Fri. & Sat.
5–1am
Price: $$
Serving: D
Cuisine: Cajun, Southern
Credit cards: Most major

This is one of the hottest places in town. If you're craving some Cajun cuisine or some soul-satisfying Southern comfort food such as jambalaya, gumbo, Cajun popcorn, crayfish, or crabcakes, come to Maxie's. It's a casual high-energy restaurant decorated in upbeat reds, purples, and lilacs. All the dishes are made from scratch. Especially popular are the raw oysters, clams, and peel-and-eat shrimp. This is a family operation owned by Chick Evans, a graduate of Cornell, and his wife, Dewi. Besides the food, one of Maxie's biggest assets is their great staff of fun, happy people. "People really like to work here," says Karen, Chick's sister who also helps in the family business. Free music is offered Sunday nights from 8pm when the place fills up with good crowd of people. No reservations. There are eight microbrews on tap and a fifty-bottle wine list which continually rotates. Happy hour is from 4 to 6 when raw oysters and clams are half price.

MOOSEWOOD RESTAURANT

607-273-9610
www.moosewoodrest
aurant.com
Dewitt Mall, 215 N. Cayuga
St., Ithaca NY 14850
Open: Mon.–Sat. 11:30–2,
café menu 2–4:30; summer Sun.–Thurs. 5:30–9,
Fri. & Sat. 6–9:30; winters
Sun.–Thurs. 5:30–8:30;
Fri. & Sat. until 9

When I received the *Moosewood Restaurant Cooks at Home* cookbook as a gift, I quickly bonded with the kind of food the folks at Moosewood celebrate: healthy low-fat vegetarian items like grains, fresh vegetables, and fruits; bold salsas in place of rich, complex sauces; dishes like Mediterranean lentil salad, roasted pepper hummus, north Indian eggplant, Mexican tomato lime soup, risotto with carrots and feta, and fish with tomato orange salsa. So it was with great anticipation that I sat down at a table on their outdoor side-

Price: $–$$
Serving: L, D
Cuisine: Vegetarian; fish on
    weekend
Credit cards: Most major

walk patio and read the menu. I was not disappointed and found it very difficult to chose just one thing. I finally decided on Thai noodle salad and a tasty orange-based soup. It was served with a wholesome grained crusty bread. Heaven. Moosewood is a collectively owned business with more than twenty members who all work together to run the restaurant and create the cookbooks. The menu changes often and draws inspiration from regional American cooking as well as ethnic cuisines. Moosewood serves great fresh fish and seafood dishes, homemade soups, salads, and pastas along with natural sodas, juices, beer, and wine. You can eat indoors in one of their two dining rooms or outdoors in season. An adjoining bar and café offers juices, speciality coffees, and a full service bar. The restaurant is designed with a clean, contemporary look. It's one of my favorites.

ROSE INN
607-533-7905;
    fax 607-533-7908
roseinn@clarityconnect.com
www.roseinn.com
813 Auburn Rd., Rte. 34,
    Ithaca NY 14850
Open: Tues.–Sun.; jazz club
    open Fri. & Sat. Apr.–Nov.
Price: $$–$$$$
Serving: B (with B&B), D
Cuisine: Regional gourmet
Credit cards: Most major

When I first arrived there, I walked right into the kitchen, which is just off the side porch, one of the main entrances. There I found the chef putting the finishing touches on some delectable-looking pastries for the evening meal. I was told that Charles, the owner, was out picking eldberberries, also to be presented at dinner. That night, dinner served in the formal dining room in front of a fireplace was elegant indeed: fine china, candles, crystal goblets, and fresh flowers. From the prix fixe menu were items such as pan-seared rare tuna loin, grilled ostrich loin, and pecan-encrusted grilled filet mignon. Fresh herbs grown in the inn's gardens and fruit from their orchards (sixteen kinds of fruit trees), along with homemade raspberry brandy preserves, often accompany the meal. The rustic Carriage House Jazz Club, also on the grounds, features live entertainment. Dinner is available à la carte. (For the Rose Inn B&B, see the entry in the Lodging section above.)

**SIMEON'S ON THE
    COMMONS**
607-272-2212
224 E. State St., Ithaca NY
    14850
Open: Daily 11–1am
Price: $–$$
Serving: L, D
Cuisine: Continental
Credit cards: Most major

In a historic 1871 Italianate building, Simeon's opened as a tavern in 1975. Its interior has been restored to its vintage splendor with lots of exposed brick, wood, and glass. You can eat inside or outside at a small table set on the sidewalk under a canopy. Generous offerings include the scooper salad with tunafish, chicken served on greens with abundant vegetables and cheese, or the Jeremiah Beebe sandwich, a classic reuben with all the trimmings. In addition to sandwiches and finger foods, you can order entrées like Jamaican jerk or island satay and pasta entrées. This is a place people come back to again and again; a good spot to see and be seen.

Seneca Falls

THE PUMPHOUSE
315-568-9109
16 Rumsey St., Seneca Falls
 NY 13148
Open: Mon.–Sat., bar daily
Price: $–$$
Serving: L, D
Cuisine: American
Credit cards: Most major

On the corner of W. Falls St. and Rumsey St., this venerable brick institution has long been known as a family kind of place with games, pool table, and dart machines. There are more than fifty beers to choose from and a number of fish, seafood, and steak items on the menu. The chef/owner prepares interesting but not bizarre dishes such as catfish in a cornbread coating served with smashed Kentucky bourbon yams. It's a favorite among locals.

Aurora

**AURORA INN AND
 RESTAURANT**
315-364-8888
Main St., Rte. 90, Aurora
 NY 13026
Open: Daily
Price: $$–$$$
Serving: L, D
Cuisine: American
Credit cards: Most major

Owned by Wells College, this lakeside inn has been an institution in the village for many years. Although the furnishings are a bit dated, the panoramic water views easily make up for any lack in decorating pizzazz. Lunch selections include items like a crabcake sandwich, quiche, and a portabella sandwich. On the dinner menu is Aurora dairy loin of veal scaloppine with maple syrup and dried cranberry chutney, traditional fisherman soup and crayfish tails, and sautéed jumbo sea scallops with corn and saffron sauce served with chickpea polenta. (Editor's note: As of the publication date, the inn was closing and expected to reopen in the spring of 2001 under new management.)

FARGO RESTAURANT
315-364-8005
Rte. 90, Main St., Aurora
 NY 13026
Open: Mon.–Sat.
Price: $
Serving: L (fish on Friday
 nights)
Cuisine: Pub style
Credit cards: Cash and
 checks only

People wait all week to run down to Jim Orman's Fargo Restaurant for fried fish on Friday nights. Their wings (Buffalo and otherwise) are also a big hit. This is a fun down-home bar with a few tables, billiards, and beer $1 and up. Don't miss the bulletin board as you enter: it's filled with a helter-skelter collection of postcards, photos, and notices. Fargo has a new deck which is used for parties and casual dining.

Other Area Restaurants

GLENWOOD PINES
RESTAURANT
607-273-3709
1213 Taughannock
　Blvd./Rte. 89, between
　Cass Park &
　Taughannock State Park,
　Ithaca NY 14850
Open: Daily 11–11
Price: $–$$
Serving: L, D
Cuisine: American
Credit cards: Most major

This is the home of the Pinesburger, a 6-ounce cheeseburger on French bread served with mayonnaise or thousand island dressing, lettuce, tomato, and onion — all for $3.75. Glenwood has huge windows both up and downstairs and a screened-in porch affording super views of the lake and countryside. This is a casual place with a very well-seasoned and friendly staff. Owned and run by the Hohwald family for more than twenty-four years, Glenwood is known for its generous portions of American staples like burgers, spaghetti, steaks, and fish. The fish fries are great.

ROGUE'S HARBOR
STEAK AND ALE
607-533-3535
Corner Rtes. 34&34B,
　Lansing NY 14882
Open: Tues.–Sat. 11–10,
　Sun. 10–9
Price: $–$$
Serving: L, D, Sun. brunch
Cuisine: American
Credit cards: Most major

In this 1830s inn the two dining rooms and pub are decorated with antiques and local memorabilia. In the winter, the fireplaces are often lit. Enjoy hand-cut USDA choice beef, local wines, microbrew drafts, and fresh seafood and fish. Shrimp and fried calamari are also specialities. There is a B&B on the second floor; see the separate listing for Rogue's Harbor B&B above. Seasonal outdoor dining is on the porch in the front of the building. Prime rib, hand-cut steaks, a wonderful baked salmon, and an excellent pork tenderloin are among the menu items. Everything is made in-house, including sauces, soups, and desserts. The chowder is especially nice. There is a selection of local wines, ten microbrews, and imports on draft.

RONGOVIAN EMBASSY
TO THE USA
607-387-3334
1 W. Main St.,
　Trumansburg NY 14486
Open: Tues.–Sun. 4–1 (bar),
　5–9 or later, seasonally
　(restaurant)
Price: $–$$
Serving: D
Cuisine: American,
　Mexican
Credit cards: Most major

In an old building, gussied up, this is a big favorite of the college set. Eclectic and casual in appointments and attire, there is a lot of brick and wood along with mismatched furniture and memorabilia. The food consists of favorite southwestern fare like great blackened salmon, Jamaican jerk, enchiladas, and a combo with your choice of fillings, mole, and guacamole. It has one of the best beer lists around: owner Eric Ott says, "If you can't find anything you like at our bar, you don't like drinking." There is live music on most evenings such as jazz on Tuesdays and Sundays, string jam on Wednesdays, and local bands for listening and dancing on weekends after dinner.

TAUGHANNOCK FARMS INN
607-387-7711, 888-387-7711
www.T-Farms.com
Rte. 89/2030 Gorge Rd. at Taughannock Falls State Park, Trumansburg NY 14486
Open: Mon.–Sat. 5–9, Sun. 3–8; Nov.–Dec. hours vary, Dec. open for private parties only; open to public New Year's Eve
Price: $$–$$$
Serving: D
Cuisine: American
Credit cards: Most major

Whether it signaled the start of summer or the occasion was a grand family outing, I remember with great pleasure the times our family dined at this lovely Victorian country inn. The prix fixe menu includes appetizer, salad, entrée, and dessert — all traditional favorites. It's next to the Taughannock Falls State Park. For accommodations here, see the entry in the *Lodging* section-above.

CASUAL FOOD

Aurora Market and Pizza (Rte. 90, Aurora NY 13021) This is more like a general store offering more than pizza . . . things like rental videos, groceries, and gifts.

Avicolli's (315-568-2233; 170 Fall St., Seneca Falls NY 13148) This is a neat, clean, no-nonsense Italian restaurant serving everything from sandwiches and pizza to full dinner. Very popular with locals.

Bailey's "It's a Wonderful . . ." Ice Cream Shop (315-568-0929; 36 Water St., Seneca Falls NY 13148) Cones, shakes, sundaes, and flurries in the "Bedford Falls" style from the movie *It's a Wonderful Life.*

Baker's Acres (607-533-3650; Rte. 34, North Lansing) The Lodge at Baker's Acres, once a feed store, has been converted into a tea room and antique and gift shop. Pleasantly decorated with hanging quilts, regional art work, and a mixture of chairs and tables, the tea room's menu has a number of creative dishes made with homegrown herbs and garnished with edible flowers. Open seasonally. For more information, see the entry in the Recreation section below.

Bubba's Dog House (315-568-8355; 2040 Rtes. 5&20, Seneca Falls NY 13148) If you're craving a quarter-pound hot dog, ice cream, burger, salt potatoes, chicken, or curly fries, Bubba's is the place to come. I was hot and tired the day I stopped at the cheerful stand; the root beer float with a huge scoop of vanilla ice cream really hit the spot. Get a peek of the canal from the porch. Open Memorial weekend–Sept. Mon.–Thurs. & Sun. 11–8, Fri. & Sat. 11–9.

Cream at the Top (315-364-7504; Rte. 90, Ledyard, King Ferry NY 13081) This is a good bet for a quick meal. Run by the Wilcox family who also own a local grocery store, the place sells good ice cream and sandwiches. Open seasonally.

Mac's Drive-Inn (Rte. 20, Waterloo NY 13165) A cheery red and white place selling light food and ice cream. There is a glass-enclosed eating area. Open seasonally.

Micawber's Tavern (607-273-9243; 118 N. Aurora St., Ithaca NY 14850) Lots of good Irish pub-style food and a good selection of beer and ale is enjoyed by locals usually early on and then college students after 8.

The Nines (607-272-1888; 311 College Ave., Ithaca NY 14850) With music every night, this place is buzzing with the young and hip. A casual place with food staples like burgers and beer. Open Mon.–Sat. 11:30am–1am, Sun. 3:30pm–1am.

Pete's Treats (315-889-7636; Rte. 90, Union Springs NY 13160) Open seasonally, Pete's is popular with locals and sells hard and soft ice cream, sundaes, and other ice cream treats plus barbecued duck, chicken tenders, and hamburgers. Take out or sit at one of the picnic tables.

The Restaurant at Knapp Vineyards (607-869-9481; 2770 Ernsberger Rd./128 County Rd., Romulus NY 14541) Open Apr.–Dec., this is a good place to stop for a bite to eat while touring the vineyards. Eat indoors or on the patio.

CULTURE

Ithaca

ARCHITECTURE

Ithaca has many outstanding buildings spanning more than 200 years. The **Clinton House** (circa 1830), at 120 North Cayuga Street, was once a grand hotel with more than 150 rooms and several elegant public area. Over the years the three-story structure has seen good times and bad, surviving several remodelings and a fire. Now this landmark building has been restored and is the headquarters for the Community Arts Project on the first floor; offices are on the top two.

The State Theatre is in the center of Ithaca's business district. This historic brick building, once a venue for theatrical performances, was built in 1915 as the Ithaca Security Company Garage, with a showroom on the first floor and copper-clad windows along the facade, many of which still exist. When the building was purchased by the Berinstein family in 1928, the interior was extensively remodeled to serve as a theater. Gargoyles, tapestries, stained glass, ornate columns, faux painted stone and an illuminated celestial ceiling turned the building into a fantasy movie palace with a glitzy marquee. Movies continued to be shown into the early 1990s, but the building had deteriorated and was badly in need of repair. In 1998 Historic Ithaca acquired the building and plans are in the works to restore it and put it back in use.

Peter Finger

The Cornell University campus, Ithaca, is one of the most beautiful in the country.

EDUCATION

Cornell University (607-255-2000; www.Cornell.edu; Ithaca NY 14850) Cornell has seven undergraduate colleges and the liberal arts quad is one of the oldest and loveliest in the state. The Herbert F. Johnson Museum of Art is a major asset. Other key sites on the campus include the Plantation with its many gardens, and the Gothic Chapel with its rose window, painted ceiling, and brass chandelier. When you walk across the center of the older campus, you may notice messages written on the sidewalks in chalk: it's a student tradition. Guided tours are given daily.

Ithaca College (607-274-3124, 800-429-4274; www.ithaca.edu; 100 Job Hall, Ithaca College, Ithaca NY 14850-7020) This is a private residential college offering 1,900 courses in more than 100 programs of study in five schools including the School of Music, School of Humanities and Sciences, School of Business, Roy H. Park School of Communications, and School of Health, Sciences, and Human Performance. More than 5,800 students attend.

MUSEUMS, EXHIBITS, AND HISTORIC SITES

Cornell Plantations (607-255-3020; www.plantations.cornell.edu; One Plantations Rd., Cornell University, Ithaca NY 14850) A 3,000 acre area of great beauty, this museum of living plants encompasses an arboretum, botanical garden, and natural areas. There are woodlands, gorges, and lakeside trails which go along the central campus. Orchids are displayed in a solarium. An educational program offers noncredit lectures, tours, and special events. The herb garden is next to a gift shop. Grounds are free and open daily from sunrise to sunset.

The Herbert F. Johnson Museum of Art is on the Cornell University campus.

Peter Finger

Herbert F. Johnson Museum of Art (607-255-6464; www.museum.cornell.edu; University Ave., Cornell University, Ithaca NY 14850) Designed by I.M. Pei, this dramatic modern structure — with 360-degree views of the countryside from galleries and patios — has a permanent collection as well as revolving exhibits. European, American, and Asian art collections span forty centuries and six continents. A sculpture garden offers a quiet place to contemplate what you have seen. Open Tues.–Sun. 10–5.

Paleontological Research Institution (607-273-6623, ext. 10; www.englib.cor nell.edu/pri or www.priweb.org; 1259 Trumansburg Rd./Rte. 96, Ithaca NY 14850) If you are interested in fossils or curious about how the glaciers formed the gorges or what kind of animals and plant life existed on this land long ago, come to this museum for the answers. Established in 1932, the museum is a combination of exhibits which change often and contain an enormous number of fossils, shells, and other natural history specimens; photographs and paintings by regional artists; and many permanent displays such as a Tyrannosaurus rex skull more than four feet long. There are lectures in the winter months, field trips and fossil hunting trips in the summer. Open Memorial Day–Labor Day Mon.–Sat. 11–4, Weds.–Sat. 11–4 the rest of year.

On the Trail of Art

More than forty-five regional artists participate in a self-guided tour to their studios, organized in the **Greater Ithaca Art Trail**. You can watch the artists working and see their finished work. Just about every media field is represented: painting, sculpture, printing, ceramics, woodworking, jewelry making, stained glass, furniture making, and more. The trail is in full operation during October, but functions as an ongoing activity throughout the year; call individual artists for an appointment. For information, check the website (www.arttrail.com) or obtain a brochure and map from a participating gallery or the Tompkins County Convention and Visitors Bureau.

Sagan Planet Walk (607-272-0600; 601 First St., Ithaca NY 14850) This walking tour, built in memory of astronomer Carl Sagan, starts with the sun at the Commons in downtown Ithaca and continues to visit all nine planets along a three-quarter-mile route to the Sciencenter Museum. Get a "Passport to the Solar System" at locations around town ($2), get it stamped along the way, and earn a free visit to the museum at the end of the walk.

Sciencenter (607-272-0600; 601 First St., Ithaca NY 14850) It's a great place to spend a day with more than 100 exhibits, many hands-on. See a boa constrictor, water flume, two-story kinetic ball, and explore the workings of a walk-in camera. Whisper into a giant dish and navigate through the outdoor science park. Open Tues.–Sat. 10–5, Sun. noon–5. Admission $4.50, children 3–12 $3.50, under 3 free.

Tompkins County Museum (607-273-8284; www.LAKENET.org/dewitt; 401 E. State St., Ithaca NY 14850) This is a vibrant museum with changing exhibits and ongoing programs: lectures, poetry readings, musical performances, workshops, storytelling, and film. The focus of the museum and its programs is Tompkins County, its people, history, and culture. Typical exhibits include "Land of Clear Water: The Early Days" and "Celebrating the Towns of Tompkins County." During the past sixty-five years, the museum has collected more than 18,000 interesting objects. Open Tues.–Sat. 11–5; Reference Room open Tues., Thurs., and Sat. 11–5.

PERFORMING ARTS

Cayuga Chamber Orchestra (607-273-8981; 116 N. Cayuga St., Ithaca NY 14850) A fall-winter chamber music series held in various locations in Ithaca. Other performances such as "Caroling by Candlelight" and "Messiah" are also offered.

Cornell Center for Theatre Arts (607-254-2700; 430 College Ave., Ithaca NY 14850) The Center is home to Cornell's Department of Theatre, Film, and Dance. Each year, a number of excellent concerts and dance and theatrical performances are held in the Proscenium Theatre. Lectures take place in the

David L. Call Auditorium and Kennedy Hall, and outdoor concerts are staged in the Arts Quad.

The Firehouse Theatre (607-277-7529; 136 W. State St., Ithaca NY 14850) This is an excellent community theater using top local talent in a variety of productions staged in a former firehouse. Each month throughout the year, a different play is performed.

The Hangar Theater, Ithaca, offers comedy, musicals, and drama.

Peter Finger

Hangar Theatre (607-273-4497; Rte. 89, Cass Park, Ithaca NY 14850) This is one of the Finger Lakes' most respected theaters. It's been in operation since 1975 and continues to produce five mainstage productions each season. Recent productions have included *The Glass Menagerie*, *The Fantasticks*, and *Blithe Spirit*. The series KIDDSTUFF, for children, runs June–mid-Aug.

Ithaca College Theatre (607-274-3920; 201 Dillingham Center, Ithaca College, Ithaca NY 14850) The Department of Theatre Arts presents drama, comedy, musicals, opera, and dance performances at the George R. Hoerner and Richard M. Clark theaters from September to May. The School of Music features concerts throughout the year.

The Kitchen Theatre Company (607-273-4497; Clinton House, Seneca and Cayuga Sts., Ithaca NY 14850) For performances up close and personal, try this year-round theater in the historic Clinton House, a renovated 170-year-old hotel. The intimate auditorium seats just seventy-three people on three sides of the stage so that no one is further than ten feet from the actors. The theater company focuses on imaginative, daring new work in a variety of theatrical styles. Talent is drawn from the local colleges and regional artists and some productions are devoted to the work of area playwrights.

Summer Concert Series (607-277-8679; the Commons, Ithaca NY 14850) Afternoon and evening concerts are held on Sundays, Tuesdays, Thursdays, and Fridays in pavilions in the Commons throughout the summer. Listen to everything from classic jazz to 50s rock and swing and blues. All concerts are free.

Seneca Falls

MUSEUMS, EXHIBITS, AND HISTORIC SITES

Elizabeth Cady Stanton House (315-568-2991; Washington St., Seneca Falls NY 13148) Elizabeth Cady Stanton (1815-1902), a leader in the women's rights movement, organized the first Women's Rights Convention in Seneca Falls in 1848. She often worked with Susan B. Anthony, co-authoring *A History of Woman Suffrage*. Her simple white frame home is now a museum containing memorabilia from her life and work. Open spring through fall.

National Women's Hall of Fame (315-568-2936; www.greatwomen.org; 76 Fall St., Seneca Falls NY 13148) Displays and exhibits focus on important women in history who have been inducted into the National Women's Hall of Fame. Women honored include Eleanor Roosevelt, Pearl Buck, Rosa Parks, and Eileen Collins. Learn how they contributed to a variety of fields such as arts, education, business, government, humanities, philanthropy, government, and science. Open daily May–Oct. 9:30–5; Nov.–Apr Weds.– Sat. 10–4, Sun. 12–4; closed Jan. except by appointment.

Seneca Falls Heritage Area Visitor Center (315-568-2703; 115 Falls St., Seneca Falls NY 13148) A good place to come first to get oriented to Seneca Falls and its important sites, buildings, and waterways. Open Mon.–Sat 10–4, Sun. 12–4.

Seneca Falls Historical Society (315-568-8412; fax 315-568-8426; www.welcome.to/sfhs/; 55 Cayuga St., Seneca Falls NY 13148) This three-story, twenty-three-room Queen Anne mansion grew from an early 1800s one-room house. It was expanded in 1855 and remodeled in the 1880s to its present style. Many of the furnishings are from the Becker family, who lived in the house for more than fifty years. Custom-designed wallpapers, carpets from France, paintings, original lighting fixtures, stained glass windows, carved golden oak woodwork, oak table and chairs, glass-globe lamps and other period lighting, and antique kitchen utensils and gadgets give visitors a good sense of what life was like during the Victorian era. Mannequins dressed in period clothing are throughout the house. There is a research library on the premises as well as an 1895 Seth Thomas Town Clock and a charming Victorian outbuilding called the Beehive now used as a gift shop. Open year-round Mon.–Fri. 8:30–4, Sat. & Sun. in the summer 1–4.

Seneca Museum of Waterways and Industry (315-568-1510; 89 Fall St., Seneca Falls NY 13148) This marvelous new museum, housed in an early 1900s masonry and brick structure right on the Cayuga-Seneca Canal,

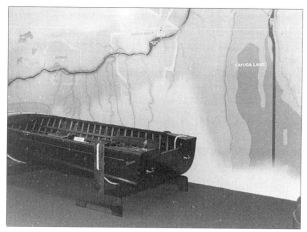

The Seneca Museum of Waterways and Industry, Seneca Falls, has exhibits about the importance of the lakes, rivers, and canals to the region.

Katharine Delavan Dyson

features hands-on presentations and an ongoing series of art and craft displays. A thirty-five-foot mural depicts this canal along with original drawings, engineers' plans, and photographs. Highly recommended for families, you can see how a pump works and how the Erie Canal was built. See the first fire engines and two-hose, people-driven carts. Children get a thrill working on an old-time loom and printing on an antique press. They can record their thoughts on the "Voices of the 20th Century," and observe how canals function by operating a working lock model. Often the site of regional arts and crafts exhibits, the museum offers periodic weaving demonstrations. A deck is planned for the back of the building where visitors may enjoy light refreshments, ice cream, or perhaps a glass of wine while watching boats glide by or tie up along the pier. Open Tues.–Sat. 10–5, Sun. 1–5 in summer.

"This is Woman's Hour . . ." The Life of Mary Baker Eddy (315-568-6488; www.marybakereddy.org; 118 Fall St., Seneca Falls NY 13148) Interactive displays tell how this woman challenged the conventional thinking of her time in theology, science, and medicine. A healer, author, and teacher, she spoke out about equal rights for women. Open May–Oct. Mon.–Sat. 9–5, Sun. 12–5; Nov.–Apr. Weds.–Sat. 9–5, Sun. 12–5.

Women's Rights National Historical Park (315-568-2991; www.nps.gov/wori; 136 Fall St., Seneca Falls NY 13148) Near the northwestern tip of the lake, this park commemorates the first Women's Rights Convention held here in 1848. See exhibits relating to women's rights and Elizabeth Cady Stanton's house. A twenty-five-minute film, *Dreams of Equality*, gives a good overview of the women's rights movement. A display of bronze figures honors those prominent in the efforts. Open daily 9–5.

Other Areas

MUSEUMS

Interlaken Historical Society Museum (Main St., Interlaken NY 14847) See eighteenth- and nineteenth-century farm tools in the Farmer's Museum and across the street on the second floor of the library, and browse exhibits of period clothing, pictures, and artifacts.

Rural Life Museum (315-364-8202; Rte. 34B, King Ferry NY 13081) Exhibits describe local agricultural life and traditions. Annual events include the Old Time Wheat Harvest Festival with wagon rides, wheat cutting, a parade, and demonstrations of harvesting.

PERFORMING ARTS

Concert in the Park Series (607-387-6739; Taughannock Falls State Park, Trumansburg NY 14486) Bring your blankets, lawn chairs, picnics, and desire to enjoy concerts under the stars on Cayuga Lake. Held July and August in Taughannock State Park. Most of the concerts take place Saturday nights and occasionally on Thursday or Friday. Recent concerts included Rock 'n' Roll Oldies, Kansas City Jump, Afro-World Beat, the U.S. Air Force Band, folk music from the Burns Sisters, and Spiegle Willcox & his All Stars.

Morgan Opera House (315-364-5437; Aurora NY 13026) Housed in a century-old Tudor-style building, the Opera House hosts a variety of productions such as puppet shows, concerts, theater productions, variety shows, children's theater, and readings.

Photo Ops

Covered Bridge: (Rte. 13, eight miles southwest of Ithaca Newfield) The only covered bridge in the Finger Lakes on a public road.

Top of Cornell Stadium: (Ithaca) Great views of the countryside.

Sunset Park: (Ithaca) Spectacular views of the valley from the south end of the lake.

The suspension bridge between Cayuga Heights and the Cornell campus (Ithaca) spans the river cut through rocks, and just below there is a winding trail down to the water — a great place for a picnic or to catch some sun on a ledge.

Cayuga-Seneca Canal: (Seneca Falls) Behind the main business block on Rtes. 5&20, with the canal boats tied up along the pier.

EDUCATION

Trumansburg Conservatory of Fine Arts (607-387-5939; Congress at McLallen Sts., Trumansburg NY 14486) In the heart of town, this is a not-for-profit learning and performing school of the arts for people of all ages.

Wells College (315-364-3264; Main Street, Aurora NY 13026) Founded in 1868 by Henry Wells, pioneer of Wells Fargo Stagecoach and American Express, Wells College is one of the oldest private liberal arts educational institutions for women in the country. The tree-shaded campus contains many red brick historic buildings.

RECREATION

BIKING

Cayuga Lake Loop: The grade is gently rolling; views are of the lake, fields, and farms. The total round trip is ninety miles. Parking is available in Cayuga Lake State Park, Rte. 89, about three miles south of Rtes. 5&20. Several B&Bs as well as hotels and inns are along the way. Key areas to overnight include Ithaca, Seneca Falls, Aurora, and Trumansburg. There are also campsites in lakeside parks.

Gorge Trail: This 30.6-mile trail starts at the Ithaca Commons and takes you by Buttermilk Falls State Park, Robert Treman State Park, and Taughannock Falls State Park. All roads are paved and there are some rolling hills. Starting on Elmira Road in Ithaca, take Rte. 13 south to Buttermilk Falls. You can spend the day here and return (a round trip of about eight miles). To continue, go right on Rte. 327 north to Halseyville Rd. and go straight to Rte. 96 (about 16.9 miles at the turn). Take Taughannock Park Rd. and follow it through the state park. At the intersection turn right onto Rte. 89 and go south returning to Ithaca.

Eastern Route: Starting in Union Springs, this 36.2-mile trail goes on mostly paved roads with several rolling hills and a few steep inclines. Attractions along the way include the Frontenac Museum, McKenzie Child, Wells College, Long Point State Park, King Ferry Winery, and Rural Life Museum. Head south on Rte. 90 through Aurora and on to King Ferry. Stay right to go into Long Point and at stoplight, turn left onto Rte. 34B and go north to Scipioville. At the turn veer left onto Ridge Rd. and follow it straight to Rte. 326. Turn left onto Rte. 326 west and follow signs to return to Union Springs.

BOATING

CRUISES:

Alcyone Charters (607-272-7963; 907 Taughannock Blvd., Ithaca NY 14850) Sail on a 1994 Hunter 35-1/2-foot sloop from Ithaca to Aurora. Half and full day charter packages are available. The four-hour cruise leaves from either Treman State Park or Johnson Boat Yard and is priced at $40 per person ($70 for full day). Overnight on board in one of the vessel's cabins or bunk in at the Aurora Inn. The overnight trip is priced from $600 for two or four guests; $950 for six.

Erie Canal Cruise Line (800-962-1771; web: www.canalcruises.com) See the entry in Chapter Two, *Transportation*, for more information.

MARINAS AND LAUNCHES:

Allan H. Treman State Marine Park (607-272-1460 summer, 607-273-3440 winter; Rte. 89, Ithaca NY 14850) One of the largest inland marinas in the state, Allan H. Treman State Marine Park provides mooring and boating access to the southern end of Cayuga Lake. There are six piers with 370 seasonal boat slips, thirty transient boat slips, thirty dry slips, and a boat launch area. Seasonal slips are assigned annually by lottery. Also on marina grounds are picnic areas, ball fields, electrical hookups, showers, and toilets.

Beacon Bay Marine (315-252-2849; 6223 Lake St., Cayuga NY 13034) This facility has twenty-five slips.

Castelli's Marine (315-889-5532; Union Springs NY 13160) This full-service marina has 160 boat slips, repair services, supply store, and fuel.

Finger Lakes Marine Service (607-533-4422; 44 Marina Rd., Lansing NY 14882) Storage, outboard ramp, and a mobile hoist are available.

Oak Orchard Marina and Campground: (315-365-3000 summer, 609-965-4647 winter; www.oakorchard.com; Rte. 89N, May's Pt., PO Box 148, Seneca Falls NY 13148) Camp on this 3,000-foot riverfront site which contains rental cottages overlooking the Erie Canal, tent and trailer sites, pool, playground, boat rentals, hiking, hayrides, boat launch, and hookup facilities.

Trade-A-Yacht Marinas (also known as Hibiscus) (315-889-5008; Union Springs NY 13160) On a protected inlet on the east side of Cayuga Lake, the marina has 205 slips, marine store, restaurant, outside deck, bathrooms, showers, pool, tenting area ($25 per night), and boat rentals. At the Wheel House Restaurant, you can eat inside or head outside and dine on a pleasant wood deck on the banks of the inlet. Live music on Sundays in season.

Troy's Marina (315-889-5560; Backus Rd., Cayuga NY 13034) The marina offers 100 slips, store, and services.

Boat launches are also at Long Point State Park (off Rte. 90, Aurora) and Deans Cove (Rte. 89, on west side of Cayuga Lake).

FISHING

Judged by *Sports Afield* magazine as one the the top ten best bass lakes in the United States, Cayuga Lake is a fisherman's dream come true. In addition to the great bass fishing, anglers pull in lake trout, land-locked salmon, brown trout, and rainbow trout. Fly fishermen have more than 102 miles of trout streams and twenty-eight miles of warm water streams to enjoy.

Cayuga Lake's AA rating means the water is fit for drinking and holds a healthy population of gamefish. The fishing season runs from April to November on the lake and September to April on the Salmon River.

For the following charters, you'll need to bring a valid NYS fishing license, seasonal clothing, soft-soled shoes, cooler to transport your catch home, snacks and beverages, and rain gear.

Eagle Rock Charters (315-889-5925; Rte. 90, Cayuga NY 13034) Half, full, and evening light-tackle fishing charters with Capt. Glenn, a full-time guide for close to twenty years. You'll fish aboard *Eagle Rock II*, a 27-foot Baha cruiser. Eagle Rock Charters also has a 100-year-old five-bedroom rental house overlooking Cayuga Lake, three and a half miles from the boat.

Release Tyme Charters (315-889-5395; Union Springs NY 13160) The company offers full and half day sport noodle rods and lite line fishing charters for trout and salmon using a 30-foot Penn Yan boat. Fish for lake trout, rainbow trout, brown trout, and landlocked salmon. Price for a full day is $275.

GOLF

Cayuga Links (315-568-6597; Rte. 89, Seneca Falls NY 13148) This course has 18 holes, a small clubhouse, driving range, pro shop, and carts.

Cedar View Golf Course (315-364-7598; 125 Cedar View Rd., Lansing NY 14882) Enjoy 9 holes with views of Cayuga Lake.

Indian Head Golf Course (315-253-6812; Rtes. 5&20 between Auburn and Seneca Falls) This rather flat 9-hole course is popular with locals. Facilities include carts, rental clubs, and snack bar. Greens fees from $9.

Wells College Golf Course (315-364-8024; Wells College Campus, Aurora NY 13026) This beautiful 9-hole course designed by Robert Trent Jones provides a pleasant round of golf. Club and cart rentals are available and there is a pro shop and snack bar on the premises. Greens fees $11–$14.

HIKING

Cayuga Trail (from Rte. 366 off the southwestern tip of Cayuga Lake, go north on Monkey Run Rd.; park at the end) This 6.5 mile loop is difficult. Follow orange blazes along an abandoned rail bed, up steep hills, through thickly planted woods, and along a creek.

Cornell Campus (Ithaca NY 14850) Pick up a map at one of the gates and walk around the campus on a self-guided tour. Cornell Plantations has a network of trails.

Esker Brook Nature Trail (315-568-5987; Montezuma National Wildlife Refuge,

Rtes. 5&20 west of Auburn) This moderately easy one and a half mile loop along dirt paths passes through woods, wetlands rich with wildlife and waterfowl, through old apple orchards, and around ponds.

Sapsucker Woods (607-254-BIRD; from Rte. 13 near the south end of Cayuga Lake, turn south on Brown Road Extension, then right on Sapsucker Woods Dr.) A wonderful area for bird lovers, this two and a half mile loop along mulched trails and boardwalks makes for easy soft walking. Press the voice boxes near the visitor center to learn about the wildlife in the area. Visit the Cornell Lab of Ornithology and the Lyman K. Stuart Observatory where you can watch birds through a large window overlooking the pond. Wander past ponds and through woods.

Sweedler Preserve (607-275-9487; from Ithaca go south on Rte. 13, left on Sand Bank Rd. and right at the "Y" on Town Line Rd.; park on the right side) White blazes mark the dirt and mulch trails of this 1.6-mile loop. Short but difficult, this part of the Finger Lakes Trail takes you down a steep hill and then back up the hill. Enjoy good views of the waterfalls in the Lick Brook gorge.

PARKS, NATURE PRESERVES, AND CAMPING

Black Rock Campgrounds (315-364-7262; Ledyard Rd., King Ferry NY 13081) This campgrounds has 100 rustic campsites, two cabins, fifty transient sites, fishing, and hiking.

Buttermilk Falls State Park (607-273-5761 summer, 607-273-3440 winter; Rte. 13, Ithaca NY 14850) Just a short drive from Ithaca, this 751-acre park contains several creeks and streams which converge to form ten waterfalls that wind through a stunning series of gorges. Larch Meadows behind the ball fields is a refuge to many species of animals and birds. There are two glens and a gorge trail that climbs more than 500 vertical feet in a mile; the grade is gentler in the upper part of the park. Swim in the pool at the foot of the waterfalls. Facilities include forty-six campsites, seven cabins, swimming in the natural pool, picnic areas, playground, ball fields, toilets, and nature programs. Segments of the early 1900s movie *Perils of Pauline* were filmed in Buttermilk Glen.

Cayuga Lake State Park (315-568-5163; 2678 Lower Lake Rd., Seneca Falls NY 13148) Level lawns, lots of trees, campsites, and a playground. Rte. 89, north end of the lake, west shore.

Frontenac Park (315-889-7341; Union Springs NY 13160) On the east shore of the lake, Frontenac has a public boat launch, swimming, and picnic facilities.

Long Point State Park (315-497-1030; Lake Rd., off Rte. 90, Poplar Ridge NY 13139) This park has two boat launches, pavilion, picnic area, swimming, dock, and fishing.

Montezuma National Wildlife Refuge (315-568-5987; 3395 Rtes. 5&20E, Seneca Falls NY 13148) Dr. Peter Clark, a well-traveled physician from New

Peter Finger

Buttermilk Falls State Park has ten waterfalls that wind through the dramatically steep gorges.

York, named this refuge after the last Aztec emperor in honor of the large marshes surrounding Mexico City. This area is rich with wildlife and plant life. Each spring and fall, ducks, geese, herons, and other shore birds are seen at this major resting and breeding area. The refuge includes a visitor center, a viewing platform from which you may be able to spot a nesting eagle or osprey, an easy-to-follow one and a half mile walking loop, and a three and a half mile mile wildlife drive.

Ridgewood Campgrounds (607-869-9787; 6590 S. Cayuga Lake Rd., Ovid NY 14521) You get lovely views of the water from this campground on the west side of the lake about twenty-five miles north of Ithaca. Facilities include tent and trailer sites, utility hookups, picnic tables, grills, restrooms, showers, camp store, playground, arcade, pavilion, fishing pond, miniature golf, horseshoe pits, volleyball, basketball, tether ball, and on-site trailer rentals.

Spruce Row Campsite and RV Resort (607-387-9225; www.campgrounds .com/sprucerow; sprucerow@clarityconnect.com; 2271 Kraft Rd., 7 miles north of Ithaca between Rtes. 89&96) Large open and shaded RV and tent sites on 125 acres. Other facilities include a pool, hayrides, playgrounds, miniature golf, recreation building, paddle boat, store, full hookups.

Stewart Park (607-273-8364; corner Rtes. 13&34; Ithaca NY 14850) This park is a major gathering place for year-round fun. There are playing fields, playground, picnic area, concession stand, tennis courts, a restored carousel, and picnic area.

Robert H. Treman State Park (607-273-3440; RD 10, off Rte. 327, Ithaca NY 14850) This 1,070 acre park runs through rustic Enfield Glen, actually two glens interwoven. It has four hiking trails, seventy-two campsites, fourteen cabins, swimming, two pavilions, a picnic area, and a camper recreation program. Twelve waterfalls can be viewed along a three-mile trail. Tours are offered to the old grist mill in the upper park. The upper and lower falls are connected by hiking trails; a stream-fed pond beneath a waterfall provides a natural swimming hole. The most dramatic part is the upper half mile where the scenery was often used as a backdrop for early Western movies before the industry moved to California. A beautiful stone path and steps lead to 115-foot Lucifer Falls. Just past this point you can look through the deep, wooded interglacial gorge as it snakes its way to the lower park.

Taughannock Falls State Park (607-387-6739; Rte. 89, Trumansburg NY 14486) Towering Taughannock Falls, the highest vertical falls east of the Mississippi River, plunge 215 feet straight down through a rock amphitheater surrounded by rock walls, some as high as 400 feet. One gorge trail runs along the rim of the gorge; another winds from the base of the falls to Taughannock Creek Outlet on Cayuga Lake. Even in the winter, the frozen and flowing ice create a visual feast and you can go whizzing down the sledding slope, skate on the rink, and hike the gorge trail. (The rim trail closes in winter.) Also on the park's 783 acres are sixteen cabins and seventy-six campsites, picnic areas, toilets, fishing in the creek, swimming, and lake and boat rentals.

Waterloo Harbor Campground (315-539-8848; 607-785-7891 off-season; right on Rte. 414W to Rtes. 5&20, Waterloo NY 13165) Facilities include a boat ramp, utility hookups, and fishing areas.

SKIING

Downhill and cross-country ski at **Greek Peak** (607-835-6111, Rte. 392, Virgil). Cross-country skiing is popular in **Robert H. Treman State Park, Taughannock Falls State Park, Upper Buttermilk Falls State Park**, and on some golf courses.

SWIMMING

The waters of Cayuga Lake are cool and clean. There are several points of entry including Wells College dock, Aurora, off Myers Point; Long Point

Peter Finger

The Taughannock Falls State Park has the highest vertical falls east of the Mississippi at 215 feet.

State Park; and Frontenac Park. Also try the rock pools formed by cascading waterfalls in Taughannock Falls State Park, Buttermilk Falls State Park, and Robert Treman Park (the best swimming is in the lower stone pool of the waterfalls).

OTHER ATTRACTIONS

Baker's Acres (607-533-3650; Rte. 34, North Lansing) What started out as in 1980 as an easy retirement business for the Baker family has evolved into a very big deal. The seventy-five acre property contains several display gardens like shade and sun perennial beds, rock gardens, an English rose garden, and vegetable gardens. There are six greenhouses, more than 100 sales frames, 600 apple trees, a cider press, and three barns for drying flowers, plus walks along a woodland path to a pond. Have lunch in the Tea Room, enjoy great barbecued chicken, and check out the antiques upstairs in the Lodge. Plus you'll find a gift shop and fruit and vegetables for sale. Classes and workshops in gardening, cooking, and herbs are offered. So much for retirement.

Cayuga Nature Center (607-273-6260; www.fcinet.com/cnc/; 1420 Taughannock Blvd., Ithaca NY 14850) This is a 241-acre fun place filled with things for kids of all ages to do and see. There is a visitor center, exhibits of live animals, a nature store, a working farm, and a number of special programs including summer camp and teen adventure. Get up close to farm animals and little creatures like snakes, turtles, and creepy-crawlers; explore the five miles of nature trails and life in the ponds; and learn about flowers.

Fallow Hollow Deer Farm (607-659-4635; 125 William Rd., Candor NY 13743) New York's largest deer farm also has exotic and traditional farm animals. You can go on a narrated hayride and check out the information center. Open May–Oct.

Iron Kettle Farms (607-659-7707; Rte. 96, Candor NY 13743) More than a farm market, kids will love coming here in the fall for hayrides, farm animals, a spook barn, and pumpkins. There is also a craft shop on the property. Open spring–Oct. Mon.–Sat. 9–7.

Ithaca Farmers Market (607-273-7109; Third St. off Rte. 13, Ithaca NY 14850) On Ithaca's waterfront where there is a pavilion, picnic area, docking facilities, and plenty of parking, the Ithaca Farmers Market sells local produce, plants, baked goods, meats and cheeses, crafts, clothing, and furniture. Everything is made or grown within a thirty-mile radius. There is also a variety of special events throughout the season such as dancing, a strawberry festival, chili contest, a bee-day, ping-pong tournament, and live performances. Open Apr.–Christmas Sat. 9–2 and mid-June–late Oct. Sun. 10–2; also open Tues. 9–1 mid-May–late Oct. at Dewitt Park, Buffalo and Cayuga Sts.

Misty Meadow Farm (607-869-9243; 2828 Vineyard Rd., Romulus NY 14541) Haywagon rides, holding and cuddling little creatures like ducklings, piglets, and other farm friends, petting ponies, touring the barns, eating hickory-smoked pork barbecue, raspberry pie, and butter cookies shaped like pig faces in the farm kitchen, and browsing through the farm shop are all part of the Misty Meadow Farm experience. Open June–Sept. Tues.–Sat. 10:30–4.

SHOPPING

Ithaca

ART GALLERIES AND STUDIOS

Etchings & Watercolors (607-277-2649; 222 the Commons, Ithaca NY 14850) Lovely watercolors and other art work as well as a nice collection of amber jewelry are sold here.

Rock Stream Studios (607-272-0116; 233 Cherry St., Ithaca NY 14850) This shop contains an intriguing collection of items including audiokinetic and wind sculpture, and gurgling fountains.

Sola Gallery (Dewitt Mall, 215 N. Cayuga St., Ithaca NY 14850) Japanese prints.

BOOKS AND MUSIC

Bookery (607-273-5055; Dewitt Mall, 215 N. Cayuga St., Ithaca NY 14850) This shop specializes in selling and obtaining old out-of-print books. If they don't have it, they try to locate it for you.

CAMPING SUPPLIES

Cayuga Outfitters (607-273-5190; Rte. 13, Ithaca Shopping Plaza, Ithaca NY 14850) Find everything you'll need for camping such as sleeping bags, fishing and hunting equipment, outdoor clothing, and work clothes.

CRAFTS AND GIFTS

Handblock (607-277-5525; 154 the Commons, Ithaca NY 14850) Beautiful linens star in this wonderful little shop. Also find children's clothes and lovely white nightwear and other clothing.

Handwork (607-273-9400; 102-106 W. State St., Ithaca NY 14850) More than forty designers and artists display and sell their work in this exceptional cooperative of working artisans who launched operations in 1976. There is artwork, baskets, clothing and accessories, glass, metals, home decor, jewelry, pottery, paper, and wood. Open Mon.–Sat. 10–6; Thurs. and Fri. until 9; Sun. 12–5.

People's Pottery (607-277-3597; 158 the Commons, Ithaca NY 14850) Looking for an interesting wedding gift? This place is filled with eclectic things like papier-mâché designs, custom glass sculptures, clever ties, and even dog-motif clocks all handcrafted by artisans from the region and beyond.

Toko Imports (Dewitt Mall, 215 N. Cayuga St., Ithaca NY 14850) This speciality store has a huge collection of drums from Africa, Asia, and elsewhere along with other ethnic items.

FARM MARKETS

Ithaca Farmers Market (607-273-7109; Third St. off Rte. 13, Ithaca NY 14850) See listing under Other Attractions above.

Ludgate Produce Farm (607-257-1765; 1552 Hanshaw Rd., Ithaca NY 14850)

This market offers local and imported fruits, vegetables, maple syrup, honey, preserves, salsa, fresh baked goods, flowers, and cider. Open daily 9–9.

FURNITURE

Contemporary Trends (607-273-5142; 121 N. Aurora St., Ithaca NY 14850) This store sells high quality Scandinavian and contemporary domestic furniture and accessories.

JEWELRY AND ACCESSORIES

Shalimar (607-273-7939; 142 the Commons, Ithaca NY 14850) Find ethnic and contemporary jewelry, clothing, and accessories from around the world.

Seneca Falls

ANTIQUES

Country Reflections (315-568-4176; 83 Cayuga St., Seneca Falls NY 13148) We're told this store is "almost always open," and sells antiques and country gifts.
Jean's Antiques & Collectibles (315-568-4444; 2146 Rtes. 5&20, Seneca Falls NY 13148) Antiques, pine furniture, glass, china, and Victorian-era items.

FARM MARKETS

Bodine Farms (315-568-9529; corner Rte. 89 & E. Baynard St., Seneca Falls NY 13148) Bodine's specializes in sweet corn but it also sells other fruits and vegetables.
Sauder's Farmer's Market (1/4 mile west of Seneca Falls on River Rd.) This market sells fresh produce, homemade baked goods, and craft items. Open year-round Thurs. 8–5, Fri. 8–9.

Aurora

ANTIQUES

The Cleavelands (315-364-7266; corner Sherwood Rd. & Rte. 34B, Aurora NY 13026) This store has an assortment of antiques, memorabilia, and just plain good old junk.
Vintage Lighting (315-364-8182; Main St., Aurora NY 13026) The company both purchases and sells antique lamps and lighting fixtures as well as repairs and restores them.

FOOD

Cravings Bake Shop (315-364-5184; Aurora Place, Main St., Aurora NY 13026)
This small shop sells delicious homemade jellies and baked goods as well as
coffee, gift baskets, and regional foods and products. Open Tues.–Sat.

GIFTS

Gratitude (315-364-3504; Rte. 90, Aurora NY 13026) The scent of soaps and
sachets deliciously pleasant lure you in. Items for sale include whimsical
homemade gift boxes from very small to shoebox-size, toys, and baby
things.

Aurora Plaza (Rte. 90, Aurora NY 13026) This is a complex of unique shops in
a group of vintage buildings on Aurora's main drag. Debbie's Corner
Bakery sells homemade muffins, breads, cookies, jams and jellies; The
Winged Chair Art & Design is filled with fanciful gaily painted furniture
and accessories designed and handpainted by artist Mnetha Warren; and
The Enchanted Florist/For the Birds tucked around in back of the complex
is a combination florist and gift shop selling balloons, gift baskets, plants,
bird feeders, hand-painted birdhouses, carved signs, toys, soaps, nature
tapes, and other items.

McKenzie Child, Aurora,
creates and sells a fanciful
collection of pottery,
glassware, and furniture.

Katharine Delavan Dyson

McKenzie Child (315-364-7123; Rte. 90, Aurora NY 13026) If you happen to
whiz by, turn around and go back. This place is worth seeing. Set on a hilltop overlooking the lake just north of Aurora, McKenzie Child is a fantasy
world of pottery, hand-painted wood furniture, glass, lamps and other
objects that are now sold in exclusive stores in the country's major cities.

And this is where is all happens. Visit a sprawling workshop, a restaurant, outlet store, self-serve snack bar, and bird aviary. Hanging from the ceiling of the restaurant are teapots, desks, a stuffed doll in a chair, tables, birdcages, tasseled chandeliers, broken pieces of colorful pottery . . . every surface space is filled. Walls are also loaded with three-dimensional objects and the floor is made of cross-sections of tree trunks and limbs. Whimsical, colorful, captivating. You'll probably leave with a few packages of loot, but beware, even in the "factory outlet," nothing is inexpensive, though bargains can be found on the seconds tables.

Other Areas

ANTIQUES

Barzilla's Barn Antiques (607-387-6820; 9402 Rte. 89, Trumansburg NY 14486) A wide assortment of antiques and memorabilia is available. Open seasonally.

The Collection (Rte. 96, Main St., Trumansburg NY 14486) Chris and Pat Whittle's shops sell antique furniture and accessories. Open Tues.–Sat. 11–5; Sun. 1–5

Turo's Treasures (315-364-8644; corner Rte. 34B & Rte. 90, King Ferry NY 13081) This shop buys and sells antiques and sells collectibles, gifts, and reproductions.

Turn of the Century (607-532-8822; 8406 Main St., Interlaken NY 14847) A large shop with three showrooms of furniture mingled with accessories, collectibles, and other things. Open Tues.–Sat. 12–5; Sun. and Mon. by chance or appointment.

ART GALLERIES AND STUDIOS

American Primitive Art Gallery (607-869-9585; Rte. 96A, Ovid NY 14521) This gallery features originals and reproductions of New York communities and landmarks. Local art displays.

Blue Heron Gallery (607-387-9476; 63B Main St., Trumansburg NY 14486) Arts and crafts by regional artisans are on sale along with antiques and books. A small shop crammed with good things.

GIFTS AND TOYS

Black Sheep Designs (607-387-7078; www.fingerlakes.net/blacksheep; 63 Main St., Trumansburg NY 14486) Local artists display their craft in a 1865 Italianate brick house. Find pottery, wood pieces, baskets, candles, jewelry, toys, handmade soaps, bath gels, and lotions as well as gourmet coffees, teas, and chocolates. Open Tues.–Sat. 10–6.

T-Burg Toys (607-387-7891; 5301 Rte. 228, Trumansburg NY 14486) Handmade wooden toys and other quality things for children are offered.

For More Information

Finger Lakes Association: 309 Lake St., Penn Yan NY 14527; 315-536-7488; www.fingerlakes.org

Seneca County Tourism: Rtes. 5&20, Box 491, Seneca Falls NY 13148; 800-732-1848; sctourmk@flare.net; www.seneca.org

Ithaca/Tompkins County Convention & Visitors Bureau: 904 E. Shore Dr., Ithaca NY 14850; 607-272-1313; 800-28 ITHACA; www.ithacaevents.com; www.visitithaca. com

Trumansburg Area Chamber of Commerce: PO Box 478, Trumansburg NY 14486; 607-387-9254

CHAPTER FIVE
Deep Waters and Gorges
SENECA LAKE

Peter Finger

This picturesque dock, popular with photographers, is about two hundred yards from downtown Watkins Glen.

The native American translation for "Seneca" — a Place of Stone — hardly does the lake justice. About twenty vineyards covering hundreds of acres are planted on the hillsides that gently slope to the water's edge. They are, quite simply, a stunning sight. More than 600,000 visitors come here each year to visit these vineyards and wineries along the Seneca Wine Trail. Many participate in special events such as December's "Deck the Halls" and June's "Pasta and Wine."

In the parks, hikers and bikers explore the vast network of trails, and campers pitch their tents. Race enthusiasts flock to Watkins Glen for motor races and residents and visitors alike attend theatrical performances and concerts, including weekly outdoor band concerts.

At thirty-five miles long and estimated to be more than 630 feet deep in some places, Seneca Lake is a coveted water playground for boaters, sailors, anglers, and swimmers. (As the second-deepest lake in the country, Seneca is a testing site for sonar equipment; a station is set about midlake.) The Seneca-Cayuga Canal, which connects Seneca Lake with Cayuga Lake, the state barge canal, and waterways beyond, gives boaters a large cruising ground — the world, in fact. From Seneca Lake, through the New York State canal system, you can literally reach the Atlantic Ocean.

Seneca Lake was once a stronghold of the Seneca nation. Many native American artifacts have been recovered around the lake including on the grounds of Belhurst Castle. The site of Kanadesaga, the capital of the nation destroyed in General Sullivan's campaign, is about where the New York State Agricultural Experiment Station now stands. In the eighteenth century, "Kanadesaga" (which means "dog town") was changed to Geneva.

The land opened up to settlers at the time of the Phelps/Gorham purchase in 1783. In 1794, Geneva was officially laid out by Charles Williamson with Water Street (now Exchange St.) as the heart of the business district. At that time, the northern shores of the lake were close to the rear of the stores, but in 1919 a portion of the land was filled in to create a park.

In the early 1800s, steamboats plied Seneca's waters, transporting agricultural products and livestock as well as passengers from one end to another. These steamboats were very important to the lake people who relied on them to get from one place to another.

Prominent companies in the early days were the Geneva Waterworks (1776), J.W. Smith Dry Goods (1847), Geneva Optical Co. (1873), the Geneva Carriage Co. (1891), and the Nester Malt House (1890). At the turn of the century, the railroads became an important means of transportation to the region. The Rochester and Eastern Rapid Roadway carried passengers and goods between Rochester and Geneva with stops all along the way.

With the advent of the automobile, the steamboat and to some extent the railroad became obsolete in the people-moving business. Highways were paved and the main route (now Rtes. 20 and 5) ran close to the shoreline. In the 1950s, this bypass highway was relocated further inland so the lakefront property could be reclaimed as a park and recreational area.

The lake is now ringed by small villages, summer houses, camps, and parks. Geneva hovers at the northern end; Watkins Glen anchors the southern end. Other towns worth noting near or around the lake include Waterloo, just west of Geneva; Dresden, a small quiet village on the lake where residents enjoy a nice beach and superb fishing; and Dundee, three miles west of Seneca Lake. Almost midway between Seneca and Keuka lakes, around Lamoka and Waneta lakes, sites of ancient native American villages are found.

A few miles south of Watkins Glen, Montour Falls is home to the beautiful SheQuaGa Falls, which plunge 165 feet into a rocky pool. At the foot of Main Street, the falls are illuminated at night, a spectacular sight. Clustered around the falls are the historic "T buildings" built in the mid-nineteenth century including the Memorial Library and museum with its lovely Tiffany glass windows. Also architecturally interesting is the Greek Revival Village Hall.

GENEVA

With a population of more than 14,000, Geneva is one of the larger cities in the region. As you drive west into the city along Routes 20 and 5, there is the expansive Seneca Lake State Park dotted with trees, picnic tables, and grills, a place you can swim, sunbathe, cycle along the trails, and laze away an afternoon. Next to this is Lakeside Park and the Chamber of Commerce Center, a good place to stop for information.

Geneva is home to several important events, including the National Lake Trout Derby held each Memorial Day and the Seneca Lake Whale Watch Festival held in August, a fun-filled weekend of crafts, food, music, and special events. (You may not glimpse a spouting whale, but you are guaranteed to have a whale of a good time.)

Recently a number of piers and boat slips have been built near the Ramada Inn, making it possible for boaters to tie up and walk into Geneva about two blocks away. Also new is a wide stone pier that protects the harbor. A tunnel walkway goes under Routes 20 and 5 and the rail tracks, but it's just as easy to cross the road. Traffic is usually light: we're not talking about Manhattan here.

Over the years, Geneva has retained its quiet village ambiance. Large lovely turn-of-the-century houses, the mini-mansions of their day with pillars, leaded windows, round towers, and generous lawns and gardens, reign along South Main Street. Rows of exquisite three-story brick Federal townhouses (circa 1820) ring tree-lined Pulteney Square, the original center of town, which sits on a hill above the lake. From the terraces and windows of the houses on the south side of the street, residents enjoy superb views of the water.

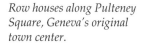
Row houses along Pulteney Square, Geneva's original town center.

Katharine Delavan Dyson

Noteworthy buildings in town include Belhurst Castle, a baronial-looking Romanesque structure, Geneva-on-the-Lake, a lakeside Italian-style villa, and

Rose Hill, an 1839 Greek Revival mansion which commands a prominent hillside position overlooking the lake.

Exchange Street, the "main drag," and the adjoining streets contain a mixture of trendy shops, restaurants, and local stores as well as old establishments that have been in the same location for decades. No chain stores are as yet evident in the center of town. The original movie house is still operating, although it now contains four smaller theaters where once there was one.

Handsome new period-style lighting, brick sidewalks, and brick-like crosswalks — along with vast renovations of the turn-of-the-century buildings — are transforming this area into one of the better small towns in the state.

The red brick buildings of the intown campus of Hobart and William Smith Colleges settle comfortably into the landscape. A liberal arts education is offered at Hobart (1882) for men, the oldest college in western New York, and William Smith (1908) for women, which are next to each other and share some facilities.

WATKINS GLEN

In 1948 the green flag waved the start of world-class motor racing in Watkins Glen. In those days, the cars raced along village streets and hillsides. Now the thunder of Grand Prix auto racing has moved to its own course, but you can use a self-guided tour map to trace the route the racers used to follow.

Peter Finger

The Columbia *offers cruises from the waterfront at Watkins Glen.*

The village's narrow main street is lined with several mid-rise buildings, housing stores and restaurants. There is a white brick hotel open seasonally and an attractive wide-board pier runs off the harbor.

WATERLOO

Two blocks of red brick buildings define the business section of Waterloo. Neighborhoods are quiet and pleasant. It's the kind of place that typifies home-town America — so it's appropriate that Waterloo is the birthplace of Memorial Day, first observed on May 5, 1866. Many Memorial Day traditions stem from this day, when flags flew at half-mast, wreaths were placed on war veteran's graves, and a parade of veterans and community leaders marched to the cemeteries and participated in ceremonies of gun salutes and speeches. A museum on Main St. is dedicated to this holiday.

Waterloo is home to other museums, including the restored Peter Whitmer Farm where the Church of Jesus Christ of Latter-Day Saints was formed in 1830.

LODGING

Seneca Lake is fortunate to have some exceptional lakefront hotels such as Geneva on the Lake and Belhurst Castle. The contemporary Ramada Inn on the north shore is within walking distance of the business area and next to the new public docking facilities. There are also a number of good bed & breakfasts in the area.

LODGING RATES

$: Up to $75 per couple
$$: $76–$150 per couple
$$$: $151–$250 per couple
$$$$: More than $250

Geneva

HOTELS AND RESORTS

BELHURST CASTLE
315-781-0201
Rte. 14S, Geneva NY 14456
Innkeepers: Duane Reeder
  family
Rooms: 13, including 2
  guest cottages
Open: Year-round

An imposing 1890s Romanesque castle on thirty lakeshore acres is graced by tall trees and gardens. At first you may think you have arrived at a private estate in the European Alps. Built by Carrie Harron Collins, who brought many of the building materials and furnishings from Europe, the rich

Price: $–$$$$
Credit cards: Most major

oak doors and woodwork, stained glass windows, and towers and turrets are indeed impressive. Over the years, Belhurst — which means "beautiful forest" — has served as a private home, a speakeasy, and a gambling casino. It is rumored that the castle even has secret tunnels and sliding panels to hidden rooms. Today Belhurst operates as an inn and restaurant. Many rooms have high ceilings with deep moldings; some have working fireplaces. The Tower Suite, often requested by honeymooners, has beamed ceilings, a large jacuzzi, a spiral stairway leading up to a lookout, and a king-size bed. The Billiards Room has a private balcony overlooking the lake and a king-size bed. Enjoy lunch and dinner in the Library, Parlor Center Room, Conservatory, or on the Veranda. The Garden Room next to the main building provides space for functions of up to 300 people.

Geneva on the Lake is an elegant villa-style inn and restaurant.

Katharine Delavan Dyson

GENEVA ON THE LAKE RESORT
315-789-7190,
  800-3-GENEVA;
  fax 315-789-0322
www.Genevaonthelake.
  com
1001 Lochland Rd., Rte. 14,
  Geneva NY 14456
Innkeeper: William
  Schickel
Rooms: 30 suites and
  studios, 10 with 2
  bedrooms
Open: Year-round
Price: $$–$$$$
Credit cards: Most major

Inspired by the Villa Lancellotti in Frascati outside of Rome, Mrs. Samuel Nester, a wealthy resident of Geneva, built this grand white mansion on a hillside above the lake in 1910. The Italian Renaissance architecture is unusual for this part of the world, a reminder of a period when European opulence was highly prized by the well-to-do. A small outdoor shrine recalls when the villa was once used as a seminary and monastery. Today Geneva on the Lake welcomes guests from around the world, including many famous artists, performers, and sports people. Beautifully renovated by Norbert and William Schickel in 1979, it continues to be refurbished. In 1995 the property was purchased by Mr. and Mrs. Alfred Audi, owners of L. & J.G. Stickley, a well-known area furniture maker. It is not surprising, therefore, to find Stickley pieces used throughout the villa in the private and public rooms. The Classic Suite, which features a fireplace in the living room and bedroom, is furnished in Stickley Chippendale with a four-poster rice-carved bed; the Loft Suite is furnished in Stickley Mission cherry and has a sixteen-foot ceiling, king-size bed, and six windows overlooking the gardens; and the former chapel has been converted into the Whirlpool Suite with a very large tomato-red jacuzzi tub, a bit out of sync with the rest of the room, but still great fun. Most suites come with parlors and kitchens. Whether you're relaxing in your room appointed with rich fabrics, Oriental rugs, tapestries, and interesting artwork, strolling in the formal gardens accented by classical sculpture, or lounging by the seventy-foot pool at the end of the gardens, your surroundings will be peaceful. The rope swing hanging from the branch of a big old tree is a particularly nice touch. Brides at receptions here like to stroll down the lawns and have their picture taken in the swing. At the end of a day, the resort's pontoon boat is ready to take you on a sunset cruise at a moment's notice. Then it's time to dine either on the Colonnade Pavilion, or in one of the intimate dining rooms where tables are set with linens, crystal, and, of course, candles. When it comes to romance, Geneva on the Lake gets a high five.

RAMADA GENEVA
315-789-0400, 800-990-0907;
fax 315-789-4351
41 Lakefront Dr., Geneva
NY 14456
Innkeeper: Victor Nelson
Rooms: 148
Open: Year-round
Price: $$–$$$$
Credit cards: Most major

With a decidedly nautical look, this four-year-old modern lakeside hotel, with its cobalt-blue roof and 148 comfortable, attractively decorated rooms, appeals to business and leisure travelers alike. Rooms come with all modern amenities and most have lake views. The lobby is spacious and opens up to marvelous lake views through large windows. Three suites have jacuzzis and there is a gym and cool-down pool. The Pier House restaurant is considered one of the better places to eat in town. The large open-air patio is a particularly good place on a pleasant summer's day. Meeting rooms can accommodate up to 220 people. The hotel is within easy walking distance of the main part of town and a tunnel running under the highway provides safe easy passage into the shopping district. New docking facilities on the shore-front invite people to come by boat.

BED & BREAKFASTS

WATERLOO HOUSE
315-539-9739, 315-568-9456
45 Virginia St., Waterloo
NY 13165
Innkeepers: Mary and Katie
Brainard

In a pleasant residential area, this 1830s Federal-style home was remodeled in the 1860s in the Victorian mode. Like many of this period, it has a front porch and walk leading to the main sidewalk.

Rooms: 4, some with
    private baths
Open: Year-round
Price: $–$$
Credit cards: Most major

The sunny Barnes Suite has a queen-size bed, private bath, feather duvet, and a sitting area. The Hudson Suite comes with a fireplace, private bath, and four-poster queen bed. Sam Bear Room has twin beds and the M'Clintock Room has a queen brass bed and is distinguished by light and flowery linens and accessories. Rooms have televisions, air-conditioning, robes, hair dryers, toiletries, and phones. A comfortable sitting room offers a selection of books and other reading materials; the guest fridge is stocked with complimentary drinks and snacks. A continental buffet or home-made breakfast is served in the dining room. Guests can use the copier and fax machine.

**WHITE SPRINGS
    MANOR**
315-781-0201
PO Box 609, Rte. 14S,
    Geneva NY 14456
Innkeepers: Reeder family
Rooms: 13
Open: Year-round
Price: $$–$$$$
Credit cards: Most major

Once the site of a native American village and later an important dairy farm and a fruit farm, this Georgian Revival home was built in the early 1900s. The house sits on the top of a breezy hill with magnificent views of the countryside and lake in the distance. Its pillared terraces, large high-ceiling rooms, sweeping grounds, and gazebo create a serene setting. Rooms are spacious and come with television/vcr, honor bar, and period furnishings. The Lewis Suite has beamed ceilings, a king-size bed, sitting room, and fireplace. The Living Room (now a bedroom) has a fireplace, canopy bed, and sitting area. There's not much going on here: even the free continental breakfast is served off the property at Belhurst Castle, the sister property nearby. So if it's solitude and good country air you're looking for, this is it.

Watkins Glen

HOTELS AND RESORTS

**GLEN MOTOR INN AND
    MONTAGE
    RESTAURANT**
607-535-2706;
    fax 607-535-7635
3380 Rte. 14, Watkins Glen
    NY 14891
Innkeeper: Victor Franzese
Rooms: 40
Open: Year-round
Price: $–$$
Credit cards: AE, MC, V

This is your basic motel setup with all ground-floor rooms, some with balconies overlooking the lake. Rooms are simply furnished and come with two double beds. There is a pool and the Montage Restaurant where you can eat inside or out on the deck. Those seeking an inexpensive, no-nonsense kind of place to use as a base to explore the region will find this a reasonable solution.

BED & BREAKFASTS

CASTEL GRISCH
607-535-9414;
  fax 607-535-2994
3380 County Rte. #28,
  Watkins Glen NY 14891
Innkeepers: Tom and
  Barbara Malina
Rooms: 3 with private
  baths
Open: Year-round
Price: $$
Credit cards: Most major

A special hideaway with lots of charm, Castel Grisch is tucked into an enclave of gardens just a short walk from the restaurant and winery. The former home on the estate, it has an octagonal tower entrance hall, and brick and timber exterior, very European in style, and very private with unending views of the vineyards and countryside. Castel Grisch has three rooms and suites, a new jacuzzi hot tub in a glass garden room, and fresh new decor in soft roses, limes, and red. There are two sitting areas, one with a large fireplace and television. The Champagne Room has a king-size bed, light off-white fabrics and carpets, and a large tub and shower. All rooms have private baths; two have balconies. Amenities include air-conditioning, ceiling fans, wine and fruit basket, robes, toiletries, and full breakfast, perhaps with Belgian waffles. A fireplace is in the sitting room and an honor bar; outside are lovely private gardens. (Also see the description in the Restaurants section below.)

CHERRY ORCHARD
607-535-7785, 607-535-9330
www.cherryorchard.com
4194 State Rte. 14, Rock
  Stream NY 14878
PO Box 145, Watkins Glen
  NY 14891
Innkeeper: Vera Giasi
Rooms: 5 with private
  baths
Open: Year-round
Price: $$
Credit cards: Most major

It comes by its name honestly: it's set in a cherry orchard and vineyard on the west side of the lake with views of the east side hills and the lake in the winter when the trees have lost their leaves. Fox Run golf course is across the street, the Arcadian Estate Winery is next door. Although the house dates back more than 100 years, extensive modernizing and additions make it more of a contemporary. Two guestrooms have cathedral ceilings and there is a very large great room/kitchen. Rooms are decorated mostly in soft neutrals and whites; beds are all different. For example, one is furnished with a 1940s pecan bed set, another pine. Three rooms have private entrances. There is an attractive stone spa accommodating nine people and an exercise room with a treadmill, weights, and other equipment. A full breakfast is served including something hot like eggs or quiche, muffins, waffles, and apple crisp.

CLARKE HOUSE B&B
607-535-7965
102 Durland Ave., Watkins
  Glen NY 14891
Innkeepers: Jack and
  Carolyn Clarke

An in-town Tudor-style house within walking distance to most shops and attractions and just about 100 yards from the Glen and ten minutes from the raceway. Furnished with antiques and reproductions, rooms have queen-size beds. Fine

Rooms: 4 with private
  baths
Open: Year-round
Price: $$
Credit cards: Most major

bed linens, comforters, and new mattresses (Carolyn says she can't stand old mattresses) assure a comfortable night's sleep. All rooms are air-conditioned and two of the rooms have a sitting area and television. There is a sitting room with a fireplace and television, a formal dining room, patio, and gardens. A full breakfast is served including hot dishes, fruit, and baked goods.

**FARM SANCTUARY
  AND B&B**
607-583-2225;
  fax 607-583-2041
www.farmsanctuary.org
PO Box 150, 3100 Aikens
  Rd., Watkins Glen NY
  14891
Managers: Lorri and Gene
  Bauston
Rooms: 3 cabins
Open: May 1–Oct. 31
Price: $–$$
Credit cards: Most major

S tay on a farm filled with animals. Each of three cabins here can sleep up to six people, with two double beds and sleeping mats for children. The cabins have wicker furniture and a porch. For more information, see the description in the Recreation section below.

LAKE HOUSE B&B
607-243-5637
46 Hunt Rd., Rock Stream
  NY 14878
Innkeeper: Dixie O'Connor
Rooms: 4, 2 with private
  baths
Open: Year-round
Price: $
Credit cards: Cash or check

F ew of the more remote B&Bs stay open during the winter months, but this one six miles north of Watkins Glen is an exception. After all, says Dixie O'Connor, "I love the winter." Her guests come here to cross-country ski, snowshoe, and get away and unwind. And what a good place to do it. This restored late nineteenth-century farmhouse, overlooking the lake, features eclectically furnished, very spacious rooms, modern baths, and a large sitting room with a good collection of books. Oriental carpets, a few Victorian pieces, and polished hardwood floors create a casual but gracious ambiance. There is beach access just a quarter of a mile walk away and a big old front porch where you can start the day with a cup of coffee or tea and homebaked breads before digging into Dixie's sumptuous breakfast.

READING HOUSE
607-535-9785
4610 Rte. 14, Rock Stream
  NY 14878
PO Box 321, Watkins Glen
  NY 14891
Innkeepers: Rita and Bill
  Newell

Y ou get superb views of the lake from this large 1820s house on the east side of the lake about five miles north of Watkins Glen. Over the years the house evolved from a Federal farmhouse to a Greek Revival with Victorian flourishes. Today it is restored to its original nineteenth-century character

Rooms: 4 with private baths
Open: Year-round
Price: $–$$
Credit cards: Most major

and contains a number of nice antiques. The grounds cover several acres with ponds, gardens, and lawns. There is an ample supply of reading matter including old and new books which you can read in your room or in one of the two parlors. Guests enjoy a full breakfast with juice, fruit, cereal, fresh baked muffins, and a main course, perhaps French toast, buttermilk pancakes with local sausage, or raised omelettes. Reading House is ideal for exploring the area. It's within five miles of the International Auto raceway at Watkins Glen, and close to wineries, Corning, Cornell, and other local attractions. It's quiet place surrounded by wonderful wildlife.

ROCK STREAM B&B
607-243-5898
www.bbhost.com/
    rockstreambb
524 Rock Stream Rd., Rock
    Stream NY 14878
Innkeepers: Carleton and
    Pauline Dailey
Rooms: 5 with private
    baths
Open: Seasonally (check
    with innkeeper)
Price: $$–$$$
Credit cards: Most major

This five-acre estate, formerly known as Peelle Farms of Rock Stream, was built in 1926 by John W. Peelle. The three-story brick house on a breezy hilltop contains spacious, well-appointed rooms decorated with designer fabrics, damask quilts, lots of pillows, pictures, and a mix of antiques and period reproductions. Some rooms have canopy beds; others king beds. One is a hand-carved mahogany Rococo-style bed. Amenities include a guest television room with a 60-inch screen, gazebo, grass tennis court, gift shop, and use of the formal living room which has a lovely fireplace. A full country breakfast is served with fruits, juices, hot casseroles, breakfast meats, baked goods, and coffee.

**SENECA LAKE WATCH
    B&B**
607-535-4490
www.bbhost.com/
    senecalakewatchbb
104 Seneca St., Watkins
    Glen NY 14891
Innkeepers: George and
    Julie Conway
Rooms: 5 with private
    baths
Price: $$
Credit cards: Most major
Open: Year-round

Built in 1820, the Seneca Lake Watch B&B is the oldest house in town, a grand Victorian home in a quiet lakeview setting. It has wide pumpkin pine floors, vintage furniture (many antique pieces), a sitting room with fireplace, a wonderful Chickering Piano circa 1880, and a comfortable lived-in feeling. A sixty-five-foot wraparound porch, a large deck, gazebo, and extensive gardens promise lots of ways to enjoy the outdoors. There are five guestrooms with queen and king beds. King rooms have private decks and views of the water. All have private baths and air-conditioning. George cooks the lavish breakfast; Julie does the baking. You can stay here for two weeks and never have the same thing twice. Unless you want to: George says he keeps a computerized account of what is served to whom so that when guests return, he knows what they like. The B&B is just a quarter-mile walk into town.

Other Area Lodging

HOTELS AND RESORTS

**THE INN AT GLENORA
    WINE CELLARS**
607-243-9500, 800-243-5513
www.glenora.com
5435 Rte. 14, Dundee NY
    14837
General manager: Pamela
    Griffith
Rooms: 30
Open: Year-round
Price: $$–$$$, packages
    available
Credit cards: Most major

Enormous barrels announce the entrance to this new inn set into a hillside overlooking the lake surrounded by vineyards. Built in a Napa, California, redwood style with lots of windows, high ceilings, and generous spaces, this inn is a departure from the B&Bs and country inns typically found in the region. There is a light, open feeling throughout. All rooms have private balconies or patios and feature cherry and pine molding, flowers, local art work, traditional Stickley furniture, and Waverly-style quilts and fabrics. Adirondack-style chairs made from the wood of former wine barrels are on the decks. Some rooms are furnished with two queen beds; others with a king, fireplace, and jacuzzi tub. All rooms have a table, clock radio, television, minifridge, hair dryer, and coffee and tea facilities. At one end of the inn, the restaurant, like all of the guestrooms, offer sweeping views of the lake. The main building of the visitor center and winery operations is farther up the hill.

**RAINBOW COVE
    RESORT MOTEL AND
    RESTAURANT**
607-243-7535
3482 Plum Point Rd.,
    Himrod NY 14842
Innkeepers: Jeff and Helen
    Ripley
Rooms: 24
Open: Mid-May–late Oct.
Price: $–$$
Credit cards: Most major

If you remember 50s-style motels, you'll get the picture. Still, the rooms have been upgraded and modernized, but the space and amount of furniture is the same. Since the road runs close to the shoreline, the buildings are just across the street. Some rooms have lake views such as the top units in the two-story building and Rooms 1–6 in the one-story buildings. There is a pool and recreation room. The beachfront has a private pier and boat slips.

**SHOWBOAT MOTEL
    AND RESTAURANT**
607-243-7434;
    fax 607-243-8050
3434 N. Plum Point Rd.,
    Himrod NY 14842
Innkeeper: John Socha

This rustic old motel is "moored" on the lake just off Rte. 14 between Geneva and Watkins Glen. The best rooms are the lakeside accommodations which have water views. Other rooms overlook the pool. Another building is across the street. The restaurant is open for breakfast, lunch, and

Rooms: 43 plus a cottage
Open: May 1–Oct. 31
Price: $–$$
Credit cards: Visa, MC

dinner in season; off-season on weekends only. You can eat inside or out on the deck. Water toys include canoes and other boats and there is a private pier.

BED & BREAKFASTS

THE COTTAGE
607-243-7194
PO Box 63, 4964 Apple Rd.,
  Rte. 14, Lakemont NY
  14857
Innkeepers: Carol and
  Bernie Kline
Rooms: 3 with private
  baths
Open: Year-round
Price: $$
Credit cards: Most major

There's no sign on Rte. 14 for the road that winds a long way down the hillside right to the lakeshore where the Cottage sits on a beautiful piece of waterfront. The house has been in Carol's family since the 50s when it was built by her father. Since then, Carol and Bernie have remodeled and added new furniture which blends with some antique family pieces to create a very comfortable retreat on the lake. The two suites on the second floor open onto a balcony overlooking the lake; the first-floor room opens onto a patio. Baths are modern and queen beds have down comforters. There is a television and phone in each room, and central air-conditioning throughout house. The green-painted cedar-sided cottage has two sitting rooms with a fireplace. Guests can swim or explore the lake using the canoe or paddle boat. A full breakfast is served. A four-wheel drive vehicle is recommended for winter visitors. No pets please.

COUNTRY GARDENS
607-546-2272;
  fax 607-546-2288
5116 Rte. 414, Burdett NY
  14814
Innkeeper: Lori Percival
Rooms: 3; 1 with private
  bath, 2 shared
Open: Year-round
Price: $–$$
Credit cards: MC, Visa

This white nineteenth-century farmhouse is perched on a hillside with super views of the lake. Rooms are large, air-conditioned, and comfortably furnished in a country style using print fabrics, paintings, and quilts. There is a phone and television in the sitting room along with books and games. The property features lovely perennial gardens, a gazebo, and swing seat. A full breakfast is served and a refrigerator is available for guests to use.

**THE INN AT CHATEAU
  LAFAYETTE RENEAU**
607-546-2062;
  fax 607-546-2069
www.clrwine.com
PO Box 238, Rte. 414,
  Hector NY 14841
Innkeepers: Dick and Betty
  Reno

This beautifully restored 1911 rustic farmhouse is next to the Chateau LaFayette Reneau Winery. The view of the countryside and lake is spectacular. Each room is different, and furnished with family antiques, double beds, and country accents. Three rooms have double jacuzzis. One sitting room has a television; the other does not and

Rooms: 5 with private
  baths
Open: Year-round
Price: $$
Credit cards: Most major

can be shut off with a pocket door. There is a front porch and a large wrap-around deck, the perfect place to see the lake. A full breakfast is served.

MAGNOLIA PLACE B&B
607-546-5338
www.magnoliaplace414.
  com
5240 Rte. 414, Hector NY
  14841
Innkeepers: Gary and
  Nancee Gross
Rooms: 5 with private
  baths
Open: Year-round
Price: $$–$$$
Credit cards: Most major

It's pink with icy white shutters, unusual for this part of the world but effective in conveying the spirit of southern hospitality. This 1830s farmhouse on seven acres is so comfortable that people return year after year. "They tell me they get a great night's sleep," says Nancee. "Perhaps it's the fact that our house is so well insulated. You can't hear anyone from the other rooms." Magnolia Place has a large porch, a Roman-style heated indoor pool with columns, and a sitting room with fireplace and library. Nancee spent many years in South Carolina, so it is not surprising that there are many pieces in the house that come from Charleston, including a handmade quilt. Air-conditioned guest rooms are on the first and second floors; second-story rooms open onto a new veranda with great lake vistas. The suite features a double jacuzzi and a fireplace. The third-story loft, which displays race car memorabilia, is the place to come to watch television and read. Breakfast is served on the porch or in the dining room, and is alway bounteous. It might be blueberry stuffed French toast or special omelets. Afternoon tea and lemonade with cakes and cookies are served; in the evening, coffee is available in the sitting room.

PEACH ORCHARD
607-546-2593
5296 Peach Orchard Rd.,
  Hector NY 14841
Innkeepers: Mary and Bill
  Musolf
Rooms: 3, 1 with private
  bath
Open: Memorial Day–Oct.
Price: $
Credit cards: Cash or check
  only

Mary Musolf is well known for her very large country breakfasts which include items like homemade jams, breads made by her husband (the old-fashioned way, by hand), hash browns, pancakes, eggs, and other good things. Then she provides visitors with doggie bags to nourish them through a day of sightseeing, inviting them to take muffins and other pastries left over from breakfast. Rooms in this old restored farmhouse are air-conditioned and all have views of the lake. The largest room has a king-size bed; the smallest room is decorated in shades of lavender and is right next to one of the shared baths. A deck built on the hill offering super lake views is set up with tables and chairs and a grill — a perfect place to sit and watch the sunsets. As Peach Orchard is not on the main road, the rooms are quiet and peaceful.

RED HOUSE COUNTRY INN
607-546-8566;
fax 607-546-4105
www.fingerlakes.net/
redhouse
4586 Picnic Area Rd.,
Burdett NY 14818
Innkeepers: Joan Martin
and Sandy Schmanke
Rooms: 5 rooms share 4
baths
Open: Year-round
Price: $$
Credit cards: Most major

Nestled on five acres in the Finger Lake National Forest next to thirty miles of hiking and cross-country ski trails, this is one of the region's loveliest restored farmsteads. The house is red, of course, with a white-painted veranda accented by latticework. Rooms are decorated in soft colors and attractively appointed with period wallpapers and fabrics, handmade quilts, four-poster full and queen beds, wicker furniture, old china, and paintings and antiques. One of the rooms has a fireplace; the Blue Room is the largest with a queen bed and two twins. There is a fully equipped guest kitchen, and two dining rooms, an inground pool with a cabana and barbecue grill, a country store, and gardens. A full country breakfast is served in the large kitchen in front of the brick fireplace, with homemade breads, pastries, jams, eggs, meat, juices, and fresh fruit. No children under twelve, please.

SOUTH GLENORA TREE FARM
607-243-7414
546 S. Glenora Rd., Dundee
NY 14837
www.fingerlakes.net/
treefarm
Innkeeper: Steve Ebert
Rooms: 5 with private
baths
Open: Year-round
Price: $$
Credit cards: Most major

Set on a sixty-eight-acre tree farm, this barn-style home with a gambrel roof is surrounded by pines, meadows, and brooks. There is a private suite along with a king and three queen-size rooms. All are centrally air-conditioned and the suite and king room have fireplaces. There is a Great Room with a large fireplace where you can relax with cocktails or a good book. In warmer weather, you can head to the wrap-around porch or picnic pavilion where there is a gas grill for casual cooking. A full breakfast is served in the dining room and the kitchen facilities may be rented for a special gathering.

WILLOW COVE
607-243-8482
www.watkinsglen.com/
bedandbreakfast
77 S. Glenora Rd, Glenora
Point, Dundee NY 14837
Innkeepers: George and
Joan VanHeusen
Rooms: 4 sharing 2 baths
Open: Apr.–Nov.
Price: $
Credit cards: Cash or check

Set on the lake at the end of Glenora Point, this big four-story house has been welcoming guests for several years. The house has wrap-around porches on the first and second stories and pleasant, moderately sized guest rooms. One room has twin beds; two have double beds and one has a king bed. Three of the rooms have lake views and the other a peek at the falls depending on the season. Willow Cove offers its guests use of a private beach and picnic area as well as a large, comfortable living room with a fireplace and two big porches overlooking the lake and countryside. The Glenora Waterfall is just across the road. A hearty continental breakfast is served with something hot from the oven and perhaps French toast or muffins.

RESTAURANTS

A side from a handful of restaurants in elegant mansions like Geneva on the Lake and Belhurst Castle, most of the places to eat are more on the casual side. Few are right on the lake, but many have lake views.

Prices are estimated per person for appetizer and dinner entrée without tax, tip, or alcoholic beverages.

$: Up to $10
$$: $11–$25
$$$: $26–$40
$$$$: More than $40

Geneva and Waterloo

ABIGAIL'S RESTAURANT
315-539-9300
1978 Rtes. 5&20, Waterloo NY 13165
Open: Mon.–Thurs. 11–2, 5–9, Fri. until 10; Sat. 5–10; Sun. 1–9:30
Price: $–$$
Serving: L, D
Cuisine: American
Credit cards: Most major

A modern, casual restaurant offering a large menu for lunch and dinner. In the warmer months you can dine on the deck overlooking the Seneca-Cayuga Canal. Typical lunch items include a veggie burger, $4.95; stir-fry chicken with rice, $5.95; and a variety of salads, wraps, and pasta dishes. An all-you-can-eat luncheon buffet is priced at $5.25. Dinner choices include several Italian specialities such as shrimp scampi, chicken parmigiana, and mussels marinara as well as staples like steak au poivre and baby back ribs. Some diners arrive by boat via the canal.

BELHURST CASTLE
315-781-0201
Rte. 14S Geneva NY 14456
Open: Mon.–Sat. 11–2, 5–9:30; Sun. brunch 11–2, 3:309
Price: $L, $$–$$$D
Serving: L, D, Sun. brunch
Cuisine: Continental
Credit cards: Most major

D ine by the lake like a baron in this 1890s Romanesque castle. The Golden Pheasant, a prized possession of Carrie Harron Collins, who built Belhurst, is the motif on the fine china that contributes to the old-world ambiance of the lakeside dining room. Leaded glass French doors, carved aged cherry, chestnut, and mahogany, mosaic-tiled fireplaces, and beamed cathedral ceilings further establish the mood. Descriptions of the dishes read like a romantic poet's work: "Fallow

Belhurst Castle, Geneva, is on the shores of Seneca Lake.

Katharine Delavan Dyson

deer rack chops roasted on cedar planks served on root vegetables, pancast and finished with forest mushrooms pesto and toasted pignoli." Fortunately, the food also tastes good. You can dine in one of the six inside rooms or outside on the veranda in warmer weather. The Garden Room next to the main building provides space for functions of up to 300 people. (Also see the description of Belhurst Castle in the Lodging section.)

At the bar in the Crooked Rooster, a popular pub and eatery.

Katharine Delavan Dyson

THE CROOKED ROOSTER
315-789-0454
459 Exchange St., Geneva NY 14456
Open: Mon.–Fri.
11:30am–midnight food,

In the refurbished Dove Block, this pub and eatery has been totally redone, retaining the tin ceiling and brick walls. Designed with lots of vintage-style glass and wood elements and plenty of good taste, this is one of the more appealing pubs around. The focus is on Irish cooking, bistro-style.

Sat. & Sun. 12–12 food;
  Mon.–Fri. bar
  11:30am–1am, Sat.
  12–2am, Sun. 12–1am
Price: $–$$
Serving: L, D
Cuisine: Irish-style pub
Credit cards: Most major

There are great crabcakes at $7.95, as well as pizza, salmon, baked Irish onion soup, potato and leek soup, and prawns served on rice with brown bread. The pub offers a number of stouts, beers, and ales on tap as well as in bottles. And in case you want to bone up on your Irish, check out the sayings on the menu such as "Croi follian agus gob fliuch" which translates to "a healthy heart and a wet mouth!"

FLOUR PETAL CAFE
315-781-2233
34 Linden St., Geneva NY
  14456
Open: Mon.–Thurs.
  7:30am–9:30pm, Fri.
  7:30am–10:30pm; Sat.
  9:30am–10:30pm
Price: $
Serving: B, L, D
Cuisine: Light meals and
  snacks
Credit cards: Cash, local
  checks

A tiny bit of perfection serving baked goods made from scratch. A wide selection of teas, sandwiches, wraps, pastries, bagels, pie, rice or bread pudding, and other tempting items make this a good place to stop for a light bite to eat. Try their Ninja Turtle or smoothie drinks: just $1.50 each.

GENEVA ON THE LAKE RESORT
315-789-7190,
  800-3-GENEVA;
  fax 315-789-0322
www.Genevaonthelake.
  com
1001 Lochland Rd., Rte. 14,
  Geneva NY 14456
Open: Daily
Price: $$–$$$$
Serving: B, L, D, Sun.
  brunch
Cuisine: Continental
Credit cards: Most major

This is elegant dining at its best. Tables are beautifully set with linens, crystal, candles, silver, and fine china. Dinner is served each evening with a choice of dining in the gracious Lancellotti Room or the more intimate smaller room next to it. Lunch is available on the Colonnade Pavilion patio in warm weather; breakfast is served daily in the Lancellotti Dining Room or in the Pavilion. Each Friday there is a wine and cheese party followed by gourmet dining. But no matter where you sit, you overlook the gardens with their neatly trimmed hedges and borders of flowers and the lake beyond. Lunch might be fresh seafood salad served in a phyllo pastry shell or perhaps a mesquite grilled tenderloin sandwich. Dinner may be fresh fish or lobster or perhaps rack of lamb or prime rib always served with the freshest of vegetables and herbs. (Also see the description in the Lodging section.)

HAMILTON 258
315-781-5323
258 Hamilton St., Geneva
  NY 14456

It has the same owner and chef, but the name and location of the former Spinnakers has been changed. Now the restaurant is housed in a reno-

Open: Daily 5–9, weekends
  until 10
Price: $–$$
Cuisine: Eclectic
Serving: D
Credit cards: Most major

vated colonial home across from Hobart College. It has four dining rooms, a bar, and a fireplace. Menu items continue to be creative — goat cheese crusted salmon with pesto cream drizzle, seared tuna with coconut steamed rice, or pork tenderloin with five spice apple chutney served with maple whipped yams.

**NONNA COSENTINO'S
  TRATTORIA**
315-789-1638
1 Railroad Place, Geneva
  NY 14456
Open: Closed Tues.
Price: $$
Serving: L, D
Cuisine: Italian American
Credit cards: Most major

Dine inside at a table or booth or outside on the deck; while you're waiting, check out the bar. Nonna's is known for homemade Italian sauces and dishes like lasagne, manicotti, braciola, and other pasta specialities as well as steak, veal, and seafood. One of the most popular items is seafood pasta. The restaurant is near the waterfront.

PARKERS
315-789-4656
100 Seneca St., Geneva NY
  14456
Open: Daily 11am–1am
Price: $–$$
Serving: L, D
Cuisine: American pub
Credit cards: Most major

Next to the Smith Opera House and a popular lunch spot for local business people, with its green-painted walls, woodwork, booths, bar, and high-top tables, Parkers has the look and feel of an old-time traditional bistro. Hot sellers on the menu include burgers, Philly steak, and homemade soups. The veggie basket is also very good. Parkers offers a very large selection of beers and ales. In the warmer weather, enjoy eating on the outside sidewalk patio.

Patti's Lakeview Diner, Geneva, is one of the few remaining traditional diners in the region.

Katharine Delavan Dyson

**PATTI'S LAKEVIEW
DINER**
315-789-6433
43 Lake St., Geneva NY
    14456
Open: Mon.–Weds.
    5:30am–3pm, Thurs. &
    Fri. 5:30–8pm, Sat.
    6:30–2:30pm, Sun.
    5:30am–12:30pm
Price: $
Serving: B, L, D
Cuisine: Diner food
Credit cards: Cash, checks

One of the last of its kind, this diner could be used in a 50s movie set. It has a counter, booths, a few tables and a location in the middle of everything. Try the "Quickie" for $3.95, liver with bacon and onions for $6.25, or burgers for $1.95. The "Big Frank" gives you three eggs, two links, two bacon strips, home fries, and toast, all for $4.95.

PIER HOUSE
315-789-0400
Ramada Geneva, 41
    Lakefront Dr., Geneva
    NY 14456
Open: Year-round
Price: $–$$
Serving: B, L, D
Cuisine: American
Credit cards: Most major

The popular Pier House is definitely into fish and seafood. Lunchtime they serve a "whale of a sandwich" (just $5.50) along with haddock, trout, steamed clams, and other fish and seafood dishes. Try the Pier House crabcakes or the fried calamari. For dinner there are tasty traditional items like veal marsala and captain's cut prime rib of beef. And while you're eating, enjoy the views of the lake through large windows or head to the patio and sit at one of the umbrella tables.

PINKY'S RESTAURANT
315-789-9753
14 Castle St., Geneva NY
    14456
Open: Mon.–Fri. 11:30–2;
    Weds. & Fri. 5–9
Price: $
Serving: L, D
Cuisine: Italian
Credit cards: Most major

The former mayor of Geneva wears many hats, including that of chef in his long-time restaurant. In fact, Pinky may just pop out from the kitchen to take or deliver an order and say hello to friends. It's not fancy or trendy. Just a favorite among locals, with a juke box in the corner. The menu includes everything from soup to nuts along with great onion rings and homemade pasta sauces. Wine by the glass is less than $3.

Watkins Glen Area

CASTEL GRISCH
607-535-9414;
    fax 607-535-2994
3380 County Rte. #28,
    Watkins Glen NY 14891
Open: Daily 11–3,
    Thurs.–Sun. 4–9, Sun.
    11–2; only open
    weekends Apr. & Nov.;

It's a couple of miles off the main lake highway (Rte. 14) but once you drive up Lovers Lane and get to the top of the hill, having passed through corn and alfalfa fields, it's worth the detour. In addition to the 138-acre vineyard, there is the chalet-style restaurant and bed and breakfast. The Alps theme of the former owners, who were Swiss, has been continued by the current owners, Tom

May–Oct. daily for lunch,
Thurs.–Sun. & some
Weds. for dinner
Price: $–$$
Serving: L, D
Cuisine: German American
Credit cards: Most major

and Barbara Malina. In the restaurant, German music plays in the background, waitresses wear blue embroidered jumpers and white blouses, flower boxes line the edge of the deck, and the menu includes items such as German potato salad, Swiss fondue, wienerschnitzel, spaetzle, sauerbraten, and strudels. You can eat on the open deck under the awning or in the open air overlooking the vineyards and the lake, or inside. Oktoberfest is particularly fun filled with oom pah pah and hearty Swiss-German food.

CURLY'S FAMILY RESTAURANT
607-535-4383
2780 Rte. 14 between
Watkins Glen & Montour
Falls
Open: Daily 6am–8pm
Price: $–$$
Serving: B, L, D
Cuisine: American
Credit cards: Most major

The Connelly family treat you to some down-home cooking in a casual atmosphere with counter and table service as well as take-out. Try their fish dinners, Italian specialities, Texas hot sandwiches, and homemade soups. This is a good place to bring mom, dad, and the kids.

DANO'S
800-803-7135
Rte. 414, Hector NY 14841
Open: June–Oct., Sat. &
Sun. 12noon–6
Price: $–$$
Serving: L
Cuisine: Light meals, wine
Credit cards: Most major

The barn-like building housing the Standing Stone Vineyard on the eastern shores of the lake is the setting for this casual restaurant where chef Dano Hutnik says, "Enjoying an afternoon of food and wine at the Heuriger is an important family event in Vienna. We hope to bring that experience to this country with Dano's." Choose from soups like goulash, a variety of spreads such as fresh herb petite Suisse and pumpkin seed oil spread; salads like Viennese potato salad and horseradish beet salad; bratwurst, fish terrine, cold poached salmon, chicken, roast pork, wienerschnitzel, and other Austrian-style foods. For dessert try strudel and seasonal fruit, bread pudding or kugelhopf. Heuriger, dry or semi-dry, is available by the glass or bottle.

THE DECOY
607-535-2607
4576 Rte. 14, Rock Stream
NY 14878
Open: Weds.–Sat.
12noon–10pm
Price: $–$$
Serving: L, D
Cuisine: American
Credit cards: Most major

A casual, friendly family-run business, with a full bar and daily and weekly specials. Rock Stream is five miles north of Watkins Glen.

**FRANKLIN STREET
  GRILLE**
607-535-2007
Franklin St., Watkins Glen
  NY 14891
Open: Daily; mid-
  Oct.–mid-May closed
  Sun.
Price: $–$$
Serving: L, D
Cuisine: American
Credit cards: Most major

It goes back to the time when racing took place in the streets of Watkins Glen. You could sit down for a bite to eat or drink and watch the action in the pits just outside the door. (Note the mural on the wall recalling those days.) Continuing in the tradition of good food reasonably priced, the Grille provides a mix of favorites like steak and burgers along with a selection of more contemporary items.

**THE PROFESSORS'
  PLACE**
607-535-8000, 607-535-4510
professorsplace@juno.com
www.netins.net/showcase
  /casata
2 N. Franklin St., Watkins
  Glen NY 14891
Open: Closed Mon. in
  season, Tues.–Sun L, D;
  closed Apr.–May;
  Jan.–Mar., Sept.–Dec.
  Tues.–Thurs. D, Fri.–Sun.
  L, D
Price: $–$$
Serving: L, D
Cuisine: Northern Italian,
  seafood
Credit cards: Most major

The restaurant in the Old Seneca Market next to the waterfront and shipyard is very popular with locals. It's a rustic kind of place with a comfortable pubby atmosphere created by a large bar, brick walls, wood paneling, low lighting, and a lot of books which can be purchased or borrowed. Gourmet sandwiches are loaded with fillings; grilled burgers including a garden burger and other light fare are available from lunchtime until 4:30. The dinner menu offers a wide range of choices: finger foods like mozzarella sticks, brew city fries, mussels and chicken fingers; and pastas with red and white sauces, grilled meats and fish, seafood, creative chicken dishes, and a vegetarian selection including tofu veggie curry. (I liked the "raspberry soy tofu.") New on the menu is tenderloin tips. Wine tastings, gift shows, bookstore, and live music are offered on various weekends.

Other Areas

**PASTA ONLY'S
  COBBLESTONE
  RESTAURANT**
315-789-8498
www.pastaonlyscobble
  stone.com
Hamilton St. at Pre-
  Emption Rd., Rtes. 5&20,
  Geneva NY 14456
Open: Daily from 5 for
  dinner; Tues.–Fri. from
  11:30 for lunch

Combine an historic 1825 farmhouse, classic Italian cooking, and a wood-fired grill and you come up with an exceptional dining experience. When the owners of the successful Pasta Only restaurant decided they needed more space, they discovered this lovely old building with porches, fireplaces, and cozy rooms. They bought it and changed the name a bit but not the quality of the food. It has a lovely garden patio, verandas, and several dining rooms. Seafood comes from Boston,

Price: $–$$$
Serving: L, D
Cuisine: Italian American
Credit cards: Most major

**VERAISONS at
GLENORA INN AND
VINEYARD**
607-243-9500
www.glenora.com
5435 Rte. 14, Dundee NY
14837
Open: Daily
Price: $–$$$
Serving: B, L, D
Cuisine: Regional fusion
with classic influences
Credit cards: Most major

produce from local farmers as much as possible, and pasta is made fresh daily. Chicken pesto, boscaida Verona, crabcakes, veal cobblestone, and sea bass are just some of the tempting selections.

Midway up the hill from the lake smack in the middle of the Glenora vineyards, this restaurant invites you to sit for hours and just enjoy the view through the large windows over the vineyards and out to the lake. Veraisons is a departure from the country-style restaurants usually found in the region. They call their cuisine "regional fusion," which translates to using the freshest of local produce combined with flavors and textures from around the world, along with wines. Breakfast might be buckwheat pancakes or Texas-stuffed French toast filled with homemade strawberry marmalade and New York State maple syrup. On the lunch menu is the caesar cannoli salad (with real anchovies) and the southwestern chicken salad made of cold spiced chicken with roasted Mexican vegetables and blue corn chips, served with a corn and salsa ranch dressing. The Baton Rouge catfish sandwich is also tempting. Dinner selections include grilled medallions of Chilean sea bass, coriander crusted ahi tuna, shredded soba duck, even barbecued bison ribs . . . and so many other things that are hard to resist. A good idea is to go with a few friends, order something different, and share. Jazz concerts, weddings, and other events are welcome. The restaurant is adjacent to the hotel, also heartily recommended (see the listing in the Lodging section).

CASUAL FOOD

Cams (315-789-6297; 476 Exchange St., Geneva NY 14456) Creative pizzas and hand-stretched fresh dough, super subs, buffalo wings, calzones, and sausage rolls: it's a winner. Open Mon.–Sat. 11–closing; Sun. 1pm–closing.

Chef's Diner (607-535-9975; Montour-Watkins Highway, Montour Falls NY 14865) Good old diner food from short orders to complete dinner served in an area institution owned and operated by Anthony Pulos. Open daily for breakfast, lunch, dinner.

Cleo's (315-781-1960; Lakeside Park, Geneva NY 14456) A weathered old sandwich board on the street announces the entrance. A couple of picnic tables, a peek of the lake across the highway, and a spot under the trees just off the main drag add up to a neat location for one of Geneva's old-time snack

Cleo's stand, a long-time favorite of locals in Geneva.

Katharine Delavan Dyson

stands. There is a huge choice of Cleo's Hots, Hoffman German Hots, red and white, served on a large rolls so you can pile on your favorite topping. Other items include BBQ chicken (just $3.85), Italian sausage sandwich ($3.75), and a Big Daddy burger with everything ($3.35). This is the place to get real frozen custards and great sundaes. Open daily 11–9.

Crow's Nest (315-781-0600; 415 Booty Hill Rd., Geneva NY 14456) Seafood and fish along with burgers and other sandwiches are served on a waterfront deck. Next to the Seneca Marina, it's very casual. Open Apr.–Dec.

Geneva Downtown Deli (315-789-4617; 30 Castle St., Geneva NY 14456) A full service deli and small restaurant selling over-the-counter and custom catering services offering giant subs, combo trays, veggie and dip trays, and hot dishes.

Ice Dreams (315-781-2558; 508 Exchange St., Geneva NY 14456) This little gem of a place features forty-plus flavors of good old-fashioned homemade ice creams with flavors like Killer Kiwi, Cannoli, and Kola Champagne as well as traditional favorites like mint chocolate chip, butter pecan, and maple walnut. People like to come here for a treat, sit at one of the few tables along the brick wall, and read their newspaper. New is a nice selection of Italian ices.

Seneca Lodge 607-535-2014; south entrance State Park, Watkins Glen NY 14891) Homemade breads, soups, and other freshly made dishes as well as a nice salad bar keep locals happy here. It's the place to come for lunch and dinner when looking for a casual meal. The Bench & Bar Tavern Room is always fun. Open May–Oct. 31.

Seneca Lake Wine Trail Events

Several vineyards and wineries are stops along the Seneca Lake Wine Trail; the wine trail map shows participating wineries and how to get there.

Special events are scheduled throughout the year, such as Wine and Cheese, Pasta & Wine, and Deck the Halls. For example, Deck the Halls takes place two weekends in the late fall. Your ticket tells you where to start. At the first winery, you get a grapevine wreath and a cookbook with the recipes for each of the items served in the vineyard. As you go from vineyard to vineyard, you taste the wine, get something to eat such as homemade squash soup, risotto, or bruschetta, and an ornament to put on your wreath. Your ticket is good for two days — trying to visit all twenty or so vineyards in one day can be a challenge. Some people get together and make a party of it, leasing a bus or chauffeur to drive them. Get your ticket early: this one sells out quickly. 315-536-9996; slwa@eznet.net

---

CULTURE

ARCHITECTURE

Geneva: The Geneva Historical Society's self-guided walking tour of South Main Street starts at 380 South Main, an 1832 Greek Revival originally built as a church. Each house of interest is described in the brochure including those of Pulteney Park, the original village green. Notable historic buildings in the area include a Victorian Gothic Revival house at 112 Jay Street built in 1862; the Smith Opera House, circa 1894, on Seneca Street, a four-story Romanesque building with arched windows and an ornate facade; and the Williamson House, an elegant Federal home built in 1827 at 839 South Main Street. Geneva's South Main Historic District, often compared to Charleston, South Carolina, contains several stately Federal-style row houses. The Durfee House, circa 1787 at 639 South Main, was the first frame structure to be built west of Rome, New York. Over the years it went through several alterations and was moved from its original location on Main Street to its present site.

Flint: Noteworthy is a saltbox-style structure on Routes 5 and 20 that in 1800 was the Ball Tavern, a stop on the stagecoach route.

Richmond: The Reed Homestead, circa 1803, is a gracious central entrance colonial brick house at 4357 Reed St.

MUSEUMS AND HISTORIC HOUSES

Geneva and Waterloo

Lee School Museum (Rte. 14 just south of Geneva) See exhibits of what life was life in the 1830s. Open by appointment only.

First Woman Doctor

In 1849 (when Hobart was Geneva College), Elizabeth Blackwell graduated from Geneva Medical College, becoming the first female physician in this hemisphere.

Mike Weaver Drain Tile Museum (315-789-3848; E. Hill Rd., Geneva NY 14456) Adjacent to the Rose Hill Mansion, this museum is contained inside the restored 1821 John Johnston farmhouse. (Johnston introduced tile drainage to America.) More than 350 tiles are on exhibit dating from 100 BCE.

Peter Whitmer Log Home (315-539-2552; Rte. 96, Waterloo NY 13165) A reconstructed 1810 log home, site of the Church of Jesus Christ of Latter-Day Saints who organized here in 1830. Period furnishings, Colonial-style chapel, and visitor center. Open daily Mon.–Sat. 9–6, Sun. 12–6.

Prouty-Chew Museum (315-789-5151; 543 S. Main St., Geneva NY 14456) The Geneva Historical Society is located in this 1829 Federal-style house which contains four period rooms and regularly changing exhibitions as well as collections of furniture, decorative arts, and period clothing. The society collects, preserves, and interprets the historic and cultural heritage of the area. Special events are held throughout the year and the society's archives are available for research. The museum shop sells local history publications and gift items, and offers a self-guided walking tour of Geneva's Historical District along South Main St. and a driving tour of noteworthy homes. Open Tues.–Fri. 9:30–4:30; Sat. (Sun. in July & Aug.) 1:30–4:30. Archives open Tues.–Fri. 1:30–4:30 or by appointment. Free.

Peter Finger

Rose Hill Mansion, a stately Greek Revival, was built in 1839.

Rose Hill Mansion (315-789-3848; Rte. 96A, one mile south of Rtes. 5 & 20, Geneva NY 14456) If you happen to be on the lake, you'll quickly notice the impressive white pillared mansion. Built in 1839, this stately Greek Revival mansion commands a prominent site overlooking Seneca Lake. The property was purchased by Robert Swan in 1850 who is famous for developing and implementing revolutionary agricultural technology in tile drainage during the mid-1800s. Furnished in the Empire style, this twenty-four-room house is considered one of America's most distinguished examples of the period. Many pieces were originally owned by the Swan family. Next door is the Mike Weaver Drain Tile Museum in the John Johnston House. Open May 1–Oct. 31, 10–4, Sun. 1–5. Admission $3 adults, $2 seniors and students, under 10 free.

Other Areas

Memorial Day Museum (315-539-9611; 35 E. Main St., Waterloo NY 13165) Recognized as the birthplace of Memorial Day because of its observance on May 5, 1866, Waterloo's museum dedicated to this occasion contains items pertaining to the day and the Civil War era. Open July 5–Sept. 15 Tues.–Sat. 1–4.

Robert Ingersoll Museum (315-536-1074; 61 Main St., Dresden NY 14441) This is the birthplace of the famous nineteenth-century orator, writer, and a founder of the Stanford & Woodstock Art Communities. See local history, exhibits, and artifacts. Memorial Day–Halloween Sat. & Sun. 12–5.

Sampson WWII Navy Museum (315-585-6203, 800-357-1814; Rte. 96A, Romulus NY 14541) Established as a naval training station in 1942, it was here that more than 411,429 young men were taught to be sailors and then sent overseas to participate in World War II. This museum, created by the thousands of members of the Sampson WWII Navy Veterans organization, is dedicated to these men. It contains artifacts from the veterans, photos, porthole displays, the ship's bell from FDR's presidential yacht *Potomac*, guns, and other memorabilia. Open May 30–Labor Day, Weds.–Sun. 10–4; Labor Day–Oct. 12 weekends only.

Schuyler County Historical Museum (607-535-9741; 108 N. Catharine St., Rte. 14, Montour Falls NY 14865) Historical museum in early nineteenth-century building. Open Mon.–Thurs., Sat. 10–4; research hours 10–3.

THEATER

Smith Opera House (315-781-LIVE; 82 Seneca St., Geneva NY 14456) This elegant theater with its ornate facade was built in 1894 and still operates today as a performing arts venue featuring dance, theater, music, and films. The interior was renovated in 1931 in the Baroque style and most recently the

Performing arts still flourish at the restored Smith Opera House, Geneva, built in 1894.

Katharine Delavan Dyson

entire theater has been refurbished. Many famous musicians have performed here, including Itzhak Perlman, who praised its magnificent acoustics.

EDUCATION

Hobart and William Smith Colleges (315-781-3000; www.hws.edu; 300 Pulteney St., Geneva NY 14456) These two four-year institutions provide programs in the liberal arts and sciences enrolling approximately 1,900 students. The two colleges share a common curriculum and some facilities but each awards its own degree and has its own dean, admission office, student government, and athletic programs. Hobart for men was founded in 1822; William Smith for women in 1908. The focal point for the campus, Coxe Hall, a grand Jacobean-style building, houses the administration and Bartlett Theatre.

RECREATION

BIKING

A bicycle path runs along both shores of the lake. The grade is gently rolling; views are of the lake, fields, and farms.

Dresden/Dundee/Dresden Route (800-868-9283; start on Main St., Dresden NY 14837) This 38.7 mile ride takes you along paved roads with some rolling hills. Highlights are the Robert Ingersoll Museum, the wineries along the Seneca Wine Trail, Wixon's Honey Stand, Dundee Historical Society, and the Windmill Farm & Craft Market (open Sat.). Cycle south on Rte. 14 for 14.9 miles, turn right at Dundee-Glenora Rd. then right on Rte. 14A in

Dundee. Stay on Rte. 14A north until you have traveled a total of 27.6 miles, then go right on Milo Center Rd. and when you reach the "T" turn left then make a quick right onto Leach Rd. and follow it to the end. Turn left at the stop sign and follow Rte. 14A north back into Dresden.

Geneva Skyline Loop (877-FUN-IN-NY; start in Geneva) This 35.7 route is mostly paved, with some dirt roads. Highlights include the Seneca Lake State Park, Smith Opera House, South Main Street Historic District, Prouty-Chew Museum, Hobart and William Smith Colleges and the NYS Agricultural Experiment Station Grounds. From Main St. (Rte. 14), turn left onto South Main St. and ride to Jay St. Right on Jay to end, left on White Springs Rd.; at stop sign, right onto Snell Rd. all the way to Slate Rock Rd. (3.1 miles to this point). Left on Slate Rock, right at Billsboro Rd., left on Wabash Rd. and follow to Alexander Rd. where you turn right. Go left on North Flat Rd. Make a quick right on Curtis Rd., cross Rte. 14A then go right on Wilson Rd. (14.5 miles at this point). Follow 14A north to #9 Rd. then turn left. Cross Rtes. 5&20, following Whitney Rd. to County Rd. 4 and turn left. Make a quick right onto Tileyard Rd., then another right onto McIvor Rd. Turn right on Johnson Rd., left onto County Rd. 4 and right onto Castle Rd. back into town.

Captain Bill's Seneca Lake Cruises depart from Watkins Glen.

Peter Finger

BOATING

Cruises:

Captain Bill's Seneca Lake Cruises (607-535-4541; 1 N. Franklin St., Watkins Glen NY 14891) The white double-decker 150-passenger boat with its bright

Sailing on Seneca Lake, the deepest of the Finger Lakes.

Finger Lakes Association

blue awning is a picturesque sight as it cruises up and down Seneca Lake. Enjoy lunch, dinner, and sightseeing cruises as well as miniature golf.

MARINAS:

A&B Marina (315-781-1755; albimarine@aol.com; 634 Waterloo-Geneva Rd., Waterloo NY 13165) A full service marina and campground offering boat rentals, hoist and dock installations, skies, kneeboards, and sales.

Roy's Marina (315-789-3094; Seneca Lake on Rte. 14, 3 miles south of Geneva) A full service facility with rentals, fishing boats, pontoon boats, hoists, launch, dockages, and storage.

Stivers Seneca Marina (315-789-5520, 401 Booty Hill Rd., Waterloo NY 13165) On the Seneca-Cayuga Canal, off Rte. 96A. The marina has a travel lift service, boat sales and repairs, and marine supplies.

FISHING

Seneca Lake provides excellent fishing grounds. For the latest fishing report, check with one of the local bait shops (for example, Barry's Bait and Tackle, Rte. 5&20, Waterloo; 315-539-5341). For example, one recent account stated that "smallmouth bass are active over rock piles at the north end of the lake and off Hi Banks in fifteen to thirty feet of water. Crabs, minnows, and worms are all catching fish. A few nice perch and pike have also been taken by bass fishermen. If you want to target the perch, use softshell crabs. If you want pike, use minnows. For lakers, drag copper at the north end in water 90 to 150 feet deep. Farther south, lakers have been hot around the barge off Dresden. Look for them 100 feet down over a 400 to 500 foot bottom." The report goes on to tell where browns, rainbows, and landlocked salmon can be found. Catharine Creek (at the head of Seneca Lake in Watkins Glen) offers anglers fishing in a thriving trout stream.

Great White Charters (315-781-1038; 301 White Springs Rd., Geneva NY 14456) Charter a boat for sport fishing on Seneca Lake or Lake Ontario and fish for salmon, steelhead, trout, bass, or perch. Boats include 26-foot and 31-foot fully equipped Penn Yan Hardtops. Ask for Capt. Jack Prutzman.

GOLF

Big Oak Public Golf Course (315-789-9419; Packwood Rd., off Rte. 14, Geneva NY 14456) This is a "Jekyll and Hyde" course with two completely different nines. The front is wide open and fairly straightforward. The more dramatic new back is cut through trees and wetlands with water on 6 holes requiring some skillful target shooting. This par 70 course plays 5,755 from the tips. There is a clubhouse, snack bar, golf carts, club rentals, and pro shop. Greens fees on weekdays are $9 for 9 holes, $15 for 18 holes, $13 and $20 for a cart; weekend greens fees are $10 and $17; $14 and $25 for a cart.

Fox Run Golf Course (607-535-4413; 4195 Rte. 14, Rock Stream NY 14878) A pretty 9-hole course providing rental clubs, pull carts, and gas carts. Restaurant and lounge.

Geneva Country Club (315-789-8786; Rte. 14S, Geneva NY 14456) A 9-hole, par 71 course playing 6,214 from the tips. Enjoy good views of the lake with your round of golf.

Seneca Lake Country Club (315-789-4681; Rte. 14S, Geneva NY 14456) An 18-hole, par 72 course playing 6,259 from the tips.

Silver Creek (315-539-8076; East River Rd., Waterloo NY 13165) This is a scenic 18-hole public course with watered fairways, tees, and greens. There is a driving range, putting green, gas carts, lounge, and pro shop. Specializing in golf tournaments and outings, the restaurant facility can seat up to 300 people.

HIKING

The Finger Lakes National Forest (607-546-4470; 5218 State Rte. 414, Hector NY 14841) This area offers a variety of hiking trails as well as primitive camping sites. The twelve-mile Interlaken Trail runs along Parmenter Road, crosses the Finger Lakes National Forest from north to south, and passes through varied terrain and vegetation. Southern portions are steeper and more wooded. On the way, stop at the Foster and Teeter Pond areas.

In the **Montour Falls** area hiking trails are in Queen Catharine Marsh, Havana Glen, the Montour Falls Historic District, and Queen Catharine's Grave.

PARKS, NATURE PRESERVES, AND CAMPING

Finger Lakes National Forest (607-546-4470; 5218 State Rte. 414, Hector NY 14841) A 15,000-acre woodland offering hiking, cross-country skiing, snow-mobiling, horse trails, camping, fishing, hunting, berry picking, and bird watching.

Havana Glen Park and Campground (607-535-9476; 135 Havana Glen Rd., PO Box 579, Montour Falls) This park offers tent and trailer sites, hiking trails, shower and toilet facilities, playgrounds, and ball fields. There are three pavilions for outings; also a magnificent gorge perfect for picnics and soaking up the beauty of the falls and surrounding countryside. Open May 15–Oct. 15

Hector Land Use Area: Operated by the US Forest Service, this area contains twenty-five miles of marked trails, water and toilet facilities, three picnic spots, and nine camping sites. Motorized sports are not allowed.

Lakeshore Park (at the north end of the lake adjacent to the state park, Geneva NY 14456) This is a pleasant grassy park where you can stroll along the water and stop by the Chamber of Commerce to get area information. There are new boat slips and a dock.

Municipal Campground and Marina (607-535-9397; Rte. 14, Montour Falls NY 14865) Ninety camp sites in this park along with 190 boat slips. On the Old Barge Canal, boats have access to Seneca Lake. Public boat launch, cable television, store, picnic pavilions, playground, and ball fields.

Sampson State Park (315-585-6392; Rte. 96A, 12 miles south of Geneva on east side of Seneca Lake, Romulus NY 14541) This park on the lake offers tent, trailer, and camping facilities as well as a marina, biking, and hiking. The Sampson WWII Navy Museum is also on the grounds.

Seneca Lake State Park (315-789-2331, Rtes. 5&20, Geneva NY 14456) On the north shore, this wide, pleasant park offers bike and walking paths, picnic areas and swimming facilities. There is also a boat launch, marina, and beach. A modest fee is charged.

Smith Park and Campground (607-546-9911, 607-546-5286 off-season; off Rte. 414, PO Box 73, Hector NY 14841) Available on this 92-acre site along 2,000 feet of Seneca Lake shoreline are boat launching facilities, swimming, hiking trails, and more than fifty-six campsites. Some of the campsites have water views, most are wooded. Open May 1–Sept. 30.

Warren W. Clute Memorial Park and Campground (607-535-4438, 521 E. Forth St., Watkins Glen NY 14891) Camp sites, tennis, playground, swimming, ball field, picnic facilities, boat launch, and a lakeside pavilion.

Watkins Glen State Park and Gorge (607-535-4511; Watkins Glen NY 14891) One of the Finger Lake's most beautiful parks, Watkins Glen is deep rock-walled canyon with nineteen waterfalls, many cascades, grottoes, and amphitheaters. There is an Olympic-size swimming pool, picnic facilities, camping, and nonstop views. As the sun sets, enjoy Timespell, a sound and light laser show depicting the birth of the gorge.

OTHER ATTRACTIONS

Community Playground Complex (S. Exchange St., Geneva NY 14456) In addition to ice skating offered in the winter, there are ball fields, playgrounds, and shuffleboard.

Farm Sanctuary and B&B (607-583-2225; fax 607-583-2041; www.farmsanctuary.org; PO Box 150, County Rte. 23, 3100 Aikens Rd., Watkins Glen NY 14891) Lorri and Gene Bauston's barns and 175 acres bordering a state forest are sanctuary for animals of all kinds. There are cows, pigs, sheep, turkeys, chickens, rabbits, and other animals and birds. Animals that have been abandoned or injured are housed in the Refuge Barn. Children can get close to a wide variety of animals here and can learn about the importance of humane care of animals at the visitor center's exhibits; guided tours are also given. To experience the farm fully, you can overnight in one of three cabins that can accommodate up to six people. The cabins contain two double beds, a sitting area, wicker furnishings, and porch. Sleeping mats for children are available. Rates are from $55 per night.

Misty Meadow Farm (607-869-9243; 2828 Vineyard Rd., Romulus NY 14541) There are many more than just three little pigs on this farm — in fact, there are more than 1,000 of the critters at Misty Meadow. Tours are available and opportunities for feeding and petting the animals.

New York State Agricultural Experiment Station (a division of Cornell University's College of Agriculture and Life Sciences, 630 W. North St., Geneva NY 14456) Group tours arranged through the Publications Office.

Seneca Grand Prix (607-535-7981; Rte. 414 S., Watkins Glen NY 14891) Take the family on a day's outing to drive the Go-Karts and bumper boats, play arcade games, and go for par on the miniature golf course. Hours vary; call ahead.

Sugar Hill Recreation Area (7 miles west of Watkins Glen) National and international archery tournaments are held here. There is also a wheelchair course designed for tournament competition. Other facilities include horse trails, campsites and shelters, picnic grounds, fishing areas, and wildflower fields.

Finger Lakes Association

Grand Prix races at Watkins Glen International Racing Circuit.

Watkins Glen International Racing Circuit (607-535-2481; www.theglen.com; 2790 County Rte. 16, Watkins Glen NY 14891) On the hills overlooking the town, the facility is the site of eight major racing weekends a year including NASCAR events and the U.S. Vintage Grand Prix.

SHOPPING

From Prime Outlets to small boutiques and gift stores in downtown Geneva, there are plenty of shopping options for the regular as well as casual shopper. There are also a number of farm markets and pick-your-own fruit places.

Do You Hear the Lake Drums?

The Senecas believed they heard the low distant booms of the drums of their ancestors, thought to be manifestations of evil spirits or divine messages from the God of Thunder. Today these booms can sometimes be heard on very still evenings but no one is sure just what causes them. Some think it's a result of gases bubbling up from the lake bottom that create the noise as they escape.

ANTIQUES

Hessney's Antiques & Used Furniture (315-789-0126; 405 Exchange St., Geneva NY 14456) A huge inventory of antiques and accessories fill more than 24,000 square feet of space in downtown Geneva. Open Mon.–Sat. 9:30–5.

One Man's Junk (716-526-6862; 4539 Rte. 14A, Geneva NY 14456) This place has lots of Victorian pieces, lighting fixtures, glass shades, and accessories. Lamp restoration and repair, too.

Rose Hill Antique Consignment Shop (315-789-5915; Rte. 96A, Geneva NY 14456) Fine antiques and collectibles are sold in this shop on the grounds of Rose Hill Mansion. Open daily July and Aug. 11–4, Sun. 1–5; June & Sept. Weds.–Sun.; May & Oct. weekends.

FACTORY OUTLETS

Famous Brands (607-535-4952; 412 Franklin St., Watkins Glen NY 14891) Three floors of merchandise offer close to twenty stores selling discounted items. Find famous names such as Timberland, Northern Isles, Dexter, Levi's, Woolrich, Duofold, and other brands. Open daily.

Prime Outlets (315-539-1100; Rte. 318 between exits 41 & 42 off the NY State Thruway, Waterloo NY 13165) A huge complex of factory outlets for just about everything including clothes, cosmetics, entertainment, food, home furnishings, housewares, jewelry, luggage, shoes, and speciality items.

FOOD

Geneva Area Farmers Market (315-789-5005; 666 S. Exchange St., Geneva NY 14456) Every Thursday from mid-June through mid-October, farmers come here to sell their produce including fruits and vegetables, breads, and flowers.

Minn's Farms (716-526-6502; Rte. 14A, between Geneva and Hall) Seasonal fruits and vegetables with sweet corn, cabbage, cauliflower, broccoli, and brussels sprouts.

Rasta Ranch Vineyard & Nursery (607-546-2974; 5882 Rte. 414, Hector NY 14841) An eclectic farmhouse experience selling all sorts of things. Greenhouses, lawns, speciality perennials and herbs, organic grapes, wine, gift shop, handcrafted jewelry, and much more. Open daily Apr.–Nov. noon–5.

Red Jacket Orchards (315-781-2749, 800-828-9410; Rts. 5&20, one mile west of Geneva) This is a big operation owned for three generations by the Nicholson family. More than 450 acres are in fruit production with several varieties of apples, strawberries, sweet cherries, prunes, plums, and apricots. Products sold in the farm store include cider, fruit butters, relishes, chili sauces, honey, cheeses, jams and jellies. In the Fruit Cellar, you can select your own fruit and often taste the different kinds as well. You can pick your own strawberries and cherries in season. Red Jacket also prepares fruit gift baskets.

Orchard Ovens (607-243-8123; 5438 Rte. 14, 8 miles north of Watkins Glen, Dundee NY 14837) Bakery, retail, gift shop.

GIFTS AND TOYS

The Attique (315-781-0529; 266 Hamilton St., Geneva NY 14456) This store is packed with interesting items: antique reproductions, garden decor, door stops, American Chestnut Collection, candles, clocks, lamps, pottery, lace, aromatherapy products, Boyd's Bears, wrought iron items, and, of course, a lot more. Open Mon.–Thurs. 10–6, Fri. 10–8, Sat. 10–5, Sun. 12–4.

A Country Basket (315-789-6163; 23 Seneca St., Geneva NY 14456) Find many unusual gifts and collectibles including Joseph Schmidt Confections, Boyd's Bears, Margaret Furlong Angels, Sheila's Collectible Houses, teapots, lace, linens, Crabtree & Evelyn, April Cornell, candles, and pottery. There are some wonderful kits by Diana Davis to make children's party hats, custom gift baskets, and a large selection of Christmas ornaments. Open Mon.–Thurs. 9–5:30; Fri. 9–8; Sat. 9–5.

Earthly Possessions (315-781-1078; 70 Seneca St., Geneva NY 14456) This small store carries lots of unique gifts such as scented candles, handcrafted jewelry, bath products, and other items. Open Tues.–Thurs. 10–6, Fri. 10–8, Sat. 10–6 (until 3 during the summer).

Kookaburra Kites (315-789-5555; 70 Seneca St., Geneva NY 14456) Every style of kite you can imagine as well as custom-made kites, accessories.

Guards Cards (315-789-6919; 60 Seneca St., Geneva NY 14456) Right on a corner in the heart of downtown Geneva, it has the ambiance of a 1920s drug store and is a wonderful place to shop. It's the only store in the state that carries Failte dolls from Ireland. Also find other popular products such as wind kites, Seagull pewter, jewelry, and greeting cards. Collectibles include Nao by Lladro, Swarovski, Lang & Wise, Hallmark, Gund animals, Anheuser-Busch steins, and Folkstones & Dollstones. Open Mon.–Thurs. & Sat. 8:30–5:30; Fri. 8:30–8; Sun. noon–4.

Seneca Hillside (607-243-9090; Rte. 14, Dundee NY 14837) Miniatures, produce, handcrafted items, and dollhouses.

Weaver-View Farms (315-781-2571; 1190 Earls Hill Rd., off Rte. 14, 7 miles south of Geneva) Amish/Mennonite quilts and country gifts in a turn-of-the century farmhouse. (See listing in Chapter Six, *Keuka Lake*.)

For More Information

Geneva Area Chamber of Commerce, Information Center: 35 Lakefront Dr., PO Box 587, Geneva NY 14456; 315-789-1776; fax 315-789-3993; www.genevany.com

Ontario County Tourism: Five Lakes Suite, 20 Ontario St., Canandaigua NY 14424; 716-394-3915; www.ontariony.com

Schuyler County Chamber of Commerce: 100 North Franklin St., Watkins Glen NY 14891; 607-535-4300; www.schuylerny.com.

CHAPTER SIX
Split Personality
KEUKA LAKE

Peter Finger

Keuka Lake branches out into a "Y" at the northern end, as seen from Skyline Drive.

To the Senecas who lived in the region long before the white man came, Keuka meant "canoe landing" — a name that ultimately prevailed even after settlers tried to change the name to Crooked Lake. Over the years, this twenty-two-mile Y-shaped lake, which forks about midway to the north, has been the epicenter of first a thriving steamship transportation company, and later an important wine producing area. The largest town, Penn Yan, lies at the tip of the northeastern branch; Branchport is nestled around the northwestern branch, and Hammondsport lies at the southern end. Keuka is on the eastern shore just where the eastern branch of the lake forks up.

Of all the Finger Lakes, Keuka's seventy miles of shoreline harbors the most lake-hugging restaurants. Many have decks literally over the water and several boat slips, so that diners can arrive by water. The lake is one of the warmest of the Finger Lakes as it is shallower in comparison, so swimming is comfortable the entire summer season.

Although most come here to visit the wineries, there are several superb museums and other attractions. The Glenn H. Curtiss Museum explores the early days of aviation; the Greyton H. Taylor Wine Museum is at the Bully Hill Winery. For a pleasant summer's day cruise, climb aboard the *Keuka Maid* which leaves from its pier in Hammondsport and offers a variety of cruises around the lake. Keuka College, a four year co-ed liberal arts school founded in 1890, has a beautiful 1,300 foot lakeshore site on the west side of the lake four miles southwest of Penn Yan. Area residents enjoy programs and events offered by the college throughout the year.

Peter Finger

Keuka College is a four-year liberal arts college on the west side of Keuka Lake.

Pleasure craft now cruise Keuka's waters, but early in the nineteenth century, the lake was the scene of a bustling commercial shipping business. The schooner *Sally* used to transport grain to Hammondsport, where it was loaded on wagons and hauled ten miles to Bath, then shipped by river to Philadelphia and Baltimore. The opening of the Erie Canal in 1825 resulted in traffic being diverted to northern ports.

For about forty years (1830–1870) the "Crooked Lake Canal" linked Penn Yan to Dresden on Seneca Lake; however, the coming of the railroad made the canal obsolete. All that remains today are traces of some of the twenty-eight locks, mill foundations, and tow path. The path of the canal is now defined by the Keuka Outlet Trail, popular with hikers and bikers.

By the late 1800s, the emphasis on transporting grains had shifted to grapes, bringing new prosperity to the region. Thanks to a spirited rivalry between steamboat companies, extensive publicity spread the word about the leisure assets of Keuka Lake, attracting affluent visitors who came and built lovely summer homes along the shores.

One of the best-known boats, the 600-passenger *Mary Bell* steamboat launched in 1892, cruised the lake for thirty years carrying passengers and grapes. The steamboat age recalls a time of romance: dances in lakeside pavilions, booming resorts at Grove Springs, Gibson's Landing and Urbana; and big name entertainers like Fred Waring and Hoagy Carmichael.

Since that time, grapes have been the most important industry around the lake. Considered the center of the champagne industry in New York State, the hills around Hammondsport are covered with vineyards, including the well-known Bully Hill Vineyards, Dr. Konstantin Frank's Vinifera Wine Cellars, and Pleasant Valley Wine Co.

It all started in an Episcopal rector's garden around 1840. Planted by the Rev. William Bostwick of Hammondsport, his Isabella and Catawba grapes flourished. Others took notice and planted their own vines. Seven years later, local entrepreneurs sent fifty pounds of grapes to the New York market. By 1860, 200 acres of vineyards were planted around the lake and, at the turn of the century, more than 23,000 acres were dedicated to growing grapes. Today the wine industry here is alive, well, and expanding.

Route 54A from Penn Yan to Hammondsport along the western shore of Keuka's western branch meanders along the shoreline providing one of the most scenic drives in the world. Middle Road, above it, gives you superb hillside views of vineyards and the lake below.

Red Jacket

On 54A just south of Branchport is a granite monument marking the burial spot for the mother of the Seneca chief Red Jacket. This famous native American orator of the Seneca tribe is believed to have been given this name (his native name was "Sagoyewatha") because of a British army jacket he was given and wore constantly. His longhouse was believed to have been at this site in 1752.

PENN YAN

On the tip of the northeastern branch of the lake, Penn Yan is a pretty peaceful place considering it was once nicknamed "pandemonium" by its neighbors because of its rowdy reputation. About 1808, looking for a real name for the town, the leaders settled on Penn Yan, satisfying two factions who were having trouble agreeing: immigrants from Pennsylvania and Yankees from New England.

One of the first founders of the town, David Wagener, came here from

Pennsylvania, a follower of Jemima Wilkinson. He built a grist mill on the site where the Birkett Mills now stand on the south end of Main Street along the Keuka Lake Outlet. Wagener's son Abraham, who is considered to be the father of the town, built the first frame house and first inn, the Mansion House, and constructed the grand manor house above Bluff Point.

In addition to grist mills, gradually shops and taverns were built both at the north end of Main Street and around the mills. The construction of the county buildings midway between the two areas tied these two commercial centers together. Since then the heart of the business district has drifted more toward the former mill areas where the Crooked Canal was built.

This National Register Historic District includes several historic buildings. A comprehensive Historic Main Street Walking Tour describes the Holowell House, a late nineteenth-century Queen Anne home at 219 Main Street, the Victorian King-Post House at 215 Main Street, the Bordwell House, a brick Italianate residence build in 1868 on the site of Abraham Wagener's first house, and others. The guide is available at the Oliver House Museum and other key sites.

HAMMONDSPORT

Finger Lakes Association

Hammondsport is centered around a small town square with a gazebo.

Hammondsport centers on a lovely compact square with shops and restaurants arranged around a park of trees, gardens, and a gazebo. Walk about a couple of blocks to the lakeshore where there is a public park and an old rail-road terminal, now housing law offices; a vintage rail car is parked alongside. During the summer months, band concerts are held in the square at 7pm on Thursday evenings.

Considered the "wine capital of the state," Hammondsport has several vine-yards within its boundaries, including the Great Western and Pleasant Valley Winery.

Site of the oldest running county fair, the buildings along Pulteney Square and Liberty Street, as well as the Erie Freight House, are especially interesting for history buffs. Several private homes are on the National Register of Historic Places. Walking tours reveal buildings in several styles: Greek Revival, Queen Anne, Italianate, and Tuscan. For a dose of the 50s, take in a movie at one of the few drive-in theaters still left in the country (open spring through fall).

BATH

South of Hammondsport, the town of Bath was named after Lady Bath of England, by founder Col. Charles Williamson, whose dream was to create the state's first planned community. Believing that Bath's pivotal location at the Susquehanna, Conhocton, and Chemung rivers would be a surefire combi-nation to creating a highway to the west, "The Baron of the Backwoods," act-ing as the agent for some wealthy Englishmen, including Sir William Pulteney, promoted the site as the next great metropolitan area.

In 1793, when fifteen families moved into the village, Williamson did not foresee that the Erie Canal and the coming of the railroad would negate the importance of the rivers. But his dynamic personality and boundless energies prevailed to some extent despite continual setbacks. Eventually, Bath was developed with a grist mill, saw mill, several residences, and even a theater and race course.

The Friend

One of the area's most interesting personalities, Jemima Wilkinson (1752–1819), an imposing figure in flowing robes with long raven hair, believed she had been reincarnated by the Divine Spirit as a Universal Friend to save sinners. Relocating from Rhode Island, she founded a community of faithful followers, first settling near Dresden at one end of the Keuka Outlet. Her group built the first grist mill in the area, harvested the first wheat sown west of Seneca Lake, and soon became the largest community in the region. Ruling with an iron hand, she forbade her subjects to marry, controlled the finances, and scorned attending such entertainments as dances, theater, and horse races. Her creed was simple: be good, go to heaven; sin and burn in hell. Eventually the settlement relocated to Branchport where The Friend built a three-story house with nine fireplaces.

Today Bath is hardly the great city Williamson imagined but it is a nice town with a most interesting history. Cemetery buffs will find the white headstones in the Bath National Cemetery adjacent to the V.A. Medical Center complex a stunning sight.

LAMOKA AND WANETA LAKES

The tiny lakes of Lamoka and Waneta, just east of the southern end of Keuka Lake, are hardly on some of the area maps. Less than four miles long, and 1,000 feet above sea level, Lamoka is the site of a prehistoric Indian settlement, one of the oldest such sites in the state. Peaceful places.

LODGING

There are no major hotels in the area. The best places to stay include bed & breakfasts and small inns or 60s-style motels. There are also cottage rentals available through reservation services. Some of the B&Bs are right on the lake and come with access to canoes and rowboats. B&Bs range from elegant estate homes with pillars and formal gardens to cozy, homey places with lots of fluff and knick-knacks.

LODGING RATES
$: Up to $75 per couple
$$: $76–$150 per couple
$$$: $151–$250 per couple
$$$$: More than $250

Branchport

OLDE TAVERN INN
888-414-5253;
    fax 315-595-2825
www.rentalplus.com
Rental Plus, 3858 County
    House Rd., Branchport
    NY 14418
President/manager: Brian
    Zerges
Rooms: 5 bedrooms, 2
    baths
Open: Year-round
Price: $$$–$$$$ for the
    entire house
Credit cards: Most major

A good place for families and small groups, this circa 1823 restored National Historic Landmark can accommodate ten people. Once a major stop on the stagecoach line from Penn Yan, the colonial-style house is in a rural setting about two miles north of Keuka Lake. Throughout the area are hiking trails. History buffs will find the native American connection fascinating: the building sits in the Gu-ya-no-ga valley named for the Seneca tribal chief who once lived on this land. The house is self-catering and completely furnished with linens and kitchenware; decor is attractive country-style with area rugs, quilts, and spreads. Check out the website for more than 100 other house, condo, cottage, and luxury home rentals on Keuka, Seneca, and Canandaigua lakes.

10,000 DELIGHTS B&B
607-868-3731
1170 West Lake, Rte. 54A,
  Branchport NY 14418
Innkeeper: Vera Van Atta
Rooms: 10, some shared
  baths
Open: Year-round
Price: $–$$
Credit cards: No

You have a delicious choice: stay in the Lake House, the apartment, or in one of the six rooms in the Greek Revival-style home. With fifty acres of woods and waterfalls, private beach, canoe, paddle boat, canoe, gardens, a Japanese tea-house, and a new treehouse with stained glass windows, there is plenty to discover outside as well. Rooms feature stenciling, wide plank floors, wood paneling, and eighteenth-century beams; furnishings include antiques, quilts, vintage dolls, and original art work. Gourmet breakfasts.

Hammondsport

MOTELS AND HOTELS

CABOOSE MOTEL
607-566-2216;
  fax 607-566-3817
caboosemotel.net
8620 Rte. 415, Avoca NY
  14809
Innkeeper: Sean O'Keefe
Rooms: 23
Open: Year-round
Price: $–$$
Credit cards: Most major

A combination of a conventional motel and 1916 train cabooses where you can sleep in one of five vintage cars (or in one of eighteen motel rooms). You get the whole caboose: bathroom, shower, air-conditioning, television, and coffee and tea service. The original cabinets, train seats, and walls are all basically in the same operating condition. There's even the sound of a train, but if you find the sound annoying rather than soothing, you can turn down the volume. There is a double or single bed on the main floor as well as bunk beds in the cupola area. Don't expect elegance. Think fun, nutty, novel. You'll remember this night. It ranks right up there with sleeping in teepees, silos, and lighhouses. There is also a heated outdoor pool and a playground. The motel, is, well, a motel (functional).

**HAMMONDSPORT
  MOTEL**
607-569-2600
PO Box 311; corner Williams
  and Water Sts.,
  Hammondsport NY 14840
Innkeepers: Ralph and
  Maxine Brown

Don't let the neon sign on the end of the building turn you off. If you're a no-frills kind of person and care mostly about being right on the shore at an economical price, this motel might be a good bet. It sits out on a little piece of land jutting into the water and is simply furnished in a 60ish style. Rooms are clean and half of the rooms come

Rooms: 17 with baths
Open: Apr. 1–mid-Nov.
Price: $
Credit cards: Visa, MC

with views of the lake. There are smoking and non-smoking rooms and they have televisions, air-conditioning, radios, and phones; coffee is available in the office mornings. There is a pretty gazebo on the end of the property near the water. Boat launch and dock space are on site; a public beach and main shopping area are within easy walking distance.

VINEHURST INN
607-569-2300
www.vinehurstinn.com
Rte. 54, Hammondsport NY
 14840
Innkeeper: Jim Heil
Rooms: 25 with private
 baths
Open: Year-round
Price: $–$$
Credit cards: All major

Ever since Jim Heil bought this place two years ago, he has been in the middle of a major renovation program to bring this circa mid-60s hotel/motel up to par. Near the southern tip of Keuka Lake, the property has a multitude of room styles, including efficiencies, apartments, and suites. All baths have been updated, the exercise room is new, and a new patio is out front with tables and trellis. Also new are the themed suites: one is based on a winery theme, another on an Adirondack cabin. Some suites come with cathedral ceilings, a king or queen bed, and sitting room with a double whirlpool. Rooms are furnished in a homey style, each one a bit different. There is a family activity area with volleyball, croquet, and other games, and a new conference room. Included in the rates is a continental breakfast.

BED & BREAKFASTS

AMITY ROSE B&B
607-569-3408, 800-982-8818
www.blushingroseinn.com
8264 Main St., Hammonds-
 port NY 14840
Innkeepers: Ellen and
 Frank Laufersweiler
Rooms: 4 with private
 baths
Open: Closed mid-
 Dec.–mid-Apr.
Price: $$
Credit cards: Cash or
 personal & travelers
 checks only

Although it's not as close to the lake as its sister property, the Blushing Rose (see below), and in fact is on a main route leading into town, this simple frame house is still a homey, comfortable B&B. Rooms are named after the Laufersweilers' daughters: Emma, Ellen, Dawn, and Hannah. Floral wallpaper, lace, and Waverly-style fabrics are used throughout. Dawn's Delight has a queen bed, sitting area, and balcony. Ellen's Retreat, on the ground floor, features a fourposter queen bed, whirlpool tub, and a private entrance. Full breakfasts are served in the simple but pleasant dining room.

BLUSHING ROSE B&B
607-569-3402, 800-982-8818
www.blushingroseinn.com
11 William St., Hammonds-
 port NY 14840

An 1843 Italianate home with period-furnished rooms on the lacey, flowery side. The Laufersweilers have used brass, four-poster, and antique queen and king beds, deep New England colors

Peter Finger

Blushing Rose B&B, Hammondsport, is the sister property to Amity Rose B&B.

Innkeepers: Ellen and
   Frank Laufersweiler
Rooms: 4 with private
   baths
Open: Closed mid-
   Dec.–mid-Apr.
Price: $$
Credit cards: Cash or
   personal & travelers
   checks only

like reds and greens, quilts, wainscoting, stenciling, wicker chairs with plump cushions, dried flower arrangements, area rugs, and lots of small accessories. The Burgundy Room has a king-size bed and sitting area; the magnificent Walnut Room has a walnut (what else) queen bed with ruffles. Just a block from the public beach and the main shopping square, this is a pleasant, well-maintained home. A large porch runs across the front of the house lined with chairs. Non-smoking, air-conditioned; no pets please.

**FEATHER TICK'N
   THYME B&B**
607-522-4113
7661 Tuttle Rd., off Italy
   Hill Rd., Prattsburgh NY
   14873 (Hammondsport
   area)
Innkeepers: Ruth, Deb, and
   Greg Cody
Rooms: 4 private and
   shared baths
Open: Year-round
Price: $$
Credit cards: Most major

This 1890s Victorian country home sits in the middle of eighty acres surrounded by open fields and trees. The rooms are furnished with a mix of antiques, quilts, and period reproductions. Sit on the wrap-around porch and sip an early morning cup of coffee. Freshly baked muffins, breads, and a full-course breakfast are provided. This B&B is non-smoking; no pets.

**GONE WITH THE WIND
ON KEUKA LAKE B&B**
607-868-4603
453 W. Lake Rd./Rte. 54A
  Pulteney; mailing
  Branchport NY 14418
Innkeepers: Linda and
  Robert Lewis
Rooms: 10, some shared
  baths, some private
Open: Year-round
Price: $$
Credit cards: Cash or check

Relax with a cup of coffee, a good book, or a cocktail on the porch of this 1887 pillared county Victorian, or simply sit back and enjoy the lovely views of the lake and countryside. Rooms are in the main house and in a log lodge on the edge of the woods; all are different. For example, one has a southwestern theme, another a rustic feeling with a headboard made by a local Amish craftsman. The Rhett and Scarlet Hideaway on the second floor of the main house has a private veranda and a king-size bed. Rooms are tastefully uncluttered. There are some antiques and period reproductions, but the furnishings complement the theme of the room. Mattresses are new and mostly queen size; bathrooms may be accented by oak, brass, and marble. There is a solarium hot tub, three fireplaces, a private cove with a gazebo and dock, and a rowboat. It's a peaceful setting with several hiking trails fanning out from the property and no televisions or phones to distract.

**J.S. HUBBS B&B &
  Stonehedge Guest
  House**
607-569-2440;
  fax 607-868-4355
www.jshubbs.com
17 Shethar St.,
  Hammondsport NY
  14840
Innkeepers: Walter Carl
  and Linda Elias-Carl
Rooms: 4 with private
  baths plus cottage on the
  lake
Open: All year
Price: $$
Credit cards: Visa, MC

Surrounded by a wrought iron fence and gardens, this historic 1840 Greek Revival in the middle of town is in the exact place where Judge Hammond had his original log cabin. The house features period furniture, antiques, a fireplace in the sitting room, original wallpaper on some walls, and high ceilings with deep moldings. The four air-conditioned guestrooms are all different. The Captain John Shethar Room has a queen-size bed and a nice free-standing mirror. The Judge Lazarus Hammond Room, named after the founder of Hammondsport, has a canopy queen-size bed and the largest bathroom in the house. The largest room in the house, the Adsit-Pierce Suite, has a queen-size bed and sitting room with a sofa bed, television/vcr, and desk. From the bright airy cupola, you get great views of the lake and town. Breakfast includes fruit and special dishes such as cheese strata or cottage cheese pancakes along with something fresh from the oven like rolls or coffee cake.

Stonehedge Cottage: The Carls also have a cottage on the lake two miles from Hammondsport. It sits on a private beach with its own swimming area, and has three floors with a spiral staircase connecting each level. The living room on the top floor has a large deck; the kitchen is fully equipped. The cottage can sleep five to six people. Cost is $875/week (includes all utilities and taxes) + $500 security deposit; cost can be pro-rated for shorter or longer stays (607-868-4358).

PLEASANT VALLEY INN AND RESTAURANT
607-569-2282
www.pleasantvalleyinn.com
7979 Rte. 54,
Hammondsport NY 14840
Innkeepers: Marianne and Tom Simons
Rooms: 4 with private baths
Open: May–Nov.
Price: $$
Credit cards: Most major

This grand 1848 Victorian is two miles out of town on a property surrounded by large trees and vineyards. Air-conditioned rooms, recently renovated, are furnished in a Victorian style, some with queen-size four-poster beds. A continental breakfast is served on the porches overlooking the vineyards. There is a restaurant in the house serving candlelight dinners Thursday through Sunday. Rack of lamb is recommended by the owner/chef; steak is also a good choice. The Simonses supply their kitchens with herbs grown from their garden and like to use local fruits and vegetables.

COTTAGE RENTALS

WRIGHT'S COTTAGES ON WANETA LAKE
607-292-6786
9472 Lakeshore Dr.,
Hammondsport NY 14840
Owners/Managers: James and Mary Ann Wright
Rooms: 5 cottages
Open: Apr.–Nov.
Price: 2 nights $$–$$$
Credit cards: Check or cash

Between Seneca and Keuka lakes, this cottage complex is popular with families and groups. There are five furnished board-and-batten cottages with fireplaces and 250 feet of lakefront. Kitchens come with a stove and refrigerator, microwave, and gas grill plus all basic appliances. There is a television/vcr in each cottage (but only two cabins have cable). Each cottage has its own lot and campfire pit ; a large common area of lawns and trees leads down to the water where there is a long dock and a raft. Kids of all ages will find plenty of water toys: rowboats, paddle boats, a raft, kayaks, and canoes. A scenic trail runs along the lake for two and a half miles and there are a lot of country roads perfect for walking. This is a quiet place — if you crave night life, you should go somewhere else. The hot entertainment here is singing around the campfire. Wood is provided for your fireplace and for campfires; bring your own towels and bedding. Wayne Market is within walking distance for ice cream, hot dogs, and hamburgers, and anything else you might need from movie rentals to steak. The nearest laundromat is in Penn Yan.

Penn Yan

MOTELS AND HOTELS

COLONIAL MOTEL AND RESORT CENTER
315-536-3056, 800-724-3008
175 W. Lake Rd., Penn Yan NY 14527
Innkeepers: Nancy and Dan Brooks
Rooms: 17
Open: Year-round
Price: $$
Credit cards: Most major

This family-owned and operated hotel is a combination of a colonial house and a two-story motel. It's just across the road from the lake. All but three of the air-conditioned accommodations are efficiencies; neat, clean, cottage-style but not elaborate. The appliances have been updated and there are coffeemakers and toasters. Many like to sit on the patio in front of the motel where a fire is lit in a fire pit each evening. If you're visiting Keuka College, this one is just a mile away. Year-round and weekly rates available.

VIKING RESORT
315-536-7061;
fax 315-536-0737
viking@vikingresort.com;
www.vikingresort.com
680 E. Lake Road, Rte. 54, Penn Yan NY 14527
Innkeeper: Ken Christensen
Rooms: 39 plus a 6- and a 3-bedroom cottage
Open: Mid-May–mid-Oct.
Price: $–$$$$
Credit cards: Most major

This no-frills cabin and motel resort has efficiencies, apartments, suites, and rooms furnished in a 50s knotty-pine mode. The whole complex is spotless: owner Ken Christensen credits his Norwegian ancestry for this. There is more than 1,000 feet of lakeshore, perfect for swimming and boating. There's also a hot tub and outdoor pool, fishing, free rowboats, pontoon boat, and power boat rentals. Guests often look forward to a late afternoon lake cruise aboard *The Viking Spirit* party boat or perhaps a sail with Ken on his 38-foot A-Scow. Docking facilities are available for privately owned boats. This is a family-oriented place with plenty of watersports and a bonfire every night.

BED & BREAKFASTS

FINTON'S LANDING B&B
315-536-3146;
fax 315-536-3791
http://home.eznet.net/~tepperd
661 E. Lake Rd., Penn Yan NY 14527
Innkeepers: Doug and Arianne Tepper
Rooms: 4 with private baths

Sitting in the restored gazebo on the lake, you can almost imagine steamboats plying the waters as they did at the turn of the century. Actually, they would have pulled into the dock here: in the 1860s, Finton's was a steamboat landing. It's the only B&B right on Keuka Lake between Penn Yan and Hammondsport. Enjoy breakfast on the spacious wrap-around porch of this pretty Victorian or simply relax in one of the rocking

Open: Please call
Price: $$
Credit cards: MC, Visa,
    checks

chairs. There are 165 feet of private beach and a marvelous redwood dock with a bench on the end, a perfect perch for romantic interludes — so perfect, in fact, that owner Doug Tepper says couples often get engaged there. There is also a hammock for two by the beach. Furnished in a comfortable Adirondacks style, all rooms are air-conditioned. The Garden Room with a queen bed looks out onto a wildflower garden filled with special plantings that attract birds and butterflies; many plants date from Victorian times. The Wisteria Room has a double bed and is directly on the lake. The Cherub Room, with a queen mahogany four-poster is also on the lake and has a larger bath. Acorn and Oak Leaves has both a brass double bed and Victorian metal twin bed. You can see the lake from the room, but the better view is of a stream and a row of grape vines. Of interest in this historic home are the many photos, maps, and artifacts dating from the days of the steamboats. Finton's Landing appeals to those who love nature; many bikers and hikers stay here. Breakfasts are not only hearty, but feature a lot of fresh produce from local farms, perhaps strawberries, peaches, or pears. Starting with fresh fruit and often sorbet, you may move on to buttermilk waffles, buckwheat pancakes, or havarti baked eggs. Along with your French batards, you are offered homemade jams made from plums, raspberries, and other regional fruits. This is a no smoking, no pets place. Children more than ten years of age are welcome.

THE FOX INN B&B
315-536-3101, 800-901-7997
cliforr@aol.com; www.yate
    sny. com/fox_inn
158 Main St., Penn Yan NY
    14527
Innkeepers: Cliff and
    Michele Orr
Rooms: 6 with private
    baths
Open: Year-round
Price: $$
Credit cards: Most major

Right on Main Street just a block from the center of town, the yellow brick Fox Inn is surrounded by wide lawns with huge trees; rose gardens bloom profusely from May through October. Built in 1820 by William Morris Oliver, the first judge of Yates County and a New York State senator, lieutenant governor, and U.S. congressman, this property should appeal to those who love traditional elegance. The new owners have furnished this gracious 1820s pillared Greek Revival house with an exceptional collection of antiques, artwork, and reproductions. Some rooms have a fireplace and whirlpool bath; all have television/vcr. The William Fox Suite has two bedrooms with a large country bathroom. There is a large billiard room, a living room with a marble fireplace, sunporch with flowers and plants, and a formal dining room. Gourmet breakfasts include fresh fruit, muffins, several types of pancakes, French toast, and eggs. The inn has rooms for small receptions and meetings. For business travelers, wordprocessing, copying, and e-mail services are available.

MERRITT HILL MANOR B&B
315-536-7682
www.merritthillmanor.com
2756 Coates Rd., Penn Yan
NY 14527
Innkeepers: Susan and
Marc Hyser
Rooms: 5 with private
baths
Open: Year-round
Price: $$
Credit cards: MC, Visa

This 1822 Federal-style country home on the crest of a hill offers spectacular views of Keuka and Seneca lakes and the hills leading to Canandaigua. On twelve acres, the house is surrounded by open pasture land and gardens; a stream runs through the property. The guestrooms are exceptionally large; rooms #1 and #5 are the ones to ask for if you want to nonstop vistas of this lovely countryside. You can also relax and soak it all up in the Adirondack chairs on the lawn. Once thought to be one of the havens on the Underground Railroad, this is one of the grander B&Bs in the area. Each of the rooms is tastefully furnished with antiques and period reproductions. Full breakfasts may include German apple pancakes or blueberry French toast, along with a large selection of fresh fruit and homemade bread or muffins.

The Trimmer House B&B in Penn Yan is a restored Victorian home with period furnishings.

Peter Finger

TRIMMER HOUSE B&B
315-536-8304, 800-968-8735
www.bbonline.com_ny_
trimmer
145 E. Main St., Penn Yan
NY 14527
Innkeeper: Gary Smith
Rooms: 5 with private
baths (1 with 2
bedrooms)

Once the home of wine merchant David Orville Trimmer, this lovely restored 1891 Victorian house is now owned by Gary Smith, a professor of hospitality management at Keuka College. His Queen Anne style home is furnished with period wall coverings and fabrics; rooms have air-conditioning and television/vcr. Special features of the house include hand-oiled oak, cypress and mahogany woodwork, marble and oak floors,

Open: Year-round
Price: $$
Credit cards: Visa, MC

painted ceilings, and chandeliers. There are two parlors, a library with fireplace, a formal dining room and music room as well as an outdoor hot tub. Guests enjoy a full breakfast, and complimentary snacks and beverages. Trimmer House is within walking distance of restaurants and shops.

TUDOR HALL B&B
315-536-9962
762 E. Bluff Drive, Penn
Yan NY 14527
Innkeepers: Priscilla and
Don Erickson
Rooms: 3 suites with
private baths
Open: Apr.–Thanksgiving;
check for off-season
Price: $$
Credit cards: Visa, MC

This Tudor-style house has a decidedly English feel inside and out. It's right on the lake at the site of a former steamboat landing — one of the suites is sited where grapes were kept in cold storage until the steamboat could transport them to market. This suite comes with a kitchen and private entrance. All suites have great views of the lake and sitting areas; the 400-square-foot Royal Suite has a four-poster canopy bed and a private balcony overlooking the lake. All come with television, phone, refrigerator, and coffeemaker. There are terraced gardens, a private beach, and three boats: a rowboat, canoe, and paddle boat. There is also a power boat that the Ericksons use to take their guests on lake cruises and a twenty-foot pontoon boat which can be rented. Gourmet breakfasts are served by candlelight using crystal and china — the whole works.

THE WAGENER ESTATE
315-536-4591;
fax 315-531-8142
www.wagenerestate.com
351 Elm St., Penn Yan NY
14527
Innkeeper: Lisa Akers and
Ken Greenwood
Rooms: 6, 4 with private
baths
Open: Year-round
Price: $$
Credit cards: Most major

Built in 1794, this gracious old colonial farmhouse is set on a magnificent four-acre property with sweeping lawns, trees, and flowering shrubs. It once contained an extensive orchard and many of these trees are still here: pear, apple, and cherry trees along with maples, sycamores, and pines — a virtual arboretum. A large porch furnished with many chairs overlooks the lawns with a peek of the lake through the trees; a hammock invites a late afternoon snooze. Furnishings include country antiques; rooms come with televisions. The Delaware Room, with its own bathroom and private deck and entrance, is a good choice. In the morning find a breakfast ranging from a country spread to a three-course gourmet deal. Fresh fruit and entrées such as banana-stuffed French toast with blueberry compote or buckwheat pancakes with apple cider syrup are offered; on Sundays you get dessert.

Vacation Rentals and Services

Lakespell Vacation Rentals (315-536-9234; www.yatesny.com/lakespell) Manager Cliff Orr offers cottages on the lake accommodating 6 to 26 people including private villa and manor. Private lake frontage, boat rentals. Open year-round, summer for weekly rentals only; off-season weekends only. Check or cash only; no credit cards.

Rental Plus (888-414-5253; fax 315-595-2825; www.rentalplus.com) President/manager Brian Zerges has more than 100 house, condo, cottage, and luxury home rentals on Keuka, Seneca, and Canandaigua Lakes. Visa, MC.

RESTAURANTS

Keuka is the star when it comes to restaurants right on the lake. Several provide docks and tie-up facilities so you can arrive by boat. Many of the wineries have restaurants with local wines prominantly featured on the menu. Regional specialities include fresh fish from the lakes and produce from the regional markets. Some restaurants offer Amish and Mennonite food.

Prices are estimated per person for appetizer and dinner entrée without tax, tip, or alcoholic beverages.

$: Up to $10
$$: $11–$25
$$$: $26–$40
$$$$: More than $40

Branchport

KNOTTY PINE INN
607-868-4664
293 W. Lake Rd.,
　Branchport NY 14418
Open: Memorial
　Day–Labor Day
Tues.–Sun.; winter hours
　vary
Price: $–$$$
Serving: D
Cuisine: Continental,
　American
Credit cards: Most major

A cozy log cabin on the water well known for serving great prime rib. Also good are the steaks, crab legs, fried fish, chicken parmesan, and stuffed mushrooms. The decor is casual with snappy hunter green table linens. Eat outdoors on the deck overlooking the lake or inside in the dining room where a fire warms you up in the winter.

Hammondsport

BULLY HILL RESTAURANT
607-868-3490
www.bullyhill.com
8834 Greyton H. Taylor Memorial Dr., Hammondsport NY 14840 (at the Wine Museum of Greyton H. Taylor)
Open: Apr.–Nov.
Price: $–$$
Serving: L 11:30–4, D Fri. & Sat. 5–9
Cuisine: American, California bistro
Credit cards: Most major

Besides good food and good portions, you have a wonderful hilltop view of the vineyards, gardens, and the lake. There are two dining rooms with copper-topped tables, as well as a large deck with umbrella tables. The Maryland blue crabcakes, grilled chicken salad with honey-Dijon mustard dressing, garlic-laced pureed eggplant with shrimp, and grilled chicken with applewood-smoked bacon and smoked mozzarella cheese are excellent. Vegetarian dishes include pizza, a garden medley vegetable burger topped with a portabella mushroom, and grilled veggies. Cuisine is prepared from fresh ingredients and local produce. While there, be sure to stop at the Greyton H. Taylor Wine Museum and the new visitor center and sample some of their wines. My favorite: Chardonnay Elise, a simple clean dry wine.

CAFÉ ALFRESCA
607-569-2009
45 Shethar St., Hammondsport NY 14840
Open: Apr.–Dec. Tues.–Sun.
Price: $
Serving: B, L, Sun. brunch
Cuisine: Bistro-style
Credit cards: Most major

Treadle sewing machines used for tables, painted wood chairs, and interesting artwork create a unique ambiance for an eclectic menu with unusual pizzas, freshly baked breads, and coffees, desserts, and sandwiches. This is a delightfully inviting small café right on the square.

LAKESIDE RESTAURANT
607-868-3636
800 W. Lake Rd., Hammondsport NY 14840
Open: Year-round
Price: $$
Serving: L, D
Cuisine: Continental, American
Credit cards: Most major

Come by car or boat and dine overlooking the west side of the lake from this restored Victorian home. You can sit on the outdoor patios or inside in the attractive dining room. New owners Jeffrey and Kathleen Bates and Jeffrey's parents, Joan and Jerry Bates, say they like using fresh, not frozen, ingredients. The lunch menu includes items such as a warm steak salad and mache greens with peppercorn chevre and frizzled leeks, and pan-seared scallops with a chipotle pepper and tomato compote. For dinner try prime rib served with garlic mashed potatoes, catfish oreganata served in a lemon-artichoke butter sauce over herbed long grain rice, or eggplant and portabella stacks. The restaurant has been upgraded with renovations to the bar area and new decks. There are seventeen boat slips and a dining room for private parties on the second floor. The Bates family also caters parties on the *Viking Spirit* cruise boat.

Peter Finger

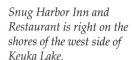
Snug Harbor Inn and Restaurant is right on the shores of the west side of Keuka Lake.

SNUG HARBOR INN & RESTAURANT
607-868-SNUG (7684),
  607-868-7684
144 W. Lake Rd.,
  Hammondsport NY
  14840
Open: Year-round
Price: $–$$
Serving: L, D; check for
  off-season hours
Cuisine: American,
  Continental
Credit cards: Most major

Right on the shores of Keuka Lake, you can arrive here by car or boat. The three-story building, dating from 1889, was once a private lakeside cottage, and later a small hotel — guests were ferried here by steamboat from the village landing. It has open decks plus indoor dining rooms; tables are attractively appointed with linen tablecloths and napkins and candles. New owner Michael Evarts emphasizes that just about everything (except ice cream and French fries) is prepared from fresh, not frozen, ingredients. Chef Dave Frascella offers items such as prime aged beef, beer battered cod, medallions of veal sautéed and served with a peppercorn demi-glaze and fresh mushrooms, and chocolate obsession cake. Everything is made from scratch including cakes, breads, pies, and dressings. An excellent selection of international wines complements the menu. Banquet facilities are available for private parties.

A two-bedroom efficiency apartment on third floor rents for $150 per night. Not luxurious, but roomy with great views of the water from the big old private deck. There are twenty-four boat slips for those coming by water.

THE VILLAGE TAVERN
607-569-2528;
　fax 607-569-3560
www.villagetaverninn.com
On the Square,
　Hammondsport NY
　14840
Open: Daily
Price: $$
Serving: L, D
Cuisine: American,
　international
Credit cards: Most major

On a corner of the village square in Hammondsport, this one pulls in the crowds especially for their Friday fish fries. You can eat at tables outside in good weather as well as inside in the restaurant next to the bar area. In addition to fish and seafood dishes, the extensive menu includes speciality items such as tournedos Rossini with truffles, Thai chicken, and roasted New Zealand lamb. A bistro menu is also available with simpler fare. Most prefer to sit in the bar area.

THE WATERFRONT
　RESTAURANT
607-868-3455
648 W. Lake Rd./Rte. 54A,
　Pulteney (6.5 miles north
　of Hammondsport)
Open: Daily Apr.–Oct. 31
Price: $–$$
Serving: L Sat. & Sun., D
　daily
Cuisine: Ribs, seafood
Credit cards: Most major

Come by boat or car for food and drink at this casual waterside restaurant that almost hangs over the water. Eleven boat slips are often full, especially on Sundays in July and August when the popular clambake is held along with a live music concert, Jimmy Buffett-style. Many anchor just off shore to listen to the concert. When all the slips have been taken, people have been known to jump into the water and swim in to pick up their clams. Sit on one of the multiple open-air decks, some right over the water, or the air-conditioned dining room. Grilled meats, fish, and pasta are popular fare as well as fish and chips; crab legs and clams a speciality. Very lively in the summer.

Penn Yan

ANTIQUE INN
315-536-6576
2940 Rte. 54A, Penn Yan
　NY 14527
Open: Sun. 12noon–8pm;
　Memorial Day–Labor
　Day Mon.-Sat. 11–9,
　after Labor Day 11–8
Price: $–$$
Serving: L, D
Cuisine: American
Credit cards: Most major

A casual, rustic family-style place with reasonably priced good food. Specialities include haddock, pasta dishes, and seafood. Try the spaghetti sauce: they make it themselves. The fried fish, fried oysters, and liver and onions are local favorites. Some prefer to eat in the bar; same menu.

LLOYDS LIMITED "A PUB"
315-536-9029
3 Main St., Penn Yan NY 14527
Open: daily, after 4
Price: $
Serving: D, late night service
Cuisine: English pub, American
Credit cards: Check or cash only

Pure Finger Lakes vintage: tin ceiling, historic photos of area on walls, beer and wine memorabilia, old Readers' Digests, blow-up beer bottles, 1910 skates, old keg taps — you name it. Starting life as a bar, Lloyds has added booths and casual pub dinners serving things like pizza, chicken wings, potato skins, and other finger foods. Loyal to the Finger Lakes, Lloyds serves wines only from area vineyards. At this community hangout, you can order a beer and some Buffalo wings, and linger in a booth reading a paper. Walls and booths are dark-stained wood. Very cozy.

MILLER'S ESSENHAUS
315-531-8260
1300 Rte. 14A, Penn Yan NY 14527
Open: Year-round Mon.–Sat. 8am–9pm
Price: $–$$
Serving: B, L, D
Cuisine: Home-baked Amish-style foods
Credit cards: Most major

When it comes to fresh and homemade it doesn't get much better. Everything possible is made right here. There's a bakery that turns out mouthwatering sticky buns, rolls, pies, apple crisp, cheesecake, and other goodies; popular dinner items include chicken and biscuits and orange-glazed pork. Local fresh produce is used whenever possible. In a new building, the decor is fresh and pleasant. Handmade quilts hang on the walls, brass lanterns provide light, and hand-painted chairs are arranged around linen-covered tables. Saturday mornings they roll out a super buffet with lots of pastries, sticky buns, fresh fruits, breakfast casserole, French toast, and oatmeal. Retail bakery and gift shop on the premises.

RED ROOSTER
315-536-9800
12 Maiden Ln., Penn Yan NY 14527
Open: Mon.–Fri. 11–closing, Sat. from 4
Price: $
Serving: L, D
Credit cards: Cash or check

Casual dining here is especially popular with families. Tables are set around a central bar. Prime rib is great here, as well as steaks, pasta, hamburgers, onion rings, and finger foods. Walls are decorated with early 1900s pictures from Penn Yan. And there's a good selection of wines and beer on tap.

CASUAL FOOD

Crooked Lake Ice Cream Company (607-569-2751; Shethar St., on the Square, Hammondsport NY 14840) Old-fashioned ice-cream parlor with original tin ceiling and soda fountain dating from 1948. Counter and booths look like the originals. The hot fudge sundaes, topped with mounds of whipped cream and a cherry, cost $2.45 to $3.25; cones are $1.25 and $2.18. Also ice-cream floats, old fashioned phosphates, sodas, shakes and other temptations. Open daily 7–7; Sun. 8–5.

Grapevine Florist and Gifts (607-569-2105; 68 Shether St., Hammondsport NY 14840) The only ice cream parlor I know of that's in a florist shop. Take out cones, milkshakes, sundaes, and floats, or eat at one of the tables just outside on the garden patio. It's really very pleasant. Open seasonally for ice cream 11–10 daily; gift and flower shop open year-round.

CULTURE

At the turn of the century, Hammondsport was buzzing with activity around the work of aviation pioneer Glenn H. Curtiss. Recognized as the father of naval aviation, Curtiss co-created the first powered aircraft, trained the first American woman pilot, built the first transatlantic aircraft, and attained a number of world speed records. And that was just the beginning. People came from all over the world to the Curtiss Motor Company in Hammondsport, where engines and aircraft were being manufactured and developed, including the famous Jenny JN-4s WWI plane.The Glenn Curtiss Museum on Rte. 54 is filled with actual planes and memorabilia from the life and achievements of this innovative hometown hero.

In 1860, the Pleasant Valley Wine Company, producer of Great Western Champagne, was founded south of Hammondsport. A comprehensive visitor center tells the story of the winery and the growth of the industry in the area. Over the years, more than a dozen wineries have been established around the lake. An important museum at Bully Hill Vineyards explores the growth of the wine industry.

Annual festivals here celebrate the grape harvest and native American customs and history.

Bath

Bath Veterans Administration Medical Center Historical Museum and National Cemetery (607-664-4772; Veterans Ave., Bath NY 14810) Red brick buildings and a large landscaped campus make the center seems more like a college than a medical center. Established in 1878, a museum on the grounds contains artifacts dating from the Civil War to the present. The cemetery holds the graves of five Medal of Honor recipients and twenty-nine unknown soldiers from the War of 1812 along with thousands of other veterans. Open Apr.–Oct. Tues., Thurs., & Fri. 10–3; Sat. by appointment.

Magee House (607-776-3582; Cameron Park, Bath NY 14810) This house contains early American artifacts such as an original mail carrier's bike. Mon.–Fri. 10–3, Sun. by appointment.

Hammondsport

The Glenn H. Curtiss Museum, Hammondsport, is filled with vintage aircraft and motorcycles along with other early transportation marvels.

Peter Finger

Glenn H. Curtiss Museum (607-569-2160; www.linkny.com/CurtissMuseum; 8419 Rte. 54, Hammondsport NY 14840) Inspired by Hammondsport's Glenn Curtiss, whose daring adventures with early motorcycles, dirigibles, and airplanes thrilled the country. His June Bug was the first aircraft to fly one mile, and he organized a Flying Circus bringing colorful barnstormers to Hammondsport. The museum, housed in a huge warehouse-like building, contains memorabilia from the early days of aviation. See June Bug II, Curtiss "Jenny," a tractor biplane 1913 "flying boat," vintage autos, motorcycles, bicycles, antique toys, and even winemaking memorabilia. More than seventeen aircraft, early motorcycles, and the first "mobile home" are here. In the workshop see how airplanes are constructed and restored. Open daily Apr.–Nov. 9–5.

Greyton H. Taylor Wine Museum (607-868-3610; www.bullyhill.com; 8843 Greyton H. Taylor Memorial Dr. off Rte. 54A, Bully Hill Vineyards, Hammondsport NY 14840) Impressive collection of eighteenth-century vineyard equipment, winemaking supplies, and brandy and cooper production in a rustic barn-like building. Also lots of memorabilia relating to the history of the area. First wine museum in America. Open daily May–Nov. Mon.–Sat. 9–5, Sun. 12–5.

Pleasant Valley Visitor Center and Great Western Winery (607-569-6111; 8260 Pleasant Valley Rd./County Rte. 88, Hammondsport NY 14840) It's not just that this is the winery that started it all in 1860 and is the home of Great

Western champagnes, but the fabulous stone buildings and Great Western Winery Visitor Center that makes this a must-see. The eight stone buildings are listed on the National Register of Historic Places and the visitor center provides a comprehensive history of wine with exhibits, displays, and wine tastings. Don't miss the Wine Cask Theater. Open Jan.–May Tues.–Sat. 10–4, Apr.–Dec. daily 10–5. (See the listing in Chapter Eight, *Wineries*, for more information.)

Penn Yan

Agricultural Memories Museum (315-536-1206; 1100 Townline Rd., Penn Yan NY 14527) See John Deere tractors, horse-drawn carriages from the 1800s, engines, toys, and other farm-related items. Open June–Nov. Sun. 1–4 or by appointment.

Birkett Mills, a historic mill in Penn Yan, still produces buckwheat flour products.

Peter Finger

The Birkett Mills (315-536-3311; 1 Main St., Penn Yan NY 14527) This imposing yellow brick building displaying a giant griddle is at the end of Main Street. Although it was constructed in 1824, the original mill operation dates back to 1796. The mill still grinds flour, including the highly prized buckwheat flour, and sells a variety of food products.

Garrett Memorial Chapel (end of Skyline Drive, Bluff Point, between Branchport & Penn Yan) A lovely Gothic stone Episcopal chapel built in memory of Charles William Garrett, the son of a wealthy wine merchant. William died in his twenties of tuberculosis. Poems the young man had loved are represented on the stained glass windows of the crypt. Known as the "Chapel on the Mount," it's set in one of the most scenic areas of the Finger Lakes.

Norton Chapel (Keuka College, W. Lake Rd., Penn Yan NY 14527) Catch the light streaming through the magnificent stained glass windows designed by Gabriel Loire of Chartres Cathedral fame.

Oliver House Museum (315-536-7318; ycghs@linkny.com; 200 Main St., Penn Yan NY 14527) The nineteenth-century brick home of the Oliver family is now filled with local history and genealogical information. Most of the rooms on the first floor are furnished with pieces from the Victorian period, including a large array of china. The second floor contains a good collection of historical materials from Yates County, often used for research by students and genealogists. Changing exhibits. Open all year Mon.–Fri. 9:30–4:30.

Photo Ops

Bluff Point (off Rte. 54A to Skyline Dr.; between Branchport & Penn Yan) At one end of an eleven-mile bluff separating the two branches of Keuka Lake. Across the top of the bluff, Skyline Drive, a scenic road, takes you to the crook of the two prongs. The Wagener Mansion is at the top of the bluff; the Garrett Memorial Chapel is barely visible in the trees on the east side of the hill. From here you can look out to the east side of the lake to Marlena Point. Some say you can see several counties and a dozen lakes on a clear day.

Hammondsport's village square: With its Tudor-style gazebo, it's classic early Americana.

Old railroad station and vintage rail car: On the waterfront (on Water Street) next to the public beach in Hammondsport.

RECREATION

Nature plays a big role in the recreational pursuits of those who come to Keuka Lake. Swimming, waterskiing, sailing, kayaking, canoeing, and fishing are all pursued on and in Keuka's clean, beautiful water. Sometimes the lake freezes over and it becomes a giant ice-skating rink.

The gentle hills, good roads, and dense forested parklands that surround the lake provide wonderful opportunities for bikers, hikers, campers, and horseback riders. Golf courses, some winding through old vineyards, treat players to spectacular views of lake and hills.

BIKING

The bike trip around the outer perimeter of the lake is forty-six miles. Grades are moderate so it's a pretty easy ride.

Hammondsport-area winery route: From the center of Hammondsport, it's about a three-mile round trip to the Great Western Winery and Pleasant Valley Visitor Center. In another direction from town, going up Middle Road to Bully Hill Winery, it's a four and a half mile round trip.

Bike Rte. 17: A stretch of a 435-mile route that goes from the Hudson River to Lake Erie. Travel through small villages along rural roads with paved shoulders. Signed with green ovals and "17."

Bluff Point: Skyline Drive, a seven and a half mile road that runs along the crest of the gently mounded peninsula between the two branches of Keuka Lake, is one way to reach the area at the fork known as Bluff Point, well worth a stop for the views and a visit to Garrett Chapel. You can also take West Bluff and E. Bluff Drives to make a loop along the shorelines. A good place to push off on this 14.3-mile trip is Keuka College in Keuka Lake State Park. The trip can take all day if you visit vineyards along the way.

BOATING

The Keuka Maid *offers a variety of lake cruises in the summer.*

Peter Finger

CRUISES:

Keuka Maid Cruises (607-569-2628, fax 607-962-9589; www.keukamaid.com; south end of lake off Rte. 54, Hammondsport; off-season: 94 Cedar St., Corning NY 14830) Up to 450 people can be accommodated on lunch, dinner, and Sunday brunch cruises aboard the 107-foot three-deck, air-conditioned, and heated boat. The *Keuka Maid*, the dream of area entrepreneur Stanley M. Clark, was built in Hammondsport using area labor. Live entertainment is featured on Saturdays for dinner and moonlight cruises. After the boat docks at 9pm, the music continues and the bars remain open. Most

Saturdays, the boat goes out for a one-hour moonlight cruise around 11, free to those on board. Costs: Two-hour lunch cruise, $22.50; Sun. brunch, $26; dinner cruise, $30–$36. Available for parties and meetings. Runs May 1–Oct. 31.

Viking Spirit Tour and Party Boat (315-536-7061; viking@vikingresort.com; Rte. 54 just south of Penn Yan at the Viking Resort) Cruise Keuka Lake aboard a two-decker boat with climate-controlled lounge area with four-foot windows and open decks. Daily cruises at 5pm and group charters. Bring your own picnic.

MARINAS AND LAUNCHES:

Basin Park Marina (315-595-8808; 46 W. Lake Rd., Branchport NY 14418) Boat rentals, dockage, pontoons, winter storage, and ski boat rentals. Also three-bedroom cottage rental.

East Bluff Harbor Marina (315-536-8236; www.keukaonline.com; 654 E. Bluff Dr., Penn Yan NY 14527) A full-service marina with twenty slips, boat rentals, Four Winns sales, shop, and boats on consignment of all kinds.

Hammondsport Motel (607-569-2600) At the corner of Water and William St.

Harbor Club Boat Storage (315-595-6669; 42 W. Lake Rd., Branchport NY 14418) This facility offers docking with eighty-four slips, repairs, and storage only: no gas sales.

H.L. Watersports in Harbor Lights Marina (607-868-4848; 797 W. Lake Rd., Hammondsport NY 14840) A full-service marina affiliated with West Branch Marina, H.L. sells gas, bait, used boats, and kayaks; it also rents boats. Convenience store and boat launch as well as thirty slips.

Keuka Bay Marine Park (607-569-2777; www.keukaonline.com; 55 W. Lake Rd., Hammondsport NY 14840) The same owners as East Bluff, this marina has more than 130 slips as well as gas sales, snack stand, and boat rentals.

Keuka Lake State Park (3370 Pepper Rd., Bluff Point NY 14478) Boat launch facilities.

Morgan Marine (315-536-8166; 100 E. Lake Rd./Rte. 54, Penn Yan NY 14527) Motor, paddle, and sail boat rentals and sales; ski sales. Full-service repairs, dockage, storage.

North End Landings and Marina (315-595-2853; 3553 Rte. 54A, PO Box 322, Branchport NY 14418) Full-service marina, boat rentals, moorings, clubhouse, bait and tackle shop, and year-round cottage rentals.

Penn Yan Boat Launch (315-536-3015; corner of Water and Keuka Sts., Penn Yan NY 14527)

West Branch Marina (607-868-4677; 803 W. Lake Rd., Hammondsport NY 14840) Primarily storage, service, and boat rentals.

FISHING

Seth Green, a world-class fisherman, proclaimed that Keuka Lake has the finest fishing grounds in the world. Although other Finger Lakes might also make the same claim, there is no doubt that these waters are mighty good for catching rainbow trout, yellow perch, black bass, pickerel, and other lake fish.

GOLF

Bath Country Club (607-776-5043, May St., Bath NY 14810) This 18-hole, 6,400 yard, par 72 course is hilly and scenic with water coming into play on six holes. Greens fees are $24, $37 with a cart. Restaurant is open to public.

Lakeside Country Club (315-536-6251; 200 E. Lake Rd./Rte. 54, Penn Yan NY 14527) At the top of Keuka Lake in Penn Yan, the course runs right through a vineyard. Older push-up-style greens tend to fall towards the lake; greens rebuilt in 1995 are more level, some two-tiered. Fairways climb up and down the slopes revealing wonderful views of the lake and Keuka College. The sixteenth par 5 dogleg, which plays 416 yards into the wind, can be wicked. Once you make the bend you're in a gully and have to hit up to the green. Eleven and fourteen follow rows of grapes; fifteen is carved through them. On your way out, stop at the clubhouse and pick up some homemade grape jam and preserves. Greens fees are $35 plus $10 for a cart. On the property is a driving range, pro shop, and restaurant.

HIKING

Outlet Trail: The Keuka Lake Outlet, a six-mile ribbon of water connecting Keuka Lake with Seneca Lake, is now banked by a linear park, a pleasant place to hike and bike. The seven and a half mile trail takes you past mill ruins, through Lock 17 and remains of other locks, and by waterfalls and bridges. It runs from Penn Yan to Dresden with entrance points at either end and along the way.

Urbana State Forest (607-776-2165) Between Prattsburg and Hammondsport west of the southern end of the lake, this trail gives you two ways to go: the long route (7.1 miles) and the shorter loop (4.8 miles). Both take you along dirt trails, up a hill to a plateau where it's easier, through woods, and by Huckleberry Bog (no huckleberries but plenty of high and low bush blueberries). The well-marked trails go over streams and follow country lanes. From Rte. 17, go north on Rte. 53, then east on Bean Station Rd. Look for FLT signs (Finger Lakes Trail) after you pass Colegrove Rd.

PARKS, NATURE PRESERVES, AND CAMPING

Birdseye Hollow Park and State Forest (607-776-2165; Birdseye Hollow Rd., Bradford NY 14815) Self-guided trails for viewing animals and birds in the forest. You can fish here from a 200-foot pier. Pavilion, picnic tables, grill.

Camp Good Days and Special Times Recreational Facility (315-595-2779; 58 W. Lake Rd., Branchport NY 14418) A summer camp for children with cancer.

Flint Creek Campground (800-914-3550; 716-554-3567 season; 716-323-2406 winter; 1455 Phelps Rd./Rte. 364, Middlesex NY 14507) Midway between Canandaigua and Penn Yan. 120 sites have fire rings and picnic tables. Playground, pool, mini-golf, showers, laundry, electric, hook-ups, pavilion.

Hickory Hill Family Camping Resort (607-776-4345, 800-760-0947; 7531 Mitchellsville Rd., Bath NY 14810) Several camping sites, two pools, playground, hiking trails, full hook-ups, miniature golf, rec room, hayrides, basketball court, plus cottage and cabin rentals.

Indian Pines Park (315-536-3015; Rte. 54A, Penn Yan NY 14527) On the west side of Keuka Lake. Swimming, pavilion, picnic area with grills, playground, and volleyball.

Keuka Lake State Park (315-536-3666; 3370 Pepper Rd., Bluff Point NY 14478) A 621-acre park with pavilion, boat launch, hiking trails, bathhouses, fishing, and 150 campsites for tents and trailers.

Outlet Trail Park (315-536-3111; Lake St., Penn Yan NY 14527) Pavilion, picnic area with grills, playground, access to Keuka Outlet Trail.

Penn Yan Boat Launch (315-536-3015; Keuka and Water Sts., Penn Yan NY 14527) Basketball court, tennis, and boat launch.

Red Jacket Park (315-536-3015; Lake St., Penn Yan NY 14527) On the east shore of Keuka Lake's eastern branch. Pavilion for rent, swimming, picnic area with grills, playground.

Wagon Wheel Campground (607-522-3270; 10378 Presler Rd., Prattsburgh NY 14873) Close to vineyards and Keuka Lake. Pool, fishing ponds, recreation hall, entertainment, showers, laundry, LP gas. Exit 37N off Rte. 17; take Rte. 53 N., right on County Rd. 74.

Wigwam Keuka Lake Campground (315-536-6352; off Rte. 54A, up James Rd. to 3324 Esperanza Rd., Bluff Point NY 14478) If you're looking for great lake views, camp here. Sixty quiet, secluded sites, family oriented, playground, fishing pond, pool, rental cabins, tents, and trailer and seasonal sites. Open mid-May–mid-Oct.

OTHER ATTRACTIONS

Keuka Karts Go-Kart Track (315-536-4833; kkarts@eznet.net; 98 W. Lake Rd./Rte. 54A, Penn Yan NY 14527) Good family fun. Take a spin on a Go-Kart. Single and double karts. Open Apr.–Oct. varying days and hours.

NY State Fish Hatchery (607-776-7087, 7169 Fish Hatchery Rd., Bath NY 14810) See fish in various stages of growth from eggs to full size. Open daily Mon.–Fri. 8–3:45.

SHOPPING

Penn Yan's shopping is mostly along Main Street, anchored by Birkett Mills. Hammondsport's stores are arranged around the village square and down a couple of side streets. Just outside town is Mehlenbacher's Taffy, an old-fashioned candy store with hand-pulled candy. For airplane models and other transportation-related items, try the shop at the Glenn Curtiss Museum. Many of the wineries have nice shops selling everything from corkscrews to books on wines.

Hammondsport

ANTIQUES

Antiques at the Warehouse (607-569-3655; 8091 County Rte. 88, Hammondsport NY 14840) Open daily Apr.–Oct. 10–4; Nov.–Mar. by chance or appointment.

Opera House Antiques (607-569-3525; 61-63 Shethar St., Hammondsport NY 14840) Showcases merchandise of several dealers selling furniture, silver, paintings, prints, glass, collectibles and much more. Open daily Memorial Day–Dec. 10–5, Jan.–Memorial Day on Sat. & Sun.

Wild Goose Chase Antiques II (607-868-3946; 10060 County Rte. 76, Hammondsport NY 14840) Housed in an old vineyard barn, lots of goodies but open by chance or appointment Apr.–Nov.

CRAFTS AND GIFTS

Browsers (607-569-2497; 33 Shethar St., Hammondsport NY 14840) A variety of items not unlike a small department store: clothing, gifts, windchimes, flags, wood bowls, glassware, and much more.

The Cinnamon Stick (607-569-2277; www.cinnamonstick.com; 26 Mechanic St., Hammondsport NY 14840) An attractive shop with two levels of gifts such as dolls, candles, teddy bears, glassware, and a whole room filled with Christmas items including limited edition pieces.

Lake Country Patchwork (607-569-3530; 67 Shethar St., Hammondsport NY 14840) A good selection of everything a stitcher needs to make a quilt.

FOOD

Mehlenbacker's Taffy (607-569-3538; 8428 Rte. 54, Hammondsport NY 14840) The owners found an old hook hanging in the small building: it was a hook for pulling taffy. Today the company makes taffy the old-fashioned way, by hand-pulling. The candy is sold to Disney as well as to local stores. It's really good and so so fresh.

Penn Yan

The Quilt Room (315-536-5964; 1870 Hoyt Rd. just off Rte. 14A, Penn Yan NY 14527) Mennonite handmade quilts, wall-hangings, and craft items. Open May–Dec. Mon.–Sat., Jan.–Apr. Thurs.–Sat.

Weaver-View Farms (315-781-2571; www.weaverviewfarms.com; 1190 Earls Hill Rd., off Rte. 14 on the west side of Seneca Lake, Penn Yan NY 14527) A neat fourteen-room farmhouse on the top of a hill houses an Amish-Mennonite store crammed with exceptional handcrafted items and gifts. Owner Pauline Weaver said she started out with just one room; now the store sprawls through several rooms up and downstairs. There are dozens of quilts designed and handmade by friends and family of the Amish-Mennonite community. Also find homespun aprons, tablerunners, pillows, furniture, art, wrought iron, pierced tin lampshades, toys, gingham dresses and bonnets, kitchen decor, pottery, and one-of-a-kind beautiful handmade dolls and miniature toy carriages. Prices are very fair. The Weavers' black carriage is parked just outside next to the red barns. Horses and cows graze in the field nearby. Don't miss this one. Open year-round; closed Sun.

The Windmill Farm and Craft Market (315-536-3032; Rte. 14A, Penn Yan) It started with just a dozen people selling Amish and Mennonite quilts, food, crafts and other items. It has been so successful, the Windmill is now regarded as a model for a running a successful collaborative. Now there are more than 250 vendors selling crafts, farm produce, plants, antiques, quilts, cheeses, baked goods, furniture. Open Sat. May–Dec., and Memorial Day Mon., July 4, and Labor Day Mon.

Note Those Mileage Markers

You can tell how far you are from major towns simply by looking at the numbers on the mailboxes. Mileage is measured from Penn Yan, Branchport, and Hammondsport. For example, the address 661 E. Lake Rd., Penn Yan (Finton's Landing), shows that you are 6.61 miles from the village of Penn Yan. Use this information to see how far you are from town.

For More Information

Greater Bath Area Chamber of Commerce: 607-776-7122; 10 Pulteney Square, West Bath NY 14810

Finger Lakes Association: 315-536-7488; www.fingerlakes.org; 309 Lake St., Penn Yan NY 14527

Hammondsport Chamber of Commerce: 607-569-2989; Box 539, Hammondsport NY 14840; open 11–3.

Steuben County Conference and Visitors Bureau: 607-974-2066, 800-284-3352; corn ingfingerlakes.com; One Baron Steuben Place, Second Floor, Corning NY 14830

Yates County Tourism: 800-868-9283; www.yatesny.com; 2375 Rte. 14A, Penn Yan NY 14527

CHAPTER SEVEN
Western Frontier
CANANDAIGUA LAKE
Canadice, Conesus, Hemlock, and Honeoye Lakes

Peter Finger

The boathouses on Canandaigua Lake's waterfront have been here for years.

The western frontier of the region is home to sixteen-mile Canandaigua Lake, along with the smallest Finger Lakes: Canadice, Honeoye, Hemlock, and Conesus, ranging from nine miles to three miles in length. The area is rich in natural beauty with many undeveloped areas of woodlands and meadows. The largest town, Canandaigua, sits at the northern end of Canandaigua Lake; Naples at the southern end is considered the heart of the wine industry.

"People of the Great Hill," the Senecas, populated the western Finger Lakes long before Columbus found his way to the New World. One of the Seneca's largest communities was on a breezy hilltop site known as Ganondagan, now a New York State Historic Site, in Victor. Here were more than 150 bark long-houses, four tall storehouses for corn, and an estimated population of 4,500. In the seventeenth century, the people of this "Town of Peace" were at the center of a thriving beaver fur trade, a vital and profitable industry. The fur was sent to such places as Holland and France to use in making beaver hats, a hot fashion item of the times. To eliminate the Seneca's competition in the fur trade, in the 1660s the Marquis de Denonville and his French troops invaded Ganondagan and destroyed it.

One hundred years later, during the Revolutionary War, the native Americans and the Loyalist rangers staged raids against the colonists until General John Sullivan, acting on orders from George Washington, retaliated and wiped out most of the other Seneca towns in the region.

At one time, this region belonged to Massachusetts; later New York State claimed sovereignty. Then congressmen Oliver Phelps and Nathaniel Gorham put together a syndicate and negotiated to purchase the land, which they then marketed and sold to settlers. Phelps and Gorham could thus be called some of the earliest land developers of our country. The settlers came and built, towns were established, communities grew.

CANANDAIGUA

Just a ten-minute drive from Exits 43 and 44 off the New York Thruway and within easy commuting distance of Rochester, the city of Canandaigua supports a substantial variety of residential services — yet, with just 10,000 people, maintains a small-town environment. The main part of town is just north of the lake.

The wide Main Street, divided by a landscaped grassy strip, is lined by stores, banks, restaurants, and service companies. However, with a few exceptions such as Nadal Glass and Renaissance Goody II Shoppe, the retail businesses are geared more to the local trade than to tourists.

The revitalized waterfront park, the weathered old boathouses that stand side by side on wooden stilts in the water, and the postage-stamp-size Squaw Island — the smallest New York State Park and the place where Seneca women and children sought refuge from Sullivan's rampage — are major assets. The Granger Homestead and Sonnenberg Gardens are important historical museums; tree-lined streets like Gibson and Howell display many gracious turn-of-the century homes fronted by deep lawns.

Canandaigua's notable citizens include Mary Clark Thompson, who gave the town a children's playground, hospital, home for the elderly, a library, historical society, and land for a post office. Her husband built Sonnenberg Gardens. And many famous visitors have come to Canandaigua for one reason or another. In 1824 the Marquis de Lafayette visited the city. In 1872, Susan B. Anthony was found guilty of violating a federal statute by voting in Rochester and was fined $100 at a hearing in the Ontario County Courthouse. Helen Keller was a guest of Antoinette Granger, a member of a prominent local family; Stephen Douglas, Lincoln's main rival, was educated at the Canandaigua Academy, and Humphrey Bogart spent summers on the lake.

Canandaigua residents and visitors alike enjoy the Finger Lakes Race Track, Captain Gray's Boat Tours, and the *Canandaigua Lady*; and performances in the Finger Lakes Performing Arts Center and band concerts in Atwater Park.

Willow Pond Aqua Farm and Ganondagan, the site of the seventeenth-century Seneca village, are also attractions.

CANANDAIGUA LAKE

Cottages, camps, and homes ring Canandaigua Lake. The native American word means "the chosen spot." It's a beautiful drive all the way around, especially on West Lake Road (County Rd. 16) and East Lake Road which generally go along the shoreline. Route 21, the middle road, called the "High Road to Naples" by the locals, is a quicker way to get from one end to another. It runs along the top of the hills on the west side, revealing some lovely scenic vistas. The further south you go, the better the views.

Between the northern end of the lake, anchored by Canandaigua, and the southern end by Naples, you pass through small villages, some merely a gas station, a few houses, and a general store or two. Cheshire is worth noting for its wonderful Company Store and, above it, an antique and gift shop housed in a former schoolhouse.

NAPLES

When you notice the purple fire hydrants, you're reminded that in Naples, grapes are big. Most of the year it's business as usual for this quiet place at the southern end of the lake, nestled in a valley of the Bristol Hills. But come September, more than 75,000 people pour into town for the annual Grape Festival. The main street is lined with booths of more than 250 artists and food vendors; jazz, country, blues, and other musical groups entertain; and, of course, everyone enjoys "The World's Greatest Grape Pie Contest."

Naples stands on the site of the original Seneca village of Nundawao and is the burial place of Conesque, the chief of the Senecas who died in 1794. A plaque notes that it is here that Washington first took command of the American army on July 3, 1775.

Original landmarks include the Ephraim Cleveland House (1794) and Memorial Town Hall. There is also the Cumming Nature Center, Bristol Valley Theatre, and several area vineyards, including Widmars.

Naples has a new golf course, Reservoir Creek; the second largest wine company in the United States, the Canandaigua Wine Company; at Sutton Company, you can buy fishing lures and gear and even learn to make your own flies.

The town's eclectic nature also appeals to artists who come here to live and work.

MIDDLESEX

On the east side of Canandaigua Lake, where Routes 364, 245, and 247 meet, you'll find Middlesex, the birthplace of the Seneca Nation. This is celebrated the Saturday before Labor Day, when Seneca Heritage Day is held at Overackers Corners Schoolhouse, culminating with a thanksgiving and bonfire on Bare Hill. This kicks off the spectacular Festival of Lights on the lake beginning around dusk as flares are lit around the shoreline.

CANADICE, CONESUS, HEMLOCK, AND HONEOYE LAKES

There is little or no commercial development on Canadice and Hemlock, which serve as water reservoirs for Rochester. Only paddle-propelled craft are allowed on these lakes, making these attractive waters to those who want to paddle their canoes and not fight the wakes of power boats.

On Honeoye Lake, the size of the motors is restricted and the lake is so small — just five miles long — you can hike around it in a day. Heading south on West Lake Road, you pass the Savoy Sandy Bottom Nature Trail, a few camps, and some lovely shoreline scenery. Nearing the south end of the lake, the terrain gets dramatically more hilly. As you round the southern part of the lake, there is a dirt road to the left that takes you to the paved road that runs along the east side of the lake. This is a good stretch of road but there's not much going on except an occasional house here and there and a marina. At the north end of the lake is the one-light village of Honeoye.

There are some cottages on Honeoye as well as on Conesus, but certainly not the density you find on Canandaigua. These smaller lakes attract those who have the attitude "I'm on vacation, leave me alone."

HONEOYE

About seventeen miles west of Canandaigua Lake, the town of Honeoye, set on its tree-fringed lake, has more than 150 historic homes and buildings, one grocery store, and one rental house. It's close to Bristol Mountain Ski Center and Harriet Hollister Spencer Park.

Folks in this pleasant residential town go about their business in a friendly yet unobtrusive manner. When their Richmond Memorial bandstand gazebo in front of the town hall was destroyed last year by arson, donations to rebuild the structure poured in totaling $18,000 — without a fundraising committee. The new gazebo will be larger and will have a Memorial Wall made out of granite and brick. There will also be a new park. Recently a group of musicians got together and created a community band which is practicing to be ready to

---

Festival of Lights

In the days of the Senecas, the start of the annual harvest was signaled by a huge council fire on top of Bare Hill on Canandaigua Lake. Smaller fires blazed along the shores. To commemorate this tradition, on the Saturday of Labor Day weekend, residents around the lake light flares at dusk.

give concerts when the gazebo is completed. A new museum has opened on Main Street, a one-room schoolhouse which contains exhibits about the area's agricultural history.

CONESUS LAKE

Quiet and pretty Conesus Lake, the most western of the Finger Lakes, is ringed by private homes and many camps, along with a few bed & breakfasts and a strip of fast-food places at the northern end. Route 256 along the western side of the lake runs less than twenty feet from the water's edge in some places. The hills at the northern end are low and gentle; at the southern end, they're higher.

LODGING

Canandaigua offers the most places to stay by far. There are large hotels such as the Inn on the Lake, chain hotels such as the EconoLodge, and many B&Bs. Naples is short on lodging. In fact, the Naples Hotel does not even have guestrooms: it's a restaurant specializing in German food. Lakeside condominiums are next to the Bristol Harbour Golf Course, and a new resort hotel is in the works on the Bristol Harbour property.

LODGING RATES

$: Up to $75 per couple
$$: $76–$150 per couple
$$$: $151–$250 per couple
$$$$: More than $250

Canandaigua

HOTELS AND MOTELS

ECONOLODGE
716-394-9000, 800-797-1222
170 Eastern Blvd./Rtes.
　5&20, Canandaigua NY
　14424
Manager: Theresa Bellows
Rooms: 65
Open: Year-round
Price: $–$$
Credit cards: Most major

A clean, efficient small chain hotel along a commercial strip where you can find all the major fast-food places including Burger King, McDonalds, and Arby's. Fifty percent of the rooms are non-smoking. Continental breakfast is included in the rates.

**CANANDAIGUA INN
ON THE LAKE**
716-394-7800, 800-228-2801
770 S. Main St.,
    Canandaigua NY 14424
Manager: Barbara Natale
Rooms: 134
Open: Year-round
Price: $$–$$$$
Credit cards: Most major

A modern resort and conference center on the shores of Canandaigua Lake. You can pull up by boat, tie up at the new docks just outside, and come in for the night or for lunch or dinner. Many rooms as well as the large dining room overlook the water. Facilities include jacuzzis, indoor and outdoor pools with spa, fitness center, restaurant, wine bar, and meeting and conference rooms. A nice deck waterside offers dining or cocktails. Ask for the lakeview rooms.

**KELLOGG'S PAN-TREE
INN**
716-394-3909
130 Lakeshore Dr.,
    Canandaigua NY 14424

Fifteen motel rooms are just behind the restaurant and within walking distance to the lakefront. Rooms are on the small side, clean and basic. They are priced from $50 to $64. (See the listing under Restaurants below for more information.)

BED & BREAKFASTS AND INNS

ACORN INN B&B
716-229-2834;
    fax 716-229-5046
http://acorninnbb.com
4508 State Rd. 64 South,
    Bristol Center,
    Canandaigua NY
    14424-9309
Innkeepers: Joan and Louis
    Clark
Rooms: 4 with baths
Open: Year-round
Price: $$–$$$
Credit cards: Most major

One of the most romantic B&Bs I have come across. Walled gardens, private brick patios, outdoor jacuzzi, a hammock tucked into a hidden corner, and stone walls provide an intimate setting for this stagecoach inn built in 1795 by Ephraim Wilder. Tastefully furnished with a mix of antiques and period reproductions, rooms are filled with interesting collections and accessories without the clutter. Oriental rugs, original paintings, shelves of books, a fireplace, and floor-to-ceiling windows make the living room a most comfortable place to linger. All guestrooms have private baths, queen-size beds, luxury bedding, sitting area, central air-conditioning, bathrobes, slippers, reading lights, a selection of books, television/vcr, radio/cd player, clock, beverage cabinets, and duvets and electric blankets in the winter. The Hotchkiss Room, perfect for honeymooners, has its own fireplace, canopy bed, French doors leading to a private garden terrace, whirlpool tub, and sitting area. The largest room, the Bristol, also has a fireplace, canopy bed, chaise longue, and huge shower as well as a window seat overlooking the flowers and lawns. In the Wilder Room the bathroom is large enough for a wicker lounge chair. A large candlelight country breakfast is served on antique English china. The Clarks have thought of everything, even complimentary beverages and snacks. Although the entire inn has been soundproofed, this is not a place for young children or smokers. It's the closest B&B to Bristol Mountain.

CLAWSON'S BED & BREAKFAST
716-396-1947, 800-724-6379
4272 County Rd. 18,
  Canandaigua NY 14424
Innkeeper: Pat Clawson
Rooms: 3 with private baths
Open: Year-round
Price: $–$$
Credit cards: Most major

On 133 acres, this Greek Revival country home features spacious rooms, full country breakfasts, and lovely lawns and gardens. One of the rooms is air-conditioned; others have fans and atrium doors opening onto a second-story veranda. Rooms are furnished with queen, twin, or king beds, comforters, and televisions. There is a guest kitchen, sitting room, and above-ground pool. Clawson's is just five minutes from downtown Canandaigua.

HABERSHAM COUNTRY INN
716-394-1510, 800-240-0644
www.HabershamInn.com
6124 Rtes. 5&20,
  Canandaigua NY 14424
Innkeepers: Raymond and Sharon Lesio
Rooms: 5, some private, some shared baths
Open: Year-round
Price: $$
Credit cards: Most major

You'll get a warm welcome from Sharon and Raymond, who obviously love helping their guests feel at home. Set on eleven acres with a pond and gardens, this restored 1840 Federal-style home is simply but tastefully furnished with a mix of reproductions and antiques. The suite has a canopy bed, fireplace, and jacuzzi and country-style furnishings. Rooms are air-conditioned and a gourmet breakfast is served. A porch and deck provide a good place to cool off on a hot summer's day.

MORGAN SAMUELS INN
716-394-9232
www.morgansamuelsinn.com
2920 Smith Rd.,
  Canandaigua NY 14424
Innkeepers: John and Julie Sullivan
Rooms: 6 with private baths, including 1 suite
Open: Year-round
Price: $$–$$$
Credit cards: Most major

You approach this beautifully maintained 1810 stone mansion by two 2,000-foot tree-lined drives. Once home to Judson Morgan of the Morgan Department Stores of Canada, and also Howard Samuels, an industrialist (he invented the plastic bag), the property features exquisite gardens with roses, other perennials, and fountains: three gardeners work full time just to maintain them. Furnishings in the house include museum-quality antiques, carpets, and oil paintings; eleven fireplaces are throughout. Guests have a choice of several common rooms, including a parlor and a glassed-in Victorian porch overlooking the gardens. Comfortable and elegant, the guestrooms all have fireplaces, antiques, and are extremely well appointed. The suite contains French inlaid wood pieces from the 1800s; another room has hand-painted furniture. Some rooms have jacuzzis, three have balconies. There is a tennis court. Full breakfasts are served and the food comes highly recommended. Arrangements can be made for a five-course gourmet dinner for eight or more people. The inn is about two miles outside of town.

OLIVER PHELPS COUNTRY INN
716-396-1650
252 N. Main St.,
　Canandaigua NY 14424
Innkeeper: Joanna Sherada
Rooms: 4 with private
　baths
Open: Year-round
Price: $$
Credit cards: Most major

On Main St., across from the Granger Homestead, this is a perfect location if you want to be in the heart of town. Because it has a large open common room, it is often used for large parties.

SUTHERLAND HOUSE B&B
716-396-0375, 800-396-0375
www.sutherlandhouse.com
3179 State Rte. 21S,
　Canandaigua NY 14424
Innkeepers: Cor and Diane
　Van der Woude
Rooms: 5 with private
　baths
Open: Year-round
Price: $$–$$$
Credit cards: Most major

Owners Cor and Diane, who bought the property in 1993, spent more than a year restoring and upgrading this gracious Victorian home just a mile and a half from Main St. Rooms have private baths and television/vcr; three rooms have king-size beds. The Parkerhouse Suite has a two-person whirlpool, its own sitting room, and fireplace. Furnishings are in keeping with the period of the house with lots of interesting memorabilia, paintings, and stenciling. Try to be there when they serve afternoon refreshments: you'll love the homemade cookies.

THENDARA INN AND RESTAURANT
716-394-4868
4356 E. Lake Rd.,
　Canandaigua 14424
Owner: Pete Stone
Manager: Julie Thomas
Rooms: 5 with private
　baths
Open: Apr.–mid-Dec.
Price: $$–$$$
Credit cards: Most major

In this wonderful setting on the east side of Canandaigua Lake, you can enjoy a meal by the water either in the casual boathouse restaurant or in the more formal dining room in the house; then spend the night in one of the comfortable rooms in this turn-of-the-century restored Victorian "cottage." The place has a decidedly homey, country feeling. Guest rooms are air-conditioned and have phones. If you want to arrive by boat, go for it. (For more information on dining here, see the entry in the Restaurants section below.)

CONDOMINIUMS/RENTALS

BRISTOL HARBOUR VILLAGE
716-396-2200, 800-288-8248;
　fax 716-394-9254
www.bristolharbour.com
5410 Seneca Point Rd.,
　Canandaigua NY 14424
Manager: Sue Ryan

This lakeside resort community with a lovely rolling Robert Trent Jones golf course occupies 454 acres along the lake. Tastefully furnished midrise condominiums, townhomes, and patio homes hang close to the water's edge, the roadway cut into the shale banks. Most have balconies looking out to the

Rooms: 240 condominiums
Open: Year-round
Price: $$–$$$$
Credit cards: Most major

lake. Other homes are along the golf course fairways. There is a marina, private beach, restaurant, tennis courts, boat slips, and ball course. Cross-country skiing on site and downhill skiing nearby, seven miles away. Golf and stay packages are available.

Naples

The Maxfield Inn B&B in Naples on Main Street was built in 1841.

Peter Finger

MAXFIELD INN
716-374-2510
105 N. Main St., Naples NY 14512
Innkeeper: Russ Cochran
Rooms: 4 with private baths
Open: Year-round
Price: $$
Credit cards: Visa, MC

Right on Main Street and one of the few good places to stay in town, this B&B occupies a large Greek Revival estate house, circa 1841.

THE VAGABOND INN
716-554-6271
3300 Slitor Rd., Naples NY 14512
Innkeeper: Celeste Stanhope-Wiley
Rooms: 5 with private baths

Those looking for quiet seclusion will find it at the Vagabond. This rustic inn on a mountain features an enormous 1,800-square-foot great room, made mostly of local woods. The fireplace is constructed of native stone and black walnut. The formal dining room looks out to the Bristol Mountains

Open: Year-round
Price: $–$$
Credit cards: Visa, MC

with a drop of 1,000 feet to the valley, a four-season masterpiece. The Bristol Suite has two decks and a private porch as well as a king-size canopy bed, two armoires, sitting areas, fireplace, and television/vcr. The bathroom has a two-person jacuzzi and fourteen-foot vanity with two sinks. The Kimberly is large and airy with wraparound windows; the Shannon, a large room with a queen-size bed, has a sitting area in front of a large glass door opening onto a patio with a mountain view; the Mahogany has a tall carved mahogany double bed, and television/vcr. A full breakfast is served and a kitchen is available for guests to use. There's an in-ground pool, too.

Honeoye, Hemlock, Canadice, and Conesus

CONESUS LAKE BED & BREAKFAST
716-346-6526, 800-724-4842
5332 E. Lake Rd., Conesus
NY 14435
Innkeepers: Dale and
Ginny Esse
Rooms: 3 with private and
shared baths
Open: Seasonally
Price: $–$$
Credit cards: Most major

Right on Conesus Lake, this B&B offers a large private dock and a pavilion set up with a barbecue and Adirondack furniture. The bedrooms, named according to their orientation to the compass, are very comfortable and come with queen-size beds and televisions. The West Room has a super balcony overlooking the water along with an enormous bathroom that is also used by North. There is a two-person whirlpool tub and guests can use the canoe, paddle boat, and rowboat. This B&B is more folksy and homey than polished; holidays the public areas are decorated to the nines. A full breakfast is served.

EASTLAKE BED & BREAKFAST
716-346-3350
5305 E. Lake Rd., Conesus
NY 14435
Innkeepers: Dennis and
Charlotte Witte
Rooms: 4 with private
baths
Open: Year-round
Price: $$
Credit cards: Most major

When the Wittes set out to build their new home, they designed it to be one of the best bed and breakfasts in the area. Their "prairie cottage," as they call it, is set on a hill with views of the lake from the large windows and the wraparound porch. Each guestroom is very spacious and extremely well decorated, some with Laura Ashley fabrics. Rooms come with central air-conditioning and television/vcr. The white-carpeted Romance Suite has a canopy queen bed, a sitting area with a see-through fireplace, a fireside whirlpool bath for two, and a large private deck.
The Garden Room has a canopy queen bed; French doors lead out onto a private deck with lake views. The Garrett, another roomy suite, is furnished with antique family treasures and has a king canopy bed, a double bed, and a full

bath with double sinks. The Study is on the main floor and features French doors opening onto the porch. The 430-foot waterfront has a pedal boat and picnic facilities. Rates include a full breakfast, complimentary refreshments, and evening dessert tray.

GREENWOODS BED & BREAKFAST INN
716-229-2111, 800-914-3559
www.greenwoodsinn.com
8136 Quayle Rd., Honeoye NY 14471
Innkeepers: Mike and Lisa Ligon
Rooms: 5 with private baths
Open: Year-round
Price: $$
Credit cards: Most major

You drive just off Routes 5&20 to reach this spacious two-story log inn which has the ambiance of an Adirondack great camp with all the comforts of a fine country house. It's a quiet, peaceful place on three acres on the top of a hill with plenty of trails to explore and three ponds just outside. Public and guestrooms are large and well appointed. The Timberlake Suite has a canopy bed, fireplace, and outside entrance leading onto a wide deck overlooking gardens and a fish pond. Great views on the top floor are a highlight of the Comstock Room, decorated in Bob Timberlake wall coverings in black and white checks and scenic calligraphy wall borders. Rooms on the back have views of the hills, those on the front get a peek out over the hills to the lake. All rooms are air-conditioned and come with queen-size feather beds and television/vcr. Public rooms include a well-stocked library, game room, and media room with a forty-inch television. There is an outdoor spa, deck, and trails cut into the hills behind the house. A full breakfast is served in the dining room. This one is a winner.

RESTAURANTS

Most of the restaurants are in the Canandaigua area, some near the lake. Teens love places like Koozinas where they chow down on pizza and pasta; the older set prefers places like the more formal Inn on the Lake and the casual Kellogg's Pan-Tree Inn, a town institution. Popular Thendara on the Lake and Lincoln Hill Inn are in historic houses in beautiful country settings. New on the scene is the nautically themed Steamboat Landing. There is Harlee's Grill on Honeoye but few other restaurants on that or the other three smaller lakes.

Prices are estimated per person for appetizer and dinner entrée without tax, tip, or alcoholic beverages.

$: Up to $10
$$: $11–$25
$$$: $26–$40
$$$$: More than $40

Canandaigua

THE BEST OF ITALY
716-396-2511
16 Lakeshore Dr.,
  Canandaigua NY 14424
Open: Mon.–Sat. from 5
Price: $–$$
Serving: D
Cuisine: Italian
Credit cards: Most major

New to the area, the well-rated Best of Italy recently moved to Canandaigua from Rochester. Already a hot spot in town, the restaurant serves mostly Italian food, with a pizzeria in front serving pizzas and subs and a deluxe dining room in the rear. Chef specialities include Gamberi Rossi al pane (large jumbo shrimp cooked over pasta with a garlic breadcrumb topping), Proveni veal dishes, and homemade soups and pasta sauces.

CASA DE PASTA
716-394-3710
125 Bemis St., Canandaigua
  NY 14424
Open:Year-round
  Sun.–Thurs. 5–9, Fri. &
  Sat. 5–10
Price: $$
Serving: D
Cuisine: Italian American
Credit cards: Most major

One of those places the locals know about, with just a few tables, a bar, and little fuss in decor. Favorite dishes include veal parmigiana, spaghetti, and other Italian specialities. If you like Northern Italian food, you'll be pleased with the menu, which features white sauces along with the usual tomato-based fare. The bar area fills up fast but is not for kids.

JULIA BEAN'S CAFE
716-394-7080
76 S. Main St., Canandaigua
  NY 14424
Open: Mon.–Sat. 7–3; Sun.
  8–12 breakfast only
Price: $
Serving: B, L
Cuisine: American bistro
Credit cards: Cash only

In a historic building next to the bank in the business area, this place is a bit different — the menu includes trendy items like wraps and speciality coffees. Though the menu is new, the ambiance is old with tin ceilings and an old-style ice cream and soda shop. It's fun and a very good deal all around.

KELLOGG'S PAN-TREE INN
716-394-3909
130 Lakeshore Dr.,
  Canandaigua NY 14424
Open: Daily
  7:30am–7:30pm
Price: $–$$
Serving: B, L, D
Cuisine: American
Credit cards: Visa, MC

It's been around since 1924, right across the street from the newly renovated Kershaw Park on the lake. Eat on the open deck or the main dining room with windows overlooking the lake. Each day there is a new special. People will drive from Rochester just to have the creamed codfish on Wednesdays; Thursday is beef stew. Pancakes are served all day. Rolls, breads, and cookies are homemade. The cinnamon buns are yummy. Some of the featured entrées include chicken pie, ham steak, French fried shrimp, and chicken parmesan, along with a large selection of homemade soups, salads, and hamburgers. You get can beer and wine here, but they

---

Grape Pie

The area around Naples is famous for grape pie. It tastes and looks much like blueberry pie, but it definitely tastes like, well, grapes. Grape pies can be purchased from local bakeries and at the Grapery. In the past, this delicious treat was available only at grape harvest time. Now the pulp is frozen for use throughout the year.

4 cups Concord grapes
3/4 cup sugar
2 tbsp. quick cooking tapioca
1-1/2 tbsp. lemon juice
1/2 tbsp. grated lemon rind
pastry for two-crust, 9-inch pie

Prepare pastry for pie. Stem and wash grapes. Squeeze grapes between thumb and forefinger, popping pulp and skins into separate bowls. Cook pulp in covered pan, stirring occasionally until seeds are loosened. Press through a sieve to remove seeds. Pour hot pulp over skins and let set until cool. Mix cooled mixture with sugar, tapioca, and lemon juice and rind. Line pie plate with pastry. Fill with grape mixture. Cover with lattice or top crust. Bake at 450 degrees for 20 minutes. Reduce to 350 degrees for 20 minutes longer. Add ice cream and enjoy.

Courtesy Ontario County Tourism

---

don't go out of their way to promote it. Diners tend to be more on the seasoned side. There are a few motel-style rooms behind the restaurant (see the section on Lodging, above).

KOOZINA'S
716-396-0360
699 S. Main St.,
  Canandaigua NY 14424
Open: Daily
Price: $–$$
Serving: L, D
Cuisine: Italian
Credit cards: Most major

It's contemporary, fun. Try their great nachos, wood-fired pizza, and pasta specials such as fettucine with broccoli. In addition to the dining area, there is a full-service bar and take-out is available. The wild colors and noise level say "yes" to young adults. They love it.

LINCOLN HILL INN
716-394-8254;
  fax 716-394-2244
www.lincolnhill.com
3365 E. Lake Rd.,
  Canandaigua NY 14424
Open: Daily in season; call
  for other times
Price: $$–$$$
Serving: D

Bill and Cheryl Ward welcome their guests to this casual, friendly 1804 farmhouse. In the warmer weather, dine on the covered decks and porches. A new garden patio is perched above the old-fashioned gardens and lawns. Inside the rooms are wonderfully inviting — even a little room set up with a table just for two. The menu features tempting items such as mandarin orange and walnut salad, shrimp martini, escargot cornucopia,

Cuisine: American
Credit cards: Most major

sesame crusted salmon filet, pan-roasted sea bass, lake trout, and herb-crusted New Zealand lamb chops. The Wards use herbs and edible flowers from their gardens in the preparation and presentation of their meals. From here you can walk to the Finger Lakes Performing Arts Center. The four-acre site is ideal for a tented garden wedding.

THE LODGE AT BRISTOL HARBOUR
800-288-8248
5410 Seneca Point Rd.,
   Canandaigua NY 14424
Open: Fri. & Sat.
   11am–10pm, Sun.–Thurs.
   11am–9pm until mid-
   Nov.; winter closed some
   days
Price $–$$
Serving: L, D
Cuisine: American
Credit cards: Most major

There's hardly a better place to appreciate the beauty of the lake than from a perch on Bristol Harbour's terrace high above the water with the rolling golf course and vineyards all around. Although the food quality and service has not yet quite caught up to the quality of the scenery, this is by far one of the nicest places to wine and dine in the area. And latest reports are that things are getting better thanks to an enthusiastic young staff. Inside the lofty dining room and bar, both made of heavy timbers and wood, the views are almost as good looking through the large windows. Chairs fit the rustic theme: they're made of bent twigs and branches.

MACGREGOR'S GRILL & TAP ROOM
716-394-8080
759 S. Main St.,
   Canandaigua NY 14424
Open: Daily 11am–1am
Price: $
Serving: L, D
Cuisine: Pub
Credit cards: Most major

Facing the waterfront and looking very colonial in its white frame building and red, white, and blue bunting, this old landmark restaurant offers sports, pub food, wine, and beer. This is a good place to get a brew and simple meal like finger foods, burgers, and sandwiches. Popular with the younger set.

NICOLE'S AT THE INN ON THE LAKE
716-394-7800, 800-228-2801
770 S. Main St.,
   Canandaigua NY 14424
Open: Daily
Price: $–$$$
Serving: B, L, D
Cuisine: New American
Credit cards: Most major

The views are great, either unobstructed from the patio or through the huge windows that overlook Canandaigua Lake. Several of the dishes have a Mediterranean flair such as the Thai grilled chicken breast stuffed with cilantro and mascarpone cheese, drizzled with mango coulis and served with couscous, or their mint pesto rubbed lamb chop. I also like the bruschetta with roasted peppers and roma tomatoes. Service is excellent and table setting is on the elegant side, with linens, candles, crystal, and charger plates. Entertainment is provided weekends. There is a wine bar.

SCHOONER'S RESTAURANT
716-396-3360
E. Lake Rd. & Lake Shore Dr., Canandaigua NY 14424
Open 11am Mon.–Sat.; closed Sun.
Price: $–$$
Serving: L, D
Cuisine: American
Credit cards: Most major

Family owned and run by the Hollys, this is a good downhome restaurant offering generous portions of pasta, steak, soups, salads, and seafood in a yacht-like setting. Friday night is fish and chips. A favorite with the older crowd.

STEAMBOAT LANDING
716-394-5365
Lakeshore Dr., Canandaigua NY 14424

On the waterfront near the *Canandaigua Lady* pier, this new restaurant on the northern end of Canandaigua Lake has been designed in the style of the steamboat era and has outdoor dining on lakeside decks. (At the time of publication, it was still under construction, but due to be completed in summer 2001.)

THENDARA INN AND RESTAURANT
716-394-4868
4356 E. Lake Rd., Canandaigua NY 14424
Open: Apr. 1–mid-Dec. from 5pm; boathouse 12noon–11pm mid-May–mid-Sept.
Price: $$–$$$
Serving: L (boathouse only), D (boathouse and main house)
Cuisine: American
Credit cards: Most major

This 1903 Victorian house, once the Canandaigua Yacht Club, is one of the only places on the lake where you can arrive by boat and then eat either casually in the converted boathouse or in the main house with plenty of good views of the water from the large dining room windows. The menu includes grilled salmon, beef filet, pasta, and other American-style specialities. Thendara also offers overnight accommodations (see the Lodging section above).

CASUAL FOOD

Catskill Bagel and Deli (716-394-5830; 103 S. Main St., Canandaigua NY 14424) Generous-sized sandwiches, fresh warm bagels with flavored cream cheese, and fresh-ground gourmet coffees. For lunch, try hot and cold soups, deli salads, and ice cream. Eat inside or on a nice day, try their "Catskill Gardens," a small but pleasant outdoor patio.

Clement's Country Store (716-229-4201; 4503 Rte. 64, Canandaigua NY 14424) At Clement's you can eat downstairs and do your gift shopping upstairs where there is an antique cooperative filled with merchandise from a variety of dealers. Have your doughnuts, pizza, and deli fare at one of the oil-cloth covered tables. The crab salad is particularly good. You can also help your-self to ice cream from the soft frozen custard machine and pick a peanut but-ter or molasses cookie or perhaps a Rice Krispie square from the basket of baked goods. Open daily. ATM machine and video rentals also in the store.

Naples

BOB 'N' RUTH'S IN THE VINEYARD
716-374-5122
Corner Rtes. 245 & 21, Naples NY 14512
Open: Daily 6am–8pm
Price: $–$$
Serving: B, L, D
Cuisine: American
Credit cards: MC, Visa

Casual downhome cooking here offers soups, desserts, baked goods, and all the usual sus-pects. Dine in the front area of counters and booths similar to Friendly's or go to the Vineyard Room in the back where tables are set with linens and crys-tal. On a recent visit, a pot roast special with pota-toes and vegetables was just $7.95. There is also the outdoor deck just off the Vineyard, especially pretty in the fall when the hill is ablaze with color. In a hurry? Go to the outside pick-up window for simple sandwiches and ice cream and take it to one of the picnic tables in the grove of trees adjacent to the restaurant.

Honeoye, Hemlock, Canadice, and Conesus

CONESUS INN
716-346-6100
5654 E. Lake Rd., Conesus NY 14435
Open: Daily July & Aug.; closed Mon. off-season
Price: $$–$$$
Serving: D
Cuisine: American
Credit cards: Most major

You can arrive by car or boat and tie up at the dock. There is a big bar, two main dining rooms, and a deck overlooking lake. People have been raving over the prime rib for many years. Also good is the lobster, tuna, swordfish, chicken Mediterranean, and king crab. It's a pretty casual place, but please no cutoffs or tank tops.

THE SHERWOOD RESTAURANT AND COCKTAIL LOUNGE
716-624-3580
60 W. Main St., Honeoye Falls NY 14472
Open: Tues.–Thurs. 5–9, Fri. & Sat. 4–9:30, Sun. noon–8
Price: $$
Serving: D
Cuisine: American
Credit cards: Most major

Thick steaks and prime ribs served in a fine old home on a creek. There are three rooms, all dif-ferent; one is a library with bookcases, one is a party room with a mural and chandeliers; one more clubby with a bar and tables where you can also eat. In addition to their prime rib, the menu includes a lot of sautéed items and a super seafood bisque.

VALLEY INN
716-229-5400
8970 Main St. W., Honeoye
NY 14471
Open: Daily 10am–11pm
Price: $–$$
Serving: L, D
Cuisine: Italian American
Credit cards: MC, Visa

Ahomestyle place with very hands-on owner-operators. You can come casual or dressy, either way you'll feel at home. A staple in the community for many years, this is a clean, very homey place. They make great homemade pastas, soups, and fresh baked pies and desserts. In addition to the popular prime ribs on Thurs., Fri., and Sat. night, chicken Romano is a long-time favorite.

CASUAL FOOD

Beachcomber Inn (716-245-9000; 5909 W. Lake Rd, Conesus NY 14435) It's right on the lake and appears to have been around for a long time, with its weathered gray siding and deck. You'll know you're there when you see the post with hand-painted signs pointing to fun places like Cancun and Nice. The deck is popular with locals who come for a casual bite to eat and a beer. Open daily in season.

Other Area Restaurants

Minnehans Restaurant and Custard (716-346-6167; corner Rtes. 20A and 256, Lakeville NY 14480) You can't miss it: it's at a major crossroads and the parking lot is usually busy with cars coming and going. Minnehans serves breakfast, lunch, and dinner and it's hard to spend more than $10. Order at the long counter and eat at tables or booths or take it out. Weekly specials include stuffed peppers, Spanish rice, meatloaf (my favorite here), goulash, chicken and biscuits, and fish fry. Burgers, battered fries, onion rings, sandwiches, breaded fried shrimp, hot roast pork sandwich, and a whole column of other items give you plenty of choices for that quick meal. There is a good selection of frozen custard and yogurt along with milkshakes, sundaes, and floats. There is a mini-golf course open seasonally as well as batter cages and laser tag. Open 8am–8pm in season.

Victor Grilling Company (716-924-1760; 75 Coville St., Whistlestop Arcade, Victor NY 14564) Sue and Mark Cupolo cook up a storm on their grill, offering beef, poultry, pork, lamb, and seafood. They try to use local cuisine whenever possible. The menu includes grilled black angus rib-eye with mashed potatoes and onion rings, and sweet corn chowder. There are three dining rooms, two fireplaces. Very cozy and casual. Open 5:30 Tues.–Sat., Sun. from 4.

Warfield's Restaurant and Bakery (315-462-7184; 7 W. Main St., off Rte. 96, Clifton Springs NY 14432) Brick and oak walls, an oak wood wine cabinet, a genuine 1800s English pub bar, and tin ceilings recall the days when people used to come to Clifton Springs to take in the health benefits of the sulphur springs, the spas of their day. Warfield's makes its own pasta and sausage, bakes its own bread every morning, smokes its own meats and seafoods, and also maintains its own gardens for growing herbs and vegetables for their meals. Special dishes include portabella mushroom steaks, stir-fried eggplant with ginger vegetables, barbecue pork chops, and sautéed lemon chicken. For desserts, there is a tempting array of pastries, pies, cakes, and puddings. Second-floor banquet rooms can accommodate up to 150 people for a sit-down dinner and there is a polished wood dance floor. In the historic red brick Warfield Block, circa 1871, in the town center. Open for breakfast, lunch, and dinner Tues.–Sat., Sun. brunch.

CULTURE

ARCHITECTURE

In the early 1800s, Federal and Greek Revival homes were built here by the wealthy, showplaces made of wood, brick, cut stone, and local cobblestone. By the mid-1800s, many homes in a "Romantic" style emerged, reflecting Asian, Swiss, and Egyptian influences. The Stick style and mansard roofs were popular. From about 1845 to 1880, Gothic Revival and Italianate styles came on the scene, followed by Queen Anne, Shingle, and Richardsonian Romanesque.

The early twentieth century ushered in Colonial Revival and Neoclassical styles for important public buildings, such as the courthouse, and gracious residences; Tudor and modern were also popular.

In Canandaigua, notable houses and buildings in the area include those along North Main Street, Gibson Street, and Howell Street; in Clifton Springs, the Foster Cottage (circa 1854) with its triple dormers and fancy fretwork; and St. John's Episcopal Church (circa 1879) made of Medina sandstone in the Gothic style and featuring windows by Tiffany; in Gorham, two houses made of Lake Ontario cobblestones, the Mapes House and the Whitman-Fox House; and in Victor, on Maple Street, the Emily Harris House (circa 1850) in the Italianate style. In Honeoye the Pennell House is a Colonial (circa 1795) at 79 East Main. In East Bloomfield, the Greek Revival Giaconia house (circa 1840) and the Holloway House (circa 1808) a Federal-style house, are on Routes 5 & 20. The Reed Homestead (circa 1803) at 4357 Reed St. is a fine brick Colonial. The Morgan Fire House, Naples, a three-story frame structure, served as a firehouse 1890–1916.

Katharine Delavan Dyson

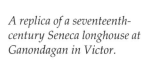

A replica of a seventeenth-century Seneca longhouse at Ganondagan in Victor.

Canandaigua

MUSEUMS AND HISTORIC SITES

Ganondagan State Historic Site (716-924-5848; County Rd. 41 at Boughton Hill, Victor NY 14564) In the seventeenth century, the largest village of the Seneca nation once occupied this hilltop mesa. When you stand on the wide meadows, you understand why they chose this site. There are magnificent sweeping views of the hills and lake all around. A bark longhouse has been recreated and depicts how the Senecas lived. Tools, clothing, cooking utensils, weapons, ornaments, and accessories have all been made by native American craftsmen selected because of their exceptional skills. At one time more than seventy-five longhouses were on the land here. There are interpretative trails and a small museum. Each summer, the Music and Dance Festival brings skilled artists to perform and demonstrate crafts, such as bow making, cornhusk doll making, wood, bone and antler carving, and other arts. A visitor center and native American gift shop are also part of the site. Peter Jemison, a descendant of Mary Jemison, a white woman captured and adopted by native Americans, is the director of the site. Open mid-May—first week of Nov.

Granger Homestead and Carriage Museum (716-394-1472; www.ggw.org/freenet/s/granger/; 295 N. Main St., Canandaigua NY 14424) A fine example of Federal architecture built in 1816 by Gideon Granger, who was postmaster general for Jefferson and Madison. Inside, there is a collection of period furnishings, some original to the house, along with lovely hand-carved woodwork.

The Granger Homestead Carriage Museum collection includes more than fifty vehicles including pleasure, sporting, and commercial conveyances.

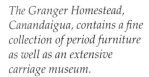

The Granger Homestead,
Canandaigua, contains a fine
collection of period furniture
as well as an extensive
carriage museum.

Peter Finger

Most have been fully restored. Of special interest are two hearses, one for summer on wheels, one on runners for winter; "The Eagle," Canandaigua's first fire engine built in 1816; a private Road Coach used by the Vanderbilts; a tinker's wagon, several sleighs, and a rare Coachee (1790s), one of only five known in the country. The house and museum are open mid-May–mid-Oct. Tues.–Fri 1–5, June 1–Aug. 31, Sat. & Sun. 1–5

Ontario County Courthouse (716-396-4239; 27 N. Main St., Canandaigua NY 14424) The venue of a number of hotly contested trials over the years, including many that challenged the Fugitive Slave Law, the courthouse has gone through several transformations. In 1794 it was a square wooden structure; in 1824, a new brick building was built (now the city hall); in 1857 a more substantial building with pillars and a dome was built and in 1909 was enlarged; in 1988 two new wings were added.

Photo Ops

Canandaigua City Pier's boathouses form a Rockport-like line of stilted buildings in the water.

Bristol Harbour: View from the restaurant's patio looking over the lake.

Harriet Hollister Spencer Memorial State Recreation Area: Stop just past the guardrails after you enter for a stunning view of Honeoye Lake. From Rte. 15A, go south on Canadice Hill Rd. and turn left into the park.

Overlook on Rte. 21, South Bristol: The town of South Bristol bought the land to preserve this great scenic spot on the lake. Look to the left and see Bare Hill (the second mound), the hill where fires announced the start of the American Indian harvest.

Ontario County Historical Society Museum (716-394-4975; www.ochs.org@ eznet.net; 55 N. Main St., Canandaigua NY 14424) See hundreds of original deeds for area lands and maps. Of particular interest is the native American copy of the 1794 Pickering treaty between the six nations of the Haudenosaunee (Iroquois) Confederacy and the U.S. government which is on display on Treaty Day, November 11. The museum contains a valuable collection of native American signatures along with artifacts and early farm and home implements. There is a huge library of family histories, photographs, and other materials. Open Tues.–Sat. 10–4:30, Weds. until 9. $2 admission for nonmembers.

The Sonnenberg Gardens, Canandaigua, feature nine formal theme gardens created between 1902 and 1919.

Peter Finger

Sonnenberg Mansion and Gardens (716-394-4922; www.sonnenberg.org; 151 Charlotte St., Canandaigua NY 14424) Built in 1887 as the summer home of bank magnate Frederick Ferris Thompson and his wife Mary Clark, who would become one of Canandaigua's most generous benefactors, the Victorian mansion features turrets, towers, stone, and heavy carved wood details. On the fifty-acre grounds are nine formal theme gardens created between 1902 and 1919, along with several species of trees and a large greenhouse complex. The forty-room mansion contains several period pieces.The house and grounds are open daily mid-May–mid-Oct.; seasonal events are offered through Dec. There is a small café on the property in one of the greenhouses.

PERFORMING ARTS

Concerts in the Park (716-396-0300; Atwater Park Gazebo, Canandaigua NY 14424) Every Friday evening during July and August, concerts are held from 6:30–8:30. Free.

Concerts and theatrical performances are presented at the Finger Lakes Performing Arts Center in Canandaigua.

Finger Lakes Association

Finger Lakes Performing Arts Center (716-222-5000; Lincoln Hill Rd., Canandaigua NY 14424) Summer home of the Rochester Philharmonic Orchestra and Rochester Performing Theatre League, performances take place on a sixty-five-foot stage at the base of a grassy hill where people can sit on blankets, picnic, and listen to great music, including classical, pop, rock, jazz and blues. A new large video screen makes the performances more accessible to those sitting on the grass. Next to the grounds of Finger Lakes Community College, the pavilion can seat 2,600; the hillside can accommodate 10,000 more.

Naples

Bristol Valley Theater (716-374-6318; 151 S. Main St., Naples NY 14512) Super summer stock productions held in a former church as well as a children's theater. See musicals, comedy, and mystery thrillers.

Mees Observatory (716-275-4385; 6486 Gannett Hill Rd., Naples NY 14512) Operated by the Rochester Museum and Science Center. Planet gazing and special programs, using a twenty-four-inch telescope. Tours Fri. and Sat. evenings, June–Aug. by appointment.

Writers and Books Gell Center (716-232-1070; www.wab.org; W. Hollow Rd., Naples NY 14512) Here at the southern end of Canandaigua Lake, writers

---

Willow Pond Aqua Farm

Is it a farm, retail outlet, or educational experience? Actually it's all three. If you're into ponds and water life, Willow Pond has everything you could ever ask for from fish, tadpoles, and crayfish to fountains. Jim Kennedy, owner of one of the newest niche businesses that have recently started up in the area, is continually coming up with new ideas for products and facilities in this water-oriented world of exotic aquatic plants and artistic water sculptures. There are more than forty ponds stocked with eight species of fish such as Japanese koi, golden orfe, and rainbow trout. Kennedy offers an ever-expanding program to teach fishing skills and gives lectures on aquaculture. The farm also sells pond and pool-related items such as handblown glass candle globes that float in the water and aerators, air and water pumps, and other accessories. Tours are offered through rough-cut trails to the ponds where you can get a close-up view of some of the more than seventy-five kinds of water lilies in all colors. (716-394-5890, 888-854-8945; www.willowpondaquafarms.com; 3581 Swamp Rd., Hopewell NY 14424; open Mon.–Fri. 10–5, Sat. 9–5, Sun. 10–3.)

---

and poets come to reflect, write, and learn. Surrounded by fields and woods, the Gleason Lodge with its large stone fireplace is used for meetings and special programs; the Gell House accommodates overnight guests.

Honeoye Falls

Peacock Oriental Antiques Museum (716-624-6058; 61 N. Main St., Honeoye Falls NY 14472) More than 700 peacocks; Chinese and Japanese artifacts from 206BCE to WWII. Extensive library is available for research. Tues.–Sun. 10am–5pm, closed Mon.

RECREATION

BIKING

Canandaigua Loop, Bristol Hills: With steep inclines and winding roads, this thirty-five-mile ride is for the experienced, fit cyclist. Start at the City Pier on Lakeshore Dr. in Canandaigua on Rtes. 5&20. Heading west, turn left on Parrish St. Go up the hill to Rte. 21S and south towards Bristol Springs. Here at almost the halfway point, you can take a break and check out the Arbor Hill Grapery and Winery. Turn right on Rte. 64N and continue to intersection of Rtes. 5&20. On the way up Rte. 64, you'll pass the Wizard of Clay Pottery. Head east (right) to Canandaigua and turn right on Pearl St., following signs for the hospital. Turn left on Parrish St. and take that road until you reach the intersection of Main St. At the stoplight turn right onto Main and follow to starting point.

BOATING AND CRUISES

The Canandaigua Lady
offers a variety of cruises.

Peter Finger

Canandaigua Lady (716-394-5365, 877-771-LADY; 215 Lakeshore Dr., PO Box
   856, Canandaigua NY 14424) Lunch, dinner, and brunch cruises as well as
   annual fall foliage cruises aboard a fanciful two-deck 150-passenger paddle-
   wheel/steamboat. Special events include New Orleans Night, Italian Fest,
   and a Hawaiian Luau. Fall foliage cruises ($28 per person) combine great
   scenery with a brief history of the area, and lunch with wine and grape pie.
   Indoor and outdoor seating for cruises that operate May–Oct.
Captain Gray's Boat Tours (716-394-5270; wwwcaptgrays.com; 770 S. Main
   St., Canandaigua NY 14424) Cruise around the lake, charter one of the two
   boats for a party, or climb on board for a morning coffee cruise. The *Jennifer
   Mac* has been piloted by Capt. Gray Hoffman for more than thirty years. His
   son, Jadon, bought the operation from his father a couple of years ago. The
   cruises' commentary on the local sites and history is especially informative:
   learn about General Sullivan's campaign, the glory days of the steamboat
   era, and area facts. Departs from the Inn on the Lake. End of May through
   Labor Day weekend; daily departures also available Sept. and Oct. weather
   permitting. Ask about the fall foliage tours.

MARINAS AND LAUNCHES:

Canandaigua Lake State Marina (S. Main St. at northern end of lake near Rtes.
   5&20 and 332, Canandaigua) $4 launch fee.
German Brothers Marina (716-394-4000; 3907 W. Lake Rd., Canandaigua NY
   14424) Full services, dockage, and winter storage. Boat rentals and sales.

Jansen Marina, Conesus (716-346-2060; 5750 E. Lake Rd., Conesus NY 14435) This facility has twenty-two slips, gas, winter storage, boat sales, and service.

Jansen Marina, Naples (716-374-2384; 7099 Rte. 21, Naples NY 14512) A full-service marina with sales, service, bait, gas, and convenience store. Fish, ski, pontoon and wave runners for rent, and seventy-five slips.

Sutter's Canandaigua Marina (716-394-0918; City Pier, Canandaigua NY 14424) On the north end of the lake. Recreational boat rentals for cruising, fishing, tubing, and sightseeing. Slip rentals, storage, store and picnic area. Not a public launching area.

Woodville Boat Launch (Rte. 21 south end of Canandaigua Lake)

FISHING

Canandaigua Lake: You can fish in the lake or from the City Pier but you must have a license. Fishing licenses can be purchased at City Hall, 2 N. Main St. or at Wal-Mart on Rtes. 5&20E.

GOLF

Bristol Harbour Golf Course (716-396-2460; 5410 Seneca Point Rd., Canandaigua NY 14424) When Robert Trent Jones came to this site more than twenty-five years ago, he said, "In all the world and of all the properties I've seen, this one has just been waiting for a golf course." The front nine plays like a links course with large bunkers, nasty rough, and fickle winds. The hilly back nine winds through woods. Many holes reveal splendid views of the lake. There is a driving range and restaurant on site. Greens fees: $45 to $52 including cart.

Centerpointe Golf Club (716-394-0346; 1940 Brickyard Rd., off Rte. 332, Canandaigua NY 14424) A semi-private 18-hole, 6,478 yd. course. Green fees including cart: $22–$27 weekdays, $35 weekends.

Reservoir Creek (716-374-6828; 8613 Rte. 21, Naples NY 14512) This new link-style course is characterized by berms and moguls which separate the fairways. There is a pro shop and restaurant with outside deck. Greens fees including cart: $31 weekdays, $36 weekends.

Victor Hills Golf Club (716-924-3480; 1450 Brace Rd., Victor NY 14564) A nice 45-hole course; restaurant and pro shop. Greens fees including cart $30 weekdays, $33 weekends.

Winged Pleasant Golf Links (716-289-8846; 1475 Sand Hill Rd., Exit 43 off NYS Thruway, Shortsville NY 14548) 18 holes, pro shop, carts, lessons, golf outings. Greens fees including cart: $22–$30 weekdays, $35 weekends.

HIKING

Bare Hill Unique Area (607-776-2165, ext. 10) Going south from Canandaigua on Rte. 364, turn right (west) on Town Line Rd., left (south) on Bare Hill Rd., and right (west) on Van Epps Rd. where it stops. This moderately difficult one and three-quarter mile loop goes along cut grass and stone trails, through woods, by a pond, and up to the top of Bare Hill. The view of the lake and valley from here is worth the trip. It is here the Senecas used to light a huge fire in celebration of a successful harvest. Today this tradition is carried out in the Genundowa Festival of Lights held on the lake each year.

Big Oak Trail and Sidewinder Trail (716-335-8111; Harriet Hollister Spencer Memorial State Recreation Area, Honeoye NY 14471) From Rte. 15A, go south on Canadice Hill Rd. and turn left into the park. The trail is marked by cross-country ski trail signs and leads north from the parking lot. Big Oak Trail, a one-mile loop through woods, over a stream, to the top of a hill, is moderately difficult on wide dirt trails with some steep climbs. Sidewinder Trail snakes 3.3 miles through the trees with some ups and downs. It's also moderately difficult.

Conesus Inlet Path (Park on the south side of Silker Hill Rd. near the intersection of Rte. 256, Conesus NY 14435) An easy one-mile walk along a mowed grass path just south of the lake. The trail starts from the parking area and is marked with round plastic discs. Walk through woods along the wetlands, stop to see wildlife from viewing platforms. You can picnic along the way. It's managed by the NYS Department of Environmental Conservation.

Cumming Nature Center (716-374-6160; 6472 Gulick Rd., Naples NY 14512) Six miles of walking trails are laced throughout the 900-acre park.

Hi Tor Wildlife Management Area (716-226-2466; from Naples take Rte. 245, cross Naples Creek Bridge, park near the Dept. of Environmental Conservation building) Several trails wind through this 6,100-acre area of steep hills, craggy outcroppings, ponds, and old logging roads. Trails can be steep and strenuous. Depending on how far you want to go, you can hike the Conklin Gully Trail, a 1.6-mile loop; the main trail, a 4.5-mile loop; or tie into several other trails along the way and backpack for several days. In the Hi Tor area of hills, forests, and wetlands, you'll be rewarded for your more strenuous climbs by some great views of gullies, lake, and cliffs. Most of the trails are marked.

Onanda Park (716-394-0315; the Upland Hiking Trail is a 1.2-mile loop from the park on W. Lake Rd. about 7 miles south of Canandaigua) Easy-to-follow dirt paths go through woods to observation platforms overlooking gorges and waterfalls. Some uphill climbing makes it moderately difficult.

Cabins and pavilion are available for rent; picnic, beach, tennis, and playgrounds also on site.

Ontario County Park at Gannett Hill (716-374-6250; 6475 Gannett Hill Rd., Naples NY 14512) Several self-guided tours, as well as playgrounds, fishing pond, picnic site, and shelters. The "Jumping Off" trail area is the highest point in Ontario County.

Quinn Oak Openings (607-776-2165, ext. 10; Honeoye Falls NY 14472; from Rte. 15, turn east on Five Points Rd. and watch for Quinn Oak Openings parking) A one and a half mile loop, moderately challenging along mowed and sometimes scruffy trails through fields of grasses surrounded by oak forests. A highly diverse area with more than 400 species of wildlife, rare prickly ash trees, and tall grasses. The trail is unmarked so get a map from the Department of Environmental Conservation or take your chances.

Seneca Trail (716-234-8226) From Rte. 96, turn west on Broughton Hill Rd., Cty. Rte. 41, and look for the parking area near the corner of Victor-Bloomfield Rd., Rte. 444; the trail is marked by red blazes and diamond-shaped, red metal markers. You can also start at the northern end of the trail at Fishers Firehall. This 5.8-mile (one way) trail recalls the time when the Senecas dominated this part of the world. Start at the Ganondagan State Historic Site and head out on several trails that loop through the region. The trail through wooded hills, meadows, and wetlands, and along abandoned rail beds, is moderately difficult. Maps are available at the center.

PARKS, NATURE PRESERVES, AND CAMPING

Bristol Woodlands Campgrounds (716-229-2290; 4835 S. Hill Rd., Bristol NY 14424; mail 3300 E. Lake Rd. #4C, Canandaigua NY 14424) From Rte. 64S, turn right at Bristol Center, go a mile and a half, then left on S. Hill Rd. to campground) Facilities include campgrounds, trails, and fishing pond on 100 acres with views of the hills. The area is often used as a camping ground for artists during the summer.

Cumming Nature Center (716-374-6160; 6472 Gulick Rd., Naples NY 14512) A vast natural environment of 900 acres with hiking and cross-country ski trails, tall red pines, and meadowland. There is an informative visitor center, gift shop, and interpretative programs with animals and birds. The nature center is an extension of the Rochester Museum and Science Center. Open 9–5 Weds.–Sun., end of Dec.–mid-Nov. Adults $4, children K–Grade 12 $1.50, seniors and college students $3.

Harriet Hollister Spencer Park (716-335-8111; Canadice Hill Rd., Honeoye; mail c/o Stony Brook State Park, 10820 Rte. 36S, Dansville NY 14437) There are several undeveloped trails and great views of the lake north toward the Rochester skyline.

Honeoye Lake State Park (716-335-8111; off Rte. 20A, four miles south of Honeoye; mail c/o Stony Brook State Park, address above) This is a boat launch area with minimal facilities and undeveloped trails.

Kershaw Park (716-396-5080; Lakeshore Dr., Canandaigua NY 14424) At the foot of the north end of the lake, this newly renovated eight-acre park has a walkway along the beach, bathhouses, picnic shelters, and gazebo. There is a sailboard and canoe launch. Beach open Memorial Day–Labor Day 9am–9pm; park open year-round.

Peter Finger

Letchworth State Park is in the western Finger Lakes region in Livingston County.

Letchworth State Park (716-493-3600; entrances at Mount Morris, Perry, Castile, Portageville, and the Parade Grounds from Rte. 436) Often called the "Grand Canyon of the East," Letchworth runs through a narrow, winding seventeen-mile bedrock canyon punctuated by three falls, including the 107-foot drop of the Middle Falls. Lights illuminate the falls after dark from May through October. The William Pryor Letchworth Museum contains a collection of native American and pioneer history items of the Genesee Valley as well as archeological and natural history displays. The statue of Mary

Jemison stands on the Council Grounds in the park, along with the Seneca Council House. Jemison's gravesite is on a bluff behind the museum. Cabins and campsites are on the grounds but those who prefer not to rough it can stay at Pinewood Lodge and the Glen Iris Inn within the park. Swimming pools, fishing areas, hiking trails, hot air ballooning, whitewater rafting, and canoeing by permit are also available.

Onanda Park (716-394-0315; W. Lake Rd., Canandaigua NY 14424) Eight miles south of the northern end of Canandaigua Lake, this park covers more than eighty acres of land, seven by the water. Activities include swimming, sledding, cross-country skiing, fishing, playground, and picnic area, along with cabins, pavilions, lodge, and tennis and ball courts. Cabin rentals are $30–$50 per night; $175–$400 (non-residents) and $100–$350 (residents) weekly. Open all year 9–9; cabins open from last frost to Oct.

Ontario County Park (E. Lake Rd, Rte. 364, Canandaigua NY 14424) The highest point in Canandaigua, this rolling grassy park with groves of very tall pines offers hiking trails, tent sites, a playground, pavilion, and great views, especially from "Jumping Off" point, which looks over the Bristol hills. This is one of the best places to view the "Ring of Fire" on Labor Day weekend.

SKIING

Bristol Mountain Ski Resort (716-374-6000; www.bristolmountain.com; 5662 Rte. 64, Canandaigua NY 14424) It's not long as ski hills go, but the 1,200-foot vertical rise is impressive. There are thirty slopes and trails, snowmaking, night skiing, ski school, rentals, babysitting, and restaurant. It's the tallest ski area between the Adirondack/Catskill region and the Rockies, and has the only Olympic-style pipe in Western New York.

OTHER ATTRACTIONS

Balloons Over Letchworth (716-493-3340; letchballoons@wycol.com; 6645 Denton Corners Rd., Castile NY 14427) Fly over the vast natural wonderland of Letchworth State Park — 14,350 acres with twenty waterfalls and cliffs up to 600 feet high. The launch site is at the Middle/Upper Falls picnic area, 1,000 feet south of the Glen Iris Inn. Prices are $189 per person; $178 per person for three or more in party.

Canandaigua Speedway (315-834-6606; www.dirtmotorsports.com; Ontario County Fairgrounds, Townline Rd,. Canandaigua NY 14424) DIRT motorsport stock racing held Sat. evenings from mid-Apr.–Labor Day. The grandstand opens at 5pm; racing begins at 7.

Copper Creek Farms (716-289-4441; 5041 Shortsville Rd., Shortsville NY 14548) You can ride horseback or in a carriage along the trails on the property. Riding and lessons for all ages; pony rides for kids. They have a surrey for use in weddings and other special occasions and sleigh rides are given in season. In the fall ride their hay wagons into the fields and pick your own pumpkin. Open year-round. Call in advance for reservations.

The Finger Lakes Race Track, Canandaigua, runs several races a day from April through early December.

Finger Lakes Association

The Finger Lakes Race Track (716-924-3232; www.fingerlakesracetrack.com; 5857 Rte. 96, Farmington NY 14425) Thoroughbred racing runs from early April through the first week in December. There are about ten races a day. One mile south of NY State Thruway Exit 44 just east of junction for Rte. 96 and 332.

Rose Park Water Park (off Rtes. 5&20) A new place in Canandaigua for family fun with water slides, river rafts, and playground is scheduled for opening spring 2001.

SHOPPING

This area is known for its grape-related products such as wines, jellies, pies, and salad dressings. Farm markets sell a variety of local produce, including fruits and vegetables, maple syrup, apples and cider, and sauerkraut. Local crafts include pottery, handblown glass, paintings, wood duck decoys, fishing lures, kites, and teddy bears. Furniture and other items made by the Mennonites and Amish are beautifully crafted. There are many antique shops where you can find good buys.

ANTIQUES

The Cheshire Union Gift Shop and Antique Center (716-394-5530; 4244 Rte. 21S, South Cheshire, Canandaigua NY 14424) Filled with an assortment of antiques and gift items, the Cheshire Union is above the Company Store. The old blackboard is still on the wall and the embossed tin ceiling is still in place, reminders that this space was once a school room, circa 1915. Tucked into nooks and crannies were collections of bears, a pair of old snow shoes, baskets, candles, an antique sled, a wood box that once held boneless salt cod, and handknit sweaters for the stuffed bears for $4.

CLOTHING

The Country Ewe (716-396-9580; 79 S. Main St., Canandaigua NY 14424) In downtown Canandaigua, this store features classic clothing including hand-knit sweaters from Ireland, Iceland, Norway, and other parts of the world. Also find fleece outerwear, oilskin dusters, Finger Lakes shirts and jewelry. Open Mon.–Fri. 9:30–8, Sat. 9:30–5:30, Sun. 11–4.

CRAFTS

East Hill Gallery (716-554-3539; 1445 Upper Hill Rd., Middlesex NY 14507) Pottery, handblown glass, handicrafts, furniture, weaving, custom clothing. Open May–Oct. Fri.–Mon.

Nadal Glass Art Studios (716-394-7850; 20 Phoenix St., Canandaigua NY 14424) Handblown glass in bright primary colors, Nadal's designs are sold in more than 200 galleries and shops around the country. Tues.–Sat. 11–5.

Silver Feather Trading Post (315-597-0097; 126 Canandaigua Rd., Rte. 21, Palmyra NY 14522) Find authentic native American artwork, craft supplies like beads, fetishes, bone and horn hairpipes, and elk and deer hide splits as well as pottery, baskets, spirit ponies, crystal bags, knives, drums, dolls, beadwork, soapstone carvings, and blankets. They also sell custom-made ribbon shirts, dresses, dance shawls, velvet bags, deer and elk hide purses, and breechcloth. If they don't have it, they can get it for you.

For More Information

Canandaigua Chamber of Commerce Tourist Center Information: 716-394-4400; www.canandaigua.com/chamber; 113 S. Main St., Canandaigua NY 14424

Finger Lakes Association: 315-536-7488; www.fingerlakes.org; 309 Lake St., Penn Yan NY 14527

Honeoye Chamber of Commerce: 716-229-4226; Honeoye NY 14471

Ontario County Tourism: 716-394-3915; www.tourismny.com; Five Lakes Suite, 20 Ontario St., Canandaigua NY 14424

Timberwood (716-374-5660; 197 N. Main St., Naples NY 14512) Handcrafted Amish and Mennonite gifts, crafts, outdoor windmills, flags, wooden garden accessories, lights, and furniture. Open daily Apr.–Dec. 31.

The Wizard of Clay Pottery (716-229-2980; 7851 Rte. 20A, 3 miles east of Honeoye Lake, Bloomfield NY 14469) Housed in geodesic domes designed and built by master potter Jim Kozlowski, the complex includes workshops with potter's wheels and kilns where every piece is individually crafted and fired. The store's shelves are filled with dinnerware, casseroles, oil-burning lamps, pie plates, pitchers, planters, bells, mugs, bowls and more. The Bristoleaf® designs are especially interesting: actual leaves gathered from the area are pressed into the soft clay before firing. When the piece is fired, the leaf burns away, leaving the impression behind. There is also a good selection of earthy red, white, and blue pottery. Workshop and store are open 9–5 daily. The pieces are reasonably priced when compared to similar pottery elsewhere; for example, a handmade ceramic fluted pie plate with an American flag motif was less than $25.

FARM MARKETS

Barrons Pratt Farm (716-394-9344; 4990 Rte. 21S, Canandaigua Palmyra NY 14522) This vineyard produces grapes primarily for people to buy by the bushel and use for pies, jellies, and other things. There is a tiny gift shop selling crafted items made by the owner such as hand-painted saws and slates.

Hanna Junction (716-394-7740; 4375 Rte. 21N just north of Canandaigua NY 14522) More than 100 vendors under one roof selling fresh vegetables, fruits, meats, baked goods, relishes, plants, furniture, crafts, antiques. Open Apr.–Dec. Thurs. 10–8

Jerome's U-Pick (800-UPICKIT; 8936 Rte. 53, Naples NY 14512) Pick your own strawberries, peas, raspberries, grapes, pumpkins, and other fruits and vegetables in season.

Joseph's Wayside Market (716-374-2380; 201 S. Main St., Rte. 21, Naples NY 14512) Every (regional) imaginable fruit is here in season along with maple syrup, honey, cheddar cheese, baked goods, jams, jellies, and locally made crafts and gifts. The market is especially known for grapes, grape pies, and juice. They also sell flowers: their hanging baskets are beautiful.

Valley View Farms: Overlooking Hi Tor at the southern end of the lake, Valley View sells a variety of local produce and baked goods including grape pies, cookies, and bread. Open seasonally.

FOOD

Arbor Hill Grapery and Winery (716-374-2870, 800-554-7553; fax 716-374-9198; www.thegrapery.com; 6461 Rte. 64, 3 miles south of Bristol Mt.,

Naples NY 14512) Grape everything: jelly, grape pies, taffy, cookbooks, salad dressings, wines (the Traminette at $11.95 a bottle is a good buy), corkscrews, pottery — you name it. John Brahm III, the founder and owner of the company, now has more than 50 products he makes, packages, and sells from his modest-sized production area next to the store. His Black Raspberry Celery Seed Dressing is one of the fourteen-year-old company's hottest items. While I was there, he invited me to sample one of his newest products, fortified teas: Strawberry Iced Tea, Peach Breezes, Lemon Delight, and Raspberry Wisp. Open daily May to Dec. Mon.–Sat. 10–5; Sun 11–5; winter weekends only.

Conesus Lake Trading Co. (716-346-2514; 5975 E. Lake Rd., Conesus NY 14435) In the spirit of the old-time general store, this store sells everything from groceries, gas, and subs to candy, "fry cakes," jellies, jams, cards, teddy bears, and seasonal gifts. Open daily 7–7.

GIFTS

Canandaigua Nature Co. (716-396-9807; 13 Niagara St., Canandaigua NY 14424) Wild bird supplies, nature gifts, wind chimes, lawn art, weather-vanes, and other items celebrate nature and the outdoors.

Cheshire Union Antique Shop and Gift Center (716-394-5530; Rte. 21, South Cheshire, Canandaigua NY 14424) Filled with an assortment of antiques and gift items, the Cheshire Union is above the Company Store. (See the listing in the Antiques section above.)

Classics (716-374-5650; 199 N. Main St., Village Corner, Naples NY 14512) As the name implies, the gift items in this store tend to be timeless in appeal: jewelry, leather goods, glassware, pottery, books, cards, porcelain dolls, kaleidoscopes, educational toys, Christmas things, garden statuary, and birdfeeders are just a sample of what you can find.

Loomis Country Shops (716-554-3154; 4942 Loomis Rd., Rushville NY 14544) A large country complex with a barn filled with home furnishings, as well as the Colonial Bouquets flower shop and Corn House Café. Rtes. 5&20 to Rte. 247 between Geneva and Canandaigua, south 7 miles to Rushville, then right on Loomis Rd.

Patch of Country (716-398-2913; 1734 Rte. 332, Farmington NY 14425) Historical items, the Cat's Meow collection, and other unique gifts.

Renaissance — the Goodie II Shoppe (716-394-6528; 86 S. Main St., Canandaigua NY 14424) In a fanciful landmark building, this store is well worth a visit, especially if you're looking for a very special gift.

1812 Country Store (716-367-2802; 4270 Rte. 15A, Hemlock) The merchandise lives up to its name. The store is filled with country gifts, quilts, Christmas things, baskets, jams, jellies, cookie cutters, lamps, cards, and antiques. Open Tues.–Sat. 10–5:30; Sun. 12–5; in Dec. also open on Mon. 10–5:30.

Types of Carriages

Coach: Private vehicle of the wealthy mostly used in urban areas. Passengers traveled in an enclosed "cabin" with windows and doors.

Phaeton: Light, four-wheeled vehicle used for personal and commercial needs. Some had roofs, some did not. Most were owner rather than coachman driven.

Surrey: Convenient two-seated family vehicles; many were outfitted with a top decorated with fringe.

Runabout: A one-seat, two-passenger utility vehicle, usually topless.

Buckboard: Simple, single-seated vehicles mounted on a board.

Game Cart: Sporting vehicles used for sightseeing and hunting excursions.

Private Drag: Resembled a commercial coach but was used privately for outings such as picnics. Under the back seat was a zinc-lined box for food and often a drawer for cutlery. It could seat fourteen people and needed four or six horses to pull.

Break: Used for recreational purposes. The seats are "on the roof."

Cutter and Sleigh: Vehicle on runners.

Speciality Vehicle: Carriage adapted for specific uses include fire wagons, hearses, traveling stores, and delivery wagons.

Judge Joseph W. Cribb of Canandaigua has collected vintage carriages and vehicles, showcased at the Carriage Museum at the Granger Homestead.

Katharine Delavan Dyson

Judge Cribb's Passion for Carriages Creates a Collection

Today's teens may dream of owning a red Mustang convertible, but, back in 1927, when the Honorable Joseph W. Cribb was but thirteen, his heart's desire was a nifty runabout for summer driving and a cutter for getting around in winter. "I think I paid about $25 for both," he recalls, pinpointing the onset of his passion for collecting horse-drawn vehicles.

Growing up in Canandaigua, New York, he explains, he was able to nurture this obsession. "After school, I used to hang around the stables at the old Granger place. I especially enjoyed Lafayette Cooper, Antoinette Granger's coachman, and liked to ride with him in Miss Granger's carriage: it was pulled by her old horse, Nero. Whenever I could, I went with Mr. Cooper when he took letters to the post office and did other errands."

When Joe was sixteen, he purchased a two-seated surrey, stripped off the body, and converted the vehicle into a buckboard. "This was my pickup truck. After school, I'd drive to the edge of town, pick carrots and beets for 5 cents a bushel, load them onto the wagon, and take them into town to sell. I could make 70 or 80 cents that way. I also earned money taking care of horses that were boarded in a barn on the Granger property."

As young Joe went on to study law at Cornell, becoming an attorney and a highly respected Ontario County surrogate judge, he diligently continued to collect and restore one carriage after another. "Whenever anyone had an old wagon or carriage for sale, no matter what state it was in, someone would say, 'Call Judge Joe. He'll take it.' I soon had close to fifty vehicles stored in sheds and barns all over town."

In the late fifties, about the time he'd just about run out of empty barns, Judge Joe ended up full circle back at the Granger Homestead. The property, once the home of Gideon Granger, postmaster general under presidents Jefferson and Madison, had been purchased in 1945 (at the urging of Judge Joe) by the the Granger Homestead Society and was being maintained by a dedicated group of volunteers as a historic home and venue for social functions.

Since some of Judge Joe's vehicles were already stored amidst the corn cobs, moldy hay, and flotsam of the old Granger barn, an idea started to germinate: Why not create a carriage museum using the Judge's carriages as the nucleus for the display? What a wonderful addition it would make to the property. Judge Joe was all for it.

So, spearheaded by Stephen Hamlin (now director of Sonnenberg Estate and Gardens), funds were raised through a series of plays and benefits, as well as contributions from Mr. Hamlin's family and other local benefactors, to be used to construct a substantial steel building to augment the smaller, wooden barn. The barnraising was a gala affair with a chicken barbecue, children's carriage rides, and a horde of volunteer workers including Arthur Hamlin, the local bank president, and Granger board member Byron Delavan, who provided hours of physical labor as well as executive expertise by suggesting that a crane might be useful to raise the heavy rafters. Thus the Granger Carriage Museum became a reality, opening its doors to the public in 1961, showcasing thirty of Judge Joe's carriages he had either donated or offered on loan to the new museum.

Continued on next page

Since that time, the Granger carriage collection has almost doubled with donations not only from Judge Joe, but also from other benefactors as well. Additional horse-drawn vehicles are displayed in the Carriage House at Sonnenberg, a turn-of-the-century "Tudor-Victorian" forty-room stone mansion, once the summer home of Mary Clark Thompson and her husband, Frederick, a banking magnate.

For a first-hand peek at some of Judge Joe's favorite carriages, I visited his private stables at the back of his Main Street property. The stables and surrounding paddocks are also home to four Morgan carriage horses: Lucy, Green Meads Emily, Pete, and the new colt J.C. Stormwatch. Judge Joe, even at eighty-five, often travels with his driver, Dale Vidler, to carriage shows around the country. It is not unusual for his stable to take top honors, as shown by the impressive display of ribbons and awards which hang on the walls. Sitting on a desk is an ornate silver bowl awarded for last year's "Best of Show" win at Walnut Hill, New York. As we walked along the corridors between more than fifteen carriages, Judge Joe put his hand on the red-painted wheel of a smart runabout. "My parents gave me this for Christmas in 1930," he says. Then he moves past a wall of sleigh bells to a Kimbal Brothers' Coach, and points out a cleverly hidden footman's seat. (Some wags refer to these as "mother-in-law" seats.)

Moving to another carriage, a game cart, he shows where hunting dogs can be contained in a specially built compartment. He points out a handsome Victoria carriage from England, a two-wheeled gig built by Studebaker (forerunner of their automobiles), and an Ointment Peddler's Wagon with advertising on the side panels.

His enthusiasm for an Essex Trap is boundless. "You're driving along with your pal and you see a couple of pretty girls. Now watch this," he says, walking to the back of the carriage to demonstrate how the back folds out to make an additional ("rumble") seat. "Now you can invite the girls to come aboard."

HARDWARE

Turner's Hemlock Farm & Home (716-367-2315; Rte. 15A, 4638 Main St., Hemlock NY 14466) A real oldie, this store sells everything you can think of: feed sacks, pet supplies, tools, burlap bags, a rabbit cage for $39.99, seeds. It's worth a stop just to get a flavor of what stores used to be like before packaged nails.

CHAPTER EIGHT
Gold Medal Grapes
WINERIES

Peter Finger

Grapes ripen in the sun in a Finger Lakes vineyard.

This is an exciting time for the wine industry in the Finger Lakes. Where just a handful of vineyards existed in the Finger Lakes in the early 60s, today there are close to eighty vineyards and wineries sprawled on the hillsides of three lakes: Seneca, Cayuga, and Keuka. A few more are huddled around the southern end of Canandaigua and, within the past two years, several acres of land on the west shores of Skaneateles have been planted with grapes.

Yet it's not just the number of vineyards but the quality of the wines being produced in the region that give cause to celebrate. After many years of ho-hum acceptance where regional wines were generally considered inferior to those from France and California, Finger Lakes wines finally are being recognized as standing with the best in the world.

As early as 1873, Great Western was the first champagne from the United States to win a gold prize at the Vienna Exposition. Glenora Wine Cellar's 1987 Chardonnay was featured at George Bush's inaugural dinner in 1989 and wines from the Hermann J. Wiemer Vineyard are served at New York City's famed Lutèce restaurant. In 1998 this winery was recognized by *Food and Wine Magazine* for producing an outstanding Riesling. Dr. Frank's Vinifera Wine Cellars won a double gold in a recent California winetasting and their semi-dry Riesling came away with a gold medal in a winetasting in Alsace. Dr. Frank's wines have been served at the White House and continue to beat French wines in blind tastings.

Unlike many winemaking regions in the world where the majority of the wineries are owned by outsiders, the Finger Lakes vineyards are usually owned and run by families whose roots are deep here. Their families and ancestors may have been farmers who sent their children to college to study marketing, business, agriculture, and viniculture. After obtaining their degrees, these sons and daughters returned armed with new knowledge of how to use the land to build a first-class winemaking business.

Jerry and Elaine Hazlitt, who opened their winery in 1985 (Hazlitt 1852 Vineyards Winery), are the sixth generation in a family that has been growing grapes in the Finger Lakes since the mid-1800s; Art Hunt (Hunt Country Vineyard) is also the sixth generation to live on his farm; Bill Wagner (Wagner Vineyards) started in 1947 as a vegetable and dairy farmer before concentrating on growing grapes and making wine; and Walter S. Taylor's (Bully Hill Vineyards) grandfather arrived in Hammondsport in the late nineteenth century and established Taylor Winery. Eventually Walter left the family fold and founded his own vineyard, going on to make superb wines and marketing with great flair and humor. His wines have names like Le Goat Blush, Thunder Road, and Happy Hen White.

HISTORY

The Rev. William Bostwick is credited with planting the first grapevines in the Finger Lakes in 1829: he planted Catawba and Isabella grapes in the rectory garden of St. James Episcopal Church in Hammondsport. But the Reverend was in another business and it wouldn't be until 1865 when the first bonded Finger Lakes winery was founded, the Pleasant Valley Winery. The Urbana Wine Company was established in 1865 and renamed Gold Seal Winery in 1887 and Taylor Winery began operations in 1880. By this time there were more than thirty vineyards in the region.

The sale of wines was banned in the 1919 Volstead Act; by the time it was repealed in 1933, all but a few wineries had gone out of business. Some like Taylor and Widmer survived by selling grape juice and sacramental wine.

One of the greatest boosts to winemaking in the Finger Lakes occurred when Vitis vinifera grapes were introduced in the early 1940s. Up until this time, the region had primarily concentrated on growing Vitis labrusca grapes like Catawba, Concord, Delaware, Elvira, and Niagara, hardy varieties which grew

Species of grapes in the region include hardy Vitis labrusca varieties like Catawba, Concord, Delaware, Elvira, and Niagara; and Vitis vinifera, classic European varieties such as Cabernet Sauvignon, Chardonnay, Gewürztraminer, Pinot Noir, and Riesling.

Peter Finger

very well in the cool climate on the protected lakeside hills. Wines produced from these grapes tended to be fruity, foxy, grapey in taste: certainly no match for the Chardonnays and Pinot Noirs from France and California. Most area winemakers were convinced that the European grapes like Chardonnay, Pinot Noir, and Cabernet Sauvignon could not survive the region's harsh winters.

In 1934 Gold Seal's president went to Rheims, France, and persuaded Charles Fournier, chief winemaker of Cliquot Ponsardin, to come to Hammondsport and rebuild the winery's Prohibition-devastated reputation. Fournier brought with him several French-American hybrid grapes which had been developed in France to withstand diseases. These new hybrids added another dimension to the quality of the grapes grown in the Finger Lakes.

In 1943, the winery's Charles Fournier Brut was introduced; the winery won a gold medal in 1950 for champagne at the California State Fair. In the following years, no non-Californian wines were allowed in the competition.

By this time, interest was escalating in growing purely European grapes — going beyond the hybrids. Only by growing the Chardonnays, Pinots, and other prized varieties, could the Finger Lakes produce better wines, some believed.

The industry received a major boost when Fournier brough Dr. Konstantin Frank, an immigrant from the Ukraine, to Gold Seal to establish a Vitis vinifera nursery. Before his arrival in the United States, Dr. Frank had studied agriculture at the Polytechnic Institute of Odessa, completing studies in enology and viticulture and going on to teach. After World War II, he came to the U.S. with his family in 1951. He had no money and could not speak English. After working at several menial jobs, he found his way to the New York State Agricultural Experiment Station in Geneva, a grape research facility. Here he was given jobs like picking blueberries and clearing fields.

It wasn't until Charles Fournier heard that that Dr. Frank had been talking about Vitis vinifera as an option for area grape growers that he approached the man from the Ukraine. Dr. Frank explained that he had seen these grapes grow in the Ukraine in temperatures 40 degrees below zero. His theory — graft the Vitis vinifera grapes to hardy root stock to make the vines winter-proof — was convincing. Dr. Frank was hired to to establish a Vitis vinifera nursery at Gold Seal.

By proving that the finest grapes in the world could be grown in the Finger Lakes, Dr. Frank triggered enormous growth in the wine industry. He eventually founded his own vineyard, Dr. Frank's Vinifera Wine Cellars Ltd., in the hills above the west side of Keuka Lake. Dr. Frank died in 1985, but the legacy continues with his son Willy and grandson Fred.

Today, Finger Lakes wineries and vineyards are producing award-winning wines from grafted, winter-hardy Chardonnays, Riesling, Pinot Noir, and other European grapes.

Wine Trails

Three of the lake areas, Cayuga, Seneca, and Keuka, have established wine trails with maps and listings of the participating wineries. All sponsor wine-related events.

Cayuga Wine Trail: 800-684-5217
Seneca Lake Wine Trail: 315-536-9996
Keuka Lake Wine Route: 800-440-4898

Following is a sampling of the many Finger Lakes wineries. It is not meant as an all-inclusive listing: several excellent books do that job well, among them *Wineries of the Eastern States* by Marguerite Thomas, another volume in the Great Destinations series. Rather, it is meant to whet your appetite for visiting the wineries and sampling their wines, and to come away with a greater appreciation for what is produced here. You will find everything from small family-run businesses to larger, sophisticated wineries with handsome facilities including shops, restaurants, lodging, and tours. Many wineries offer wine tastings and participate in events throughout the year. Be sure to call for hours; some are open for visitors year-round; others seasonally.

WINERIES AND VINEYARDS

Cayuga Lake

Cayuga Ridge Estate Winery (607-869-5158, 800-598-WINE; crew@epix.net; www.cayugaridge.com; 6800 Rte. 89 at Elm Beach, Ovid NY 14521) Owners

Cayuga, Seneca, and Keuka lakes offer well-signed wine trails.

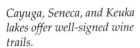

Peter Finger

Susie and Tom Challen feature Chardonnay, Riesling, Cayuga White, Chancellor (French-American hybrid), Pinot Noir, Vignoles, and Cabernet Franc; also Cranberry Essence and Cranberry Frost. Cayuga Ridge is set on thirty-eight acres with winetasting facilities in a gigantic old barn with a deck. Picnic tables are also on the grounds. The winery sponsors special events and a vigneron, a "rent-a-grapevine" program. Learn how to grow, tend, and harvest rented vines, then take the grapes or sell them to the vineyard and pay to have them made into wine.

Frontenac Point Vineyard (607-387-9619; cdj4@cornell.edu; 9501 Rte. 89, Trumansburg NY 14886; 12 miles north of Ithaca) Winetastings and tours by appointment are offered by owners Jim and Carol Doolittle. Their wines include Vinifera varieties such as Chardonnay, Pinot Noir, and Riesling and French-American hybrids including Chambourcin, Chelois, and Vidal Blanc. Blends include Proprietor's Reserve Red, oak-aged Proprietor's Reserve White, and Chateau Doolittle made with Riesling and Chambourcin. Frontenac Red is a blend of four varieties. Brut champagne is produced in the méthode champenoise where fermentation generating the bubbles takes place in the bottle. The vineyard is on the west side of the lake.

Goose Watch Winery (315-549-2599; www.goosewatch.com; goosewatch@ flare.net; 5480 Rte. 89, Romulus NY 14541; 15 minutes south of Seneca Falls) Owners Dick and Cindy Peterson feature classic premium European-style wines such as Merlot, Brut Rosé Champagne, Pinot Gris, Villard Blanc, Viognier, and Finale White Port. Traminette and Melody, from newer grape varieties developed by Cornell University, are also offered. Half mile north of Dean's Cove on the western shore of the lake, Goose Watch is accessible

Helpful Terms

Barrel fermented: Wine is aged in oak barrels which creates a more complex flavored, full-bodied wine.

Brut: A measure of the dryness of a champagne (extra dry, brut, or natural).

Enology: Winemaking.

Enophile: A lover of wine.

Estate bottled: Wine made from grapes grown on the property.

Finish: Indicates flavors that remain in the mouth after the wine is consumed.

French-American hybrid: A cross (hybrid) of American and European grape varieties.

Grafted Vitis vinifera: European grapes grafted to hardier root stock to help survive low temperatures.

Late harvest: Grapes picked very ripe at the end of the season. Used to produce sweet dessert wines.

Méthode champenoise: When making champagne, the second fermentation takes place in the bottle.

Nose: The smell of a wine.

Reserve: Wines marked as special by the producing vineyard.

Varietal wines: Wines of one grape variety.

Viniculture: Grape growing, winemaking, and marketing wine.

Vinification: The fermentation process by which juice is converted into wine.

Vitis labrusca: Hardy grapes like Catawba, Concord, Delaware, Elvira, and Niagara known for their foxy/grapey taste. Because of their ability to survive harsh winters, these were the first grapes grown in the Finger Lakes region.

Vitis vinifera: Classic European varieties like Chardonnay, Pinot Noir, Gewürztraminer, Riesling, Sauvignon Blanc, Cabernet Sauvignon, Cabernet Franc, Merlot, and Meunier.

by boat. The winery is in a restored 100-year-old barn set in a grove of chestnut trees. Visitors can enjoy a picnic area, boat dock, and agriculture tram tours; the winery also sells a selection of cheeses, smoked trout, and other gourmet items. In addition to producing wines, Goose Watch has a aquaculture trout operation.

Hosmer Winery (607-869-3393, 888-HOSWINE; fax 607-869-9409; 6999 Rte. 89, Ovid NY 14521) Cameron and Maren Hosmer offer Cayuga White, Riesling, Seyval Blanc, Chardonnay, and Pinot Noir; visitors can enjoy winetastings, picnic tables, a gift shop, and snack foods. The winery is set on forty acres on the western shore of the lake. A new wine, Raspberry Rhapsody, is made from fresh raspberries and grape wine.

King Ferry Winery (315-364-5100, 800-439-5271; fax 315-364-8078; www.treleavenwines.com; 658 Lake Rd., King Ferry NY 13081; 16 miles north of Ithaca) Owners Peter and Tacie Saltonstall offer winetastings and sell most of their production at the winery. However, some of their wines are available in restaurants and New York City stores. King Ferry has a retail store at Prime Outlets in Waterloo. Featured wines are Treleaven Chardonnays aged in French oak, Treleaven Rieslings, Pinot Noir, and Gewürztraminer. The winery is on the eastern shore of Cayuga Lake.

Harvesting grapes at Knapp Vineyards, Romulus.

Peter Finger

Knapp Vineyards Winery and Restaurant (607-869-9271, 800-869-9271; fax 607-869-3212; www.knappwine.com; 2770 Ernsberger Rd./County Rte. 128; Romulus NY 14541) Featured are classic European wines such as Barrel Reserve Chardonnay; Cayuga Lake Chardonnay; Dutchman's Breeches, a combination of Vidal and Vignoles; Ruby Port; and Sangiovese, a red wine originating in Tuscany. The stylish modern winery is set on ninety-nine acres and offers winetastings, picnic facilities, and a harvest festival. The excellent restaurant on site features American cuisine and European dishes as well as winemaker's dinners. Guests can eat indoors or on the outdoor garden patio. Knapp also concocts brandy and grappa in a hand-hammered copper onion-dome distillery.

Lakeshore Winery (315-549-7075; fax 315-549-7102; www.lakeshorewinery.com; 5132 Rte. 89; Romulus NY 14541) On the west side of the lake with beautiful views, this is a friendly, relaxed place with a large stone fireplace and rocking chairs. Outside are picnic tables and a boat dock. Owners John and Annie Bachman feature Vinifera varieties such as Cabernet Sauvignon and Pinot Noir, and French-American hybrids including Baco Noir and Cayuga White. Aunt Clara and Uncle Charlie are blends of Labrusca grapes, based on the Catawba variety. Food is served with wine at the sit-down tastings; special activities include Lakeshore Nouveau Weekend in early November to celebrate the harvest.

Lucas Vineyards (607-532-4825, 800-682-WINE (NY only); fax 607-532-8580; www.babylonvillage.com\lucas.htm; 3862 County Rd. 150, Interlaken NY 14847; 18 miles north of Ithaca) The oldest winery on Cayuga Lake, Lucas Vineyards is set on sixty-eight acres on the west side of the lake with beautiful views of the water from the tasting room. Owner Ruth Lucas features Vinifera, French-American varietals, and sparkling wines. The tugboat wines — Captain Belle Blush, a blend of five hybrids; Blues, a blend of Cayuga White and Seyval Blanc; and Harbor Moon, a blend of Cayuga White and Vidal Blanc — recall founder Bill Lucas's early years as a tugboat captain on the eastern seaboard. Visitors can enjoy winetastings, gift shop, picnic facilities, special events.

Swedish Hill Winery (315-549-8326, 888-549-WINE; fax 315-549-8477; www. fingerlakes.net/swedishhill; 4565 Rte. 414, Romulus NY 14541; 8 miles south of Seneca Falls on the west side of the lake) Although owners Dick and Cindy Peterson make wine from European varieties, they have successfully produced excellent wines from Labrusca and French-American hybrids. Notable wines include Rieslings, Svenska White, Svenska Red, Late Harvest Vignoles, Optimus (a Bordeaux-style blend), Cynthia Marie Vintage Port, and Eaux-De-Vie grape brandy. Set on thirty-five acres, the winery's rustic red barn has a deck overlooking a pond. An old still sits near the entrance. And be sure to walk over to the pasture near the picnic area and say hello to the miniature donkey. The large winetasting room has three separate tasting bars. Amish-baked breads and gift wine packs are also available at Swedish Hill. In addition to the gift shop, tours, and tastings, the winery hosts many annual events, including the Scandinavian Festival, a Wine and Art Festival, and a Champagne and Dessert Wine Festival.

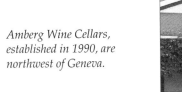

Amberg Wine Cellars, established in 1990, are northwest of Geneva.

Peter Finger

Seneca Lake

Amberg Wine Cellars (716-526-6742; fax 315-462-6512; www.ambergwine.com; 2200 Rtes. 5&20, Flint NY 14561; 6 miles west of Geneva) The Amberg family has been growing grapes for more than thirty years. Eric Amberg, winemaker, offers Chardonnay, Pinot Noir, Riesling, and Chambourcin, a French-American hybrid. Blends include Blanc, Burgundy, Pearl, Gypsy, and Red Panda, a semi-sweet wine. Red Baron is a rich fruity wine. When the original barns of the family farm (circa 1795) burned down, a new winery was built. A huge wooden wine cask serves as a sign to announce the entrance. Winetastings and a shop are offered to visitors.

Anthony Road Wine Company (315-536-2182, 800-559-2182; fax 315-536-5851; anthonyroad@flare.net; 1225 Anthony Rd., Penn Yan NY 14527) Owners John and Ann Martini feature Chardonnay, Riesling, Cabernet Franc, Seyval Blanc, and late harvest Vignoles; blends include Poulet Rouge, Tony's Red, Vintner's Red, and Vintner's Select. Winetastings and the Standing Stone Café are in an attractive new building with high ceilings, blue and tan stencils, and a good view of the lake.

Arcadian Estate Vineyards (607-535-2068, 800-298-1346; fax 607-535-4692; www.arcadianwine.com; 4184 Rte. 14, Rock Stream NY 14878) Winetastings, an art gallery, a gourmet food court, and special events are offered in a 170-year-old knotty-pine barn set on seventy-two acres. Owners Mike and Joanne Hastrich feature Dechaunac (French-American hybrid), Pinot Noir, Chardonnay, Riesling, and Cabernet Sauvignon; blends include Sail Away (Chardonnay and Cayuga), Pinot Rougeon, and Flora de la Noche. They suggest trying their Simple Pleasures fruit wines like blackberry, black raspberry, cherry, and pear.

Castel Grisch Estate Winery (607-535-9614; fax 607-535-2994; www.finger lakes-ny.com/CastelGrisch; 3380 County Rte. 28, Watkins Glen NY 14891) The Malina family offers Chardonnay, Gewürztraminer, Johannisberg Riesling, Blanc Noir, Chablis Grand Cru, Baco Noir, Estate Reserve Burgundy, Cabernet Frank, Seneca Blush, Seneca Dream Red and White, Vidal Blanc Ice Wine, and Riesling Ice Wine. Their 138-acre vineyard has an Alps-style chalet winery, an adjacent bed and breakfast, and an open-decked restaurant which serves Swiss-German cuisine.

Chateau LaFayette Reneau (607-546-2062, 800-469-9463; fax 607-546-2069; http://members.aol.com/clrwine/; Box 238, Rte. 414, Hector NY 14841) Owners Dick and Betty Reno offer hayrides through the vineyards here; the site encompasses 140 acres of grapevines, meadows, woodlands, and ponds on the east side of the lake. Featured wines are Chardonnay, Riesling, Cuvee Rouge, Pinot Noir, Vidal Blanc, Blanc de Blanc, and Pinot Noir Blanc. Visitors can enjoy winetastings, picnic tables, and a terrace overlooking the lake.

Earle Estate Meadery (607-243-9011; fax 607-243-9058; www.meadery.com; 3586 Rte. 14, Himrod NY 14842) This large retail store and winetasting facility has its own beehives and honey. Owners John and Esther Earle are known for their honey and fruit-influenced wines such as Pear-Mead, Peach Perfection, Cherry Charisma, Raspberry Reflections, and Strawberry Shadows, as well as a light fruity Chardonnay, Riesling, Cayuga White, and Seyval Blanc. The wine bottles alone are worth the price. The family also owns the new Torrey Ridge Winery down the road.

Four Chimeys Farm Winery (607-243-7502; fax 607-243-8156; 211 Hall Rd., Himrod NY 14842) At the first organic winery in the region, owner Scott R. Smith features Reserve White (mostly Chardonnay), Alsatian-style Dry Cayuga, Kingdom White and Red, Reserve Reds, Eye of the Bee (from

Fox Run Vineyards, on the west side of Seneca Lake, specializes in wines made from European varieties of grapes.

Peter Finger

Concord), Coronation, organic champagne, and speciality fruit wines. On the property is an Italianate villa with four chimneys, and a large Victorian barn. Winetastings are offered.

Fox Run Vineyards (315-536-4616, 800-636-9786; www.foxrunvineyards.com; 670 Rte. 14, Penn Yan NY 14527) Winner of the 1997 Governor's Cup for the Best New York State Wine, Fox Run features Riesling, Pinot Noir, Chardonnay, Cabernet Sauvignon, Cabernet Franc, Merlot; Reserve Chardonnay and Reserve Pinot Noir; also Ruby Vixon, a semi-dry blush, Arctic Fox, and Port. Owners Scott Osbourn and Andy Hale preside over a lovely barn with a deck overlooking the lake, a large winetasting area, gift shop, and wine tours.

Glenora Wine Cellars (607-243-5511, 800-243-5513; www.glenora.com; 5435 Rte. 14, Dundee NY 14837) Owners Gene Pierce, Ed Dalrymple, and Scott Welliver feature Chardonnay, Chardonnay/Barrel Fermented, Pinot Noir, Riesling, Merlot, Cabernet Sauvignon, and Gewürztraminer; sparkling wines including Brut (blend of Pinot Noir, Pinot Blanc and Chardonnay), Blanc de Blancs, and Brut Rosé; and French-American hybrid wines such as Cayuga White and Seyval Blanc. The magnificent lakeside setting includes a large winetasting room, gift shop, deck, restaurant, and inn; the winery often hosts special events.

Hazlitt 1852 Vineyards (607-546-9463; fax 607-546-5712; www.hazlitt1852.com; 5712 Rte. 414, PO Box 53, Hector NY 14841) The Hazlitt family features Chardonnay, Riesling, Gewürztraminer, Schooner White, Cabernet, Merlot, Pinot Gris, and Red Cat, a blend of Catawba and Baco Noir. The winery is in a wonderful rustic barn filled with antiques and memorabilia. Tastings take place around two U-shaped bars. It's a lively, friendly place run by a fun group of people.

Lamoreaux Landing Wine Cellars specializes in wines for the premium market.

Peter Finger

Lakewood Vineyards (607-535-9252; fax 607-535-6656; www.lakewoodvine yards.com; 4024 Rte. 14, Watkins Glen NY 14891) Three generations of the Stamp family pour their souls into making this vineyard work. Featured are Labrusca wines such as Delaware, Niagara, and White Catawba; French-American hybrids Long Stem White and Long Stem Red; Chardonnay, Riesling, and Ice Wine. The winery and tasting room is in a long, modern wood building on the east side of the lake near fields full of sunflowers. This is a kid-friendly place, with tours, picnic facilities, and a playground.

Lamoreaux Landing Wine Cellars (607-582-6011; fax 607-582-6010; www.finger lakes.net/lamoreaux; 9224 Rte. 414, Lodi NY 14860) Owner Mark J. Wagner targets the ultra-premium market and produces a full-bodied Pinot Noir, as well as Chardonnay, Gewürztraminer, Riesling, Merlot, Cabernet Franc, and Brut; blends include Estate White and Estate Red. The winery and tasting room, a striking tall narrow building with four square columns, resembles a Greek temple, and is set on 130 acres overlooking the east side of the lake. Picnic tables are available.

New Land Vineyard (315-585-4432; 577 Lerch Rd., Geneva NY 14456) Owner Nancy Newland was one of the last students of Dr. Konstantin Frank. Her small, new winery, tucked into ten acres on a bluff on the east side of the lake, is worth the trip. The winetasting room is small but cozy. Featured wines are premium varietals in the European tradition: Chardonnay, Merlot/Cabernet blend, Sauvignon Blanc, and Pinot Noir.

Prejean Winery (315-536-7524, 800-548-2216; fax 315-536-7635; 2634 Rte. 14, Penn Yan NY 14527; just south of Dresden) Owners Elizabeth and Tom Prejean feature Merlot, semi-dry Gewürztraminer, premium Chardonnay, Riesling, Cayuga, Vignoles, and Port. Winetastings and a gift shop are in a weathered old barn with a deck overlooking the west side of the lake. Prejean is one of the top producers of Gewürztraminer, a wine known to go well with Cajun food. (Prejean is a Cajun name).

Red Newt Cellars Winery and Bistro (607-546-4100; fax 607-546-4101; www. rednewt.com; 3675 Tichenor Rd., Hector NY 14841; ten miles north of Watkins Glen) This new winery features Chardonnay, Riesling, Red Newt White, Cabernet Franc, Merlot, and Cabernet Sauvignon. Co-owner David Whiting is well known for his winemaking skills at other local vineyards where he created award-winning wines. The winery, set on the east side of the lake with stunning views, also houses a restaurant run by co-owner Debra Whiting, who comes from the catering business. You can eat inside or out on the deck.

Seneca Shores Wine Cellars (315-536-0882; 929 Davy Rd. & Rte. 14; Penn Yan NY 14527) Owner David DeMarco offers Cabernet Franc, Gewürztraminer, barrel-fermented Chardonnay, Riesling, White Castle blend, Cabernet Sauvignon, Merlot, and Red Castle blend. A new modest-size blue building with rocking chairs and a covered deck overlooks the lake; tours and a picnic area are also available. The winetasting room features a medieval theme complete with battle axes and shields to complement its "medieval wines."

Standing Stone Vineyards (607-582-6051, 800-803-7135; fax 607-582-6312; 9934 Rte. 414, Hector NY 14841) In a nifty restored chicken coop with a spacious terrace, this winery features Chardonnay, Gewürztraminer, Riesling, Cabernet Franc, Merlot, Pinnacle blend, and Dry Vidal Blanc aged in oak. Owners Marti and Tom Macinski's Riesling and Gewürztraminer have won several awards; Cabernet Franc was awarded the Governor's Cup at a recent New York Wine and Food Classic. Winetastings and picnic tables are offered.

Torrey Ridge Winery (315-536-1210; 2770 Rte. 14, Penn Yan NY 14527) Owners John and Esther Earle feature Chardonnay, Riesling, Cayuga White, Seyval Blanc, Baco Noir; native American varieties such as Concord, Diamond, and Niagara; and Bandit Red, Virtue, Bandit Blush, and Summer Delight, a semi-sweet fruit wine. This new winery, owned by the Earle Estates Meadery family, is in a handsome white building with winetasting rooms on both floors; don't miss views of the lake from the second floor balcony. Educational tours are offered.

Wagner Vineyards, on the east side of Seneca Lake.

Peter Finger

Wagner Vineyards (607-582-6450; fax 607-582-6446; www.wagnervineyards.com; 9322 Rte. 414, Lodi NY 14860) Featured wines are Chardonnay, Gewürztraminer, Riesling, Cabernet Franc, Cabernet Sauvignon, Merlot, and Pinot Noir. Also Brut Champagne, Riesling Ice Wine, Vignoles Ice Wine, OCR (Octagon Cellars Reserve), and Reserve Red and White. Unique to the area are the fruity beer varieties, such as Captain Curry's Lager, Grace House Honey

Wheat, Mill Street Pilsner, Seneca Trail Pale Ale, and Caywood Station Stout. One of the largest operations in the Finger Lakes, the winery is in a striking octagonal building set in the 250-acre vineyard, along with a twenty-barrel German-style brewery. Owner Bill Wagner also presides over beer and wine-tastings, a large gift shop, and café.

Hermann J. Wiemer (607-243-7971, 800-371-7971; fax 607-243-7983; www. wiemer.com; 3962 Rte. 14, PO Box 38, Dundee NY 14837; halfway between Geneva and Dundee on the west side of the lake) Owner Hermann Wiemer features wines only from Vitis vinifera grapes: Chardonnay, Alsace-style Gewürztraminer, Riesling, Sparkling Wine, Brut Champagne, Late Harvest Riesling, Merlot, and Pinot Noir. The handsome winery is designed within an old dairy barn set on beautiful grounds overlooking the lake. Wiemer also grows vines for other wineries. Winetastings and a picnic area are offered.

Keuka Lake

Barrington Cellars (315-536-9686; 2772 Gray Rd., Penn Yan NY 14527) This small, family-owned winery features wines made from Vitis labrusca grapes (native American) and French hybrids. Owners Ken and Eileen Farnan offer Pink Cat, Isabella Rosé, and dessert wines; Bliss, Isabella, and Niagra Ice Wines. Visitors can enjoy winetastings, wine shop, and the 100-year-old farmhouse.

Bully Hill Vineyards above Keuka Lake has a visitor center, gift shop, restaurant, and museum.

Peter Finger

Bully Hill Vineyards (607-868-3610, 607-868-3210; fax 607-868-3205; www.bully hill.com; 8843 Greyton H. Taylor Memorial Dr., Hammondsport NY 14840-1458) Owner Walter S. Taylor, a creative pioneer in winemaking and a grandson of the founder of the Taylor Wine Company, has produced many award-winning wines. Wines from French-American hybrids include

Aurora, Baco Noir, Cayuga White, Ravat (Vignoles), Seyval Blanc, and Vidal Blanc. Blends carry often humorous names like Meat Market Red, Miss Love White, Space Shuttle Rosé, and Le Goat Blush. Flying Fortress pays tribute to the National Warplane Museum in Elmira. Champagnes include Mother Ship Over Paris Champagne Rouge and Seyval Blanc Brut Champagne. The winery's lovely weathered barns in hillside gardens look out over marvelous lake views; the Bully Hill Restaurant has both indoor and deck dining. Winetastings, gift shop, retail store, and the Greyton H. Taylor Wine and Grape Museum also enhance the visit. Bully Hill's colorful and distinctive wine labels are worthy of collecting.

Dr. Frank's Vinifera Wine Cellars and Chateau Frank (607-868-4884, 800-320-0735; fax 607-868-4888; www.drfrankwines.com; 9749 Middle Rd., Hammondsport NY 14840) The Frank family winery, set on seventy-nine hillside acres overlooking Keuka lake, features barrel-fermented Chardonnay, Gewürztraminer, Riesling, Pinot Noir, Rkatsiteli, Cabernet Sauvignon, and a sparkling Riesling, Célèbre. Chateau Frank is a premium sparkling wine made in the méthode champenoise style. The winery was founded in 1962 by one of the Finger Lakes' most important winemakers, Dr. Konstantin Frank, who showed how the prized European grape varieties could be grown in the region and how world-class table wines could be produced. His Pinot Noir vines are the oldest in the Finger Lakes, producing a more complex, full-bodied wine not possible with younger vines. It is no wonder his wines have been critically acclaimed. After Dr. Frank's death in 1985, his son Willy Frank took over the operations. Willy's son, Fred, is president of the company. Winetastings are offered daily.

Heron Hill Winery (607-868-4241, 800-441-4241; fax 607-868-3435; www.heron hill.com; 9249 County Rte. 76, Hammondsport NY 14840) A handsome new building with a winetasting room and other facilities showcases a breathtaking view of the lake. Owners John and Josephine Ingle feature Chardonnay, Johannisberg Riesling, Pinot Noir, Eclipse, Baco Noir, Seyval Blanc, Harmony Red and White, blends from hybrid and Vitis vinifera grapes; the Rockin' Robin series uses native American grapes. The Game Bird series comes with recipes for preparing game. Visitors can enjoy winetastings, a shop, restaurant, deli, conference room, banquet space, oak barrel room, and patio.

Hunt Country Vineyards (315-595-2812, 800-946-3289; fax 315-595-2835; www. uncorknewyork.com; www.huntcountryvineyards.com; 4021 Italy Hill Rd., Branchport NY 14418) Scenic trails here are open to hikers and cyclers, who are invited to bring their lunch for picnicking. The operating family farm, with horses grazing near the entrance road, includes a renovated 1820s barn with a winetasting room, deck, and shop. Owners Art and Joyce Hunt focus on speciality wines, and feature Riesling, Barrel Reserve Chardonnay, Foxy Lady (blush), Classic Red and White, Seyval, Cayuga, Vignoles, and Vidal Ice Wine. Tours and winetastings are offered.

Varieties of wines produced at Hunt Country Vineyards on Keuka Lake include Foxy Lady (blush), Barrel Reserve Chardonnay, and Vidal Ice Wine.

Peter Finger

Keuka Overlook Wine Cellars (607-292-6877; http://members.aol.com. keukaoverl/; 5777 Old Bath Rd., Dundee NY 14837) Owners Bob and Terry Barrett feature barrel-fermented and aged Chardonnay, Gewürztraminer, Riesling, Cabernet Sauvignon, Cabernet Franc, Pinot Noir and Merlot. Blends include Meritage and Triumph. The winery is set on one of the highest hillsides overlooking Keuka and Waneta lakes; there are winetastings, a large gift shop, picnic area, and the Keuka Overlook Bed & Breakfast Inn. Weekend getaway packages are offered with dinner and stay at the B&B.

Keuka Spring Vineyards (315-536-3147; 716-620-4850 off-season Nov.–May; www.keukaspringwinery.com; ksvwine@frontiernet.net; 273 E. Lake Rd./Rte. 54, Penn Yan NY 14527) Owners Judy and Len Wiltberger's gambrel-roofed barn houses the winetasting room; also on the historic property overlooking the lake is an 1840s homestead, and a picnic area. Featured wines are Chardonnay, Riesling, Cayuga Whites, Seyval Blanc, Vignoles, Cabernet Franc, Cabernet Sauvignon, Merlot, Pinot Noir, and Crooked Lake Red.

McGregor Vineyards and Winery (800-272-0192; fax 607-292-6929; www.l inkny.com/~mcg; 5503 Dutch St., Dundee NY 14837) Set on a hill overlooking Bluff Point, one of the most scenic overviews in the state, the winery is in a modest-sized barn. Owners Robert and Margaret McGregor feature Chardonnay, Pinot Noir aged in French oak, Alsatian-style Riesling, Gewürztraminer, Johannisberg Rieslings, Blanc de Noir, Muscat Ottonel, Lake Harvest Vignoles, Black Russian Red, Highlands Red, Chardonnay Blanc de Blanc Champagne, and Sunflower White, a blend of Vitis vinifera and French-American hybrid grapes. Verdelet and Muscat Ottonel are produced by only a few other vineyards in the Finger Lakes. Visitors can enjoy winetastings and a picnic terrace.

Pleasant Valley Wine Company/Great Western Winery, Keuka Lake.

Katharine Delavan Dyson

Pleasant Valley Wine Company/Great Western Winery (607-569-6111; fax 607-569-6112; GWWinery@InfoBlvd.net; 8260 Pleasant Valley Rd., Hammondsport NY 14840) Owner Michael Doyle features Great Western Champagne, Chardonnay, Riesling, Verdelet, Port, Sherry, Marsala, Madeira, Brut Rosé, and Labrusca grape varieties. The eight stone buildings here, very European in feeling, are listed on the National Register of Historic Places. Their ornate interiors have elaborate carved wood paneling and molding, and period furniture. The storage areas house enormous wine vats and barrels. Caves are carved into the valley's hillside, and a working model of the Bath-Hammondsport Railroad is on the grounds. Visitors can also enjoy winetastings, tours, and the Great Western Winery visitor center, with a theater, memorabilia, and wine equipment spanning 140 years. Established in 1860, this was the first bonded United States winery. In 1873 Great Western became the first American champagne to win a gold medal in Europe at the Vienna exposition.

Canandaigua

Arbor Hill Grapery (716-374-2406; www.thegrapery.com; 6459 Rte. 64, Bristol Springs, Naples NY 14512) John and Katie Brahm preside over eighteen acres and feature Chardonnay, Riesling, Pinot Noir, Cayuga White, Maréchal Foch, Traminette, Vidal Blanc, Catawba, Niagara, and Celebration sparkling wine. Winetastings are offered and the shop sells everything remotely connected to grapes. Try their homemade grape pies and other gourmet foods using wine and grapes.

Peter Finger

Widmer's Wine Cellars in Naples, at the southern end of Canandaigua Lake, was one of the first wineries in the region to offer varietal wines (one-grape wines) and dated vintage wines. Here almost a thousand barrels of sherry are stored on the winery's roof, where it ages in the sun from four to six years, a technique derived from the Spanish solera system.

Widmer's Wine Cellars (716-374-6311, 800-836-5253; fax 716-374-2028; www.widmerwine.com; 1 Lake Niagara Lane, Naples NY 14512) On the hills overlooking the Naples valley, the Canandaigua Wine Company offers sherries, sparkling wines, Lake Niagara, Crackling Lake Niagara, and Port. Visitors can enjoy winetastings, tours of underground cellars and the bottling facility, and the gift and wine shop. The Widmer Antique Museum displays a collection of old winemaking equipment. Manischewitz, a line of kosher premium varietals, is made here.

CHAPTER NINE
Host Cities
SYRACUSE, CORTLAND, ELMIRA, CORNING, AND ROCHESTER

Five major cities anchor the Finger Lakes region. Starting in the northeast corner is Syracuse, a city on the move to rebuild and recharge the vitality of its downtown. Further south on the eastern border of the region and just off Rte. I-81 is Cortland, hub of downhill skiing for the eastern Finger Lakes.

Elmira, once the home of Samuel Clemens (Mark Twain), sits on the southern fringe just off Rte. 17. Corning, home of the extraordinary Museum of Glass, is just west of Elmira. At the northwestern corner is Rochester, a vibrant city of high-tech business, museums, and upscale suburbs.

I have lived in Rochester and grew up just a half hour from Syracuse. Still, it was only in revisiting

Peter Finger

The Corning Museum of Glass offers an extensive overview of the history of glass and demonstrations in the art of making beautiful glass objects.

these and other cities for the purpose of writing this book that I realized just how much these places had to offer. Hence this chapter "Host Cities." Although these cities do serve as gateways to the Finger Lakes region, it would be a pity simply to pass through to get where you're going — each one of these cities is worth a good long linger.

SYRACUSE

Syracuse is perhaps best known as the home of Syracuse University and the site of the New York State Fair, which brings close to a million visitors to the fairgrounds each year. Increasingly, however, the city has much more to offer.

At the crossroads of two interstate highway systems, the east-west New York State Thruway and the north-south I-81, Syracuse has important businesses such as New Process Gear, Carrier Corporation, Niagara Mohawk, and Lockheed Martin, three major newspapers, an international airport, and excellent hospitals including SUNY Upstate Medical Center. Forty-four private and state colleges are in the Greater Syracuse region; in Onondaga County alone, there are eight schools including Syracuse University, with more than 18,000 students, and Le Moyne College.

On the cultural scene, Syracuse has its own symphony orchestra, opera company, and several museums and art galleries including the Everson Museum of Art. The Carrier Dome, a venue for athletic and other events; the gigantic New York State Fair; Oncenter, a multi-purpose facility; and the many parks and golf courses are further assets residents and visitors enjoy.

Syracuse has its own lake, Onondaga, but unfortunately it is not yet safe for swimming or drinking. In the past, companies on the lake's shore haphazardly allowed their industrial waste to run into the lake and pollute its waters. A massive effort is underway to clean it up, but experts predict it will take several years before the lake is back to where it should be. Still, it is a pleasant visual asset with a recreational area, Onondaga Lake Park, which runs for five miles along the west shore of the lake. The park has three trails: one for walking and running, one for biking and rollerblading, and another for exploring. The Onondaga Lake Parkway is closed to traffic in the summer months on Sunday for hikers, rollerbladers, joggers, etc.

Fifty years ago, Salina Street in downtown Syracuse was the place to come for fashionable shopping. Those looking for clothes and gifts shopped in department stores like W.E. Addis Co. (1916), E.W. Edward, and Dey Brothers, stopped for hot fudge sundaes at Schrafts, and dined at the Hotel Syracuse. When the malls opened in the suburbs, shoppers left town. One after another, the retailers either moved to the malls or closed their doors completely.

Now Syracuse's downtown area is making a comeback. Armory Square, an area of buildings in the center of town, has been reclaimed and now houses chic shops and restaurants. The Syracuse Hotel and other in-town hotels and buildings are being renovated; the striking Art Deco Niagara Mohawk building is illuminated by layers of color when the sun sets and there are plans to light up the entire downtown area at night.

Clinton Square is the site of summer concerts and other events; automobile enthusiasts are being drawn into the city with such events as the Syracuse

National 2001 Show, which will bring up to 6,000 people to the Empire Exposition Center. Street rod events will also bring more than 10,000 antique cars into town for a five-day event in July.

The Carousel Center, already the largest mall in the region, may get even bigger if a major new project goes through to build a complex just across from the Center. The plans call for three hotels, an aquarium, entertainment facilities, and a sky bridge connecting it to the Carousel Center.

LODGING

Syracuse is represented by most major hotel chains. Several of the in-city hotels are undergoing restoration. The Syracuse Hotel, listed as one of the Historic Hotels of America and now a part of the Radisson group, has renovated its grand ballroom and its guestrooms. The following speciality hotels and B&Bs provide other options.

The Craftsman Inn (315-637-8000; 7300 E. Genesee St., Fayetteville NY 13066) The ninety-three rooms and suites are furnished in the simple Arts and Crafts mode with clean lines, rich colors, wood moldings, and Stickley tables and chairs. Rooms are equipped with the latest in communications equipment.

Crest Hill Suites (315-463-0258, 888-723-1655; www.cresthillsuites.com; 6410 New Venture Gear Dr., E. Syracuse NY 13057) At Carrier Circle near I-81, the NY State Thruway, and major area employers, this all-suite hotel is designed for extended-stay business travelers and frequent guests. Suites are spacious and come with work areas equipped with free high-speed internet access, multiple telephone lines with speaker phones, and voice mail. There are studios, and one- and two-bedroom suites.

Dickerson House on James (315-423-4777; 1504 James St., Syracuse NY 13203) The five guestrooms in this B&B are on the top floor of this gracious old house on one of the best residential streets in the city.

Giddings Garden B&B (315-492-8542, 800-377-3452; 290 E. Seneca Tpk., Syracuse NY 13207) The three rooms in this historic 1810 house feature four-poster beds, down comforters, and marble baths. Guests also enjoy fireplaces, gardens, and a full breakfast.

Hotel Syracuse/Radisson Plaza (315-422-5121, 800-333-3333; www.hotelradisson.com or http://www.hotelsyracuse.com; 500 S. Warren St., Syracuse NY 13202) 600 guestrooms in this historic hotel in the heart of Syracuse; an indoor pool, fitness facility, three ballrooms, and meeting rooms.

Sheraton University Hotel and Conference Center (315-475-3000, 800-395-2105; www.syracusesheraton.com; 801 University Ave., Syracuse NY 13210) This 231-room hotel with an indoor pool and fitness facility is on the campus of Syracuse University.

RESTAURANTS

Alto Cinco (315-422-6399; 526 Wescott St., Syracuse) Mexican cuisine: the real thing.

Arad Evans Inn (315-637-2020; 7206 E. Genesee St., Fayetteville) Serving French American food beautifully presented. Desserts are over the moon.

Aunt Josie's Restaurant (315-471-9082; 1110 N. Salina St., Syracuse) Tradition, tradition, tradition, Italian style. Red and white checkered table cloths and a simple setting with excellent homemade pasta and sauces.

Brick Alley Grille House (315-472-3990; 317 Montgomery St., Syracuse) A café-style restaurant serving creative cuisine inside or out.

Coleman's Authentic Irish Pub (315-476-1933; 100 S. Lowell Ave., Syracuse) A super pub with a long wooden bar and full-service restaurant housed in a wonderful old building on the west side of town. Great pub fare, ales, and beer.

The Craftsman House (315-637-9999; 7300 E. Genesee St., Fayetteville) The interior is furnished in the simple Arts and Crafts mode — clean lines with lots of wood and Stickley tables and chairs. Food is American traditional with items like steak, brook trout, and prime ribs.

The Dark Room (315-446-2072; E. Genesee St., Dewitt) A small place that packs a powerful punch when it comes to fresh, eclectic cuisine.

Dinosaur Bar-B-Q (315-476-4937; 246 Willow St., Syracuse) It's been called the best place to get barbecue in the east. One thing is for sure: portions are huge and the ribs are finger-lickin' good and the decor featuring biker memorabilia is fun. The place is full all the time. Outside Harleys are parked next to BMWs and SUVs.

Empire Brewing Company (315-475-2337; 120 Walton St., Syracuse) Enjoy a casual meal and a glass of Stout or "Skinny Atlas Light" while watching beer being brewed behind the glass wall.

Glen Loch Restaurant (315-469-6969; 4626 North St., Jamesville) What a setting: an 1827 mill alongside a stream and waterfall. Food is hearty American traditional.

Hyde's of Liverpool (315-451-0786; 305 Oswego St., Corner of Old Liverpool Rd. and Onondaga Lake Parkway, Liverpool) It's been here for years serving up coneys, bratwurst, and all the fixin's.

The Inn Between Restaurant (315- 672-3166; 2290 W. Genesee Turnpike, Rte. 5, Camillus) See Chapter Three, *Skaneateles.*

Kahunaville (315-422-4500; Carousel Center, Syracuse) There's a gushing waterfall with a periodic sound and light show, a dark jungly rainforest ambiance, and lots of plants and bird sounds. The menu includes exotic drinks garnished with flowers, tortilla wraps, burgers, nachos, stir fries, and other such fare. Kids get a kick out of it.

Lemon Grass Grille (315-475-1111; 238 W. Jefferson St., Syracuse) Pacific Rim cuisine including Thai specialities. In the Armory Square.

The Mission Restaurant (315-475-7344; 304 E. Onondaga St., Syracuse) It looks like a tiny church with a steeple; inside, red brick, stained glass, and hand-painted walls add to the sense of mission. Food is south of the border and island Caribbean with super margueritas and fajitas.

Pascale's Wine Bar and Restaurant (315-471-3040; 204 W. Fayette St., Syracuse) An elegant little place specializing in continental cuisine. Fabulous bakery scones.

Pastabilities (315-474-1153; 311 S. Franklin St., Syracuse) The name says it all. Homemade bread, too, from their bread and bake shop across the street.

Spaghetti Warehouse (315-475-1807; 689 N. Clinton St., Syracuse) It's huge with lots of brick and wood and lofty ceilings but the booths make it more intimate. Serves spaghetti and much more.

To the Moon (315-478-1003; 305 Burnet Ave., Syracuse) A nice bistro-style place with superb creative cuisine from one of Syracuse's best chefs.

ATTRACTIONS

Beaver Lake Nature Center (315-638-2519; 8477 E. Mud Lake Rd., Baldwinsville) Explore forest, meadows, and wetlands along miles of trails and boardwalks. Paddle a canoe across the lake, learn about maple sugaring, go snowshoeing, and tour the visitor center.

Clinton Square (in the center of downtown Syracuse near Armory Square) This is the venue for a variety of outdoor musical and theatrical events in the summer such as jazz nights and blues festivals. During the Blues Festival, every bar and restaurant in the area features entertainment. In the winter Clinton Square becomes an ice skating rink.

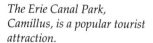
The Erie Canal Park, Camillus, is a popular tourist attraction.

Peter Finger

Erie Canal Museum (315-471-0593; 318 Erie Blvd., E. Rte. 5 at Montgomery St., Syracuse) Find out about the history of the canal in the nineteenth-century Weighlock Building. You can view the story of Syracuse in the theater, take a historical walking tour, and explore the *Frank B. Thomson*, a 65-foot replica of an old canal boat. A reconstructed vintage tavern has a bar and a gift shop. The research library contains more than 40,000 prints. The museum is also available for private parties.

Erie Canal Park and Sims' Store Museum (315-488-3409; Devoe Rd., Camillus) Set on the banks of the old Erie Canal, cruises include a summer dinner cruise Wednesday, boat rides Sunday. Open weekends May–Oct.

Everson Museum of Art (315-474-6064; 401 Harrison St., Syracuse) Designed by I.M. Pei, this museum contains a fabulous collection of ceramics as well as other arts and revolving exhibits. Ten galleries on three levels. Special exhibitions, tours, lectures, workshops, and film series. Open Tues.–Fri. & Sun. 12–5, Sat. 10–5.

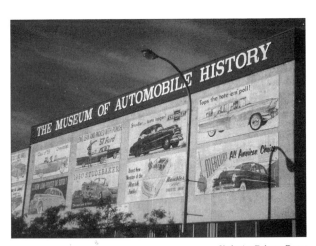

The Museum of Automobile History, Syracuse, is filled with memorabilia from the world of cars.

Katharine Delavan Dyson

Museum of Automobile History (315-478-CARS; 321 N. Clinton St., Syracuse) It's the world's largest collection of automobilila in the world, jump-started by Walter Miller's love of the automobile and his passion for collecting anything remotely related to cars. See old billboards, license plates, fine art memorabilia, old magazines, the last speeding ticket James Dean received before dying in a car crash that same night, toys, prototypes of manufactured cars, and more than 10,000 bits of history.

MOST: Milton J. Rubenstein Museum of Science and Technology (315-425-9068; 500 S. Franklin St., Syracuse) Buzzing with activity, this handsome brick building is filled with exhibits, many interactive. Go through the giant maze, thrill to dinosaurs, climb the rock wall, see how your lungs work as you navigate your way through the human body, stand inside a humungous bubble, and learn about the universe at the Silverman Planetarium. The only domed IMAX theater in the state, the Bristol Omnitheater, with its six-story screen, puts you in the middle of the action of sweeping films about climbing Mt. Everest or diving into the depths of the ocean.

Nascar Speedway (315-479-7223, 877-633-3773; www.smsonline.com; Carousel Center, Syracuse) You get not only the thrill of driving a car fast, but you also learn how to drive it, feel the tension, and hear the sounds. And all from your stationary car in this novel new attraction. A big screen in front of your windshield gives you the illusion you are actually racing. See if you can beat the masters.

Oncenter (315-435-8000; 800 S. State St., Syracuse) This multi-purpose facility combines the Onondaga County Convention Center, Onondaga County War Memorial, and John H. Mulroy Civic Center. It's used as a convention center, sports arena, meeting place, banquet hall, ice rink, concert hall, showroom, and theater.

Onondaga Historical Association Museum (315-428-1864; 311 Montgomery St., Syracuse) Filled with historical information, paintings, maps, and rare artifacts spanning 300 years of history. Of special interest are letters home from Civil War soldiers. The OHA's Research Center contains thousands of photos, maps, and other documents.

Ontrack (800-424-1212; platforms at Carousel Center, Armory Square, Syracuse University) Originally started to get Syracuse University students around, its services have been expanded to include an extensive network of routes taking in historic areas, fall foliage tours, even cowboy holdups and a Santa's train.

P&C Stadium (315-474-7833; Hiawatha Blvd., Syracuse) Home of the Toronto Blue Jays affiliated with Syracuse SkyChiefs and venue for many events.

Plainville Farms Pioneer Learning Center (315-635-3427; 7830 Plainville Rd., Plainville) Tour a replica of a primitive log cabin and see items used by our early settlers. Indoor animal petting area with lots of live turkeys and favorite farm animals. Light lunches served. Open late May until late Nov., Mon.-Sat. 10–5:30, Sun. 12–5; free.

Relyea Brewing Company (315-428-9794; 222 Teall Ave., Syracuse) Tour the microbrewery facility which specializes in Erie Canal–themed products such as Double Lock Lager.

Rosamond Gifford Zoo at Burnet Park (315-435-8511; One Conservation Place, Syracuse) Recent improvements to the original Burnet Park facility have resulted in a first-class zoo. One of the favorite attractions is Preya, a baby elephant born in the zoo. See Siberian tigers, penguins and seals, a rainforest with birds, and 600 other animals which live in spacious, natural-looking environments.

The Burnet Park Zoo, Syracuse, is popular with all ages.

Finger Lakes Association

Sainte Marie among the Iroquois (315-453-6767; Rte. 370, on Onondaga Lake Parkway, Liverpool) Established by Jesuit missionaries in the 1600s to foster friendly relations with the Iroquois, the site overlooking Onondaga Lake contains a museum and a re-created seventeenth-century village. Villagers and native Americans in period dress tell visitors about their life as they go about their business. There is a garden, cookhouse, forge, and other buildings.

The Salt Museum (315-453-6715; Rte. 370, Liverpool) Covers 150 years of the salt industry.

Syracuse Opera (315-476-7372; 411 Montgomery St., Syracuse) This year-round opera company offers three productions each season in addition to ongoing educational programs.

Syracuse Stage (315-443-3275; www.syracusestage.org; 820 E. Genesee St., Syracuse) This professional theater produces seven or more mainstage play during the season which runs from Sept. through May. It also features productions for young people.

Syracuse Symphony Orchestra (315-424-8222; 411 Montgomery St., Syracuse) The symphony offers concerts at various venues around the city.

RECREATION

Syracuse has several excellent 18-hole golf courses, including the following:

Drumlins: 315-446-5580; 800 Nottingham Rd., Syracuse
Foxfire North Golf and Tennis: 315-638-2930; One Village Blvd., Baldwinsville
Radisson Community Golf Course: 315-638-0092; Potter Rd., Baldwinsville
West Hill Golf and Country Club: 315-672-8677; West Hill, Camillus

Peter Finger

Sainte Marie among the Iroquois, in Syracuse, is a living museum of the time when native Americans and French lived together on the shores of Onondaga Lake.

SHOPPING

Armory Square (Headquarters: 500 S. Franklin St., Syracuse) Located in an area taking in Walton St., S. Clinton St., W. Jefferson St., and S. Franklin, Armory Square is highly recommended for more intimate speciality shopping where you can get away from the mall crowds. Browse small boutiques, crafts shops, and other speciality stores such as Artifice Gallery, Dobbs Glassworks, Eureka Crafts, and I've Been Framed. Gift shops include The Added Touch, Enchanted Bazaar, Just for You Design, M.O.S.T. Gift Shop, P'Liptin's Something Special, and Suzie Q. Gift Shoppe. There are also jewelry stores, clothing stores, and other speciality retailers as well as restaurants and pubs.

The Carousel Center (315-466-7000; www.carouselcenter.com; 9090 Carousel Center Dr., Syracuse) With close to 250 retail outlets and services as well as a working carousel and food court, this is the largest mall in the Northeast. It contains a nineteen-screen cinema complex, banquet and meeting facilities, and a 1909 antique carousel.

Muench-Keuzer Candle Company (315-423-0319; 617 E. Hiawatha Blvd., Syracuse) It's small and hard to find (four blocks from the Carousel Center), but with prices from about 20 cents and up for tapers, votives, and novelty candles, it's worth the effort.

Pascale's Bake House & Café (315-471-3050; 304 Hawley Ave., Syracuse) A small café and bakery where the smell of freshly baked breads and pastries entice you to indulge.

Syracuse China Factory Outlet Store (315-455-4581; 2900 Court St., Syracuse) Syracuse China and Libbey Glass at 20 to 70 percent off. Open Mon.–Weds. 10–7, Thurs.–Fri. 10–9, Sat. 10–6, Sun. 11–5.

CORTLAND

On the southeastern corner of the Finger Lakes region, Cortland is home to the State University at Cortland and is close to three popular ski areas: Greek Peak at Virgil, Song Mountain at Preble, and Labrador at Truxton. Just north of Cortland around Preble are several natural lakes, including Tully Lake, Song Lake, Goodale Lake, and Little Green Lake. Little York Lake is part of Dwyer Memorial Park where you find Little York Pavilion, a National Historical Preservation site, and the Cortland Repertory Theatre.

Just west of Cortland, the historic district of Homer Village contains dozens of lovely nineteenth-century homes in the Greek Revival and Queen Anne style. The village green is the scene of year-round activities: concerts, fairs, sporting events, ice skating. At 26 Clinton Street, there is an excellent example of an octagonal house, a popular architectural style during the mid-1800s. The Salisbury-Pratt Homestead, on Rte. 281 between Homer and Little York, was part of the Underground Railroad.

ATTRACTIONS

Cortland Country Music Park (607-753-0377; Rte. 13N, Cortland) Dance Hall, Hall of Fame Museum, campground, and outdoor performance center.

Cortland Repertory Theatre (607-756-2627, Rte. 281, Pavilion Theatre, Little York Lake) Professionals perform from June through August.

1890 House Museum and Center for Victorian Arts (607-756-7551; 37 Tompkins St., Cortland) A castle-like stone manor with a round tower houses artifacts, furniture, and memorabilia from the Victorian era.

Suggett House Museum and Kellogg Memorial Research Library (607-756-6071; 25 Homer Ave., Cortland) Home of the Cortland County Historical Society.

RECREATION

GOLF:

Elm Tree Golf Course (607-753-1341; State Rte. 13, Cortland) 18 holes, weekday specials.

Maple Hill (607-849-3285; Conrad Rd., Marathon) Highest rated of 18-hole area courses from the back tees with ponds and dog-legs. Pro shop, restaurant.

Walden Oaks Country Club (607-753-9452; 3369 Walden Oaks Blvd., Cortland) Highest rated from the white and red tees for area 18-hole courses. Watered tees and fairways; ponds, restaurant, clubhouse, locker rooms, and showers.

Willow Brook Golf Club (607-756-7382; 3267 Rte. 215, Cortland) 18 holes, restaurant, pro shop, and weekday specials. A pleasant family-owned course.

HIKING:

Lime Hollow Nature Center (607-758-LHNC; Gracie Rd., Cortland) An interpretive center, hiking trails.

SKIING:

Greek Peak Ski Resort (607-835-6111, 800-955-2754; www.greekpeak.net; 2000 Rte. 392, Cortland) Home of the Magic Carpet lift, Greek Peak has close to thirty trails, seven ski lifts, a tubing center, more than 200 instructors, night skiing, cross-country trails, Children's Learning Center, slopeside accommodations, lodge, and restaurants.

Labrador Mountain (607-842-6204, 800-446-9559; Rte. 91, Truxton) Twenty-two slopes, downhill skiing, snowboarding, night skiing, three base lodges, instruction, babysitting, and ski rentals.

Song Mountain (315-696-5711; 1 Song Mountain Rd., Tully) Song has twenty-five trails and five lifts.

Toggenburg Ski and Board Center (315-683-5842; Toggenburg Rd., Fabius) Trails and lodge.

ELMIRA

Samuel Clemens, better known as Mark Twain, spent several summers in this quiet town with his wife, Olivia Langdon, an Elmira native. Here he wrote much of such beloved novels as *The Adventures of Huckleberry Finn* and *Tom Sawyer*. He did much of his work in an octagonal study now on the Elmira College Campus.

Those interested in the life and work of this famous author can visit the Mark Twain Exhibit in Hamilton Hall and see his grave in Woodlawn Cemetery.

Elmira is also known as the "Soaring Capital of America." From 1930 to 1946, the city hosted national soaring contests. Today you can visit the National Soaring Museum and take a sailplane ride at Harris Hill Soaring Corp.

Other area attractions include the Clemens Center, a great venue for plays, concerts, and other cultural performances; Arnot Art Museum, exhibiting current work as well as old masters and nineteenth-century paintings; Tanglewood Nature Center, site of walking and hiking trails, and picnic areas; and the Near Westside Historic District, featuring guided and self-guided tours of historic houses.

LODGING

Halcyon Place Bed & Breakfast (607-529-3544; 197 Washington St., Chemung NY 14825) On pleasant grounds with herb and flower gardens, this lovely Greek Revival home built in 1820 is furnished with antiques and period reproductions. A full breakfast is served.

Holiday Inn (607-734-4211; Elmira-Riverview, 760 E. Water St., No. 1 Holiday Plaza, Elmira NY 14901) Convenient for business or leisure travelers.

Lindenwald Haus (607-733-8753; 1526 Grand Central Ave., Elmira NY 14901) Set on five acres with an outdoor pool, this 1875 Italianate mansion is conducive to relaxing in the huge living room or cooling off in the pool.

Rufus Tanner House (607-732-0213; 60 Sagetown Rd., Pine City NY 14871) A B&B with four rooms with private baths and moderate rates. Like many old houses in the area, this 1864 farmhouse sits in a grove of 100-year-old sugar maples producing enough maple syrup for pancake breakfasts. Furnishings are mostly antiques; one room has a queen-size bed and a fireplace. Another has a jacuzzi. Rooms are air-conditioned.

RESTAURANTS

Hill Top Inn (607-732-6728; 171 Jerusalem Hill Rd., Elmira) The oldest licensed restaurant in Elmira, Hill Top serves American cuisine indoors or outdoors where diners enjoy beautiful views of the countryside.

Pierce's 1894 Restaurant (607-734-2022; 228 Oakwood Ave., Elmira Heights) Serving American and continental cuisine, Pierce's is on the elegant side with period furnishings.

ATTRACTIONS

Arnot Art Museum (607-734-3697, 235 Lake St., Elmira) European and American art exhibits as well as contemporary traveling exhibits are housed in a neoclassical mansion.

Chemung Valley Living History Center (607-732-3944; Newtown Battlefield) Historic reenactments and encampments in May, Aug., Oct.

The Clemens Center (607-733-5639; 207 Clemens Center Pkwy., Elmira) This is a major performing arts center offering international touring artists, Broad-

Finger Lakes Association

Mark Twain's study is on the Elmira College campus.

way musicals, concerts, jazz, rock'n'roll, dance, stand-up comedy, and children's theater.

Harris Hill Soaring (607-796-2988, 607-734-0641; Harris Hill, Rte. 17, Soaring Hill Dr., Elmira) Soar above the countryside with FAA-certified pilots.

Mark Twain Study and Exhibit (607-735-1941, Elmira College campus, One Park Place, Elmira) The octagonal study where Samuel Clemens wrote some of his well-known books while a summer resident in the town. Nearby an exhibit contains photographs and Mark Twain memorabilia.

National Soaring Museum (607-734-3128; Harris Hill, Exit 51, Rte. 17, 51 Soaring Hill Dr., Elmira) This aviation-orientation museum has a glider cockpit simulator, sailplane collection, and other exhibits.

National Warplane Museum (607-739-8200; near Elmira-Corning Regional Airport, 17 Aviation Dr., Horseheads) Here military aviation history comes to life through a series of exhibits and a collection of twenty-three vintage aircraft. You can watch old airplanes being restored, look inside the cockpits and gunners' areas, and walk under the wings of a PBY Catalina flying boat. Take a ride in "Fuddy Duddy," a restored B-17 aircraft with flights offered from May through October. The annual Wings of Eagles Air Show features more than 150 military aircraft in a thrilling two-day air show.

Trolley Tour (800-MARK TWAIN, leaves from Riverview Holiday Inn on E. Water St., Elmira) Ride in a turn-of-the-century green and gold trolley on this guided ninety-minute historic tour of the area. Stop at Mark Twain's study and Harris Hill.

RECREATION

GOLF:

Mark Twain Golf Course (Harris Hill, 2275 Corning Rd., Elmira) An 18-hole
Donald Ross–designed course with a large clubhouse and snack bar.

SHOPPING

Arnot Mall (607-739-8704; 3300 Chambers Rd. S., Horseheads) A major mall com-
plex with more than 100 stores, several theaters, food court, and restaurants.
The Christmas House (607-734-9547; 361 Maple Ave., Elmira) This 1894 Queen
Anne mansion features fifteen rooms full of holiday ornaments and gifts.
Santas, nutcrackers, decorated trees, and much more.
A Touch of Country (607-737-6945; 1019 Pennsylvania Ave., Elmira) A seven-
teen-room Victorian home filled with antiques, gifts, collectibles, and
Christmas items.

CORNING

*Centerway Square, Corning,
a beautiful market area in
town.*

Katharine Delavan Dyson

Thousands come to Corning each year to visit the Museum of Glass which
has expanded considerably over the past few years, and for this reason is
called "The *New* Corning Museum of Glass."

Corning is also home to the Hall of Science and Industry and the Steuben
Glass Factory, as well as a Historic Market Street with more than 100 craft
shops, artists' studios, gift stores, boutiques, cafés, and restaurants. This tree-

shaded street and Centerway Square are listed on the National Register of Historic Places and are graced by period lighting, hanging baskets of flowers, brick walkways, and restored nineteenth-century buildings. The Market Street restoration has been cited as a benchmark for Main Street America, a national program.

Market Street and Centerway are the venue for many special events including art and crafts fairs, street parties, jazz festivals, a festival of lights parade, and seasonal celebrations. The annual "Sparkle of Christmas" closes the streets to traffic so you can shop, take buggy rides, and enjoy the ice carving and live entertainment.

The old City Hall houses the Rockwell Museum, currently undergoing a major renovation. It contains a fabulous collection of art of the American West.

Shuttle bus service carries passengers from Market Street to the Corning Museum of Glass and other stops. This is a visitor-friendly town. You even get two free hours of parking.

LODGING

In addition to a number of chain hotels, including a Holiday Inn, Radisson Hotel, Best Western, and other chain properties, there are several inns and B&Bs.

1865 White Birch Inn B&B (607-962-6355; 69 E. First St., Corning NY 14830) Innkeepers Kathy and Joe Donahue's 1860s Victorian home has four guest-rooms. A full breakfast is served and the inn is within walking distance to town.

Rosewood Inn B&B (607-962-3253; www.rosewoodinn.com; 134 E. First St., Corning NY 14830) Suzanne and Stewart Sanders's lovely Victorian house is within walking distance of Market Street. The seven rooms have private baths; many of the rooms are decorated in soft warm colors like mauve and gray. The rooms are elaborately furnished with period antiques and memorabilia and all rooms are air-conditioned. Most have queen beds and all feature luxurious 300-thread-count linens. A full breakfast is served in the formal dining room.

Villa Bernese (607-936-2633; www.southerntier.net/vb; 11860 Overlook Dr., Corning NY 14830) Four rooms feature European-style amenities in a home that overlooks the Chemung River valley.

RESTAURANTS

Beauregard's Bakery and Café (607-962-2001; 23 W. Market St., Corning) The place for wedding cakes, cookies, strudels, sticky buns, croissants, and other yummy desserts. It's also popular for lunch where you eat in a cozy little café with brick walls, small counter, and booths. Sandwiches, box lunches, and soups are available.

Boomers/Boomers' Bistro (607-962-6800; 35 E. Market St.; 607-936-1408, 58 W. Market St., Corning) These two restaurants offer an extensive menu of American and California-style food. Children eat for 99 cents.

Ellis' Ice Cream Parlor and Eatery (607-936-2133; 1 Baron Steuben Place, W. Market St., Corning) Most of the fixtures and furnishings, including the hardcarved mahogany woodwork, come from an ice cream parlor of the 1800s. There is an old-fashioned soda fountain counter, marble-topped round tables, tile floor, and pressed metal ceiling. In addition to ice cream, there are salads, sandwiches, soup, hamburgers, and deli combos.

DeClemente's Deli (607-937-5657; 30 W. Market St., Corning) Eat at wrought iron tables outside or inside. This is one of the area's best delis.

Green Shingles Inn Restaurant and Lounge (607-523-7784; Rte. 15, Lindley) Watch your favorite teams on a 50-inch big screen television while you eat your wings and burgers. Popular with sports fans.

Lining up for ice cream from Jim's Texas Hots, Market Street, Corning.

Katharine Delavan Dyson

Jim's Texas Hots (607-936-1820; 8 W. Market St., Corning) There's no sign on the building, but there probably will be a line of customers outside to buy ice cream, hot dogs, and sandwiches. Texas Hots is hot.

London Underground Café (607-962-2345; 69 E. Market St., Corning) Serving regional American and European cuisine, this unique three-tiered restaurant has earned awards for its food and service. Everything is cooked in an open-style kitchen.

Pelham's Upstate Tuna Co. (607-936-TUNA; 73 E. Market St., Corning) If you want to cook your own fish or steak here, go for it. Pelham's features many unique items on its menu, but as you might guess, fish and seafood are big.

Sorge's Restaurant (607-937-5422; 66-68 W. Market St., Corning) This family-owned and operated Italian American restaurant is known among the locals for its homemade pasta dishes and friendly service.

Spencer's Restaurant and Mercantile (607-936-9196; 359 E. Market St., Corning) A busy, fun place with pasta cooked to order, seafood, fish fry, and many other items served in an intimate rustic setting a bit off the beaten track.

ATTRACTIONS

Benjamin Patterson Inn Museum Complex (607-937-5281; 59 W. Pulteney St., Corning) Guides in period costume show you through this restored 1796 inn, 1784 log cabin, 1878 one-room schoolhouse, and a nineteenth-century agricultural exhibit. Open Mon.–Fri. 10–4.

The New Corning Museum of Glass (800-732-6845; One Museum Way, Corning) Take the day or more to explore this intriguing complex. Start with the fifteen-minute film for an introduction to glass and what you'll be seeing. Learn about the history of glass-making, check out the Glass Innovation Center where the mysteries of creating windows, optical glass, and vessels are revealed, and purchase glass items like a giant lightbulb lamp, a glass putter, or Christmas ornaments in one of the seven shops (even if you've seen the museum a hundred times, this is a great place to come for unique gifts). A new gallery displays a dazzling array of contemporary glass sculptures from minute to towering; the studio provides instruction in all aspects of glass blowing and the Hot Glass Show enables you to watch master craftspeople transform gobs of molten glass into exquisite objects. Children and adults alike will enjoy the interactive exhibits.

Newly installed is a glass sculpture by Dale Chihuly, a thirteen-foot-high piece of green flame-like blown glass pieces inserted in a tree-like structure. (Another of his works is in the park in front of the Monte Carlo Casino.) There are two places to eat, including an outdoor patio, and a shuttle that runs back and forth from the Market Street area every fifteen minutes. And it seems they've thought of everything: even the jitney path and sidewalk are heated to make sure things keep moving even in the winter. Open daily 9–5; in July and Aug. open 9–8.

The Fun Park (near the intersection of E. Corning Rd./Rte. 352 & Gorton Rd., East Corning) This new family fun place on a thirty-two-acre site offers an 18-hole miniature golf course, a 32-foot hydraulically operated climbing rock, a petting zoo, pony rides, bumper boat ride, video game arcade, a 250-yard golf driving range, and a concession stand.

Rockwell Museum (607-937-5386; 111 Cedar St., Corning) At the time of publication, the Rockwell Museum was in the process of beginning a major renovation project to enhance the impressive collection of American Western

The Rockwell Museum, Corning, contains a splendid collection of art of the American West.

art. Artists represented include Frederic Remington, Thomas Moran, C.M. Russell, N.C. Wyeth, and painters from the Taos Society of artists. Special exhibits are designed to help children understand the importance of the heritage of the American West. Open Mon.–Sat. 9–5, Sun. 12–5.

SHOPPING

Market Street is a great place to get unique gifts and crafts. Then grab an ice cream or table in one of the small restaurants and ponder your purchases.

Bacalles Glass Shop (607-962-3339; 10 W. Market St., Corning) Everything glass like oil lamps, crystal, jewelry, and other items.

Books of Marvel (607-962-6300; 94 E. Market St., Corning) This store buys and sells thousands of out-of-print books for young people as well as National Geographic. Enter through Glass Menagerie.

Comics for Collectors (607-936-3994; 60 E. Market St., Corning) Superman, Wonder Woman, and hundreds of other old-time favorites.

Culture Shock (607-937-4358; 10-1/2 W. Market St., Corning) This store sells one-of-a-kind items like batiks, woven blankets, baskets, and jewelry.

The Glass Menagerie (607-962-6300; 37 E. Market St., Corning) Features hundreds of kaleidoscopes and paperweights along with crystal ornaments, jewelry, stained glass, bottles, animals, and other things.

Lost Angel Glass (607-937-3578; 79 W. Market St., Corning) Handcrafted glass in the contemporary mode.

Vitrix Hot Glass Studio (607-936-8707; 77 W. Market St., Corning) Glass artist Thomas Kelly works and sells his glass creations here.

West End Gallery (607-936-2011; 12 W. Market St., Corning) A fine art gallery selling paintings, prints, and contemporary work.

ROCHESTER

As the sixty-ninth largest city in the United States, with a population of more than a million people, Rochester offers all the cultural attractions and facilities you'd expect from a major urban area. Home of companies like Bausch & Lomb, Kodak, and Xerox, and with its own international airport, Rochester and its attractive suburbs are considered one of the nation's most desirable places to live.

As early as the mid-1800s, Rochester's thriving horticulture industry and gardens caused it to be called the "Flower City." Each May, the hundreds of varieties of lilacs planted in Highland Park — the largest public collection of lilacs in the world — are the focal point of the ten-day Lilac Festival.

Cultural attractions include the Geva Theatre, the Rochester Philharmonic Orchestra, the Eastman School of Music, The George Eastman House and International Museum of Photography and Film, the Memorial Art Gallery, the Rochester Museum and Science Center with its impressive planetarium, and the Strong Museum, a hands-on history center for families.

You can trace the history of the women's rights movement at the Susan B. Anthony House and Museum, see wild animals at the Seneca Park Zoo, and spend hours at the entertainment centers at High Falls Complex, one of Rochester's newest nightlife extravaganzas.

Among the many major players on the sports scene are the Rochester Redwings, an AAA baseball team, the Rochester Raging Rhinos, a champion soccer team, and the Rochester Americans hockey team, winner of several Calder Cups. With Lake Ontario on its northern boundaries and the many rivers and lakes in the region, Rochester residents enjoy a plethora of water sports. Bristol Mountain offers good downhill skiing, with a vertical drop of 1,200 feet, twenty-two trails, and five lifts. There are also many fine golf courses in the area including Greystone Golf Club.

Education plays a strong role in the city. Colleges include the Colgate Rochester Divinity School, Monroe Community College, Nazareth College of Rochester, Roberts Wesleyan College, Rochester Institute of Technology, and the University of Rochester.

Rochester was an important station on the Underground Railroad: Maplewood Park was part of the Railroad where slaves boarded boats headed from Rochester across Lake Ontario to Canada and freedom.

Famous residents include Frederick Douglass, African American orator, reformer, abolitionist, and publisher of the North Star newspaper; and George Eastman, who founded the Eastman Dry Plate Company, precursor to the Eastman Kodak Company. In 1888, the easy-to-use Kodak camera was introduced, as well as a flexible film that would help launch the motion picture industry. Another famous Rochester citizen, Susan B. Anthony, founded the Women's Educational and Industrial Union. Anthony worked all her life to secure rights for women.

LODGING

Most of the major hotel chains are represented in Rochester. There are also several small inns and bed and breakfasts in the area.

Avon Inn (716-226-8181; 55 E. Main St., Avon) This nineteenth-century country inn has fifteen rooms with private baths as well as a restaurant.

428 Mt. Vernon (800-836-3159; 716-271-0792; 428 Mt. Vernon St. at the entrance to Highland Park, Rochester) This B&B, a gracious Victorian home, is set on two acres. All rooms have private baths, phones, and televisions. A full breakfast is served.

Oliver Loud's Inn (716-248-5200; 1474 Marsh Rd., Pittsford) In a restored 1812 stagecoach inn on the canal, this inn is next to Richardson's Canal House restaurant.

RESTAURANTS

Bacco's Ristorante (716-442-5090; 263 Park Ave., Rochester) Italian cuisine in the Northern style starts with complimentary bruschetta and homemade bread. Delicious.

The Clark House (716-385-3700; 600 Whalen Rd., Penfield) Furnished in the colonial style and serving gourmet cuisine. The original structure, built in 1832, now houses the Blue and Clark rooms.

Daisy Flour Mill (716-381-1880; 1880 Blossom Rd., Penfield) In a restored 1848 post and beam gristmill overlooking Irondequoit Creek, Daisy's featured items include angus beef and seafood.

Dinosaur Bar-B-Q (716-325-7090; 99 Court St., Rochester) Super ribs and Cajun and Cuban food have gained Dinosaur a solid reputation for great meals and value.

Edwards Restaurant (716-423-0140; 13 S. Fitzhugh St., Rochester) In the historic Academy Building, Edwards serves French and American food in a rich British-club-style setting. Very elegant with excellent service.

The Grill at Water Street (716-454-1880; 175 N. Water St., Rochester) Sophisticated yet casual, the Grill serves innovative American cuisine with flair.

The Olive Tree (716-454-3510; 165 Monroe Ave., Rochester) The Olive Tree, in a historic brick building, is known for its superb Greek cuisine.

Park 54 (716-442-8890; 54 Park Ave., Rochester) A creative menu combining American and continental cuisine, art exhibits, and good service make this place a winner.

Richardson's Canal House (716-248-5000; 1474 Marsh Rd., Pittsford) On the roster of the National Register of Historic Places, this restored Erie Canal tavern offers a prix fixe meal featuring French and American regional food and a great location on the canal.

The Spring House (716-586-2300; 3001 Monroe Ave., Rochester) An early nineteenth-century four-story Southern Colonial-style inn with gardens and patio. Traditional American cuisine an old favorite among locals.

Tokyo Japanese Restaurant (716-424-4166; 2930 W. Henrietta Rd., Rochester) Great sushi, tempura, and other Japanese specialities.

Tapas 177 (716-262-2090; 177 St. Paul St., Old Rochesterville) An eclectic menu of Mediterranean food served by candlelight along with music on weekends for a warm, romantic ambiance.

ATTRACTIONS

Center at High Falls (716-325-2030; 60 Brown's Race, Rochester) Built on the banks of the Genesee River, this new urban cultural park features interactive 3-D exhibits such as a room-size "supermap," taxi tour, flour mill, and talking camera. There is the Triphammer Forge with multi-level views of 1816 factory ruins and an art gallery.

Eastman School of Music's Eastman Theatre (716-274-1100, 716-274-1400; 26 Gibb St., Eastman School of Music, Rochester) More than 700 concerts during the year are offered by students.

Genesee Country Village Museum (716-538-6822, 1410 Flint Hill Rd., Mumford) This is the third largest collection of historic buildings in the country, with fifty-seven restored structures portraying life in the Genesee region from the 1790s to the 1870s. There are houses, schools, farms, blacksmiths, and stores along with heirloom gardens and craftspeople on 400 acres. Costumed villagers, restaurants, ships, and picnic areas. Open May–Oct.; closed Mon.

Geological Tours (716-271-7368; PO Box 18937, 57 Clovercrest Dr., Suite 100, Rochester) This company features a full range of geologic and environmental tours throughout the Finger Lakes led by Mariana Rhoades.

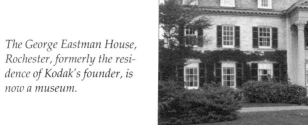

The George Eastman House, Rochester, formerly the residence of Kodak's founder, is now a museum.

Peter Finger

George Eastman House (716-271-3361, 900 East Ave., Rochester) This fifty-room historic turn-of-the-century house, which George Eastman called home, is filled with important collections of films, cameras, books, and photography in changing exhibits. The house and gardens have been restored to their early 1900s appearance. Closed Mon. and major holidays.

Geva Theatre (716-232-GEVA, 75 Woodbury Blvd., Rochester) This professional regional theater produces a variety of performances including comedies, musicals, and world premieres.

The Memorial Art Gallery, Rochester.

Peter Finger

Memorial Art Gallery (716-473-7720; 500 University Ave., Rochester) This gallery contains an enormous collections of art work spanning 5,000 years including works by Edgar Degas, Mary Cassatt, Henry Moore, Jacob

Lawrence, Hans Hofmann, the French impressionists, and many others. See revolving exhibits from the gallery's permanent collections plus exceptional art from leading contemporary and regional artists.

New York Museum of Transportation and the Rochester & Genesee Valley Railroad Museum (New York Museum of Transportation: 716-533-1113; http://www.nymt.mus.ny.us/; 6393 E. River Rd., West Henrietta NY 14586; Rochester & Genesee Valley Railroad Museum: 716-533-1431; http://www. rgvrrm.mus.ny.us/; 282 Rush-Scottsville Rd./Rte. 251, Rush NY 14543) See historic rail cars and vintage vehicles including a 1909 Erie Railroad depot, cabooses, trolleys, and a large HO model train. The two museums are connected by a railroad.

The Rochester Museum and Science Center is a popular attraction for families.

Peter Finger

Rochester Museum and Science Center (716-271-1880, 657 East Ave., Rochester) This museum focuses on archaeology, science, and technology, cultural heritage, and anthropology, and features a computerized star theater and CineMagic 870 theater at the Strasenburgh Planetarium, and a Seneca Iroquois display. Large-screen science/nature films are shown daily.

Rochester Philharmonic Orchestra (716-454-2620; Eastman School of Music's Eastman Theatre, 100 East Ave., Rochester) This critically acclaimed orchestra offers classical, pops, and special children's concerts including traditional favorites like the Nutcracker Ballet.

Seneca Park Zoo (716-467-WILD; 2222 St. Paul St., Rochester) River otters, polar bears, penguins, and other animals live in settings that approximate their natural environments. See Africa elephants, Bornean orangutans, wolves, kangaroos, and more than 300 other animals.

Strong Museum (716-263-2702, 1 Manhattan Sq., Rochester) A great museum with hands-on exhibits for kids who have fun while learning about history. Step onto Sesame Street, pilot a giant helicopter, shop for food in a king-sized

Sesame Street, a popular exhibit at the Strong Museum.

Greater Rochester Visitors Association

supermarket, and board a whaling ship. See collections of dolls, toys, miniatures, a 1950s diner, a 1918 carousel, and an old-fashioned ice cream fountain.

Susan B. Anthony House (716-235-6124; 17 Madison St., Rochester) This red brick house was the home for women's rights champion Susan B. Anthony from 1866 until her death in 1906. Today, the house is a museum filled with memorabilia from Anthony's life and the women's suffrage movement.

Seabreeze Park and Raging Rivers Waterpark (800-395-2500, 4600 Culver Rd., off I-590N, Rochester) Rides, slides, fun, games, soak zone, carousel, bumper cars, water park, giant Jack Rabbit roller coaster, food, entertainment. Four roller coasters. Open weekends May to mid-June; daily mid-June to Labor Day.

Victorian Doll Museum (716-247-0130; 4332 Buffalo Rd., North Chili) If you love dolls come here and browse through exhibits of thousands of collector's dolls of bisque, china, wood, wax, and paper. See Kewpie dolls, Noah's Ark toys, and a puppet theater.

RECREATION

CANAL CRUISES:

Colonial Belle (716-223-9470, 400 Packett's Landing, Fairport) A 246-passenger double-deck boat cruising the Erie Canal. On-board restaurant. Three cruises daily. Private charters.

Fairport Lady (716-223-1930, 10 Liftbridge Lane West, Fairport) An 80-passenger paddle-wheeler offering lunch and dinner cruises along the Erie Canal. Charters available.

Sam Patch (716-262-5661; Corn Hill Navigation, Ste. 7, 12 Corn Hill Terrace, Rochester) Canal cruises including lunch, brunch, and dinner cruises are offered aboard a replica of an authentic Erie Canal packet boat.

SHOPPING

More than 500 stores and services are at Rochester's four major malls: EastView Mall, Greece Ridge Center, Irondequoit Mall, and Marketplace Mall. Trendy Park Avenue, which runs from Alexander Street to Culver Road, contains a number of stylish shops, boutiques, and cafés. In the summer months, the street is a lively place with sidewalk cafés in full swing.

A.D. Flint Luggage and Leather Goods (716-325-5544; 111 Midtown Plaza, Rochester; 3400 Monroe Ave., Pittsford Colony Plaza) This store sells top quality leather goods, gifts, clocks, desk accessories, and travel items.

Irish Import Shop (716-225-1050; 3821 W. Ridge Rd., Rochester) This shop sells all things Irish from Belleek china and Celtic brass to sweaters and Waterford.

Stever's Candies (716-473-2098; 623 Park Ave., Rochester) For more than fifty years, Stever's has been making homemade candy on the premises including chocolates, nuts, brittles, truffles, jellies, and sugar-free candy.

For More Information

Chemung County Commerce Center: 800-MARK TWAIN; fax 607-734-4490; www.chemungchamber.org; 400 E. Church St., Elmira NY 14901-2803

Cortland County Convention and Visitors Bureau: 607-753-8463, 800-859-2227; 34 Tompkins St., Cortland NY 13045

Greater Corning Area Chamber of Commerce: 607-936-4686; www.Corning-Chamber.org; Baron Steuben Place, Second Floor, Corning NY 14830

Greater Rochester Chamber of Commerce: 716-454-2220; 55 St. Paul St., Rochester NY 14604

Syracuse Convention and Visitors Bureau: 315-470-1910, 800-234-4797; fax 315-471-8545; www.syracusecvb.org/; 572 S. Salina St., Syracuse NY 13202

CHAPTER TEN
Finger Lakes Facts and Figures
INFORMATION

Peter Finger

Finger Lakes tourist organizations offer information on everything from fruit and vegetable stands to museums.

In this chapter are facts and figures selected to enhance your Finger Lakes stay — a sampling of information from temperatures and newspapers to listings of annual events and visitor organizations.

AMBULANCE, FIRE, POLICE

Cayuga County Sheriff's Office: 315-253-1222
Seneca County Sheriff's Office: 315-539-9241
Steuben County Emergency Services/Control Center: 607-776-4099
Tompkins County Sheriff's Office: 607-272-2444
Tompkins County Ambulance/Fire: 607-273-8000
Tompkins County City Police: 607-272-3245
All other counties: 911

BOOKS

BIKING AND HIKING

Biking & Hiking in the Central Destinations of the Finger Lakes Region features detailed routes for every lake region; 800-CALL-NYS.

Take a Hike by Rich and Sue Freeman, Footprint Press, PO Box 645, Fishers NY 14453; 1999. A fabulous resource for serious as well as novice walkers and hikers. Highly detailed descriptions of trails, how to get there, contact information, maps, photos and historic information. $16.95.

30 Bicycle Tours in the Finger Lakes Region by Mark Roth and Sally Walters is a must-have for bicycle enthusiasts. Details include mile-by-mile directions, excellent maps, and history notes for each tour. $15.

HISTORY

Ontario County, compiled by Valerie Knoblauch, Ontario County Four Seasons Development Corp., 248 S. Main St., Canandaigua NY 14424; 1989. A marvelous history of Ontario County loaded with photos of notable people and places in the region's history and development.

As We Were, volumes 1 & 2, compiled by the Seneca Falls Historical Society, 1979. A random collection of early twentieth-century photographs of Seneca Falls. Available at the Seneca Falls Historical Society, 55 Cayuga St., Seneca Falls. $10.

WINERIES

Wineries of the Eastern States by Marguerite Thomas, Berkshire House Publishers; and *Wineries of the Finger Lakes Region* by Emerson Klees, Friends of Finger Lakes Publishing; excellent companions for exploring the wineries.

CLIMATE AND WEATHER

The climate in the Finger Lakes region can be fickle indeed. June, July, and August are usually gloriously warm and sunny. Fall comes around mid-October or even earlier, providing all the wonderful color and bright blue skies — perfect football weather. Snow usually comes in November, but has arrived as early as mid-October. When the snow rudely makes an early debut, it usually doesn't stay around long — kids have barely enough time to get their sleds out before the weather moderates and the snow melts.

Winter usually delivers deep snow — blustery, huddle-around-the fire-type stuff; temperatures can plunge below zero. The lakes often freeze. Some days the lakes are dotted with skaters and ice boaters.

One winter, driving above Skaneateles Lake, along Rte. 41 just outside of Scott, a small community of weathered buildings time forgot, I came upon a breathtaking sight. Apparently others thought so too. Drivers had parked their cars along the road so they could marvel at the icy wonderland suddenly created. Every twig, grass blade, and telephone pole wire was sheathed in a dazzling coat of ice which glistened in the sun.

The long-anticipated spring usually appears before Easter, but there have been years when the Easter bunny needed snowshoes. And times when the lakes have still not thawed out.

In summer, the temperatures are warm and balmy and in fact can get quite hot, sometimes into the 90s but seldom more than 100 degrees. Generally, the temperature average 75 degrees and the lakes warm up mid-July. There are exceptions. In 1996, a heat wave in June warmed the lakes so fast that people were swimming before the parks were open and rafts were out.

Summer fun at Fillmore Glen State Park, Moravia.

Peter Finger

Average Temperatures in the Finger Lakes

Summer: day mid-80s; night 50s to 60s
Fall: day mid-60s; night mid-40s
Winter: day mid-30s; night teens to mid-20s
Spring: day mid-60s; night mid-40s

(From the Finger Lakes Association)

LAKE FACTS AND FIGURES

Each Finger Lake is unique; all are named after a Native American word or phrase. The list below goes from east to west.

Otisco

Length: 6 miles
Depth: 66 feet
Elevation: 784 feet
Characteristics: Ringed by small lakeside camps and homes.
Meaning: "Waters much dried away"
Largest town: Amber

Skaneateles

Length: 15 miles
Depth: 350 feet
Elevation: 867 feet
Characteristics: Cold, clean water, shale base, steep hillsides at southern end; large homes and mansions hug northern shores.
Meaning: "Long Lake"
Largest town: Skaneateles

Owasco

Length: 11 miles
Depth: 177 feet
Elevation: 710 feet
Characteristics: More laid back than its neighbor, Skaneateles.
Meaning: "Floating bridge" or "Crossing place"
Largest town: Auburn

Cayuga

Length: 40 miles
Depth: 435 feet
Elevation: 384 feet
Characteristics: Long and wide, it can get very rough on windy days. Large stretches of open rolling land between towns; many vineyards.
Meaning: "Boat Landing"
Largest town: Ithaca

Seneca

Length: 36 miles
Depth: 632 feet
Elevation: 444 feet
Characteristics: The deepest of the Finger Lakes and the second deepest in the
    country. Ringed by hills and vineyards.
Meaning: "Place of stone"
Largest town: Geneva

Keuka

Length: 22 miles
Depth: 187 feet
Elevation: 709 feet
Characteristics: Branches into a Y shape; many vineyards.
Meaning: "Canoe landing"
Largest town: Penn Yan

Canandaigua

Length: 16 miles
Depth: 262 feet
Elevation: 686 feet
Characteristics: Mostly lined by homes.
Meaning: "Chosen Spot"
Largest town: Canandaigua

Honeoye

Length: 5 miles
Depth: 30 feet
Elevation: 818 feet
Characteristics: Small, some nice houses.
Meaning: "Finger lying"
Largest town: Honeoye

Canadice

Length: 3 miles
Depth: 91 feet
Elevation: 1099 feet
Characteristics: The highest elevations, yet the smallest lake.
Meaning: "Long Lake"
Largest town: Canadice

Hemlock

Length: 8 miles
Depth: 96 feet
Elevation: 905 feet
Characteristics: No motor crafts are allowed on this pristine reservoir.
Meaning: This is the only lake the white man named; it refers to the native American word "Onehda."
Largest town: Hemlock

Conesus

Length: 9 miles
Depth: 59 feet
Elevation: 818 feet
Characteristics: Small, quiet, and pretty; surrounded by meadows and woodlands.
Meaning: "Always beautiful"
Largest town: Lakeville

More Finger Lakes Data

Hotel rates: Most range from $45 to $200
Restaurant rates: Dinners range from $8 to $30 per person; lunches range from $5 to $20
Family income: Average income ranges from $29,800 (Yates County) to $45,400 (Monroe County)
Average cost of family home: $68,000

(From The Finger Lakes Association)

MEDICAL FACILITIES

Auburn Memorial Hospital: 315-255-7011
Cayuga Medical Center at Ithaca: 607-274-4011

Syracuse

Community General Hospital: 315-492-5011
Crouse Hospital: 315-470-7111
St. Joseph's Hospital Health Center: 315-448-5111
University Hospital: 315-464-5540

Taylor-Brown Health Center, Waterloo: 315-787-4553

NEWSPAPERS

Auburn, *The Citizen*: 315-253-5311

Canandaigua, *The Daily Messenger* **and** *Sunday Messenger*: 716-394-0770; 800-724-2099

Dundee, Finger Lakes Media (*The Dundee Observer* **and** *Watkins Review*): 607-243-7600

Geneva, *Finger Lakes Times* **and** *Sunday Finger Lakes Times*: 315-789-3333

Ithaca Times: 607-277-7000

Rochester, *Democrat and Chronicle*: 716-232-7100

Skaneateles, *Press-Marcellus Observer*: 315-685-8338

Syracuse

Syracuse Post Standard: 315-470-0011

Syracuse Herald Journal: 315-470-0011

Sunday Herald American: 315-470-0011

RECREATION FACTS AND FIGURES

Ice fishing is popular on the Finger Lakes.

Finger Lakes Association

The extreme changes of climate, along with the dramatic landscape of hills, lakes, gorges, and meadows, have created a great range of recreational activities: sailing and boating, swimming, fishing, waterskiing, downhill and cross-country skiing, snowmobiling, climbing, hiking, biking, and ice skating.

*Skiing at Greek Peak,
Cortland.*

Kristian S. Reynolds

Hikers and bikers will find the Finger Lakes region laced with trails, both well traveled and off the beaten path. Some roads are still unpaved.

Hiking: The Finger Lakes Trail covers more than 559 miles running south of the lakes from Allegheny State Park in southwestern New York State to the Catskill Mountains. There are six spurs running from the main trail north with a total of 238 miles. All these trails, with the campsites along the way, are maintained by the Finger Lakes Trail Conference. Many are good for cross-country skiing, biking and horseback riding. Motorized vehicles are not allowed. (716-288-7191; PO Box 18048, Rochester NY 14618-0048; www.finger lakes.net/trailsystem).

Biking: Cyclists can enjoy an excellent network of well-paved back roads as well as roads ringing the lakes. You can ride a loop around ten of the lakes with distances ranging from twelve miles (Canadice) to ninety miles (Cayuga). The terrain in the northern part of the lake is generally easier, more level, less rugged than the southern ends of the lakes. And cycling in the direction the lakes run, north and south, is for the most part less strenuous than riding in an east-west direction.

Unless you have skies on your wheels, avoid cycling in the winter, when icy roads and drifting snow make it slow going. Always bring a rain parka: you can start your ride in the blazing sun only to have a fast-moving storm take over. The weather in the Finger Lakes can be fickle indeed.

Fishing: The lakes and rivers are a fisherman's paradise. Fed by underground streams and rivers that flow from Lake Ontario, the Finger Lakes harbor a variety of fish. Whether you troll, fly fish, or simply drop a line over the side of a boat, you can pull in rainbow trout, rock bass, sunfish, lake trout, perch, panfish, bluegills, pickerel, smelt, and other species that thrive in the cool clean lakes and feeder streams.

TOURISM ORGANIZATIONS

COUNTY TOURIST BOARDS

Cayuga County Office of Tourism: 315-255-1658, 800-499-9615; fax 315-255-3742; cctourism@cayuganet.org; www.cayuganet.org/tourism; 131 Genesee St., Auburn, NY 13021

Chemung County Commerce Center: 800-MARK TWAIN; fax 607-734-4490; ccomerc@stny.rr.com; www.chemungchamber.org; 400 E. Church St., Elmira NY 14901-2803

Cortland County Convention and Visitors Bureau: 607-753-8463, 800-859-2227; cortcvb@odyssey.net; www.cortlandtourism.com; 34 Tompkins St., Cortland NY 13045

Monroe County, Greater Rochester Visitors Association: 716-546-3070, 800-677-7282; fax 716-232-4822; grva@frontiernet.net; www.visitrochester.com; 45 East Ave., Ste. 400; Rochester NY 14604-2294

Onondaga County: 315-470-1910, 800-234-4797; fax 315-471-8545; 572 S. Salina St., Syracuse NY 13202

Ontario County Tourism: 716-394-3915; fax 716-394-4067; info@tourismny.com; www.tourism.com; Five Lakes Suite, 20 Ontario St., Canandaigua NY 14424

Schuyler County Chamber of Commerce: 607-535-4300; fax 607-535-6243; chamber@schuylerny.com; www.schuylerny.com; 100 N. Franklin St., Watkins Glen NY 14891

Seneca County Tourism: 315-568-8687, 800-732-1848; fax 315-568-1730; sctourmk@flare.net; www.seneca.org; Box 491, Rtes. 5&20, Seneca Falls, NY 13148

Steuben County Conference and Visitors Bureau: 607-936-6544; fax 607-936-6575; sccvb@corningsteuben.com; http://corningsteuben.com; 21 W. Market St., Ste. 201, Corning NY 14830

Tompkins County Convention and Visitors Bureau: 607-272-1313, 800-28-ITHACA; fax 607-272-7617; jodi@tccofc.org; www.ithacaevents.com; www.visitithaca.com; 904 E. Shore Dr. Ithaca NY 14850

Yates County Tourism: 800-868-9283; fax 315-536-3791; info@yatesny.com; www.yatesny.com; 2375 Rte. 14A, Penn Yan NY 14527

OTHER TOURISM ORGANIZATIONS

Bath Chamber of Commerce: 607-776-7122; 10 Pulteney Sq. West; Bath NY 14810

Camillus Chamber of Commerce: 315-488-1919; 4600 W. Genesee St.; Camillus NY 13219

Other Useful Numbers

New York State

Empire State Bed and Breakfast Association of New York State: 716-882-6116; mail @ esbba.com, http://www.esbba.com
NYS Canal Corporation: 800-4-CANAL-4
NYS Department of Environmental Conservation: 518-457-3521 (for hunting and fishing information)
NYS Office of Parks, Recreation, and Historic Preservation: 518-474-0456
NYS Parks: 800-456-CAMPS (for camping and cabin reservations)
NYS Thruway Information: 800-225-5697

Rochester

Cinemark IMAX: 716-426-2629
City of Rochester Special Events: 716-428-6697
The Dome Center: 716-334-4000
Greater Rochester International Airport (716-464-6000; www.rocairport.com)
Fishing Advisory Hotline: 716-987-8800
Rochester Events: 716-546-6810
Rochester Information for the Deaf: 716-546-8484
Rochester Riverside Convention Center: 716-232-3362

Syracuse

Carrier Dome Box Office: 315-443-2121
Empire Expo Center/NYS Fairgrounds: 315-487-7711, 800-475-FAIR; www.nysfair.org
Fishing Information: 315-472-2111, ext. 2645
Golf Information: 315-472-2111, ext. 3672
Oncenter Complex: 315-435-8000; www.oncenter.org
Onondaga County Parks & Recreation: 315-451-PARK
ONTRACK: 315-424-1212
Ski Information: 315-472-2111 x 7547
Syracuse Events Hotline: 315-470-1978
Syracuse Newspapers Newsline: 315-472-2111 (includes fishing, golf, and ski information)
Syracuse Hancock International Airport: 315-454-4330
Syracuse University Information: 315-443-5500

Rental and Reservation Services

Bed & Breakfast Network of Central New York: 800-333-1604
The Finger Lakes Bed & Breakfast Association: 800-695-5590
Vacation Rentals: (888-414-5253; www.rentalplus.com) A service providing a variety of rental properties in the Finger Lakes region including condominiums, B&Bs, cabins, and single houses.

Canandaigua Chamber of Commerce Tourist Center Information: 716-394-4400; fax 716-394-4546; www.canandaigua.com; 113 S. Main St., Canandaigua NY 14424

Greater Corning Area Chamber of Commerce: 607-936-4686; www.corning ny.com; 1 Baron Steuben Place, Second Floor, Corning NY 14830

The Finger Lakes Association: 800-KIT-4-FUN; www.fingerlakes.org; 309 Lake St., Penn Yan NY 14527

Geneva Area Chamber of Commerce Information Center: 315-789-1776; fax 315-789-3993; www.genevany.com; 35 Lakefront Dr., PO Box 587, Geneva NY 14456

Greater Bath Area Chamber of Commerce: 607-776-7122; 10 Pulteney Square, W. Bath NY 14810

Greater Rochester Chamber of Commerce: 716-454-2220; 55 St. Paul St., Rochester NY 14604

Greater Syracuse Chamber of Commerce: 315-470-1800; fax 315-471-8545; chamber@cny.com; http://chamber.cny.com; 572 S. Salina St. Syracuse NY 13202-3320

Information Center of Corning: 607-962-8997; One Baron Steuben Place, Corning NY 14830

Hammondsport Chamber of Commerce: 607-569-2989; Box 539, Hammondsport NY 14840

Honeoye Chamber of Commerce: 716-229-4226; PO Box 305, Honeoye NY 14471

Moravia Locke Chamber of Commerce: 315-497-1966; 102 Main St., Moravia NY 13118

Skaneateles Chamber of Commerce: 315-685-0552; www.Skaneateles.com; PO Box 199, Skaneateles NY 13152

Trumansburg Area Chamber of Commerce: 607-387-9254; PO Box 478, Trumansburg NY 14486

WINERY INFORMATION

New York Wine and Grape Foundation: 315-536-7442; 350 Elm St., Penn Yan NY 14527

WINE TRAILS

Three of the lake areas, Cayuga, Seneca, and Keuka, have established wine trails with maps and listings of the participating wineries. All sponsor wine-related events.

Cayuga Wine Trail: 800-684-5217; www.cayugawine.com

Seneca Lake Wine Trail: 315-536-9996
Keuka Lake Wine Route: 800-440-4898

YEARLY EVENTS

SKANEATELES, OWASCO, AND OTISCO LAKES

MAY

Memorial Day Parade (Genesee St., Skaneateles) A hometown parade with veterans, scouts and local dignitaries.

SUMMER

Annual Book Sale (315-685-5135; Skaneateles Library, 49 E. Genesee St., Skaneateles) Lots of books, old and new, for all ages.

Annual Summer Arts and Crafts Show (Marcellus) Park off Rte. 175. Sale and exhibit of art work by a variety of artisans.

Concerts at Emerson Park Pavilion (315-253-5611; Emerson Park, Rte. 38A, Auburn) Live entertainment through August including concerts by bands such as the Dean Brothers and the Joe Whiting Band. Everything from rock'n'roll to Irish step dancers.

Concerts in the Park (Clift Park, Skaneateles) Every Friday evening at 7:30pm throughout the summer outside in the park, or at the Allyn Arena if it rains.

Made in NY (315-255-1553; Schweinfurth Memorial Art Center, 205 Genesee St., Auburn) A juried show of artwork by artists and artisans living and working in New York State.

Polo Matches (Andrews St., Skaneateles) Held every Sunday through the summer at 3pm. Small parking fee.

AUGUST

Skaneateles Classic and Antique Boat Show (315-685-0552; Clift Park and pier, Skaneateles) More than sixty antique and classic boats in and out of the water. Activities include concerts, boat parade, and shopping.

Skaneateles Festival (315-685-7418; Skaneateles) Twenty or so concerts are scheduled throughout August and September. They are held in a stone church and under the stars at Brook Farm.

SEPTEMBER

Labor Day Celebration (Allyn Arena and Austin Park, Jordan St., Skaneateles) The town's largest parade is followed by barbecues, games, rides, and fireworks.

NOVEMBER

Quilt Exhibition (315-255-1553; Schweinfurth Memorial Art Center, 205 Genesee St., Auburn) Outstanding handmade quilts. Early November through early January.

DECEMBER

Costumed musicians enliven the streets of downtown Skaneateles during Dickens Days.

Katharine Delavan Dyson

Dickens Days (Genesee St., Skaneateles) The town and townspeople are dressed for the holidays as Dickens characters. Very festive.

CAYUGA LAKE

MARCH

Maple Sugar Festival (607-273-6260; Cayuga Nature Center, 1420 Taughannock Blvd., Ithaca) See how maple syrup is tapped and made into sugar.

MAY

Cayuga Wine Trail Fresh Herb and New Wine Festival (800-684-5217; Cayuga Lake wineries) Visit participating wineries, taste new wines, sample foods made with fresh herbs, and take home potted herbs ready for planting.

JUNE

Annual Finger Lakes Carp Derby (315-568-5112, Peoples Park, Seneca Falls) More than $2000 in prizes to catch the big one.
Canalfest (315-568-8687; Seneca Falls Canal Promenade) Arts and crafts show with artisans, entertainment, food, antique boats, steamboats, and fireworks.
Ithaca Festival (607-273-3646, Ithaca) An enormous festival with crafts, singing, theater, mimes, fireworks, food.

Old Home Days (607-532-8731; Interlaken) Great family fun with parade, auctions, yard sales, entertainment.

Vintage Car Show (607-277-8979; On the Commons, Ithaca) Antique cars on display.

July

Finger Lake Grassroots Festival (607-387-5144; Trumansburg Fairgrounds, Trumansburg) Four days, usually the third weekend in July, of musical concerts on three stages.

August

Cayuga Wine Trail Chardonnay Weekend (800-684-5217; Cayuga Lake wineries) Taste and compare various styles of Chardonnay from participating wineries.

Empire Farm Days (716-526-5356; Rodman Ltd. & Sons Farm, Seneca Falls) A huge farm show.

October

Apple Harvest Festival (607-277-8679; Ithaca) A gala weekend filled with local produce including apples, cider, and pies; craft fair, entertainment, and storytellers.

December

Cayuga Wine Trail Shopping Spree (800-684-5217; Cayuga Lake wineries) Taste wine, sample holiday hors d'oeuvre, and take home recipes.

Trumansburg Festival of Lights (607-387-6292; Trumansburg) The village Christmas tree is the center of attention as it is lighted with a sing-along, music, crafts, horse and carriage rides, and dessert contest. Held the first weekend in December.

SENECA LAKE

February

Chocolate and Wine (315-536-9996; Seneca Lake wineries) Visit wineries and taste gourmet chocolate delights paired with select wines; receive a gift.

April

Spring Wine and Cheese Weekend (315-536-9996; Seneca Lake wineries) Follow a route around the lake sipping wine and nibbling cheese and crackers as you go.

MAY

National Lake Trout Derby (315-789-8634, Seneca Lake, Geneva) Fish for prizes, fun. Memorial Day weekend.

Memorial Day Celebrations (Waterloo) Parades, picnics, music, fairs in the "birthplace" of Memorial Day.

JUNE

Pasta and Wine, Seneca Lake Wine Trail (315-536-9996) Visit twenty-one wineries along Seneca Lake and enjoy pasta dishes paired with wine.

Waterfront Festival (607- 535-4300, Seneca Harbor Park, Watkins Glen) Regatta, kayak rides, bands, chicken, BBQ.

Watkins Glen Historic Race (607-535-2481, Watkins Glen) Watkins Glen International, races with vintage cars.

SUMMER

Concerts in the Park (607-535-4300; Watkins Glen) Every Tuesday evening through mid-August.

Geneva Lakefront Park Concert Series (315-789-5005; Lakefront Park, Rtes. 5&20, Geneva) Free concerts at 7pm through the summer.

JULY

American Legion Fireworks and July 4th Festival (315-789-5165; American Legion, Lockland Rd., Geneva) Festival of fun, games, food.

Dundee Day (downtown Dundee) Twenty-four miles of yard sales, arts and crafts, food, fun. First Sat. after July 4th.

Ontario County Fair (315-462-3168; Ontario County Fairgrounds) 4-H fair with activities, stock car races, demolition derby, and more.

PBA's Classic Auto and Sports Car Show (315-789-1852; Lakeshore Park, Rtes. 5&20, Geneva) More than 500 vintage cars on display, plus arts and crafts vendors, flea market, food, entertainment, vintage boat regatta, and fireworks.

St. Mary's Annual Festival (315-539-2944; Waterloo) Entertainment, fire engine rides, games, and food under tents.

Summerfest: Street Rod Rally (Geneva) Classic, vintage, and sports car show plus food and arts and crafts booths, flea market. 1950s music and entertainment.

AUGUST

Fingerlakes Dixieland Jazz Festival (607-546-8296; Rte. 414, Hector Fairgrounds, east side of lake) Several Dixieland and swing bands treat you to a concert on the grounds. Pack a picnic, bring blankets and chairs, and find a spot under a big tent. Food, wine, crafts, and local vendors. Mid-Aug.; admission.

Seneca Lake Whale Watch (315-781-0820; PO Box 226, northern end of lake, Geneva Area Chamber of Commerce, Geneva; slww@fltg.net; www.whale-watch.org) No whales in this fresh-water lake but a weekend promising whales of fun. Crafts, games, food, water ski show, boating excursions, musical performances, displays, fireworks, wine tastings. Third weekend of Aug.

SEPTEMBER

Ikepod Watkins Glen Grand Prix Festival and Zippo US Vintage Grand Prix (607-535-3003; PO Box 65, Franklin St., Watkins Glen) Sports car events, live music, Concours d'Elegance (vintage and classic car show), race re-enactment of vintage cars from the 1948-1952 circuit, wine tastings, family fun, kidracer school and derby, road rally, food vendors, and more.

NOVEMBER

Deck the Halls (315-536-9996; around the lake) Visit each of the wineries along the Seneca Lake Wine Trail and collect ornaments, recipes, and a wreath as you go. Each place offers wine tastings and something to eat. Early reservations a must.

KEUKA LAKE

FEBRUARY

Be Mine with Wine (800-440-4898; Keuka wineries) Each winery offers a dessert paired with different wines.

APRIL

Easter Egg Hunt (607-569-2989; Village Square, Hammondsport) Children hunt for hidden eggs and prizes.

JUNE

Finger Lakes Historic Boats Show (800-868-9283, Fireman's Field, Penn Yan) Antique boat display, Finger Lakes–built boats.

JULY

Keuka Lake Art Association Show (607-569-2989; downtown Hammondsport) Local and regional artists show and sell their work.

SEPTEMBER

Buckwheat Festival (Penn Yan) Celebrates the importance of buckwheat in the area; with food, music, entertainment, and more.
The Genundowa Festival of Lights (607-569-2989; Village Square, Hammondsport) Native American dancing, drums, singing, storytelling, crafts, food, and art.

OCTOBER

Fall Foliage Festival (Cohocton) Family fun, fireworks, parade, games, food.
Rhineland Oktoberfest (800-440-4898; Keuka Lake wineries) Enjoy German music and food; taste world-class German-style wines at participating wineries.

NOVEMBER

Keuka Holidays (800-440-4898; Keuka Lake wineries) As you visit each winery along the Keuka Lake Wine Trail, enjoy hearty winter foods and wine. Gift and recipe booklet also included.

CANANDAIGUA and Canadice, Conesus, Hemlock, and Honeoye Lakes

JANUARY

Festival of Lights (716-394-4922; Canandaigua) Sonnenberg mansion grounds filled with designs in lights; house and greenhouse decorated for holidays.

MARCH

Maple Sugaring (716-374-6160; Cumming Nature Center, Naples) Demonstrations in the process of maple sugaring.

MAY

Mercy Flight Balloon Festival (716-396-0584; Brickyard Rd., Canandaigua) Balloons, rides, helicopter rides, and crafts.
Naples Art and Music Festival (716-394-3915; Memorial Town Hall Park, Main St., Naples) An arts and crafts show with more than 200 vendors. Food, crafts, plants, fiddler contest, entertainment.

JUNE

Antique Market (716-394-1472; Granger Homestead, 295 N. Main St., Canandaigua) Antiques, treasure table, and bake sale.
Canandaigua Lake Trout Derby (716-394-4400; weigh-in stations at Inn on the Lake, Canandaigua) Prizes given for best catches.

SUMMER

Concerts in the Park (716-396-0300; Atwater Park, Canandaigua) Free concerts through the summer on Fri. at 6:30.

JULY

Canandaigua Art Festival (716-396-0300; S. Main St., Canandaigua) Juried show with more than 300 art and craft exhibits and food vendors.

Civil War Re-enactment (716-396-1417; Bristol Woodlands Campground) Living encampment and scenarios, infantry, artillery, cavalry, battles, food. Ongong through month.

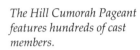

The Hill Cumorah Pageant features hundreds of cast members.

Finger Lakes Association

Hill Cumorah Pageant (315-597-2757, Rte. 21, Exit 43 NYS Thruway, Manchester, near Palmyra) Religion-based outdoor theatrical production with a cast of 600 and recorded music from the Mormon Tabernacle Choir.

July 4th Celebration (716-396-5000; Kreshaw Park, Lakeshore Dr., Canandaigua) Family entertainment, activities, food, fireworks.

Native American Dance and Music Festival (Ganondagan Historic Site, 1488 Victor-Holcomb Rd., Victor) Native American foods, wonderful crafts and demonstrations, dance, and exhibits.

AUGUST

Pageant of Steam (716-394-8102; Gehan Rd., 5 miles east of Canandaigua) This weekend-long festival celebrates antique vehicles powered by steam. The 100-acre site is the venue for a number of events including saw-mill demonstrations, parades, live music, pedal tractor pull, grain threshing, shingle making, antique car show, garden tractor pull, and a giant craft and flea market.

Steuben County Fair (607-776-4801, Bath) Six days of fun, carnival, rides, livestock, exhibits, shows, truck pull, music, and demolition derby.

Waterfront Art Festival (716-383-1472; Kershaw Park, Lakeshore Dr., Canandaigua) More than 200 art and craft exhibits, demonstrations, cloggers, puppet shows, concerts, and face painting.

SEPTEMBER

Naples Grape Festival (716-374-2240; Memorial Town Hall Park, Main St., Naples) More than 250 exhibitors, live entertainment, juried arts and crafts, food, Grape Pie contest.

Ring of Fire Around the Lakes (Lakeside, Canandaigua/Honeoye Lakes) Residents light up the lakes with flares, signifying the end of the summer season.

OCTOBER

Fall Festival (315-986-9821; Macedon) See Doug's giant straw-bale maze and pumpkin land, and ride haywagons into the fields.

Haunted Gardens (716-394-4922; Sonnenberg Gardens, Canandaigua) Ghosts, vampires, goblins, and monsters lurk in the gardens and walkways of this turn-of-the-century mansion.

NOVEMBER

Festival of Lights (716-394-4922; Canandaigua) Sonnenberg mansion grounds filled with designs in lights; house and greenhouse decorated for holidays. Through January.

Festival of Trees (716-394-1472; Granger Homestead, 195 N. Main St., Canandaigua) Theme decorated trees, silent auction of trees and wreaths.

HOST CITIES

Syracuse

MARCH

St. Patrick's Day Parade (downtown area, Syracuse) Wear green and watch the parade to celebrate this festive Irish holiday.

JUNE

Coors Light Balloon Fest (315-451-7275; Jamesville Beach, Syracuse) The sky fills with close to fifty colorful balloons. Rides, family activities, entertainment, food.

Jazz Fest (315-422-8284; Clinton and Hanover Squares, Syracuse) National and international jazz greats perform throughout the month. (Check for possible alternate sites.)

JULY

Pops in the Park (315-473-4330 ext. 3006; Hiawatha Lake Gazebo, Onondaga Park, Syracuse) Free concerts throughout the month and sometimes beyond.

AUGUST

Central New York Scottish Games and Celtic Festival (315-463-8876; Long Branch Park) Scottish and Celtic music and dancing, bands, clan genealogy.

Great New York State Fair (NYS Fairgrounds, Syracuse) Almost two weeks of fun and exhibits in late Aug.–Sept. featuring car races, craft fairs, amusements, animals, horticulture, ethnic celebrations, food.

New York State Rhythm & Blues Festival (315-469-1723; Clinton, Armory and Hanover Squares and Hotel Syracuse/Radisson Plaza, Syracuse) Great performers entertain throughout several days.

SEPTEMBER

Golden Harvest Festival (315-638-2519; 8477 E. Mud Lake Rd., Beaver Lake Nature Center, Baldwinsville)

NOVEMBER–JANUARY

Lights on the Lake (800-243-4797; Syracuse Chamber of Commerce, Syracuse) Flares are lit around the lake.

Cortland

APRIL

Central New York Maple Festival (Cortland) When the sugar maples start running in the spring, it's time to celebrate. One of the highlights is a marathon.

JUNE

Apple Jazz Festival (Dwyer Memorial Park, Little York) Great music plus food and craft stands.
Firemen's Field Days (Homer)

SEPTEMBER

McGraw Harvest Festival (607-836-6107; Recreation Center, McGraw) Crafts, parade, entertainment.

OCTOBER

The Great Cortland Pumpkinfest (800-859-2227; Courthouse Park, Cortland) Pumpkins everywhere, wagon rides, carving contests, food. Lots of fun for the whole family.
NYS Draft Horse Show and Sale (607-533-4160; Cortland County Fairground, Cortland)

NOVEMBER

Ice skating (Homer) On a sunny winter day, the village green is filled with skaters of all ages.

Corning

MARCH

Spring Antique Show and Sale (607-937-5281; Greg Elementary School, Corning) Many vendors show and sell a wide assortment of furniture, glassware, memorabilia, and other old things.

Rochester

MAY

Lilac Festival (716-256-4960; Highland Park, Highland Ave., Rochester) Thousands of lilacs and other spring flowers plus a parade, races, arts and crafts, activities, entertainment, and horticultural exhibits.

JUNE

Maplewood Rose Festival (716-428-6697; Maplewood Rose Garden, corner Lake Ave. and Driving Park, Rochester) A three-day floral celebration centered around more than 5,000 roses. Tours, entertainment, and rose culture workshops.

JULY

Corn Hill Arts Festival (716-262-3142; streets of Corn Hill neighborhood, Rochester) An eclectic variety of arts and crafts, live music, food and entertainment.

Renaissance revelry in Sterling, in July and August.

Finger Lakes Association

Renaissance Festival (800-879-4446; Farden Rd., Sterling) Live jousting, food, period music and dance, knights in shining armor, stage and street performances, games and marketplace; through Aug.

The Rochester Music Fest (716-428-6697; High Falls area, Rochester) A two-day festival of American music featuring a variety of internationally known musicians from jazz to blues artists.

AUGUST

Monroe County Fair (716-334-4000; Monroe County Fairgrounds and Dome Center, corner E. Henrietta and Calkins Rds., Rochester) A good old country-style fair with agricultural exhibits, rides, games, and entertainment.

Park Ave. Summer Art*Fest (716-234-1909; along the one-mile stretch of Park Ave., Rochester) Music, juried arts and crafts exhibits, outdoor dining, shopping.

SEPTEMBER

Clothesline Festival (716-473-7720; Memorial Art Gallery, 500 University Ave., Rochester) Hundreds of local and statewide artists sell and show their goods at one of the oldest and largest outdoor art show in the country.

OCTOBER

Rochester River Romance (716-428-6697; Genesee Valley Park and University of Rochester river campus waterways, Rochester) A weekend party along the city's waterways with hiking, boating, special activities, and historical fun. On Sunday there is a collegiate invitational regatta for college rowing teams.

IF TIME IS SHORT

The best thing of all would be to spend several days in the Finger Lakes with enough time to see and do everything you want to do as well as eat in the best restaurants and overnight in the greatest places in the area. In the real world, time is often much too short to accomplish all this. So if your trip to the region is all too brief, here is a quick list of my favorite places for you to consider. Please check out the listings in the book for more details.

HOTELS, INNS & B&Bs

Geneva on the Lake Resort (800-3-GENEVA; 1001 Lochland Rd., Rt. 14, Geneva NY 14456) A lovely European-style villa on Seneca Lake with gardens, terraces, restaurant, pool and waterfront. Each room is elegant, different. A favorite for romantic escapes.

Mirbeau (877-MIRBEAU; www.mirbeau.com; 851 West Genesee Street, Skaneateles NY 13152) A luxurious new inn with an old European ambiance and a Monet-style pond is but a five minute walk from the lake, park and shops of Skaneateles, one of the regions loveliest towns. An exceptional spa and restaurant pamper privileged guests.

Acorn Inn B&B (716-229-2834; 4508 State Road 64 South, Bristol Center, Canandaigua NY 14424) This 18th-century stagecoach inn features wonderful enclosed gardens and patios, fireplaces, floor-to-ceiling windows, and tastefully arranged antiques, orientals, art work and period furniture. Truly a romantic setting of character without clutter.

The William Henry Miller Inn (607-256-4553; 303 North Aurora St., Ithaca NY 14850) Tudor styling, stained glass windows, impressive antiques, and craved chestnut moldings create an elegant oasis in the heart of downtown Ithaca.

RESTAURANTS

Doug's Fish Fry (315-685-3288 8 Jordan St, Skaneateles) The place is about the size of a one-car garage, but *the* place to come for fish and chips. The fish sandwich with slaw and fries ($6.25) is a huge seller.

Lincoln Hill Inn (716-394-8254, 3365 East Lake Rd., Canandaigua) Gardens and terraces surround this 1804 farmhouse. Eat outdoors or in one of the candlelit dining rooms by the fireplace.

Maxie's Supper Club & Oyster Bar (607-272-4136; 635 West State St.,

Ithaca) Soul-satisfying Southern comfort food including New Orleans-style Cajun dishes have made this one of the hottest spots in town. Free music, good prices also help.

Moosewood (607-273-9610, Dewitt Building, 215 North Cayuga St., Ithaca) Vegetarian cuisine starring grains, fresh vegetables, and fruits along with bold salsas, fish and seafood are yummy enough to be the subject of several best-selling cookbooks.

Rosalie's Cucina (315-685-2200, 841 West Genesee St., Skaneateles) Great Italian fare with a pedigree.

CULTURAL ATTRACTIONS

Sonnenberg Mansion and Gardens (707-255-1144; 716-394-4922; 151 Charlotte St., Canandaigua) This magnificent late 19th-century Victorian mansion with several formal gardens is perfect for any who love flowers and relish a glimpse as to how the rich used to live. With 40 rooms and 50 acres, you will have plenty to explore.

Museum of Waterways and Industry (315-568-1510, 89 Fall Street, Seneca Falls) This new museum gives you a crash course in the importance of the canals and waterways in the Finger Lakes. Current art exhibits are a bonus.

The Corning Museum of Glass (315-568-1510; 800-732-6845; One Corning Glass Center, Corning) If you have time only for one museum, go to this one. Learn about glass making from prehistoric to the present. See incredible glass sculptures and exhibits. Plan to spend many hours.

WINERIES

For history: **Pleasant Valley Wine Company/Great Western Winery** (607-569-6111; County Rt. 88, Hammondsport) Established in 1860, this was the first bonded U.S. winery. A large museum and magnificent buildings with huge wine cellars recall the early days of wine production. Still produces an award-winning bubbly.

For wine buffs: **Dr. Frank's Vinifera Wine Cellars & Chateau Frank** (800-320-0735; 9749 Middle Rd., Hammondsport) This distinctive winery was founded by the man who upgraded the Finger Lakes wine by proving that prized European grape varieties could be grown in the region to produce world-class table wines. Makes a superb barrel-fermented Chardonnay and Pinot Noir.

For creative folks: **Bully Hill Vineyards** (607-868-3610; 8843 Greyton H. Taylor Memorial Drive, Hammondsport) With names like Space Shuttle Rose and Meat Market Red, you've got to appreciate the creativity of the founder, Walter Taylor, who has produced many award-winning wines as well as wine labels worth collecting. The Greyton H. Taylor Wine and Grape Museum and an excellent restaurant is also on

For class: **Glenora Wine Cellars** (800-243-5513; 5435 Rt. 14, Dundee) Glenora enjoys a magnificent lakeside setting, spacious wine tasting room, restaurant, winery, and hotel. The barrel-fermented Chardonnay is very good.

RECREATION

Getting Close to Nature: The many spectacular parks in the region showcase deep gorges, waterfalls and miles of hiking trails. Some of the best are **Watkins Glen State Park** at the south end of Seneca Lake; **Taughannock Falls State Park** on the southwestern side of Cayuga Lake and **Fillmore Glen State Park** in Moravia south of Owasco Lake.

Dinner & Canal Cruising: Take a lunch or dinner cruise on one of the lakes or cruise New York State's Canal system for a day or a week. Check out the Introduction Chapter as well as lake chapters for details.

SHOPPING

There are many shops and boutiques throughout the Finger Lakes. Some that come immediately to mind that are those located in downtown Corning, Ithaca, Skaneateles, and Armory Square in Syracuse. Some shops are so unusual that they're worth a side trip. These include **Arbor Hill, Bristol Springs** (Canandaigua Lake), where everything is grape-related; **Mehlenbacher's Taffy**, an old fashioned candy store with hand-pulled candy in Hammondsport (Keuka Lake); **Weaver-View Farms,** selling Amish and Mennonite crafts, foods and gifts (Seneca Lake); **McKenzie Child,** Aurora (Cayuga Lake), a fantasy land of whimsically-painted pottery, glass and furniture; **Aardvarks and Zippers**, Auburn (Owasco) a small store filled with original gifts, some hand crafted; and **Vermont Green Mountain Specialty Company**, Skaneateles, homemade candy and other goodies that are impossible to resist.

Index

LODGING BY PRICE CODE

RESTAURANTS BY PRICE CODE

*Skaneateles, Owasco,
     Otisco Lake region*

$
Johnny Angel's Heavenly
     Hamburgers, 36
Parker's Grill and Tap House,
     42
Swaby's Kangaroo Court, 41

$–$$
Auburn Family Restaurant, 40
Balloons, 41
Blue Water Grill, 35

Cristy's Lake House, 41
Doug's Fish Fry, 35
Kabuki, 36
Millard's at the Summit, 38
Pioneer Restaurant, 42

$–$$$
Sherwood Inn, 39

$$
Mandana Inn, 37
Marietta House, 38
Riordan's, 42

$$–$$$
Curley's Restaurant, 41
Inn Between restaurant, 36
Lasces, 41
Springside Inn, 42

$$$
Rosalie's Cucina, 39

$$$–$$$$
The Krebs, 37
Mirbeau, 38

RESTAURANTS BY CUISINE

Canandaigua Lake region

American
Bob 'N' Ruth's in the Vineyard,
     198
Casa de Pasta, 194
Conesus Inn, 198
Julia Bean's Cafe, 194
Kellogg's Pan-Tree Inn, 194
Lincoln Hill Inn, 195
Lodge at Bristol Harbour, 196
Nicole's at the In on the Lake,
     196
Schooner's Restaurant, 197
Sherwood Restaurant and
     Cocktail Lounge, 198
Thendara Inn and Restaurant,
     197
Valley Inn, 199

Bistro
Julia Bean's Cafe, 194

Italian
Best of Italy, 194
Casa de Pasta, 194
Koozina's, 195
Valley Inn, 199

Pub Food
MacGregor's Grill & Tap Room,
     196

Cayuga Lake region

American
Aurora Inn and Restaurant, 91
Glenwood Pines Restaurant, 92

Ithaca Yacht Club, 87
Just A Taste Wine and Tapas
     Bar, 88
The Pumphouse, 91
Rogue's Harbor Steak and Ale,
     92
Rongovian Embassy to the
     USA, 92
Rose Inn, 90
Taughannock Farms Inn, 93

Asian fusion
Madeline's Restaurant and Bar,
     89

Cajun
Maxie's Supper Club and
     Oyster Bar, 89

Continental
Simeon's on the Commons, 90

Italian
Angelina Centini's Italian
     Restaurant, 86
Giovanni's Osteria Paesana,
     87
Joe's Restaurant, 87

Mexican
Rongovian Embassy to the
     USA, 92

Pub Food
Fargo Restaurant, 91

Southern regional
Maxie's Supper Club and
     Oyster Bar, 89

Spanish
Just A Taste Wine and Tapas
     Bar, 88

Steaks
John Thomas Steak House, 88

Vegetarian
Moosewood Restaurant, 89

Keuka Lake region

American
Antique Inn, 170
Bully Hill Restaurant, 168
Knotty Pine Inn, 167
Lakeside Restaurant, 168
Lloyds Limited "A Pub," 171
Red Rooster, 171
Snug Harbor Inn & Restaurant,
     169
Village Tavern, 170
Waterfront Restaurant, 170

Amish
Miller's Essenhaus, 171

Bistro
Bully Hill Restaurant, 168
Café Alfresca, 168

Continental
Knotty Pine Inn, 167
Lakeside Restaurant, 168
Snug Harbor Inn & Restaurant,
     169

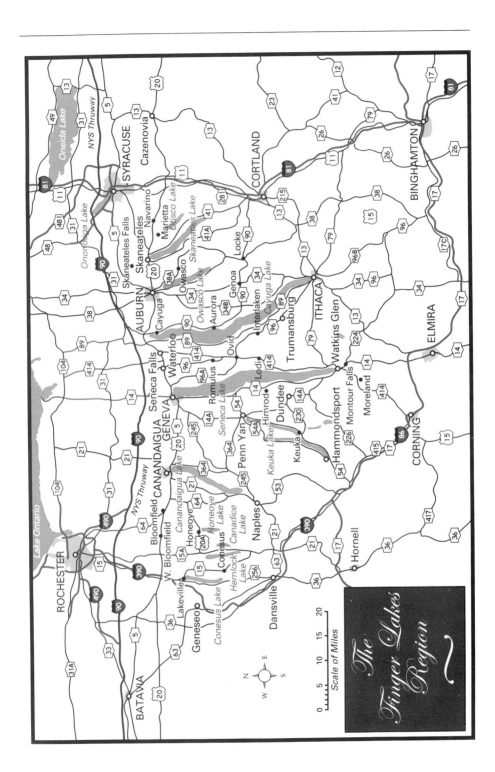

The Finger Lakes Region

Scale of Miles
0   5   10   15   20

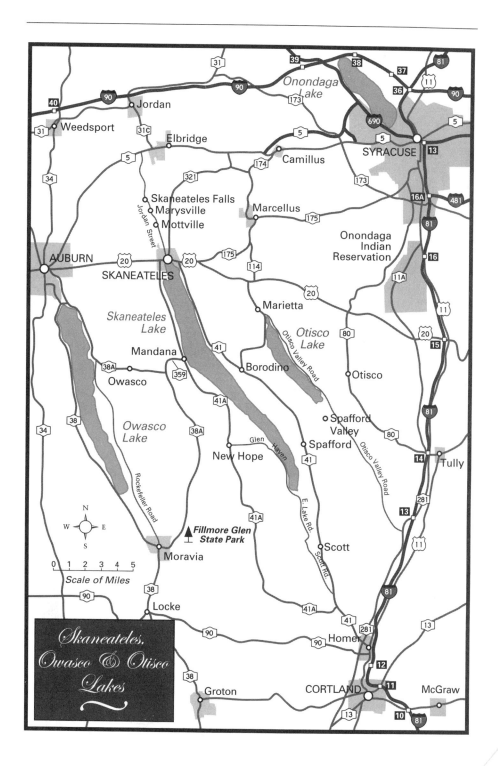

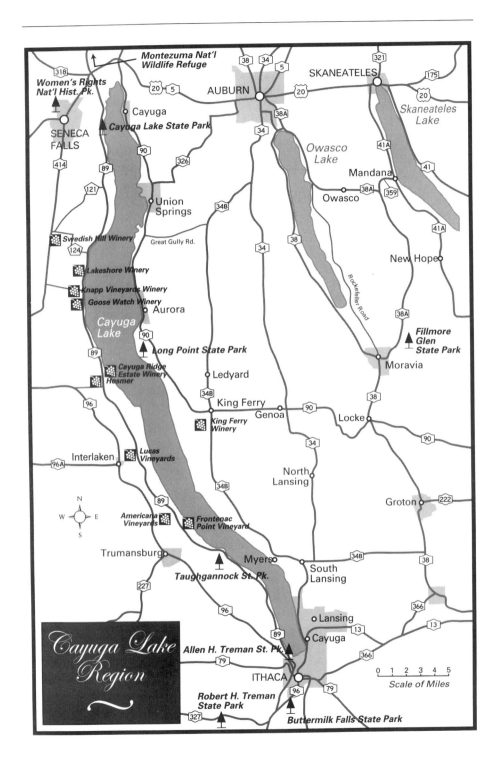

Montezuma Nat'l
Wildlife Refuge

Women's Rights
Nat'l Hist. Pk.

SENECA
FALLS

Cayuga

Cayuga Lake State Park

Union
Springs

Great Gully Rd.

Swedish Hill Winery

Lakeshore Winery

Knapp Vineyards Winery

Goose Watch Winery

Aurora

Cayuga
Lake

Long Point State Park

Cayuga Ridge
Estate Winery
Hosmer

Ledyard

King Ferry
Winery

King Ferry

Genoa

Lucas
Vineyards

Interlaken

North
Lansing

Americana
Vineyards

Frontenac
Point Vineyard

Trumansburg

Myers

Taughgannock St. Pk.

South
Lansing

Lansing

Cayuga

Allen H. Treman St. Pk.

Robert H. Treman
State Park

ITHACA

Buttermilk Falls State Park

AUBURN

SKANEATELES

Skaneateles
Lake

Owasco
Lake

Mandana

Owasco

New Hope

Rockefeller Road

Fillmore
Glen
State Park

Moravia

Locke

Groton

N
W   E
S

0 1 2 3 4 5
Scale of Miles

Cayuga Lake
Region

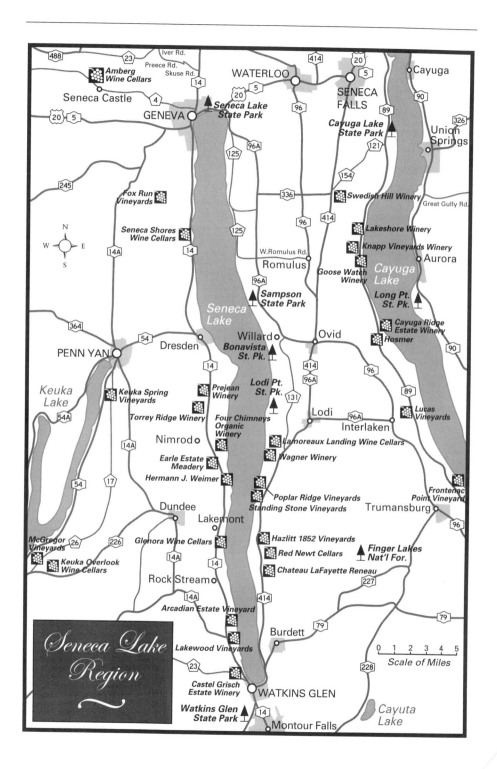

488

23 Iver Rd.
Preece Rd.
Skuse Rd.

Amberg
Wine Cellars

Seneca Castle

14

WATERLOO

414

20

5

Cayuga

20 5

4

GENEVA

20

5

96

SENECA
FALLS

89

90

Seneca Lake
State Park

Cayuga Lake
State Park

326

Union
Springs

96A

125

121

245

Fox Run
Vineyards

336

154

Swedish Hill Winery

Great Gully Rd.

N

W   E

S

14A

Seneca Shores
Wine Cellars

125

14

125

W.Romulus Rd.

Romulus

96

414

Lakeshore Winery

Knapp Vineyards Winery

Aurora

96A

Goose Watch
Winery

Cayuga
Lake

364

Seneca
Lake

Sampson
State Park

Long Pt.
St. Pk.

54

Dresden

Willard

Ovid

Cayuga Ridge
Estate Winery

Hosmer

PENN YAN

Bonavista
St. Pk.

90

Keuka
Lake

14

Lodi Pt.
St. Pk.

414

96A

96

89

54A

Keuka Spring
Vineyards

Prejean
Winery

131

Lodi

Lucas
Vineyards

Torrey Ridge Winery

14A

Nimrod

Four Chimneys
Organic
Winery

96A

Interlaken

Lamoreaux Landing Wine Cellars

54

17

Earle Estate
Meadery

Hermann J. Weimer

Wagner Winery

Dundee

Lakemont

Poplar Ridge Vineyards

Standing Stone Vineyards

Frontenac
Point Vineyard

Trumansburg

96

McGregor
Vineyards

26

226

Glenora Wine Cellars

Hazlitt 1852 Vineyards

Finger Lakes
Nat'l For.

Keuka Overlook
Wine Cellars

14A

14

Red Newt Cellars

Rock Stream

Chateau LaFayette Reneau

227

14A

414

Arcadian Estate Vineyard

79

79

Burdett

Lakewood Vineyards

0 1 2 3 4 5

Scale of Miles

23

Castel Grisch
Estate Winery

WATKINS GLEN

228

Watkins Glen
State Park

14

Cayuta
Lake

Montour Falls

*Seneca Lake
Region*

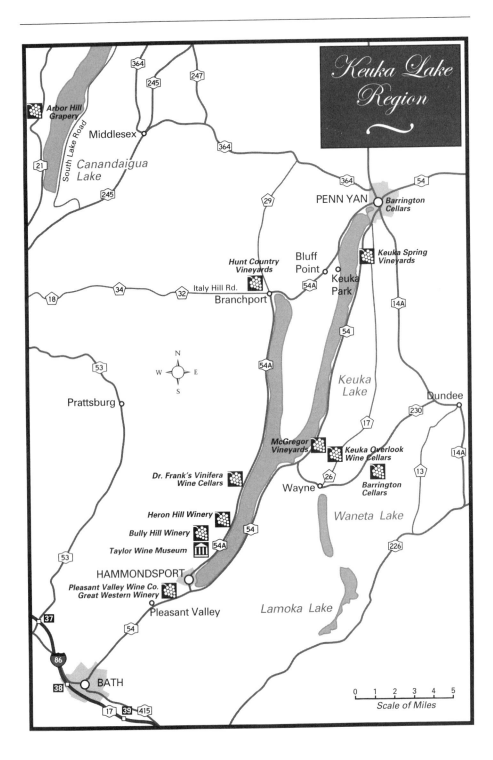

Keuka Lake Region

Arbor Hill Grapery

Middlesex

South Lake Road

Canandaigua Lake

364
245
247
364
21
245
29
364

PENN YAN
Barrington Cellars

54

Keuka Spring Vineyards

Bluff Point

Hunt Country Vineyards

Italy Hill Rd.
Branchport

Keuka Park

54A

14A

18
34
32

53

Prattsburg

N
W   E
S

54A

Keuka Lake

Dundee

230

McGregor Vineyards

Keuka Overlook Wine Cellars

17

14A

Dr. Frank's Vinifera Wine Cellars

26
Wayne

13

Barrington Cellars

Heron Hill Winery

Waneta Lake

Bully Hill Winery

Taylor Wine Museum

54
54A

226

53

HAMMONDSPORT

Pleasant Valley Wine Co.
Great Western Winery

Lamoka Lake

Pleasant Valley

37

54

86

38

BATH

17   39   415

0   1   2   3   4   5
Scale of Miles

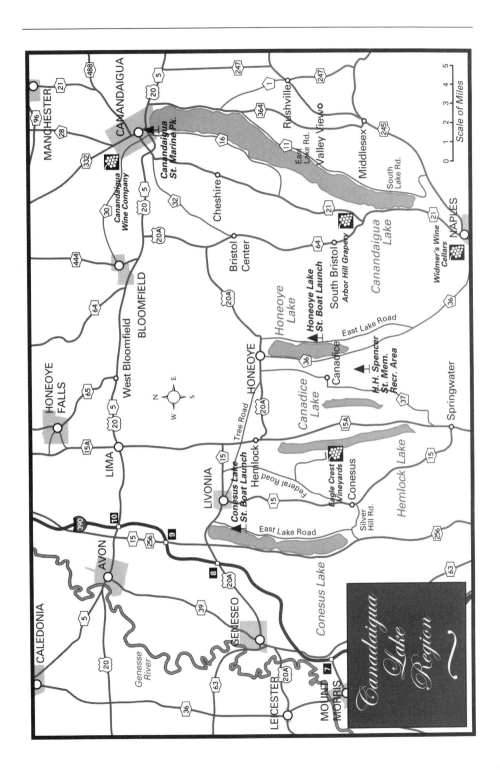

About the Author

Katharine Delavan Dyson, born and raised in Skaneateles, can trace family roots in the Finger Lakes back for six generations. As a travel writer, she has been all over the world. She is the author of *100 Best Honeymoon Resorts of the World* and *100 Most Romantic Resorts of the World*, and she has contributed to many travel and lifestyle publications, including *Caribbean Travel & Life*, *Bride & Groom*, *Country Victorian*, *Country Collectibles*, *Westport Magazine*, *Skywritings*, *Island Scenes*, *Where to Retire*, *American Express' Golf Annual*, *Modern Bride*, *Garden Traveler*, and *Specialty Travel Index*. She has been publisher/editor of *Great Family Guide to Connecticut* and *Yankee Hosts*, and she was editor-in-chief of *Jax Fax Travel Marketing Magazine*. A winner of the Garden Writers Association's Quill and Trowel Award, she is also a member of the Society of American Travel Writers. She lives with her husband in Connecticut, where she writes two columns, "Travel Savvy" and "Food and Drink," for Hersham/Acorn Press, seven papers in Fairfield and Westchester Counties.